Microsoft®
Word 2016

by Jill Murphy, Custom Performance Solutions

COMPREHENSIVE

LABYRINTH
LEARNING™

Microsoft Word 2016: Comprehensive

Copyright © 2017 by Labyrinth Learning

Labyrinth Learning
PO Box 2669
Danville, CA 94526
800.522.9746
On the web at lablearning.com

Product Manager:
Jason Favro

Development Manager:
Laura Popelka

Senior Editor:
Alexandra Mummery

Junior Editor:
Alexandria Henderson

Assessment and Multimedia Content Development:
Ben Linford, Judy Mardar, Andrew Vaughnley

Production Manager:
Debra Grose

Compositor:
Happenstance Type-O-Rama

Indexer:
Valerie Perry

Interior Design:
Debra Grose

Cover Design:
Mick Koller

ebook only ITEM: 1-59136-833-2
                ISBN-13: 978-159136-833-5

ebook with printed textbook ITEM: 1-59136-834-0
                ISBN-13: 978-159136-834-2

Manufactured in the United States of America

QGI   10 9 8 7 6 5 4 3 2 1

Contents in Brief

Table of Contents

Preface

This textbook is part of our brand-new approach to learning for introductory computer courses. We've kept the best elements of our proven instructional design and added powerful, interactive elements and assessments that offer enormous potential to engage learners in a new way. We're delighted with the results, and we hope that learners and educators are, too!

Why Did We Write This Content?

In today's digital world, knowing how to use the most common software applications is critical, and those who don't are left behind. Our goal is to simplify the entire learning experience and help every student develop the practical, real-world skills needed to be successful at work and in school. Using a combination of text, videos, interactive elements, and assessments, we begin with fundamental concepts and take learners through a systematic progression of exercises to reach mastery.

What Key Themes Did We Follow?

We had conversations with dozens of educators at community colleges, vocational schools, and other learning environments in preparation for this textbook. We listened and have adapted our learning solution to match the needs of a rapidly changing world, keeping the following common themes in mind:

Keep it about skills. Our content focus is on critical, job-ready topics and tasks, with a relentless focus on practical, real-world skills and common sense as well as step-by-step instruction to ensure that learners stay engaged from the first chapter forward. We've retained our proven method of progressively moving learners through increasingly independent exercises to ensure mastery—an approach that has been successfully developing skills for more than 20 years.

Keep it simple. Our integrated solutions create a seamless and engaging experience built on a uniquely dynamic instructional design that brings clarity to even the most challenging topics. We've focused our content on the things that matter most and have presented it in the easiest way for today's learners to absorb it. Concise chunks of text are combined with visually engaging and interactive elements to increase understanding for all types of learners.

Keep it relevant. Fresh, original, and constantly evolving content helps educators keep pace with today's student and work environments. We have reviewed every topic for relevancy and have updated it where needed to offer realistic examples and projects for learners.

How Do I Use This Book?

We understand that we are in a time of transition and that some students will still appreciate a print textbook to support their learning. Our comprehensive learning solution consists of a groundbreaking interactive ebook for primary content delivery and our easy-to-use eLab course management tool for assessment. We want to help students as they transition to a digital solution. Our interactive ebook contains learning content delivered in ways that will engage learners. Students can utilize a print text supplement in conjunction with the ebook that provides all the textual elements from the ebook in a full-color, spiral-bound print format.

Our eLab platform provides additional learning content such as overviews for each chapter, automatically graded projects and other assessments that accurately assess student skills, and clear feedback and analytics on student actions.

 This textbook carries the ProCert Certified logo, indicating that the content covers all course objectives included in the Microsoft Office Specialist (MOS) Core exam.

Included with Your Textbook Purchase

▶ *Interactive ebook*: A dynamic, engaging, and truly interactive textbook that includes elements such as videos, self-assessments, slide shows, and other interactive features. Highlighting, taking notes, and searching for content is easy.

▶ *eLab Course Management System*: A robust tool for accurate assessment, tracking of learner activity, and automated grading that includes a comprehensive set of instructor resources. eLab can be fully integrated with your LMS, making course management even easier.

▶ *Instructor resources*: This course is also supported on the Labyrinth website with a comprehensive instructor support package that includes detailed lesson plans, PowerPoint presentations, a course syllabus, test banks, additional exercises, and more.

▶ *Learning Resource Center*: The exercise files that accompany this textbook can be found within eLab and on the Learning Resource Center, which may be accessed from the ebook or online at: **www.labyrinthelab.com/lrc**.

▶ *Overview chapter content*: The "Overview Chapter ISM" folder in the Instructor Support Materials package and the "Overview Chapter Files" folder in the Student Exercise File download include the helpful "Introducing Microsoft Office and Using Common Features" chapter. In addition to providing a discussion of the various Office versions, this chapter introduces a selection of features common throughout the Office applications. **We recommend that students complete this "overview" chapter first.**

We're excited to share this innovative, new approach with you, and we'd love you to share your experience with us at www.lablearning.com/share.

Display Settings

Multiple factors, including screen resolution, monitor size, and window size, can affect the appearance of the Microsoft Ribbon and its buttons. In this textbook, screen captures were taken at the native (recommended) screen resolution in Office 2016 running Windows 10, with ClearType enabled.

Visual Conventions

This book uses visual and typographic cues to guide students through the lessons. Some of these cues are described below.

Cue Name	What It Does
`Type this text`	Text you type at the keyboard is printed in this typeface.
Action words	The important action words in exercise steps are presented in boldface.
Ribbon	Glossary terms are highlighted with a light yellow background.
Note!　Tip!　Warning!	Tips, notes, and warnings are called out with special icons.
(!)	Videos and WebSims that are a required part of this course are indicated by this icon.
Command→Command→ Command→Command	Commands to execute from the Ribbon are presented like this: Ribbon Tab→Command Group→Command→Subcommand.
≡ **Design→Themes→Themes** [Aa]	These notes present shortcut steps for executing certain tasks.

Acknowledgements

Many individuals contribute to the development and completion of a textbook. We appreciate the careful attention and informed contributions of Carol Rogers, Accounting Program Chair at Central New Mexico Community College, and Rick Street, Spokane Community College, for their assistance in the development of this book.

We are also deeply grateful to the instructors and professionals who reviewed the text and suggested improvements.

This book has benefited significantly from the feedback and suggestions of the following reviewers:

Pam Silvers, *Asheville-Buncombe Technical Community College*

Ramiro Villareal, *Brookhaven College*

Teresa Loftis, *Inland Career Education Center*

Kim Pigeon, *Northeast Wisconsin Technical College*

Lynne Kemp, *North Country Community College*

Tom Martin, *Shasta College*

Karen LaPlant, *Hennepin Technical College*

Kay Gerken, *College of DuPage*

Colleen Kennedy, *Spokane Community College*

1 | Creating and Editing Business Documents

The business letter is one of the most common business documents. It's different from sending a casual email, which tends to be more conversational. Business letters are formal; however, they shouldn't be stuffy. You want to engage the reader while maintaining a professional tone. Before you start writing, analyze your audience. Your readers want to know what's in it for them, so you need to tell them, and you need to convey the purpose clearly and succinctly. In this chapter, you will create business letters using proper formatting.

LEARNING OBJECTIVES

▸ Navigate in a document

▸ Create and save documents

▸ Enter and edit text

▸ Create numbered and bulleted lists

▸ Save documents as different file types

▸ Create envelopes

▸ Use document views

▸ Print documents

📁 Project: Creating a Well-Formatted Business Letter

School is over, and it's time to line up some interviews. You are seeking a retail computer sales position. You've scanned lots of computer company ads and websites, and now you're ready to write a cover letter in the proper format that states your desired position and highlights your educational and professional experience. Your goal is to create an impressive cover letter that gets you noticed right from the start.

Elements of a Professional Business Letter

There are several acceptable styles of business letters. All business letters contain similar elements but with varied formatting. The following block style is the most common business letter style. All elements are left aligned and single spaced, except for double spacing between paragraphs.

Date: two inches from top of page but may vary based on letterhead

Inside address: two to four lines below the date

Salutation: Followed by a colon

Body

Complimentary close: Followed by a comma

Signature

Enclosures notification

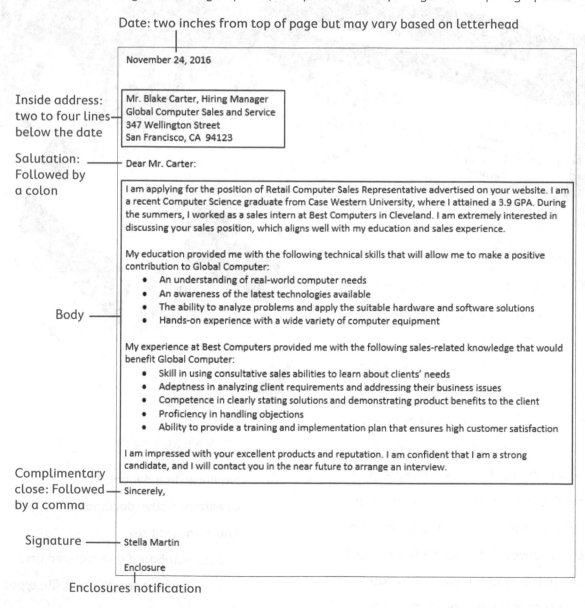

November 24, 2016

Mr. Blake Carter, Hiring Manager
Global Computer Sales and Service
347 Wellington Street
San Francisco, CA 94123

Dear Mr. Carter:

I am applying for the position of Retail Computer Sales Representative advertised on your website. I am a recent Computer Science graduate from Case Western University, where I attained a 3.9 GPA. During the summers, I worked as a sales intern at Best Computers in Cleveland. I am extremely interested in discussing your sales position, which aligns well with my education and sales experience.

My education provided me with the following technical skills that will allow me to make a positive contribution to Global Computer:
- An understanding of real-world computer needs
- An awareness of the latest technologies available
- The ability to analyze problems and apply the suitable hardware and software solutions
- Hands-on experience with a wide variety of computer equipment

My experience at Best Computers provided me with the following sales-related knowledge that would benefit Global Computer:
- Skill in using consultative sales abilities to learn about clients' needs
- Adeptness in analyzing client requirements and addressing their business issues
- Competence in clearly stating solutions and demonstrating product benefits to the client
- Proficiency in handling objections
- Ability to provide a training and implementation plan that ensures high customer satisfaction

I am impressed with your excellent products and reputation. I am confident that I am a strong candidate, and I will contact you in the near future to arrange an interview.

Sincerely,

Stella Martin

Enclosure

📖 What's Important in a Cover Letter

Now that you know the fundamentals of a proper business letter, you will explore the best approach to creating a cover letter to go with your résumé. Keep the following points in mind:

▶ *Purpose:* Use a cover letter to introduce yourself and explain why you fit the job requirements.

▶ *Application Tracking System (ATS):* The first review of your application documents (cover letter and résumé) is likely to be done by an ATS software program. The software searches your documents for job-specific skills and keywords. You may wish to conduct an Internet search to become familiar with ATSs and how best to write your documents so that they will not be overlooked by an ATS.

▶ *File Types:* Some file types work better than others relative to an ATS, and some employers may request that you submit your documents using a specific file type. If you are not sure what file type to use, contact the prospective employer and ask if it has a preference.

▶ *Audience Awareness:* Study the job description and conduct an online search of the company to learn as much as you can. You need to know *what* your audience members are interested in so you'll know *how* to get their attention.

▶ *Beginning, Middle, and End:* Introduce yourself and include an attention grabber (I believe I could make an excellent contribution to your company); highlight, but don't duplicate, outstanding points from your résumé; close the letter expressing your enthusiasm for the company and position.

▶ *Importance of Fresh Eyes:* An error in your documents could eliminate you. Ask friends or colleagues to proof your documents with fresh eyes.

Navigating in a Document

If you are working in a multipage document, it's helpful to know various techniques for moving through it quickly. You can navigate using the scroll bar at the right side of the screen, or you can use keystrokes.

Navigating with the Scroll Bar

The scroll bar lets you navigate through documents; however, it does not move the insertion point. After scrolling, you must click in the document where you want to position the insertion point. There are several ways you can use the scroll bar. You can click the up and down arrows at the top and bottom of the scroll bar to scroll one line at a time. You can drag the scroll box to move quickly through a multipage document, and you can click below or above the scroll box to move up or down one screen at a time.

When the mouse pointer is in the text area, it resembles an uppercase "I" and is referred to as an I-beam. The insertion point is positioned at the location where you click the I-beam and it begins flashing. Wherever the insertion point is flashing is where the action begins.

 View the video "Using the Scroll Bar to Navigate."

Keyboard Navigation Tips

Whether you use the mouse or the keyboard to navigate is up to you. Navigating with the keyboard always moves the insertion point, so it will be with you when you arrive at your destination. Here are some handy keyboard navigations tips:

▸ Ctrl + End to move to the end of the document

▸ Ctrl + Home to move to the beginning of the document

▸ End to move to the end of the line

▸ Home to move to the beginning of the line

DEVELOP YOUR SKILLS: W1-D1

In this exercise, you will use the scroll bar and keyboard to navigate in a document. When you use the scroll bar, you have to position the insertion point. When you use the keyboard, the insertion point moves with you.

Before You Begin: *Be sure to visit the Learning Resource Center at labyrinthelab.com/lrc to retrieve the exercise files for this course before beginning this exercise.*

1. Click **Start**.
2. Type **Wo** and then choose **Word 2016** from the list of suggestions.
3. Click the **Blank Document** template on the Word start screen.
4. Make sure the Word window is **maximized** 🗗.

   When you hover the mouse pointer over the button, if the window is already maximized, the ToolTip will say Restore Down.

   Next you will open an existing document so you can practice navigating.

5. Choose **File→Open** to display the Open screen in Backstage view (which is what Microsoft calls the contents of the File tab).
6. Navigate to your **Word Chapter 1** folder and open **W1-D1-MyVirtualCampus**.
7. Move the mouse pointer in the body of the document and notice that it looks like an I-beam I .
8. Move the mouse pointer into the left margin area, and now the white selection arrow ⇗ is visible.

Navigate with the Scroll Bar and Keyboard

9. Click below the scroll box to move the document down one screen.

   Notice that the insertion point has not moved.

10. Click the **I-beam** $\boxed{\text{I}}$ in the document to position the insertion point.

    The insertion point appears where you clicked. If the background is highlighted, you accidentally selected the text. Deselect by clicking the I-beam in the document background.

11. Drag the **scroll box** toward the bottom of the scroll bar until you see the end of the text and then position the insertion point at the end of the text.

12. Drag the **scroll box** to the top of the scroll bar and position the insertion point at the top of the document.

13. Position the insertion point at the beginning of the first paragraph.

14. Tap $\boxed{\text{End}}$ to move the insertion point to the end of the line; tap $\boxed{\text{Home}}$ to move the insertion point to the beginning of the line.

15. Press $\boxed{\text{Ctrl}}$+$\boxed{\text{End}}$ to move the insertion point to the end of the document.

16. Choose **File→Close**, and if you are prompted to save changes, just click **Don't Save**.

    The document screen is now a new blank document.

Entering Text

You always insert text at the flashing insertion point. Therefore, you must position the insertion point at the desired location before typing. When you insert text, existing text moves to the right as you type. You should not tap $\boxed{\text{Enter}}$ at the end of each line. Text will automatically wrap to the next line when you reach the right-hand margin.

You use the $\boxed{\text{Enter}}$ key to begin a new paragraph or to insert blank lines in a document. Anything that ends by tapping $\boxed{\text{Enter}}$ is considered to be a paragraph. Thus, short lines such as a date line, an inside address, or even blank lines themselves are considered paragraphs.

Tapping $\boxed{\text{Enter}}$ inserts a paragraph symbol in a document. These and other symbols are visible when you show formatting marks.

Showing and Hiding Formatting Marks

Although formatting marks appear on the screen, you will not see them in the printed document. Viewing these symbols can be important when editing a document. For example, you may need to see the formatting marks to determine whether the space between two words was created with the $\boxed{\text{Spacebar}}$ or $\boxed{\text{Tab}}$.

Paragraph symbols appear when you tap $\boxed{\text{Enter}}$.

¶
¶
Mr.·Blake·Carter,·Hiring·Manager¶
Global·Computer·Sales·and·Service¶
347¡Wellington·Street¶
San·Francisco,·CA··94123¶
¶
Dear·Mr.·Carter:¶
¶
I·am·applying·for·the·position·of·Retail·Computer·Sales·

Dots appear between words when you tap $\boxed{\text{Spacebar}}$.

DEVELOP YOUR SKILLS: W1-D2

In this exercise, you will turn on the Show/Hide button to show formatting marks and type a paragraph, allowing Word Wrap to end lines automatically at the right-hand margin. Then you will use the Enter *key to end the first paragraph and start another paragraph.*

1. If necessary, choose **File→New**.
2. Click the **Blank Document** template to start a new document.
3. Choose **File→Save As** and navigate to your **Word Chapter 1** folder.
4. Name the file **W1-D2-CoverLtrTips** and then click the **Save** button at the bottom of the dialog box.
5. Choose **Home→Paragraph→Show/Hide** ¶ to show formatting marks.

   All new documents contain a paragraph symbol; you won't see it if you don't turn on the Show/Hide feature. Paragraph symbols carry formatting in them. In this example, the Blank Document template formatting includes the default Calibri font and 1.08 line spacing.

 Feel free to turn the Show/Hide button on and off as needed.

6. Type the following text and let Word Wrap do its thing:

   Your cover letter may be the first impression a company has of you. You want to be certain it's a good impression. Research the company on its website before preparing a cover letter. The more you know about what a company is doing, the better you can explain how you can contribute to the company.

   If you make a typo, use Backspace *or* Delete *to remove it. Remember to position the insertion point next to the typo.*

7. Tap Enter.

   Notice the paragraph symbol ¶ *. Also notice the extra space between the end of the paragraph and the insertion point. That is due to the default spacing of 1.08. You will learn more about spacing soon.*

8. Type the following text:

   Proofreading is critical. Errors in a cover letter will likely eliminate you. Don't go it alone. Ask others to proof your letter as well.

9. Save and close the file.

   The document window is now blank.

Spacing in Letters

The default line spacing in Word 2016 is 1.08 rather than the traditional 1.0 single spacing. It adds an extra 8% more space between lines than regular single spacing. It also adds 8 points of space after paragraphs. Therefore, rather than tapping Enter twice at the end of a paragraph, you just tap Enter once, and Word adds the extra spacing.

When you choose the Blank Document template on the Start screen or on the New screen in Backstage view, you are using the default spacing. Some documents, however, typically require single spacing, such as business letters, reports, and proposals. These methods are available for applying single spacing:

- Single Spaced (Blank) template
- Line and Paragraph Spacing button

Applying Traditional Spacing Using the Single Spaced (Blank) Template

Choosing the Single Spaced (Blank) template from the Start screen or from the New screen opens a single-spaced document. This is a good choice if the majority of your document will be single spaced. If you use single spacing in only part of your document, the Line and Paragraph Spacing button is a good choice.

Changing Spacing Using the Line and Paragraph Spacing Button

If you start a new document using 1.08 spacing and then decide to apply single spacing to a portion of the document, you can choose the 1.0 option in the Line and Paragraph Spacing button menu. You must select (highlight) the text to be single spaced or, at a minimum, position the insertion point in the paragraph before changing the spacing. If you wish to use other spacing such as double or triple spacing, the Line and Paragraph Spacing button is the place to go.

≡ Home→Paragraph→Line and Paragraph Spacing ⌁ | Right-click in the text→ Paragraph→Line Spacing

DEVELOP YOUR SKILLS: W1-D3

In this exercise, you will use the Single Spaced (Blank) template, and you will modify spacing in your cover letter.

1. Choose **File→New** to display the templates.
2. Click the **Single Spaced (Blank)** template to start a single-spaced document.

   A window appears describing the template.

3. Click the **Create** 🗋 button to start the document.

Tip!   *If you double-click the template, the document will open immediately.*

   Now you will save the document in your student exercise folder.

4. Choose **File→Save As**, navigate to your **Word Chapter 1** folder, and save the file as **W1-D3-CoverLtr**.
5. Type **Nove**, but stop typing when AutoComplete displays a pop-up tip.
6. Tap Enter to automatically insert *November* in the letter.

   Word recognizes certain words and phrases, such as names of the months and days, and offers to complete them for you.

7. Finish typing the date as **November 24, 2016**.
8. Tap Enter three times to provide space between the date and the inside address.
9. If necessary, choose **Home→Paragraph→Show/Hide** ¶ to display formatting marks.

   Notice the paragraph symbols that were created when you tapped Enter.

10. Type the following inside address and salutation, tapping Enter wherever you see a paragraph symbol.

If you catch a typo, you can tap Backspace *enough times to remove the error and then continue typing.*

Mr.·Blake·Carter,·Hiring·Manager¶
Global·Computer·Sales·and·Service¶
347·Wellington·Street¶
San·Francisco,·CA··94123¶
¶
Dear·Mr.·Carter:¶
¶
¶

11. Type the following body paragraphs, letting Word Wrap do its thing and tapping Enter twice at the end of each paragraph.

Remember, you are using the single-spaced template now and there is no additional spacing when you tap Enter *at the end of the paragraph. You have to tap* Enter *twice to create white space between paragraphs.*

I·am·applying·for·the·position·of·Retail·Computer·Sales·advertised·on·your·website.·I·am·a·recent·
Computer·Science·graduate·from·Case·Western·University,·where·I·attained·a·3.9·GPA.·During·the·
summers,·I·worked·as·an·intern·in·the·sales·department·at·Best·Computers·in·Cleveland.·I·am·extremely·
interested·in·discussing·your·sales·position,·which·aligns·well·with·my·education·and·sales·experience.¶
¶
I·am·impressed·with·your·excellent·products·and·reputation.·I·am·confident·that·I·am·a·strong·
candidate,·and·I·will·contact·you·in·the·near·future·to·arrange·an·interview.¶
¶
¶

Change Line Spacing

12. Position the insertion point anywhere in the first main paragraph.

13. Choose **Home→Paragraph→Line and Paragraph Spacing** ⸬.

14. Slide the mouse pointer over the menu options and notice that Live Preview shows how the selected paragraph will look if the formatting is applied.

Notice the Add Space Before Paragraph and Add Space After paragraph options. These options add an extra 12 points of space before or after a paragraph.

15. Choose **3.0** (triple space).

Remembering that single spacing is appropriate for a business letter, you decide to change back to single spacing.

16. Choose **Home→Paragraph→Line and Paragraph Spacing** ⸬ and choose **1.0**.

17. Save your letter.

 Always leave the file open at the end of an exercise unless instructed to close it.

Aligning Text Horizontally and Vertically

You can control how text aligns horizontally on the page using the paragraph alignment buttons in the Paragraph group on the Home tab. You can determine vertical alignment of text on a page using the Vertical Alignment feature in Page Setup.

TEXT ALIGNMENT OPTIONS

Horizontal Alignment	Vertical Alignment
• Align Left (default) • Center • Align Right • Justify (text distributed evenly between left/right margins)	• Top (default) • Center • Justified (text distributed evenly between top/bottom margins) • Bottom
☰ Home→Paragraph→Choose the desired alignment	☰ Layout→Page Setup ⌐ dialog box launcher→ Layout tab→Page→Vertical Alignment

---

DEVELOP YOUR SKILLS: W1-D4

In this exercise, you will change the horizontal and vertical alignment in your letter.

1. Choose **File→Save As** and save your file as **W1-D4-CoverLtr**.
2. Position the insertion point anywhere in the date line.
3. Choose **Home→Paragraph→Center** ☰ to center the date between the margins.

   Notice that the Center button on the Ribbon is highlighted, indicating that center alignment is in effect at the insertion point.

4. Choose **Home→Paragraph→Align Right** ☰ to place the date at the right-hand margin.

   You've decided you prefer to have the date left-aligned.

5. Choose **Home→Paragraph→Align Left** ☰.

   Now you will type the complimentary close, the signature, and an enclosures notification.

6. Position the insertion point next to the last paragraph symbol in the document.
7. Type the end of the letter as shown, tapping Enter wherever you see a paragraph symbol.

```
Sincerely,¶
¶
¶
¶
Stella·Martin¶
¶
Enclosure¶
```

Center the Letter Vertically

8. Scroll down to the end of the page.

   There is too much white space at the bottom of the letter, so now you will center it vertically on the page.

9. Click the **Layout** tab on the Ribbon.

WORD

10. Click the **dialog box launcher** in the bottom-right corner of the Page Setup group to open the Page Setup dialog box.

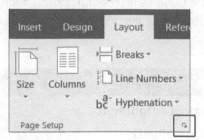

11. Follow these steps to center the letter vertically on the page:

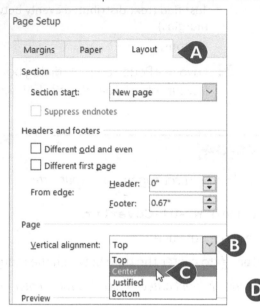

Ⓐ   Click the **Layout** tab.

Ⓑ   Click the **Vertical Alignment** field to display the menu.

Ⓒ   Choose **Center** from the menu.

Ⓓ   Click **OK** at the bottom of the dialog box to close it.

Now you will use the zoom controls to zoom out so you can see the entire page.

12. Click the **Zoom Out** button (at the bottom-right corner of the screen) enough times to see the entire page.

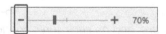

The letter is centered vertically on the page.

13. Click the **Zoom In** button enough times to return to 100%.

14. Save the letter.

Selecting Text

You must select (highlight) text if you wish to perform an action on it. Suppose you want to delete a line. You select the line first and then delete it. Whether you use the mouse or the keyboard to select text is up to you.

 The Mini toolbar appears when you select text. It contains frequently used commands. You can choose a command or ignore the toolbar, and it will fade away.

View the video "Selecting Text with the Mouse."

Here are some handy mouse and keyboard selection tips:

▶ Use the shortcut click+ Shift +click to select awkward amounts of text, such as the end of one line and the beginning of the next. It's as simple as clicking at the beginning of a text block, holding down Shift , and clicking at the end of the text block.

▶ Press Ctrl +click to select a sentence.

▶ Press Ctrl + A to select the entire document.

DEVELOP YOUR SKILLS: W1-D5

In this exercise, you will practice various selection techniques.

1. Follow these steps to select text using the left margin:

 Mr. Blake Carter, Hiring Manager
Global Computer Sales and Service
347 Wellington Street
San Francisco, CA 94123

 Dear Mr. Carter:

 I am applying for the position of Retail Computer Sales advertised on your website. I am a recent Computer Science graduate from Case Western University, where I attained a 3.9 GPA. During the summers, I worked as an intern in the sales department at Best Computers in Cleveland. I am extremely interested in discussing your sales position, which aligns well with my education and sales experience.

   Ⓐ Place the **selection arrow** in the margin to the left of the first line of the inside address; click to select the line. The Mini toolbar appears; you can ignore it for now.

   Ⓑ Use the **selection arrow** to select this line. (Notice that the previously selected line is no longer selected.)

   Ⓒ Select this paragraph by double-clicking the **selection arrow** in the margin to the left of the paragraph.

2. Using the selection arrow, drag down the left margin to select text.

3. Click anywhere in the body of the letter to deselect.

4. Triple-click with the selection arrow anywhere in the left margin to select the entire letter and then deselect it.

5. Double-click any word to select it.

6. Double-click a different word, notice that the previous word is deselected, and then deselect the latest selection.

Select Nonadjacent Text

You can select multiple locations simultaneously.

7. Double-click to select one word.

8. Press and hold Ctrl as you double-click another word; release Ctrl .

   Both selections are active. You can select as many nonadjacent areas of a document as desired using the Ctrl key.

9. Move the I-beam $\boxed{I}$ to the start of the first main paragraph, click to position the insertion point, and then hold down $\boxed{\text{Shift}}$ and click after *Sales*.

I am applying for the position of Retail Computer Sales advertised
Computer Science graduate from Case Western University, where
summers, I worked as an intern in the sales department at Best Co
interested in discussing your sales position, which aligns well with

10. Click to deselect.

Using Numbered and Bulleted Lists

Numbered and bulleted lists are effective in drawing your reader's attention to items of interest. You can turn them on before you begin typing or apply them after you typed the list. Numbered lists are automatically renumbered if you insert or delete an item. A good example of when to use a numbered list is when sequence is important, as in a series of steps in a procedure. Items in a bulleted list have no sequence.

 Be sure to check whether the ATS used by a prospective employer can read numbered and bulleted lists.

 View the video "Promoting and Demoting Lists."

≡ Home→Paragraph→Bullets ⊟

≡ Home→Paragraph→Numbering ⊟

DEVELOP YOUR SKILLS: W1-D6

In this exercise, you will create and format numbered and bulleted lists. Because correctness is important, you'll also work with proofreading tools.

1. Choose **File→Save As** and save your letter as **W1-D6-CoverLtr**.
2. If necessary, choose **Home→Paragraph→Show/Hide** $\boxed{¶}$ to display formatting marks.
3. Position the insertion point at the end of the last line in the first body paragraph.
4. Tap $\boxed{\text{Enter}}$ twice, type this paragraph, and then tap $\boxed{\text{Enter}}$ once more.

My·college·education·provided·me·with·the·following·technical·skills·that·will·allow·me·to·make·a· positive·contribution·to·Global·Computer:¶

Type a Numbered List

5. Choose **Home→Paragraph→Numbering** ⊟ to turn on numbers.
6. Type the following text, tapping $\boxed{\text{Enter}}$ at the end of each item to generate the next number:

1.→ An·understanding·of·real-world·computer·needs¶
2.→ An·awareness·of·the·latest·technologies·available¶
3.→ The·ability·to·analyze·problems·and·apply·the·appropriate·hardware·and·software·solutions¶

Notice the arrow formatting marks following the numbers. They represent tabs, which were automatically generated by the numbering system.

7. Tap ⌈Enter⌉ at the end of the line to generate the next number.

8. Begin typing the last item, purposely misspelling *experience*, but don't tap ⌈Spacebar⌉ yet:

> 4.→ Hands-on·experence¶

9. Now, as you tap ⌈Spacebar⌉, watch how AutoCorrect fixes the misspelling for you.

This is another proofreading tool that makes corrections automatically. It also fixes common punctuation errors and capitalizes the names of days and months if you do not.

10. Finish typing the fourth item:

> 4.→ Hands-on·experience·with·a·wide·variety·of·computer·equipment¶

11. Tap ⌈Enter⌉ three times at the end of item 4: once to generate the next number, once to turn off numbering, and once again to add space between paragraphs.

12. Type the following paragraph and then tap ⌈Enter⌉ once:

> My·experience·at·Best·Computers·provided·me·with·the·following·sales-related·knowledge·that· would·benefit·Global·Computer:¶

Continue a Numbered List

13. Choose **Home→Paragraph→Numbering** ☷.

Notice that numbering restarted at 1. The system assumes you are starting a new list. There may be times when you want to continue numbering even though some regular text is entered within the list.

A smart tag pop-up appears next to the number.

14. Click the **AutoCorrect Options** �☲ smart tag and then click **Continue Numbering** to continue the previous list with the number 5.

Another smart tag appears.

15. Click the **AutoCorrect Options** ⚡ smart tag and then choose **Restart Numbering**.

Remember that numbered lists are typically used when sequence is important. In this example, the items you type are not in sequence, so you will change to a bulleted list.

16. Choose **Home→Paragraph→Bullets** ☷.

17. Type the following list:

> •→ Skill·in·using·consultative·sales·skills·to·learn·about·clients'·needs¶
> •→ Adeptness·in·analyzing·client·requirements·and·addressing·their·business·issues¶
> •→ Competence·in·articulating·solutions·and·demonstrating·product·benefits·to·the·client¶
> •→ Proficiency·in·handling·objections¶
> •→ Ability·to·provide·a·training·and·implementation·plan·that·ensures·high·customer·satisfaction¶

Because numbering is typically used when sequence is important and in this case the list is not in sequential order, you decide to use bullets for the first list as well.

18. Move the mouse pointer to the left margin next to the first numbered item, press and hold down the **mouse button**, and drag down through the fourth item.

19. Choose **Home→Paragraph→Bullets** ☷ to apply bullets.

20. Click in the body to deselect the bullets and then save your letter.

Editing Text

There are many tools for editing documents, allowing you to insert and delete text. Remember, you must position the insertion point before you begin typing. You can use `Backspace` and `Delete` to remove one character at a time. If you select a block of text, you can use `Backspace` or `Delete` to remove the entire block, or you can type over the selected text to replace it.

Spell checker and grammar checker automatically help you edit text on the fly by placing a squiggly red line under words that might be misspelled and a squiggly blue line under words that may be grammatically incorrect. Right-clicking on underlined words presents possible options for correcting the potential error. Spell checker and grammar checker are only editing aids; you must use your own good judgment when deciding what action to take.

You can look up synonyms from within the document you are editing in order to enhance your word choice. You can view a list of synonyms by right-clicking a word and choosing Synonyms from the menu. For a more extensive list, choose Thesaurus from the submenu to open the Thesaurus task pane.

 View the video "Using the Thesaurus Task Pane."

DEVELOP YOUR SKILLS: W1-D7

In this exercise, you will insert and delete text, and you will use the pop-up menu to find synonyms.

1. Choose **File→Save As** and save your file as **W1-D7-CoverLtr**.
2. In the first line of the first main paragraph, click the **I-beam** `I` in front of *advertised* to position the insertion point.

> I·am·applying·for·the·position·of·Retail·Computer·Sales·advertised·
> Computer·Science·graduate·from·Case·Western·University,·where·

3. Type **Representative** `Spacebar`.
4. In the third line of the first paragraph, position the insertion point between the *a* and *n* in *an*.

> I am applying for the position of Retail
> a recent Computer Science graduate fr
> the summers, I worked as an intern in

5. Tap `Delete` to remove the *n* and then tap `Spacebar`.

   The a is underlined in blue indicating a grammar error, but you can ignore it, and it will eventually go away.

6. Type **sales**.
7. In the third line of the first paragraph, drag the mouse pointer across *in the sales department* to select (highlight) the words.

> I am applying for the position of Retail Computer Sales Representa
> a recent Computer Science graduate from Case Western University
> the summers, I worked as a sales intern in the sales department at

8. Tap `Delete` to remove the selected words.

9. In the first line of the second paragraph, double-click *college* to select it and then tap $\boxed{\text{Delete}}$ to remove it.

10. In the third bullet point in the second bulleted list, double-click *articulating* to select it.

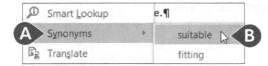

11. Type **clearly stating** in its place.

Work with Synonyms

12. In the third bullet point in the first bulleted list, right-click *appropriate* to display the pop-up menu.

13. Follow these steps to choose a synonym:

Ⓐ Drag the mouse pointer in the menu to **Synonyms**.

Ⓑ Drag over to the submenu and choose *suitable* from the list of synonyms.

The word Suitable *replaces* appropriate.

14. In the first bullet point in the second list, right-click *skills* and then follow these steps to choose a synonym:

Ⓐ Drag the mouse pointer to **Synonyms**.

Ⓑ Drag over to the submenu and choose *abilities* from the list.

15. Save your document.

Creating an Envelope

Creating envelopes is an easy task. When you type a business letter with the recipient's name and address at the top, it is recognized as the delivery address. You can choose to include a return address or not depending on whether there is a preprinted address on the envelope.

 Word generates an envelope by pulling the recipient address from the letter exactly, including format and text case. The USPS recommends that addresses on envelopes appear in all caps and without punctuation.

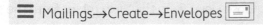 Mailings→Create→Envelopes 🗔

In this exercise, you will create an envelope and add it to your letter.

1. Choose **File→Save As** and save your file as **W1-D8-CoverLtr**.
2. Position the insertion point at the top of the document.
3. Choose **Mailings→Create→Envelopes** .

   Notice that the inside address of the letter displays as the delivery address. Remembering that the USPS prefers solid caps and no punctuation, you will now make those changes.
4. Click the **Options** button.
5. Click the **Font** button in the Delivery Address area.
6. In the Font tab, choose **All Caps** in the Effects area.

Effects	
☐ Strikethrough	☐ Small caps
☐ Double strikethrough	☑ All caps
☐ Superscript	☐ Hidden

7. Click **OK** twice.
8. Follow these steps to complete the envelope:

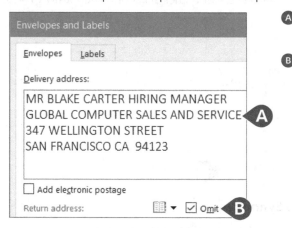

Ⓐ Edit the delivery address to remove the punctuation.

Ⓑ If necessary, check **Omit** to not include a return address on the envelope. (You would likely use this option when you have pre-printed envelopes that include the return address.)

9. Click the **Add to Document** button at the bottom of the dialog box and look over the envelope.

 If the Show/Hide button is turned on, you will see a section break code at the top of the envelope. You can just ignore it for now.

10. Save your document.

Working with Views

You can view your documents in several ways. Each view is optimized for specific types of work. The views change the way documents appear on the screen, but in most cases they have no impact on the appearance of printed documents. You can choose views from the View tab or from the status bar at the bottom right of the screen.

DOCUMENT VIEWS

View	Description
Read Mode (View tab) Read Mode (status bar)	This view provides a book-like reading experience with pages laid out side by side. The Ribbon disappears to display more of your document. You navigate horizontally as in a book.
Print Layout (View tab) Print Layout (status bar)	With this default view, your documents look similar to the way they will look when printed. You can see graphics, headers and footers, and multi-column layout.
Web Layout (View tab) Web Layout (status bar)	This view displays your document as it would look as a web page. It appears as one long page without page breaks.
Outline (View tab)	Outline view is useful for organizing long documents.
Draft (View tab)	This view simplifies page layout by eliminating elements such as headers and footers and graphic elements. This view is useful when you want to focus on content.

 View the video "Using Views."

DEVELOP YOUR SKILLS: W1-D9

In this exercise, you will try out various views.

1. If necessary, position the insertion point at the top of the document.
2. Locate and mouse over the View buttons on the status bar at the bottom right of the screen and notice the ToolTips that appear.

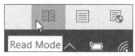

3. Click the first button, **Read Mode** , and notice how the look of your letter has changed.
4. Click the arrow at the right side of the window to move to the end of the document.

Note! *Depending on your screen's resolution, both pages may already be visible, in which case the arrow on the right side is not active.*

5. Click the **Print Layout** button on the status bar to return to the previous view.
6. Choose **View→Views** on the Ribbon to display all available views.

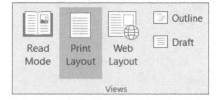

Notice that additional view options appear in the Views group.

Saving Your Work in a Different Format

You can save a document in many different formats. Prospective employers may ask you to send your application documents in one of several different formats. The format of a file is specified by the extension added at the end of the filename.

 You may or may not see a file extension in your filenames. There is a Windows option to hide extensions.

Document Files

Earlier versions of Word saved documents in the *.doc* file format. The current version uses the *.docx* file format. Users of earlier *.doc* formats may not be able to read files in the *.docx* format. However, you can choose to save your document in the older *.doc* format so users of earlier versions can read the document.

When you open a document created in earlier versions, the title bar displays *[Compatibility Mode]* next to the title. This means features not compatible with older versions are turned off while working in the document.

PDF Files

Using a PDF file (**.pdf*) is great when sharing files with others. If you're not sure what hardware and software the other person has, save as a PDF file, and the layout and fonts will look the same on various types of computers, software, and operating systems. A prospective employer may ask you to submit your employment application documents as PDF files.

Saving a Document for ATS Analysis

Text files (**.txt*) contain very little formatting, and thus they may be the best format when you are submitting employment application documents that are likely to be scanned into a computer. Text files can be read by ATS software. It's always a good idea to check with prospective employers if they haven't specified a particular file format.

It's great to have nicely formatted, paper-based documents to hand to an interviewer, if necessary. In addition, many prospective employers may ask to receive your documents electronically. In this exercise, you will assume the employer has asked to receive the document as a PDF file.

1. Choose **File→Save As** and navigate to your **Word Chapter 1** folder.

2. Click the **Save As Type** field toward the bottom of the dialog box to display the list of possible file formats.

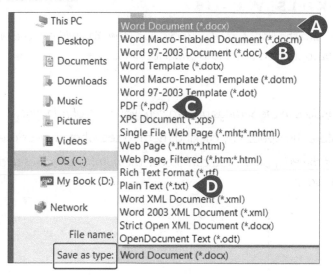

Ⓐ Default format

Ⓑ Older document versions

Ⓒ PDF format

Ⓓ Plain Text format

3. Choose **PDF (*.pdf)** from the menu.

   Notice that your file now has a .pdf file extension.

   Remember, you may or may not see a file extension in your filenames. There is a Windows option to hide extensions.

4. Change the filename to **W1-D10-CoverLtr.pdf** and then click the **Save** button at the bottom of the dialog box.

   Your document now appears in Adobe Acrobat Reader.

5. Click the **Close** ☒ button in the upper-right corner of the Adobe screen.

   Your original .docx file is still open on the screen.

Working with Print and Print Preview

The Print command and Print Preview feature are available in Backstage view. Here you can choose various ways to print your document, and the Print Preview feature allows you to preview your document to see how it will look when printed.

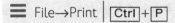 ☰ File→Print | Ctrl + P

DEVELOP YOUR SKILLS: W1-D11

In this exercise, you will work with the Print screen in Backstage view. You will explore printing options, and you will preview the document to see how it will look when it prints.

1. Choose **File→Print**.

   There are a number of options in the Settings area to help you control printing.

2. Take a moment to explore the options by clicking them to see what choices are available.

   Notice the top portion of the Print panel. You can choose the number of copies and any printer properties you want to modify.

   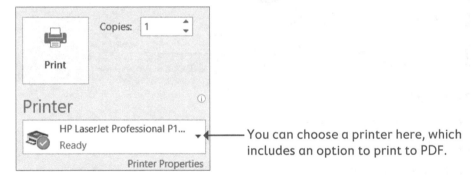 —— You can choose a printer here, which includes an option to print to PDF.

3. If directed, click the **Print** button. If you want to stay green and not print a page, you might print to PDF or simply click the **Back** ⬅ button.

    If you printed to PDF, be sure to change back to your default printer the next time you print.

4. Exit Word.

Self-Assessment

 Check your knowledge of this chapter's key concepts and skills using the Self-Assessment in your ebook or eLab course.

Reinforce Your Skills

Create an Informal Letter

In this exercise, you will create a letter from Kids for Change to local residents, announcing an upcoming recycling pickup. Because this does not have to be a formal business letter, you will use a more casual style. You will also practice selection and navigation techniques.

1. Start Word.

2. Create a new document based on the **Blank Document** template and save it as **W1-R1-RecycleLtr**.

    Next you will center the return address at the top of the page.

3. Use the **Center** ≡ button on the Ribbon, type the return address, and then tap Enter twice:

```
           Kids·for·Change¶

          159·Park·Boulevard¶

         Atlanta,·GA··30313¶

                  ¶

                  ¶
```

4. Click the **Align Left** ≡ button on the Ribbon.

5. Type **Nove** to begin the date, use **AutoComplete** to finish entering the month, and then complete the date as **November 19, 2016**.

6. Tap Enter twice.

    Using the default 1.08 line spacing in the Blank Document template may cause the letter to be more than one page. Next you will change to single spacing.

7. Use two keystrokes to select the document and then use the **Line and Paragraph Spacing** ⬘ button to change to single spaced.

8. Use the **Line and Paragraph Spacing** ⬘ button again and choose **Remove Space After Paragraph**.

9. Complete the letter shown in the following illustration, tapping Enter wherever a paragraph symbol appears:

    Notice when you type the website address in the second paragraph that it is automatically recognized and formatted as a hyperlink.

```
Current·Resident¶
123·Peach·Blossom·Lane¶
Atlanta,·GA··30313¶
¶
Dear·Neighbor,¶
¶
I·am·the·recycling·representative·for·Kids·for·Change,·and·our·motto·is·Think·Globally,·Act·Locally.·We·
know·that·recycling·large·objects·takes·extra·effort·since·they·do·not·fit·in·your·city-provided·recycle·
cans.·We·would·like·to·give·you·a·hand.¶
¶
On·Tuesday,·November·22nd,·we·will·collect·recyclable·objects·in·your·neighborhood.·Visit·
http://recycleatlanta.org·to·ensure·you·are·following·the·city's·recycling·guidelines.·Please·place·your·
recyclables·at·the·curb·in·front·of·your·house·before·9:00·a.m.¶
¶
Thank·you·for·caring·about·our·planet!¶
¶
Sincerely,¶
¶
¶
¶
Tania·Tulip¶
Recycling·Representative¶
```

10. Use two keystrokes to position the insertion point at the top of the document.

11. Use the **selection arrow** in the margin to select the return address at the top of the page.

12. When the Mini toolbar appears, click the **Bold** $\boxed{\text{B}}$ button to bold the return address.

    It might look nice to justify the body of the letter.

13. Select the first two body paragraphs and then click the **Justify** $\boxed{\equiv}$ button on the Ribbon.

    The body of the letter now has a straight right-hand margin.

14. Click the **Zoom Out** button at the bottom right of the screen enough times to see the entire page.

    The letter is a little too high on the page.

15. Use the **Zoom In** button to return the screen to 100% and then click the **Layout** tab on the Ribbon.

16. In the Page Setup dialog box, click the **Layout** tab and choose **Center** in the Vertical Alignment field.

17. Use two keystrokes to position the insertion point at the bottom of the letter and then scroll down and notice that there is now less white space at the bottom.

18. Use two keystrokes to position the insertion point at the top of the letter.

19. Save and close your letter.

Edit a Document

In this exercise, you will edit a letter from Kids for Change to local residents inviting them to celebrate Mother Nature Day at Camp Cuyahoga. The group has planned many exciting activities. In the letter, you will create lists and use proofreading tools. You will create an envelope for your letter and then save the letter in an older version of Word.

1. Open the file **W1-R2-CuyahogaCamp** and save it as **W1-R2-CuyahogaCampRevised**.

   You can see the wavy red and blue lines indicating typos and grammar errors. There's a wavy blue line in the inside address indicating that there are two spaces between the state and zip. This is the format recommended by USPS guidelines.

2. Instruct the grammar checker to ignore the double space by right-clicking the underlined state and zip and choosing **Ignore Once**.

3. Correct the spelling of *leeding*.

4. In the second line of that paragraph, use the grammar checker to replace *receiving* with *receive*.

5. In the first line of the next paragraph, replace *convening* with *convene*.

6. Correct the spelling of *buug*.

7. In the second line of the next paragraph, right-click *accordingly* and then display the Thesaurus task pane.

8. In the Thesaurus task pane, hover the mouse pointer over *appropriately*, click the **drop-down arrow**, and choose **Insert** to replace *accordingly*. **Close** ☒ the Thesaurus task pane.

Create a Bulleted List

9. In the second line of the first paragraph, delete the comma following *scheduled* and type a colon in its place.

10. Use an **arrow key** to position the insertion point in front of *including* and tap ⌷Enter⌷.

11. Turn on the **Bullets** ⌷☰ feature.

12. Delete *including* and the space following it.

13. Delete the *h* in *hiking* and replace it with an uppercase **H**.

14. Delete the comma and space following *Hiking* and then tap ⌷Enter⌷.

15. Continue editing the list of activities until it looks like the following illustration.

   - Hiking
   - Bird watching
   - Tree planting
   - Bug hunting

Create an Envelope

16. Position the insertion point at the top of the letter and create an envelope.

17. Modify the delivery information to conform with USPS guidelines and then add the envelope to the document.

18. If necessary, position the insertion point at the top of the document.

19. Display the document in **Read Mode** 📖 and then return to **Print Layout** 🗐 view.

Change Format and Print

Some recipients will get the letter as an email attachment. For those who may not have the latest version of Word, you will save the letter in an older format.

20. Choose the **Save As** option in Backstage view and navigate to your **Word Chapter 1** folder.

21. Use the *Save as Type* field to save the file in the Word 97-2003 Document (*doc) format and then click **Save** at the bottom of the dialog box.

Notice [Compatibility Mode] *in the title bar.*

22. Position the insertion point in the envelope.

23. Choose the **Print** option in Backstage view and notice the Settings option Envelope #10.

How you print an envelope varies depending on the model of your printer.

24. If directed, click the **Print** 🖨 button. If you want to stay green and not print, you might print to PDF as a Printer option or simply click the **Back** ⬅ button.

 If you printed to PDF, be sure to change back to your default printer the next time you print.

25. Save and close the letter.

REINFORCE YOUR SKILLS: W1-R3

Edit a Letter and Navigate in a Three-Page Document

In this exercise, you will create a letter for Kids for Change members announcing a fundraiser to adopt a seal. Donations help to fund research and educate the public about ocean health. In the letter, you will work with line spacing, text alignment, lists, and proofreading tools. You will save your letter as a PDF file, and then you will navigate in a longer document.

1. Start a new single-spaced document and save it as **W1-R3-Fundraiser**.

2. Begin typing the letter.

Remember to use AutoComplete to help with the dates, and let Word Wrap do its thing.

> August·5,·2016¶
> ¶
> ¶
> ¶
> MEMBER·NAME¶
> STREET·ADDRESS¶
> CITY·STATE··ZIP¶
> ¶
> Dear·MEMBER:¶
> ¶
> Our·local·chapter·of·Kids·for·Change·will·hold·a·car·wash·fundraiser·to·collect·$300·to·adopt·a·seal·at·the·Center·for·Seals.··We·are·scheduling·the·car·wash·for·August·17th.··The·next·monthly·meeting·will·be·a·planning·session.··Here·are·some·things·to·think·about·before·the·meeting:·¶
> ¶
> ¶

Use Numbering and Bullets

3. Type the following list using the **Numbering** ▤ feature:

> 1.→ Choose·a·location.··Our·options·are·the·parking·lots·at·the·following·businesses:·Jake's·Gas·
>   Station,·Beulah's·Diner,·or·Dick's·Grocery·Store.¶
> 2.→ What·hours·can·you·volunteer·on·August·17th?¶
> 3.→ Let·me·know·if·you·can·supply·any·of·the·following:·hose,·vacuum,·soap,·brushes,·sponges,·or·
>   rags.¶
> 4.→ Should·we·set·a·price·or·request·a·donation?¶
> 5.→ Can·you·design·a·flyer·for·the·car·wash?¶

Now you will demote, or indent, some of the items in the list.

4. In the first item, position the insertion point in front of *Jake's*, tap ⎡Enter⎤, and then demote the line by tapping ⎡Tab⎤.

5. Position the insertion point in front of *Beulah's* and tap ⎡Enter⎤ to generate the next item.

6. Continue modifying the list, deleting extraneous punctuation and words as shown.

> 1.→ Choose·a·location.··Our·options·are·the·parking·lots·at·the·following·businesses:·¶
>   a.→ Jake's·Gas·Station¶
>   b.→ Beulah's·Diner¶
>   c.→ Dick's·Grocery·Store¶

7. In item 3, position the insertion point in front of *hose*, tap ⎡Enter⎤, and then demote the line.

8. Organize the list as shown, deleting unnecessary punctuation and words.

> 3.→ Let·me·know·if·you·can·supply·any·of·the·following:·¶
>   a.→ hose¶
>   b.→ vacuum¶
>   c.→ soap¶
>   d.→ brushes¶
>   e.→ sponges¶
>   f.→ rags¶

Remembering that numbering is typically used when sequence is important, you decide to change to a bulleted list.

9. Select items 1 through 5 and apply **Bullets** ▤ to the selected text.

10. Position the insertion point at the end of the last bulleted item and then tap ⎡Enter⎤ three times to turn off bullets and create a blank line.

11. Type the following sentence making the grammar error and typo as shown.

> ¶
> Were·looking·forward·to·a·great·planning·sassion.··See·you·at·the·meeting!¶

Proofread Your Letter

12. Correct the grammar and spelling errors.

13. Right-click the word *businesses* at the end of the first bullet point and display the **Thesaurus** task pane.

14. Use the task pane to replace *businesses* with *establishments* and then click the **Close** ⊠ button on the task pane.

Change Line Spacing and Vertical Alignment

Now you will add a little white space between the sub-bulleted items.

15. Select the three items in the first sublist, use the **Line and Paragraph Spacing** 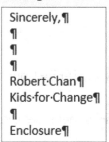 button to change to **1.15** spacing, and then use the same technique to add white space to the second sub-list.

16. Move the insertion point to the end of the document, tap ⌐Enter⌐ twice, and then type the letter closing:

> Sincerely,¶
> ¶
> ¶
> ¶
> Robert·Chan¶
> Kids·for·Change¶
> ¶
> Enclosure¶

17. Display the letter using the **Print** option in Backstage view and notice that the letter is a bit high on the page.

18. Return to the document window.

19. Click the **dialog box launcher** in the **Page Setup** group on the **Layout** tab on the Ribbon.

20. Change the Vertical Alignment to **Center** and then click **OK**.

Add an Envelope and Save the Letter in PDF Format

21. Position the insertion point at the top of the letter, create an envelope, and then add it to the document.

22. Save the file in PDF format and then close Adobe Acrobat Reader.

23. Save and close the Word file.

You've discovered a document that gives some helpful hints on car washing, and you plan to include it with the letter to the members.

24. Open the three-page document named **W1-R3-HowToWashACar**.

25. Using the following notes, navigate through this longer document.
- Use **two keystrokes** to position the insertion point at the end of the document.
- Use **two keystrokes** to move the insertion point to the top of the document.
- Use an **arrow key** to move down one line.
- Use **one keystroke** to move to the end of the line and then **use one keystroke** to move to the beginning of the line.

26. Use the following text selection techniques:
- Position the insertion point at the top of the document and use mouse clicks to select **Introduction**.
- With *Introduction* still selected, select **How** and **Wash** in the next heading and then click to deselect.
- Use **two keystrokes** to select the entire document.

27. Use the following notes to observe the document in various views:

- Position the insertion point at the top of the document.
- Display the document in **Read Mode** 📖, using the status bar button, and then page through the document.
- Display the document in **Web Layout** 📄 using the status bar button.
- Switch back to **Print Layout** 🖹 view using the status bar button.

28. Close the document and exit Word.

Apply Your Skills

Create a Business Letter

In this exercise, you will create a letter from a Universal Corporate Events representative inviting the sales winners at Reukert Enterprises to an orientation meeting for their Paris tour. You will work with proofreading tools and use navigation and text selection techniques.

1. Start Word, create a new single-spaced document, and save it as **W1-A1-LeeLtr**.

2. Create the following letter using AutoComplete with the dates and making the spelling and grammar errors indicated with wavy underlines:

   Note that in the company name, Reukert, is correctly spelled; it just is not in Word's dictionary. You can ignore it.

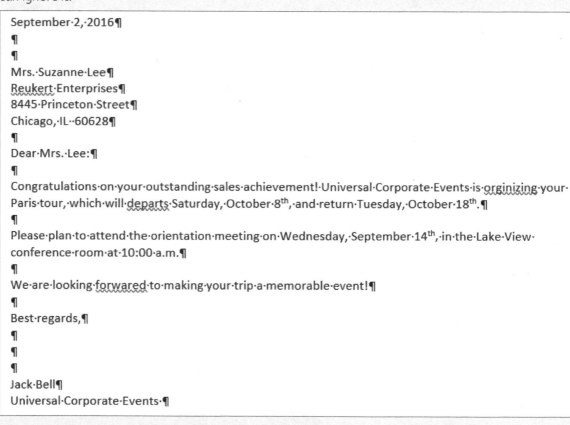

```
September·2,·2016¶
¶
¶
Mrs.·Suzanne·Lee¶
Reukert·Enterprises¶
8445·Princeton·Street¶
Chicago,·IL··60628¶
¶
Dear·Mrs.·Lee:¶
¶
Congratulations·on·your·outstanding·sales·achievement!·Universal·Corporate·Events·is·orginizing·your·
Paris·tour,·which·will·departs·Saturday,·October·8th,·and·return·Tuesday,·October·18th.¶
¶
Please·plan·to·attend·the·orientation·meeting·on·Wednesday,·September·14th,·in·the·Lake·View·
conference·room·at·10:00·a.m.¶
¶
We·are·looking·forwared·to·making·your·trip·a·memorable·event!¶
¶
Best·regards,¶
¶
¶
¶
Jack·Bell¶
Universal·Corporate·Events·¶
```

3. Correct the grammar and spelling errors.

4. In the first sentence, use the Synonyms feature to replace *achievement* with *attainment*.

5. Use the following navigation techniques:

Scroll Bar	Keyboard
• Move down one screen. • Move to the top of the document and then position the insertion point at the beginning of the first main paragraph.	• Use two keystrokes to move to the end of the document. • Use one keystroke to move to the beginning of the line. • Use one keystroke to move to the end of the line.

6. Use the following selection techniques:
   - Use the **white selection arrow** to select the first line of the first paragraph.
   - Use the **keyboard** to select the entire document and then deselect.
   - Use the **white selection arrow** to select the entire document and then deselect.
   - Select three nonadjacent words simultaneously and then deselect.
7. Save and close your letter.

APPLY YOUR SKILLS: W1-A2

Work with Lists and Make Editing Changes

In this exercise, you will create a letter from a Universal Corporate Events representative to a client suggesting ideas for side trips during its annual kickoff meeting in San Francisco. You will create a bulleted list and make line spacing and editing changes. Then you will save the letter in the older version .doc format.

1. Open **W1-A2-SFTours** and save it in the older .doc format as **W1-A2-SFToursRevised**.
2. Position the insertion point at the end of the letter and type the following bulleted list:

   - → Yacht·Charters¶
   - → Napa·Valley¶
   - → Sausalito¶

3. Tap ⏎Enter three times to turn off bullets and create a blank line.
4. Use cut and paste to rearrange the list in alphabetic order.
5. Position the insertion point after Napa Valley, generate a new bullet, and then demote the bullet one level.
6. Modify the list as shown.

   - → Napa·Valley¶
     - ○ → Napa·Wine·Train¶
     - ○ → Hot·air·balloon·rides¶
     - ○ → Top-ranked·restaurants¶
   - → Sausalito¶
     - ○ → Ferry·boat·ride·from·San·Francisco¶
     - ○ → Docks·and·marinas¶
     - ○ → Boutiques·and·art·galleries¶
   - → Yacht·Charters¶
     - ○ → Sunset·cruise¶
     - ○ → Sail·under·Golden·Gate·Bridge¶
     - ○ → Alcatraz·and·Angel·Island¶

7. Position the insertion point at the end of the document and type the closing:

   Sincerely,¶
   ¶
   ¶
   ¶
   Geoff·Simons¶
   Universal·Corporate·Events¶

8. Make the following changes:
   - Center the letter vertically on the page.
   - In the first line of the first paragraph, select *needs regarding your* and replace it with `annual`.
   - In the second line of the same paragraph, insert `San Francisco` to the left of *meeting*.
   - In the first bullet point under Yacht Charters, insert `dining` between *Sunset* and *cruise*.
9. Change the line spacing for the sub-bulleted items to **1.15**.
10. Add an envelope to the top of the document, adjusting the delivery address to comply with USPS recommendations.
11. Display your letter in **Read Mode** 📖, page through to the end if your screen resolution allows it, and then return to **Print Layout** 🗏 view.
12. Save and then close the file.

APPLY YOUR SKILLS: W1-A3

Edit and Format a Letter

In this exercise, you will draft a letter to a Universal Corporate Events employee detailing his responsibilities relative to the Vaughn Storage Device's Kauai event. You will use proofreading tools and the Thesaurus, work with alignment, and add a bulleted list to a letter. You will use navigation and selection techniques, work with line spacing, and save the document in PDF format. Finally, you will work with different views.

1. Open **W1-A3-WilliamsLtr**, save it as **W1-A3-WilliamsLtrRevised**, and then correct the spelling and grammar errors.
2. In the first line of the first paragraph, use the **Synonyms** feature to change *ambassador* to **representative**.
3. In the same line, select *Hawaiian* and replace it with `Kauai`.
4. At the beginning of the second paragraph, insert `and Martin` between *You* and *will*.
5. At the end of the second paragraph, change *entertainment* to **entertainers**.

Align Text and Complete the Letter

6. Use the keyboard to move the insertion point to the top of the letter and then tap [Enter] four times.
7. Move the insertion point to the top of the letter again and center-align the address:

   23 Park Ave.

   San Jose, CA 95119
8. Use the **selection arrow** in the margin to select the second paragraph and then deselect.
9. Use a keyboard and mouse combination, [Ctrl]+click, to select the first sentence in the first paragraph.
10. Use the **selection arrow** to select the entire document and then change the line spacing to **1.0**.

11. Move the insertion point to the end of the document and add the following text:

> The·side·tours·will·take·place·on·September·13th,·14th,·15th,·and·16th.·Here's·a·list·of·the·side·
> tours·that·attendees·will·sign·up·for·during·the·arrival·dinner.¶
>
>   •→ North·Shore·Bike·Tours¶
>   •→ Snorkeling·at·Salt·Pond·Beach·Park¶
>   •→ Catamaran·Tour·on·Na·Pali·Coast¶
>   •→ Surfing·at·Hanalei·Bay¶
>   •→ Kekaha·Beach·Luau¶
> ¶
> Sincerely,¶
> ¶
> ¶
> ¶
> Jose·Ramirez¶
> Universal·Corporate·Events¶

12. Center-align the letter vertically on the page.

Save the File in PDF and Print

Bill is on assignment out of the country, so to be sure the letter reaches him, you will send it as a PDF email attachment, but you will also create an envelope and send the letter to his snail mail address.

13. Save the file in **PDF format** and then close Adobe Acrobat Reader.

The .docx file is still open.

14. Create an envelope formatting the delivery address to conform with USPS recommendations and add the envelope to the top of the document.

15. Use the **View** tab on the Ribbon to view the document in **Read Mode** 📖 and then switch back to **Print Layout** 📄 view.

16. Move to **Backstage** view and choose the **Print** option.

17. If directed, click the **Print** 🖨 button. If you want to stay green and not print, you might print to PDF as a Printer option or simply click the **Back** ⬅ button.

 If you printed to PDF, be sure to change back to your default printer the next time you print.

18. Save and close the file and then exit Word.

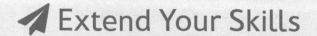 # Extend Your Skills

These exercises challenge you to think critically and apply your new skills. You will be evaluated on your ability to follow directions, completeness, creativity, and the use of proper grammar and mechanics. Save files to your chapter folder. Submit assignments as directed.

W1-E1 That's the Way I See It

You have decided to start your own landscaping business, and you are going to conduct online research to see what's involved. Your friend is studying for his MBA, and you will send him a letter containing the results of your research and ask him what he thinks of your idea.

Create a block-style, single-spaced letter, including a list of five landscaping tools that your research shows you will need to purchase. Then research what is involved in becoming a certified landscape professional and explain how you plan to earn your certification. Finally, list three tips for running a successful landscaping business. The letter should include at least three paragraphs (one to give an overview of the business, one or more to discuss certification, and one for the conclusion) and a list of three tips. Add an envelope using USPS-recommended formatting. Save the file in the older version *.doc* format, naming it **W1-E1-NewBusiness**.

W1-E2 Be Your Own Boss

You own Blue Jean Landscaping, a service that helps customers be their own landscapers. You provide the plans and directions and then the customer helps with the labor. A customer would like you to help her landscape her front yard. Use your imagination to decide on your business's location and climate. Conduct online research to determine what plants work well for the climate you chose. Send the client a block-style letter with traditional letter spacing to propose four plant options that would work well for the location and climate. The letter should contain both an introductory and concluding paragraph, as well as a list of four plant options, and each option should be associated with a sentence or two explaining why it is a good choice. Add an envelope to the document and save the file in PDF format as **W1-E2-NewClient**.

W1-E3 Demonstrate Proficiency

Stormy BBQ is a local BBQ restaurant featuring fresh, locally grown vegetables and local grass-fed pork and beef. As the marketing manager of Stormy BBQ, you've decided to hold a chili cook-off to attract new clients. Use online research to learn how to have a successful cook-off and also research rules for the chefs to ensure that they are competing on a level playing field.

Create a correctly formatted business letter to send to prospective chili chefs listing three important guidelines for a successful cook-off and three competition rules for your chefs. The letter should include both an introductory and concluding paragraph, as well as the rules that have been established. Make up the name and address for the first chef you want to invite. Create an envelope to go with the letter. Save your letter in Plain Text format as **W1-E3-ChiliChef**.

2

Creating a Résumé in a Table

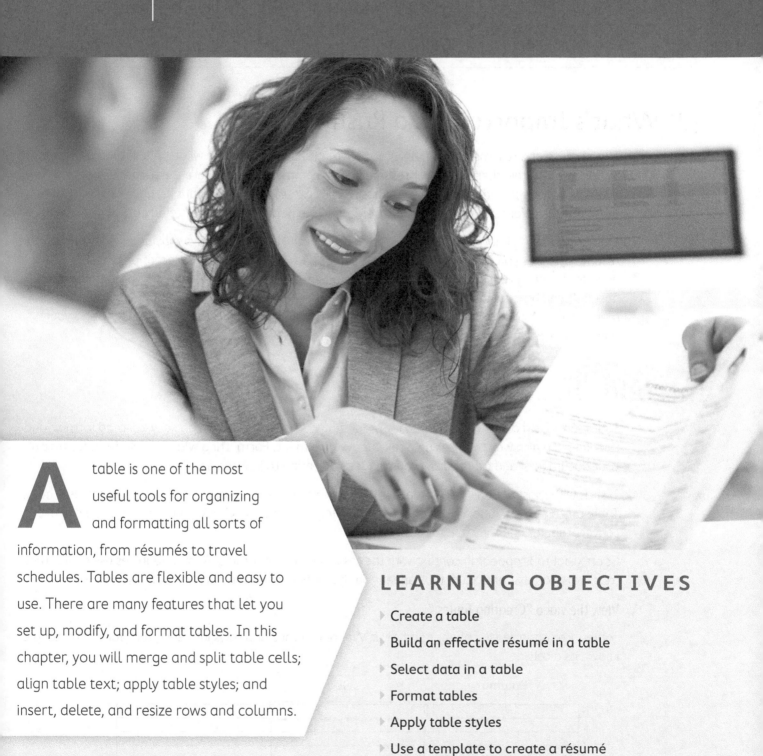

A table is one of the most useful tools for organizing and formatting all sorts of information, from résumés to travel schedules. Tables are flexible and easy to use. There are many features that let you set up, modify, and format tables. In this chapter, you will merge and split table cells; align table text; apply table styles; and insert, delete, and resize rows and columns.

LEARNING OBJECTIVES

▸ Create a table

▸ Build an effective résumé in a table

▸ Select data in a table

▸ Format tables

▸ Apply table styles

▸ Use a template to create a résumé

📁 Project: Landing the Perfect Job

Your cover letter is complete, and now it's time for your résumé. You are pursuing a position in retail computer sales. You need to summarize your qualifications and experience, focusing on skills that target the position you are applying for. You also need to demonstrate that your skills fit the needs the employer has expressed. You decide to use a table for your résumé since it will make your résumé easy for a hiring manager to quickly read.

You also intend to make as many professional contacts as possible in the next few months, and using a table to track those contacts will be very helpful. You'll take advantage of the table's Sort feature to organize the data and apply formatting that will make it attractive and, more important, easy to read.

📖 What's Important in a Résumé?

The purpose of a résumé is to win an interview. Many hiring managers will take less than a minute to review a résumé; therefore, your résumé needs to immediately capture the reader. It needs to be dynamic, targeted, and designed to emphasize your experience, qualifications, and skills, particularly those that transfer to the job. Like the cover letter, one page is generally preferred.

There are three primary types of résumés: *chronological*, *functional*, and *combination*. A chronological résumé assumes you are continuing along a career path, listing your most recent position first. It is good for showing your growth within a profession. A functional résumé is skill and accomplishment based. It can be used by those just out of school, career changers, or those with gaps in their employment history. A combination résumé is a combination of chronological and functional, listing your skills and experience first, followed by your employment history.

Introducing Tables

Tables provide a convenient method for organizing and aligning data in an easy-to-read format, and they afford a nice way to break up a text-heavy document. Formatting with table styles adds flair to your documents, and tables draw your reader's attention to key items.

Just as with most actions on a computer, there are multiple ways to insert a table. You can use the Table button on the Ribbon, the Insert Table dialog box, and the Quick Tables gallery. You can even convert tabular columns to a table.

Contextual tabs appear in context with the task you are performing. A lot of features use contextual tabs. With tables, contextual tabs appear on the Ribbon when the insertion point is in a table.

 View the video "Creating Tables."

Tables are organized in columns and rows. Where columns and rows intersect, they form a rectangle known as a cell.

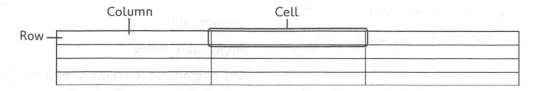

Navigating and Selecting Data in a Table

You can move the insertion point by clicking in a cell, or you can use keystrokes for navigating. Here are the keystrokes you are likely to use most often:

▸ `Tab` for moving to the next cell

▸ `Shift`+`Tab` for moving to the previous cell

Just as in a regular text document, if you want to format or modify something in a table, you select it first. The mouse pointer changes shape depending on whether you're selecting a cell, row, column, or the entire table.

 View the video "Selecting Data with the Mouse."

DEVELOP YOUR SKILLS: W2-D1

In this exercise, you will insert a table in a document and use selection and navigation techniques. Then you will enter data in your table.

1. Start Word and create a new document using the **Single Spaced (Blank)** template.
2. Navigate to your **Word Chapter 2** folder and save the document as **W2-D1-StellaResume**.
3. Choose **Home→Paragraph→Show/Hide** ¶ to display formatting marks.
4. Follow these steps to insert a **2×4** table from the Ribbon:

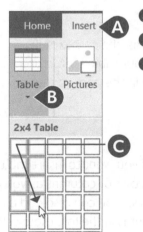

    Ⓐ   Click the **Insert** tab.

    Ⓑ   Click the **Table** button.

    Ⓒ   Drag in the grid and click the fourth cell in the second column.

Notice that the insertion point is in the table and that the contextual Table Tools' Design and Layout tabs appear on the Ribbon.

Select Table Elements and Navigate in a Table

Remember, the Mini toolbar appears when you select table data, just as when you select regular text.
It contains frequently used commands. You can choose a command or ignore the toolbar, and it will fade away.

5. Apply the following selection techniques:
   - Use the selection arrow to select a row.
   - Click the **move** handle 田 in the upper-left corner of the table to select the entire table. (The insertion point or the mouse pointer must be in the table for the move handle to appear.)
   - Use the down-pointing black mouse pointer to select a column.

6. Deselect by clicking anywhere in the table and then use the following notes to navigate in a table:
   - Use [Tab] and [Shift]+[Tab] to move forward and back one cell at a time.
   - Position the insertion point at the end of a row (not the last row) and tap [Tab] to move to the beginning of the next row.
   - Press [Alt]+[Page Up] to move to the top of the column.
   - Press [Alt]+[Page Down] to move to the end of the column.

Enter Data in a Table

7. Enter the following information:

Stella·Martin¶ 127·Stevens·Street¶ Cleveland,·OH··44113¶ 216-555-1212¶ SSMartin5@yahoo.com¤	¤
OBJECTIVE¤	¤
QUALIFICATIONS¤	¤
EXPERIENCE¤	¤

8. Save the document.

Modifying a Table

Whenever you click in a table or select cells, rows, or columns, the contextual Layout tab appears. All the features you'll need to modify your table's structure are located here. Also, some of these features are available in the pop-up menu when you right-click in a table.

Inserting Rows and Columns

You can insert new columns and rows in an existing table. If you want to insert multiple rows or columns, you must first select the same number of existing rows or columns as you want to insert. For example, to insert two new rows, select two existing rows first. You can also add a row to the bottom of a table with a tap of the [Tab] key when the insertion point is in the last table cell.

A quick and easy way to insert a single row or column is with the insert control that appears when the insertion point is in the table and the selection arrow is pointing between rows or columns.

≡ Table Tools→Layout→Rows & Columns | Right-click in the table and choose Insert

Merging/Splitting Cells and Aligning Data

You can merge two or more adjacent cells in the same row or column into a single cell. The merge option is often used to create a heading row that spans the width of the table. You can also split a single cell into multiple cells.

You can split the entire table, if desired. The first step is to position the insertion point anywhere in the row that you want to become the first row of the second table. Then, execute the Split Table command. When formatting marks are visible, you will see a paragraph between the two tables. To rejoin the table, delete the paragraph symbol.

≡ Table Tools→Layout→Merge→Merge Cells *or* Split Cells | Right-click in the table and choose Merge Cells *or* Split Cells

≡ Table Tools→Layout→Merge→Split Table

Aligning Table Data

You can align data horizontally or vertically, and you can change the direction of text. You can also modify the cell margins thereby customizing the spacing between cells.

≡ Table Tools→Layout→Alignment

DEVELOP YOUR SKILLS: W2-D2

In this exercise, you will use several techniques to insert and delete rows. You will also merge cells and align data within cells.

1. Choose **File→Save As** and navigate to your **Word Chapter 2** folder.
2. Name the file **W2-D2-StellaResume**.

Insert and Delete Rows

3. Make sure the insertion point is in the table.
4. Move the mouse pointer to the left edge of the table between the first and second rows until the insert control appears as shown.

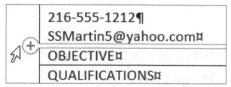

5. Click the **insert control** to add a row to the table.

   You will leave this row blank to add white space between the heading row and the rest of the table.

6. Position the insertion point in the last table cell (last column, last row) and then tap `Tab` to generate a new row.

   If you want to add several columns or rows at once, you must select the number of columns or rows that you want to add.

7. Use the selection arrow in the left margin to select the *QUALIFICATIONS* and *EXPERIENCE* rows.

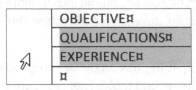

8. Follow these steps to insert two rows in the table:

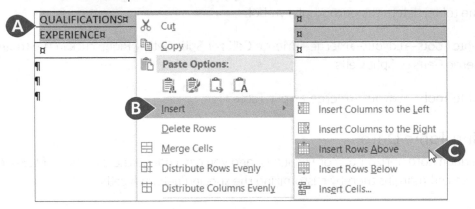

Ⓐ Position the mouse pointer within the selected rows and right-click to display the menu.

Ⓑ Drag the mouse pointer to the **Insert** command.

Ⓒ Choose **Insert Rows Above** from the submenu.

Two rows are inserted because two rows were selected. Now you will delete one of the rows.

9. Select the second blank row, position the mouse pointer in the selected row, and right-click to display the menu.

10. Choose **Delete Rows** from the menu.

Now you will insert another blank row.

11. Use the selection arrow to select the *EXPERIENCE* row and then click the right mouse button in the selected row.

12. Choose **Insert** from the menu and then choose **Insert Rows Above** from the submenu.

13. Use the **insert control** to insert another row at the bottom of the table.

Merge Cells and Align Data

14. Position the selection arrow to the left of the first row and click to select the row.

15. Choose **Table Tools→Layout→Merge→Merge Cells** ▦.

Row 1 is now one cell that spans the width of the table.

16. Choose **Table Tools→Layout→Alignment**.

The alignment options on the left of the Alignment group offer several ways of aligning data within the cells.

17. Follow these steps to center the heading data:

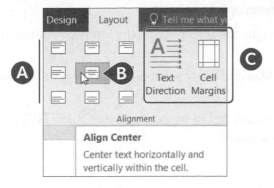

Ⓐ Hover the mouse pointer over the buttons in the group on the left and notice the ToolTips that describe the alignment options.

Ⓑ Choose the **Align Center** option.

Ⓒ Hover the mouse pointer over the two buttons on the right and read the ToolTips.

18. Save the file.

Sizing Columns and Rows

There are a number of techniques for resizing columns and rows. The adjust pointer, which is a double-headed arrow, appears whenever you position the mouse pointer on a row or column grid-line. You can adjust the column width or row height by dragging the gridline. The Cell Size group in the contextual Table Tools' Layout tab provides handy tools for precise sizing.

≡ Table Tools→Layout→Cell Size

DEVELOP YOUR SKILLS: W2-D3

In this exercise, you will continue modifying the table by resizing columns and rows. Then you will finish entering data in the résumé.

1. Save your file as **W2-D3-StellaResume**.

The left column is wider than it needs to be.

2. Choose **View→Show→Ruler**.

3. Follow these steps to narrow the left column:

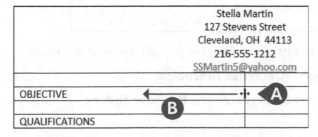

Ⓐ Position the mouse pointer on the center vertical gridline; it changes to the adjust pointer (a double-headed arrow).

Ⓑ Drag left until the column is approximately 1½" wide. You can use the ruler at the top of the page as a guide.

4. Position the mouse pointer on the bottom border of the *OBJECTIVE* row and notice the adjust pointer is a double-headed arrow pointing up and down.

5. Drag down a bit to increase the row height and then position the insertion point in the *OBJECTIVE* row.

6. Choose **Table Tools→Layout→Cell Size** and hover the mouse pointer over the buttons to observe their purpose.

These buttons offer more precise sizing options. Notice the height of the OBJECTIVE row in the Table Row Height field. (Your measurement may differ.)

7. Position the insertion point in the next row and notice the default row height is 0.18".

Now you will resize the OBJECTIVE row to the same size as the other rows.

8. Position the mouse pointer in the *OBJECTIVE* row, then click in the **Table Row Height** field, type **0.18**, and tap Enter .

Enter Data

9. Position the mouse pointer in the second cell of the *OBJECTIVE* row and type **Retail Computer Sales**.

10. Position the insertion point in the second cell of the *QUALIFICATIONS* row.

Now you will type a bulleted list of Stella's qualifications.

11. Choose **Home→Paragraph→Bullets** ☷ and type **Hardware/Software** Enter .

The next bullet will need to be demoted one level; however, inside a table, you cannot use the Tab key to demote. Remember, using Tab in a table moves the insertion point to the next cell.

12. Choose **Home→Paragraph→Increase Indent** ☷.

13. Complete the list, including the last bullet:

> • → Hardware/Software¶
>   o→ In-depth·knowledge·of·computer·hardware·and·peripherals¶
>   o→ Understanding·of·computer·operating·systems·and·end-user·applications,·including·Windows·and·Microsoft·Office·Suite¶
>   o→ Maintain·hardware·and·software·knowledge·via·blogs,·newsletters,·and·conventions¶
>   o→ ¤

Now you need to promote the last bullet. This time you will decrease the indent.

14. Choose **Home→Paragraph→Decrease Indent** ☷.

15. Type the following list, remembering to use the **Increase Indent** ☷ button to demote:

> • → Sales¶
>   o→ Ability·to·build·good·customer·relations¶
>   o→ Good·presentation·skills¶
>   o→ Familiar·with·sales·proven·strategies¶
>   o→ Ability·to·close·the·sale¤

16. Position the insertion point in the second cell of the *EXPERIENCE* row and type **Sales Intern, Best Computers (Summers, 2013–2016)** Enter.

17. Type the remaining lists, remembering to use **Increase Indent** and **Decrease Indent** to demote and promote bullet points:

> Sales·Intern,·Best·Computers·(Summers,·2013–2016)¶
> - → Presales¶
>   - → Prepared·demonstrations·describing·hardware·and· software·features·and·benefits¶
>   - → Prepared·proposals·and·sales·contracts¶
> - → Sales¶
>   - → Sold·various·brands·of·PCs,·tablets,·notebooks,·including· IBM,·Hewlett·Packard,·Compaq,·and·Macintosh¶
>   - → Recommended·software·based·on·customer·needs¶
>   - → Performed·follow-up·activities·necessary·to·close·sales¶
>   - → Closed·difficult·deals·and·exceeded·sales·goals¶
>   - → Assisted·in·promotional·events¶
>   - → Recognized·as·Intern·of·the·Month·on·three·occasions¶
> - → Post·Sales¶
>   - → Scheduled·delivery·and·installation·and·implemented· training·schedules¶
>   - → Followed·up·with·customers·to·ensure·satisfaction¤

18. Position the insertion point in the first cell of the last row and type **EDUCATION**.

19. In the second cell of the *EDUCATION* row, type **Computer Science Graduate, Case Western University**.

20. Choose **File→Print** to view your document in the Print screen.

Notice that the résumé is too high on the page.

21. Click **Back** to return to the Word screen.

22. Choose **Layout→Page Setup→dialog box launcher**, click the **Layout** tab, then choose **Center** from the Vertical Alignment field and click **OK**.

23. Save and close the file.

Formatting with Borders, Shading, and Styles

Borders, shading, and styles can enhance the readability of a table, and they add pizzazz. Whenever you click in a table or select cells, row, or columns, the contextual Design tab appears. The features you need to modify your table's formatting are located here.

The Borders and Shading buttons have memory, meaning they reflect the last option chosen in the current session. This is handy if you want to apply the same effect multiple times.

Just like regular text, you can also format tables using the formatting tools on the Home tab. Or, use the Mini toolbar, which provides convenient formatting tools right at your mouse pointer when you select data.

In this exercise, you will open a table and apply formatting using borders, shading, and styles. Stella has started a list of hiring managers she plans to contact. Because she intends to make many contacts, a table is the perfect tool for staying organized.

1. Navigate to your **Word Chapter 2** folder, open **W2-D4-JobContacts**, and save it as **W2-D4-JobContactsRevised**.

2. Click the move handle in the upper-left corner of the table to select the entire table.

   Remember, the insertion point has to be in the table, or you have to hover the mouse pointer over the table for the move handle to appear.

3. Choose **Table Tools→Design→Borders→Borders ⊞ menu button ▼** and choose **No Border**.

   You may see gridlines within the table, but they won't print; they are there just to guide you. The Borders menu button ▼ on the Design tab provides the option to turn gridlines on or off.

4. Select the first table row, choose **Table Tools→Design→Borders→Borders ⊞ menu button ▼**, and then choose **Outside Borders**.

5. Keep the first row selected and choose **Table Tools→Design→Table Styles→Shading ▨ menu button ▼**.

6. Choose **Light Gray, Background 2, Darker 10%**.

Use Table Styles

7. Make sure the insertion point is in the table and choose **Table Tools→Design→Table Styles**.

8. Click the **More** button to display the full gallery of styles.

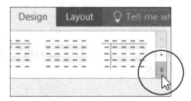

9. Move the mouse pointer over several styles and notice that Live Preview displays the styles in the table.

10. Choose **Grid Table 5 Dark**.

    The style overrides your cell margin spacing, borders, and shading. In turn, you can override Table Styles formatting by applying direct formatting.

11. Select the first row of the table; choose **Home→Font→Font menu button ▼→Century Gothic**.

12. Save the file but leave it open.

Remove Table Borders

Now that you know about table borders, you can remove the default borders on the résumé to give it a sleeker look.

13. Open **W2-D3-StellaResume** and save it as **W2-D4-StellaResume**.

14. Click the move handle to select the entire table.

15. Choose **Table Tools→Design→Borders→Borders** ⊞ **menu button** ▼.

16. Choose **No Border** from the menu and then deselect.

17. Choose **File→Print** to see how neat and professional the résumé looks.

18. Click **Back** ⬅ to return to the Word screen.

19. Save and close the résumé.

Sorting Data in a Table

When sorting a table, you can choose to sort one or more columns in ascending or descending order and specify whether the first row of the table is a header row. You can sort a table by up to three levels. For example, say you have a table containing column headings for city, state, and zip. You can sort the table first by state, then by city within state, and then by zip code within city.

		Second sort level (City)	First sort level (State)	Third sort level (Zip)
Name	Address	City	State	Zip
Laurie Chu	61 Granger Road	Flagstaff	Arizona	86002
Martin Hernandez	45 Priscilla Court	Holbrook	Arizona	86025
Maria Valera	254 Part Street	Colorado Springs	Colorado	80840
Ella Goodspeed	32 Ash Lane	Denver	Colorado	80215
Adam Chaffee	51 Stony Lane	Denver	Colorado	80226

DEVELOP YOUR SKILLS: W2-D5

In this exercise, you will sort data in the Job Contacts file. You will want to sort the contacts table as it continues to grow so you can easily locate information. In this example, the table will be sorted by city and by company name within city. You could also sort the table by company name if you're looking for a particular company, or by contact date if you want to locate a company you contacted on a certain date.

Before You Begin: *The W2-D4-JobContactsRevised file should still be open on the screen.*

1. Save the file as **W2-D5-JobContactsRevised**.

2. With the insertion point in the table, choose **Table Tools→Layout→Data→Sort** ⬙↓ to open the Sort dialog box.

As the list grows longer, it will be convenient to have the cities sorted together so you can focus on one geographic area at a time.

Sorting Data in a Table **43**

3. In the **Sort By** field, click the drop-down arrow and choose **City** from the menu.

Notice the Ascending and Descending option buttons on the right. Because you won't change that option, the cities will be sorted in Ascending (A to Z) order.

4. In the **Then By** field, choose **Co Name**.

This will sort the company names alphabetically within city.

Notice the Header Row button in the bottom-left corner of the dialog box. This option indicates that the table has a header row, which prevents the row from being sorted in with the rest of the data.

5. Click **OK** and observe the sorted table.

 As new rows are added to the bottom of the table, simply execute the sort again to re-establish the sort order.

6. Save and close the file.

Using Templates

All documents are based on a template, which can include text, formatting, graphics, and other objects. The default template is Blank Document. The benefit of templates is that they do not change when documents *based on them* change. When you start a new document, you are opening a *copy* of the template. This lets you use templates repeatedly as the basis for new documents. Word provides a variety of ready-to-use templates, or you can create your own personal templates.

Templates are located in the Start screen or in Backstage view when you are starting a new file. Basing a new document on a template can save you a lot of time as much of the work is already included for you.

≡ File→New

DEVELOP YOUR SKILLS: W2-D6

In this exercise, you will search for a résumé template and use it as the basis for a new résumé file.

1. Choose **File→New** and then follow these steps to locate a résumé template:

 Ⓐ Type **resume** in the search field at the top of the screen.

 Ⓑ Click the **Start Searching** button.

2. Scroll through the templates and locate a functional résumé of your choice.

You can open and close several until you decide which one you want.

3. Use data from Stella's résumé if you wish, or create your own data to complete the new résumé.

You can add or delete template elements and change formatting as desired.

4. Save the file as **W2-D6-MyResume** and then close it.

Saving Personal Templates

When you create a document containing specific formatting, you can save it to use later as a template. You should save the template in the Custom Office Templates folder unless instructed to do otherwise, because saving your templates there makes them appear when you click the Personal link on the templates screen.

This Personal category refers to Word-supplied templates such as personal letterhead.

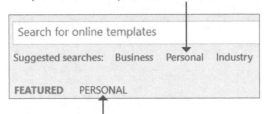

This PERSONAL category refers to templates you create yourself.

 Some users of MS Office Professional Plus 2016 might not see the Personal link as shown here.

DEVELOP YOUR SKILLS: W2-D7

In this exercise, you will open a copy of a personal budget and save it as a template, so you can use it over and over every month. The variable text of the budget has been removed; however, other elements are still in place, including the expense items and the formatting.

1. Navigate to your **Word Chapter 2** folder, open **W2-D7-PersonalBudget**, and notice the elements that are in place that will be helpful each month when you create a new budget.

2. Choose **File→Save As**, double-click the file path above the current filename to open File Explorer, and choose **Word Template (*.dotx)** from the Save As Type list at the bottom of the dialog box.

   Notice the file path that appears at the top of the Save As dialog box, which leads to the default Custom Office Templates. Unless instructed to do otherwise, you should use this folder if you want your template to appear when you click the Personal link on the templates screen. Word defaults to the Custom Office Templates folder in the Documents folder as the file storage location.

3. Save the file.

4. Close the template file and then choose **File→New**.

5. Follow these steps to open a copy of your template:

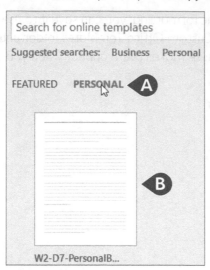

W2-D7-PersonalB...

Ⓐ Click the **PERSONAL** link (if you do not see the link, skip to step #6).

Ⓑ Click your template to open a copy.

Notice the DocumentX filename in the title bar at the top of the window. This indicates that you are working on a copy of the template rather than the template itself.

6. Close the file and exit Word.

📖 What to Do Before a Job Interview

Many job search sites, such as Monster.com and Careerbuilder.com, offer career advice including interviewing tips. Or do a web search of *interview tips*, and you'll get lots of tips to steer you in the right direction. Here are a few things to keep in mind:

▶ Anticipate the interviewer's questions and prepare your answers. You can even search for interview questions that are typical for a specific career, such as *interview questions for electrical engineers*.

▶ Practice, practice, practice. Get a friend or colleague to role play interviews with you. The more you practice, the more confident you will be during the interview.

▶ Think of questions you would like to ask the interviewer, especially those that demonstrate your interest in the job and company.

▶ Decide on your wardrobe. Conduct an Internet search for *how to dress for an interview*. Also, it's fine to ask the person scheduling the interview what the company dress code is. When in doubt, err on the side of conservatism.

▶ What to take with you: driving directions and contact information, folder/briefcase, paper copies of your résumé, pen, and notepad.

▶ What to not take with you: ear buds, cell phone that is not turned off, baseball cap, chewing gum, food or drink, distracting jewelry.

Self-Assessment

Check your knowledge of this chapter's key concepts and skills using the Self-Assessment in your ebook or eLab course.

Reinforce Your Skills

REINFORCE YOUR SKILLS: W2-R1

Insert Tables and Format Table Elements

Kids for Change is partnering with the local Center for Environmental Health to identify products in the home that present a risk to babies. In this exercise, you will create and enter data in a table. You will resize columns, rows, and cell margins and change alignment. You will use a Quick Table, convert a tabular document to a table, and split and merge cells.

1. Start Word and create a document using the **Single Spaced (Blank)** template saved as **W2-R1-RiskToBabies**.
2. Choose the **Insert→Tables→Table** 🏢 button and create a **3×6** table.
3. Enter the data shown here, select the first row, and choose **Home→Font→Bold** B :

 Remember, you can add rows to the bottom of a table by tapping Tab *when you reach the last table cell.*

Member Name	School	Research Assignment
Stacey	Highland	Harmful chemicals
Jacob	Lincoln	Cribs
Noah	Tri-way	Baby slings
Emma	Blue Ridge	Bath seats
Olivia	Springville	Highchairs
Nanda	Arlington	Infant swings

Now you will resize the columns.

4. Position the mouse pointer on the border between *Member Name* and *School*.
5. When the mouse pointer changes to the adjust pointer, drag to the left about ¾".
6. Resize the second and third columns to be just as wide as they need to be to fit the data without allowing any text to wrap within the cell.
7. Position the adjust pointer on the bottom border of the top row and drag down until the row is about twice its original height.
8. Select the first row and choose **Table Tools→Layout→Alignment→Align Center** 🔲 .

Next you will insert a calendar Quick Table so you can keep track of meetings with the Center for Environmental Health.

9. Position the insertion point at the end of the document and tap Enter twice.
10. Choose **Insert→Tables→Table** 🏢 , slide the mouse pointer down to **Quick Tables**, and insert **Calendar 2**.

Now you will copy a tabular table from another file and paste it into your document.

Convert a Tabular Document to a Table

11. Open **W2-R1-FoodRisk** and then select the entire document.
12. Choose **Home→Clipboard→Copy** 🗋 and then close the file.
13. Position the insertion point at the end of the **Risk to Babies** document and tap Enter .

14. Choose **Home→Clipboard→Paste** 🗐 and, if necessary, display formatting marks.

    Notice that the columns in this tabular table are separated by a single tab. Remember, there must be only one tab between columns for the conversion to work properly.

15. Select the entire tabular table and choose **Insert→Tables→Table** ⊞**→Convert Text to Table**.

16. Accept the defaults in the dialog box and click **OK**.

17. Use the mouse pointer to select the *Food* and *Risk Factor* columns.

18. Choose **Table Tools→Layout→Alignment→Align Center**.

19. Choose **Table Tools→Layout→Alignment→Cell Margins** ⊞.

20. In the Table Options dialog box, change the top and bottom margins to **0.04** and click **OK**.

    This increases the vertical space between cells.

21. Click in the first table row.

22. Choose **Table Tools→Layout→Rows & Columns→Insert Above** ⊞ and then position the insertion point in the first cell of the new row.

23. Choose **Table Tools→Layout→Merge→Split Cells** ⊞.

24. In the Split Cells dialog box, change the number of columns to **4**; click **OK**.

25. Select the first row.

26. Choose **Table Tools→Layout→Merge→Merge Cells** ⊞.

27. Click in the new row and type **Food Risk**.

28. Save and close the file.

REINFORCE YOUR SKILLS: W2-R2

Format and Sort a Table

Kids for Change members are planning a demonstration of safe cleaning products at the Community Center. They plan to distribute a table document that lists safe products you can use in the kitchen. In this exercise, you will use table formats to design a professional-looking table that is engaging and easy to read. Because you need to share this and other materials with other Kids for Change members, you will create a personal fax cover template to save time later.

1. Open **W2-R2-SafeClean** and save it as **W2-R2-SafeCleanRevised**.

2. Make sure the insertion point is in the table.

3. Choose **Table Tools→Design→Table Styles**, open the **Table Styles gallery**, and choose **Grid Table 4 – Accent 6**.

    Hint: It's a green style.

4. Select the table and choose **Table Tools→Design→Borders→Borders** ⊞ **menu button** ▼→ **Outside Borders**.

5. Select the first row and choose **Table Tools→Design→Borders→Borders** ⊞ **menu button** ▼→ **Bottom Border**.

6. With the first row still selected, choose **Table Tools→Design→Table Styles→Shading** 🖎 **menu button** ▼.

7. Choose **Green, Accent 6, Darker 50%** (last green color in the right column).

8. Select the entire table and choose **Home→Font→Font menu button** ▼ →**Comic Sans MS**.

9. Select in the first column starting at *Clean coffee pot* through the end of the column.

10. Choose **Home→Font→Italic** I .

11. Save and close the file.

Sort a Data Table

Dylan, a Kids for Change member, volunteers at a green cleaning supply company so he can become familiar with safe cleaning products. He has been asked to take inventory this month, which is a good way to get to know the products. Dylan plans to sort the inventory list by Category and then by Sub-Category. This will make it easier to locate the items in the warehouse.

12. Open **W2-R2-Inventory** and save it as **W2-R2-InventoryRevised**.

13. Select the entire table and choose **Table Tools→Layout→Data→Sort** ; if necessary, choose the **Header Row** option in the bottom-left corner of the Sort dialog box.

14. Choose **Sort By menu button** ▼ →**Category** and then choose **Then By→Sub-Category**; click **OK**.

    It will now be easier for Dylan to inventory the cleaning supplies.

15. Save and close the file.

Create a Table with a Template

16. Open the table template **W2-R2-Fax Cover (Green Design)** and save it as **W2-R2-KidsFaxCover**.

17. When you see a message asking if you want to save the template, click **Yes**.

> **Tip!** Hover the mouse pointer over the fax cover thumbnail to see the full template name in a ToolTip. Some names are similar, so be sure to select the exact above description.

18. You will not include a logo in the fax cover, so click the **YOUR LOGO HERE** icon, and when you see small circles indicating the object is selected, tap ⌑Delete⌑ to remove it.

19. In the second row, click the **Your Company Slogan** control and type **Think Globally, Act Locally**.

20. Scroll to the bottom of the page and fill in the following contact information, clicking each corresponding field:

    [Your Company Name]: **Kids for Change**

    [Street Address]: **159 Park Boulevard**

    [City, ST ZIP Code]: **Atlanta, GA 30313**

    Phone [000-000-0000]: **404-555-0100**

    Fax [000-000-0000]: **404-555-0101**

    [Email]: **Kids@Yahoo.com**

    Now that you have customized the fax cover with Kids for Change information, you will save it as a personal template so you can use it over and over without typing the company slogan and contact information repeatedly.

21. Choose **File→Save As**, navigate to any file storage location, and choose **Word Template (*.dotx)** from the Save As Type list.

Notice that the file path at the top of the dialog box leads to the default Custom Office Templates. Unless instructed to do otherwise, you should use this folder if you want your template to appear when you click the PERSONAL link on the templates screen.

22. Save the file and then close the template file.

Now you'll test your new template.

23. Choose **File→New**, click the **PERSONAL** link as shown, and then click your template.

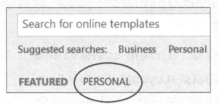

24. Click the **W2-R2-KidsFaxCover** thumbnail to open a copy of the template.

Notice that the default file name in the title bar is DocumentX, *indicating that this is a copy of your template.*

25. Close the file and choose **Don't Save** when prompted to save changes.

REINFORCE YOUR SKILLS: W2-R3

Insert and Format Tables

This holiday season Kids for Change members are working with the local fire department to collect toys for needy kids. The members will be assigned to different neighborhoods for collecting toys. In this exercise, you will format a table that tracks how many toys each member collects. In preparation for sending out mailing lists and tracking additional donations, you will sort a table, insert a Quick Table, convert text to a table, and finally use a template.

1. Open **W2-R3-Toys** and save it as **W2-R3-ToysRevised**.
2. Select the second and third columns of the first table.
3. Choose **Table Tools→Layout→Alignment→Align Center** ▣.
4. Select the entire table and choose **Table Tools→Layout→Alignment→Cell Margins** ▦.
5. Change the top and bottom margins to **0.06** and then click **OK**.

Merge Cells, Format the Table, and Sort Data

6. Select the four *Sycamore* cells in the third column.
7. Choose **Table Tools→Layout→Merge→Merge Cells** ▦ and then delete three of the *Sycamore* entries.
8. Use the same technique to merge the *Homestead Valley* and *Middle Ridge* cells and then delete three *Homestead Valley* and three *Middle Ridge* entries.
9. Select the entire table.
10. Choose **Table Tools→Design→Borders→Borders** ▦ **menu button** ▾**→No Border**.

Only the gridlines, which do not print, are visible—unless they were turned off. (Remember, you can turn gridlines on and off via the Table Tools' Design tab and the Borders menu button ▾*.)*

11. Choose **Table Tools→Design→Table Styles→More** ⊡→**Grid Table 4 – Accent 5** style.

Hint: It's a blue style.

Several Kids for Change regional directors plan to meet following the toy collection to discuss plans for next year's collection. They compiled a mailing list of directors who will be notified of the meeting. Now you will sort the mail as presorted mail results in lower postage rates.

12. Scroll to the table on page 3 and position the insertion point in the table.

13. Choose **Table Tools→Layout→Data→Sort** ⊞.

14. Ensure that **Header Row** in the Sort dialog box is chosen and then choose to sort first by **State**, then by **City**, and finally by **Zip**. Click **OK**.

The California cities sorted in ascending alphabetic order within State, and the Dallas Zip codes sorted in ascending numeric order within City.

Insert Rows and Resize Columns

15. Scroll to the table on page 4.

Region 5 was accidentally omitted.

16. Position the mouse pointer to the left of, and between, the last two rows until the insert control appears.

Region
1
2
3
4
6

17. Click the **insert control** to insert a blank row between the last two rows and then enter the following data in the new row:

5	1,951	2,543

18. Select the entire table and choose **Table Tools→Layout→Cell Size→AutoFit** ⊞→**AutoFit Contents**.

Insert a Quick Table and Convert Text to a Table

Kids for Change members decided to take up a collection from friends and family to purchase additional toys. You will insert a Quick Table for tracking the donations.

19. If necessary, display formatting marks and then position the insertion point next to the last paragraph symbol on page 4.

20. Choose **Insert→Tables→Table** ⊞→**Quick Tables→Tabular List**.

21. Select the *ITEM* heading and type **MEMBER** in its place; select the *NEEDED* heading and type **AMOUNT** in its place.

22. Select the remaining rows, tap Delete, and then enter the new data as shown.

MEMBER	AMOUNT
Ella	$20
Tom	$17
Roger	$32
Stella	$15
Jennifer	$22
Max	$29
Jose	$35
Albert	$40

23. Scroll to page 2 and select the rows in the tabular table.

24. Choose **Insert→Tables→Table →Convert Text to Table**.

25. When the Convert Text to Table dialog box appears, click **OK** and then save and close the file.

Use a Template

Kids for Change had a successful toy collection campaign, and now the employees are ready to celebrate. You have volunteered to create a flyer announcing the event.

26. Choose **File→New** and choose the **Event** category of templates.

Search for online templates							🔍
Suggested searches:	Business	Personal	Industry	Print	Design Sets	Education	Event

27. Double-click the **Winter Holiday Event Flyer** and save it as `W2-R3-HolidayFlyer`.

28. Use the following notes to complete the flyer.

What to select	What to type
Your Holiday Event	Celebration!
Date	December 17th
Time	7:00 p.m.
Address	159 Park Boulevard, Atlanta
Paragraph below address	Our toy collection was a great success, and we hope you'll join us to celebrate. Egg nog, hot cider, and munchies will be served. See you there!
Your Organization	Kids for Change

29. Save and close the file and then exit Word.

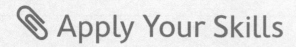# Apply Your Skills

APPLY YOUR SKILLS: W2-A1

Insert and Modify a Table

Universal Corporate Events is finalizing its schedule for the autumn cruises. You have been asked to complete the September cruise schedule for the Bahamas. In this exercise, you will insert a new table, align data, and resize columns and cell margins.

1. Start Word; open **W2-A1-CorpEvents** and save it as **W2-A1-CorpEventsRevised**.

2. If needed, display formatting marks and then position the insertion point on the first blank line below *Oceanic Cruise Lines*.

3. Insert a **4×4 table** and enter the data shown:

Date	Itinerary	Ship	From
09/02/16	4-night Bahamas Cruise from Miami	Oceanic Star	$560
09/09/16	3-night Bahamas Cruise from Miami	Oceanic Jewel	$600
09/30/16	7-night Bahamas Cruise from New York	Oceanic Odyssey	$1159

You accidentally overlooked the September 22 cruise, so you'll add that now.

4. Use the **insert control** to add a row between the last two rows and then enter this information:

09/22/16	7-night Bahamas Cruise from New York	Oceanic Star	$1120

5. Select the last two columns and then center-align the text.

6. Use the adjust pointer to resize the columns to the approximate width shown in the following figure.

Date	Itinerary	Ship	From
09/02/16	4-night Bahamas Cruise from Miami	Oceanic Star	$560
09/09/16	3-night Bahamas Cruise from Miami	Oceanic Jewel	$600
09/22/16	7 night Bahamas Cruise from New York	Oceanic Star	$1120
09/30/16	7-night Bahamas Cruise from New York	Oceanic Odyssey	$1159

7. Set the top/bottom margins to **0.08"**.

8. Insert a new row at the top of the table.

9. Merge the cells in the new row and type **Travel Special** as the table heading.

   Next, you will convert a table to text.

10. Scroll to page 2 and select the entire table.

11. Choose **Table Tools→Layout→Data→Convert to Text** and then click **OK**.

12. Save and close the file.

Format and Sort Tables

A Universal Corporate Events sales rep has asked you to prepare two tables of travel packages that he will present to two different clients. In this exercise, you will format the tables with borders, shading, and table styles and then you will sort the data. Finally, you will customize a template that you will use for gathering traveler information.

1. Open **W2-A2-Universal** from your **Word Chapter 2** folder and save it as **W2-A2-UniversalRevised**.
2. Remove the borders from the table on page 1.
3. Select the first row and use the **Borders** ⊞ **menu** button ▼ to apply a bottom border.
4. Apply a bottom border to the last row of the table.
5. Select the first row and then choose **Table Tools→Design→Table Styles→Shading** ⬛ **menu button** ▼ **→Gold, Accent 4, Darker 25%**.
6. Select the third row and apply **Gold, Accent 4, Lighter 60%**.
7. Apply the same color you used in the third row to the fifth row.
8. Scroll to page 2, position the insertion point in the table, choose **Table Tools→Design→Table Styles**, and open the Table Styles gallery.
9. Choose **Grid Table 6 Colorful — Accent 4**; it's a yellow style.

Sort Data and Insert a Row

10. Using the page 2 table, specify that the table has a header row and sort by the **Travel Package** column in ascending order.
11. Using the page 1 table, insert a blank row at the top of the table, merge the cells in the first row, and type **Universal Corporate Events**.
12. Use **Align Center** ▣ to center the heading and then apply shading, **Gold, Accent 4, Lighter 40%**.
    The black print in the second row is a bit hard to read.
13. Change the Font Color **A** to **white**.
14. Save and close the file.

Use a Template

15. Choose **File→New** and use the search field to locate templates in the travel category.
16. Open a copy of the **Client Travel Planning Form** and save it as a template, naming it **W2-A2-TravelerInfo**.
17. Select *Travel Agency Name* and type **Universal Corporate Events** in its place.
18. Use your imagination to complete the two rows at the top of the form.
19. Scroll down and delete the rows at the bottom of the form, starting with *Tour Information*.
20. Save and close the file.

Create and Format Tables

The Universal Corporate Events marketing manager has asked you to create a list of the day tours from Paris. She also asks that you reformat the list of African trips and modify and reformat the Asian tour table. In this exercise, you will create a table, convert a table to text, and sort and reformat a table.

1. Open **W2-A3-Travel** from your **Word Chapter 2** folder, save it as **W2-A3-TravelRevised**, and, if necessary, display formatting marks.
2. Position the insertion point next to the first paragraph symbol at the top of the page.
3. Insert a **4×5 table** and enter the data as shown:

Day Tours	From	When	Duration
Versailles	$70	Daily except Mon	4 hrs.
Eiffel Tower	$75	Daily	3 hrs.
Louvre Museum	$65	Daily except Tue	2.5 hrs.
Moulin Rouge Show	$153	Daily	4.5 hrs.

4. Scroll to page 3 and select the table.
5. Convert the table to text; ensure that the *Tabs* option is chosen in the dialog box.

Sort a Table

6. Scroll to page 2 and position the insertion point in the table.
7. Open the **Sort** dialog box, indicate that the table has a header row, and sort by the **Dates** column in ascending order.
8. Delete the **Discount** column and use the **insert control** to add a column between *Dates* and *Duration*.
9. Enter the information shown in the following figure:

Departure
San Francisco
Los Angeles
Los Angeles
San Diego
San Francisco

10. Select **columns 2—5** and position the adjust pointer between two of the selected columns.
11. Double-click to autofit the columns to the width of the longest entry in each of the selected columns.
12. Insert a row at the top of the table and merge all cells in the row.
13. Type **Universal Corporate Events** in the row and center align the text.
14. Select the table and remove all borders.
15. Select the first row, apply outside borders, and apply a blue shading color of your choice.
16. Save and close the file; exit Word.

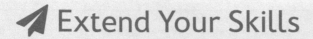 Extend Your Skills

These exercises challenge you to think critically and apply your new skills. You will be evaluated on your ability to follow directions, completeness, creativity, and the use of proper grammar and mechanics. Save files to your chapter folder. Submit assignments as directed.

W2-E1   That's the Way I See It

You own a hardware store, and a few building contractors order from you in large quantities. Track their contact information in a ten-row table with column heads for Name, Address, City, State, and Zip. Your business covers four states: Utah, Arizona, New Mexico, and Colorado. Include each state and sort by State, then by City, then by Zip. Add a column at the end of the table for Phone and enter the new data. Add a header row centering your company name. Apply a table style and then save the file as **W2-E1-Contractors**.

You want to market to other contractors and will use a template to track them. Search for online **name and address list** templates. Open the Party Guest List template and modify it for your needs. For example, delete the image at the top and change the title. Change the column headings as needed and then apply a table style. Enter three new prospects. Save the file as **W2-E1-Prospects**.

W2-E2   Be Your Own Boss

Business is blooming at Blue Jean Landscaping; you need to get control of inventory. Decide how many landscapers work for you and the number of items needed to keep them supplied. Create a six-row table listing tools, such as spades and hoes. Note how many you have and how many you need to add. Include headings for Item, Location, Units Needed, Units in Stock, Units to Add, and Price. Add five rows of data, sort by item, and resize the columns as needed. Add a header row centering the company name. Add borders and shading for readability. Save the file as **W2-E2-Inventory**.

You've landed a big corporate client, and you'll need lots of plants to landscape the property. You will use an inventory template to help you keep track of plants to buy. Search for online **inventory** templates. Open a copy of the Physical Inventory Count Sheet template. Modify the title, column headings, and any other parts of the template to suit your needs. Start your list by entering five plants you'll need to purchase for the job. Save the file as **W2-E2-PlantsNeeded**.

W2-E3   Demonstrate Proficiency

The chef at Stormy BBQ will introduce a new dish. Decide on the dish and then create a document named **W2-E3-Order**. Set up a table for the food order including item, price, quantity, and cost and then enter five food items. Sort the table in an order you think most useful. Add a heading row and enter the restaurant name centered. Size the table so it's easy to read and apply a table style of your choice.

New dishes mean a new menu will be needed. Search for a menu template and modify it to include standard BBQ items as well as the new item you created the food order list for. Format it in a way that is attractive and will be easy for customers to read. Save your menu as **W2-E3-BBQMenu**.

3 | Creating a Promotional Brochure

In this chapter, you will add graphic elements, such as WordArt, to a brochure. SmartArt graphics provide a gallery of predesigned diagrams such as lists, processes, cycles, hierarchies, and relationships that help you communicate ideas clearly and vividly. Borders and page color add a polished look to your brochure. Live preview galleries allow you to quickly test many choices while deciding what looks best for your brochure. All these and more help you create materials that are both dynamic and informative.

LEARNING OBJECTIVES

▸ Create an eye-catching brochure

▸ Insert shapes in a document

▸ Add pictures, text boxes, and WordArt to a document

▸ Choose page setup features

▸ Communicate information with SmartArt

▸ Format the page background

📁 Project: Promoting an Ergonomics Seminar

As the owner of Ergonomic Office Solutions, you have decided to create a presentation about the benefits of an ergonomic office. Your friend, Tommy Choi, owner of Green Clean, has provided you with his customer database. Knowing Tommy's customers are already interested in the environment, you believe they would be interested in your products. (You are already beginning the process of understanding who your audience is.) You decide to create a brochure to mail to local businesses promoting a seminar. You will use product pictures as well as shapes, WordArt, and SmartArt to create a brochure that is both informative and visually appealing.

📖 Designing an Engaging Brochure

Knowing your audience is the path to successful communication. This principal applies to almost everything you write. The readers want to know what's in it for them. Analyze them; walk in their shoes. What interests them? What would they want from you? What can you do for them? How can you engage them?

Design is critical. Use photos, shapes, and graphics that grab the audience's attention. And be sure to incorporate blank space. Without it, your page will look cluttered and hard to read. Space provides balance and symmetry. Don't get complicated. People tend to skim, so keep it simple. Your message should be clear, crisp, and concise. Decide which points are priorities and use bullets to focus the reader's attention. Limit the number of fonts to two or three and use fonts that are clean and easy to read.

Color is significant. Use a color scheme that reflects your photos and graphics. Color also conveys feeling and mood. Direct the reader's eye by highlighting important elements with prominent placement and distinctive colors. Take time to think about the colors you use; you may want to conduct an Internet search of the *psychology of color*.

Branding is important. Express your brand with a consistent logo, tagline, and color scheme that complement your company's other brand assets, such as packaging, your website, and media campaigns.

Working with Shapes

There is a large gallery of graphic shapes available to you, including lines, text boxes, rectangles, ovals, and many others. They can add interest to documents, such as flyers and brochures, and you can type text in most shapes. You can also rotate, resize, and move shapes. You insert shapes from the Shapes gallery. When a shape is selected (displays round handles), the contextual Drawing Tools and Format tabs appear, where you can choose many styles and designs for your shape.

≡ Insert→Illustrations→Shapes 🔲 | Drawing Tools→Format→Insert Shapes

☁️ View the video "Using Shapes."

☁️ View the video "Adding Text to and Formatting Shapes."

In this exercise, you will draw, size, and move shapes. You'll maintain a shape's proportions with the Shift *key when resizing, and you'll see how the mouse pointer changes appearance based on various ways you work with shapes.*

1. Open **W3-D1-Brochure** and save it as **W3-D1-BrochureRevised** in your **Word Chapter 3** folder.

2. If necessary, turn on formatting marks.

   Notice that a number of paragraph symbols are already in the document. It can be easier to work with graphics if some spacing is already set up.

3. Choose **Insert→Illustrations→Shapes** ⬡ to display the Shapes gallery.

4. Choose the **Rounded Rectangle** from the Rectangles category.

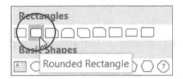

   After you choose a shape, the mouse pointer changes to a crosshair icon resembling a plus sign (+), which you click or drag in the document to create the shape.

5. Click and drag anywhere in the document to draw a rounded rectangle.

6. Choose **Insert→Illustrations→Shapes** ⬡ and then choose the **Rounded Rectangle** again.

7. Hold the Shift key and drag to draw another rounded rectangle.

   This time you drew a perfect square with rounded corners instead of an elongated rectangle, even though you started with the same shape. Holding down the Shift *key while drawing maintains the proportional relationship between the shape's width and height.*

Resize and Rotate Shapes

8. With the square shape selected (displaying round handles), follow these steps to resize the shape:

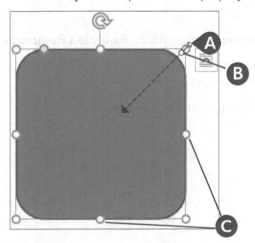

   Ⓐ Position the mouse pointer on the top-right corner sizing handle.

   Ⓑ Hold Shift and drag diagonally toward the center of the shape to resize while maintaining proportions.

   Ⓒ Drag from a side handle to change only the height or width of the object.

9. Follow these steps to rotate the shape:

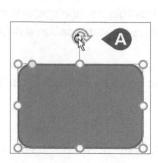 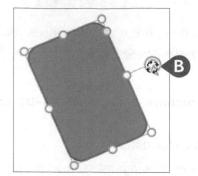

Ⓐ Position the mouse pointer on the rotation handle; the mouse pointer appears as a circular arrow.

Ⓑ Click and drag to the right about 45 degrees; the mouse pointer appears as four small arrows when rotating.

 Holding Shift *allows you to select multiple shapes at once. Then you can delete, move, or format them all at once.*

10. If necessary, click one of the shapes to display the handles and then hold Shift and click the other shape.

11. Tap Delete to remove both shapes.

You can use the ruler to help align and size shapes and other graphic images. It may or may not be visible on your screen.

12. If necessary, choose **View→Show→Ruler**.

Notice that there are two rulers: one at the top and one at the side of the screen. The margin areas (1" by default) are the gray areas at the left, right, top, or bottom ends of the rulers. The typing areas are white.

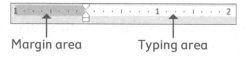

Margin area   Typing area

13. Choose **Insert→Illustrations→Shapes** 🔲 and choose **Rounded Rectangle** again.

14. Starting about 1" from the top of the page and about 1" from the left-hand margin, draw a 1" tall rectangle that spans the page but remains within the margins.

15. Position the mouse pointer on the shape until the pointer appears as a four-headed arrow.

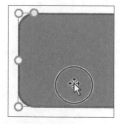

16. Practice dragging the shape to move it and then return it to its original position.

17. Save the file.

Adding Text and Formatting Shapes

You can add text to shapes you draw. This is handy if, for example, you want to create a flyer announcing an event. Just select the shape and begin typing the announcement. Text is automatically centered horizontally and vertically, and it wraps within a shape as you type.

The contextual Format tab contains many tools you can use to add pizzazz to a shape, including Shape Styles, Shadow effects, and 3-D effects. The contextual Format tab also has its own Shapes gallery in the Insert Shapes group. It contains the same shapes as the Shapes gallery located in the Illustrations group on the Insert tab.

 Drawing Tools→Format→Shape Styles

DEVELOP YOUR SKILLS: W3-D2

In this exercise, you will add text to a shape and format the text. Then you will format the shape using the Shape Styles gallery.

1. Save your file as **W3-D2-BrochureRevised**.
2. If necessary, select the rectangle shape at the top of the page by clicking anywhere on it.
3. Tap ⌐Caps Lock⌐, type **ERGONOMIC OFFICE SOLUTIONS**, tap ⌐Enter⌐, and type **PRESENTS**. Tap ⌐Caps Lock⌐ once more to turn it off.

   Notice that the text was automatically centered in the shape.
4. Click the border of the shape, taking care not to drag.

 Selecting a shape by clicking the border selects everything inside the shape. Thus, the text in the shape is selected, although it is not highlighted.

5. Choose **Home→Font→Font menu button ▼→Tahoma**.
6. Keep the shape selected and apply **Bold 22 pt** font.
7. If your shape is not big enough for the larger text, drag a sizing handle to enlarge it.

   Next, you will use the Shape Styles gallery to format the shape.
8. Make sure the object is selected so the contextual Format tab is available and then choose **Drawing Tools→Format→Shape Styles**.
9. Click the **More** button on the Shape Styles gallery to open the gallery.

10. Choose **Subtle Effect – Blue, Accent 1**.
11. Save the file.

Using WordArt and Inserting Pictures

WordArt is great for creating smart-looking text objects. It's wonderful for creating special effects such as logos and headings in newsletters, flyers, and brochures. You can use the built-in designs as they are, or you can customize them.

You can browse through your computer, or other computers, to locate pictures and other images for your document, or you can search online.

Search for pictures saved as files on a computer.

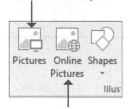

Search online for pictures and other images.

WordArt and pictures can be rotated, resized, and moved like other objects. The cropping tool can be used to remove any unwanted parts of a picture making portions of the image transparent, allowing anything under it to show through.

 View the video "Enhancing Pictures."

≡ Insert→Text→WordArt 🄰

≡ Insert→Illustrations→Pictures 🖼 *or* Online Pictures 🖼

Aligning Objects

You can manually drag and drop objects to align them, but using the Align feature on the contextual Format tab is more precise. Select the objects you want to align and then choose the desired alignment.

 The terms object and image are both used when referring to graphical elements such as shapes, WordArt, and pictures.

≡ Drawing Tools→Format→Arrange→Align 🗒

DEVELOP YOUR SKILLS: W3-D3

In this exercise, you will add a WordArt object and align it with a shape. You will insert and resize a picture and make its background transparent. Then you will format and move the table.

1. Save your file as **W3-D3-BrochureRevised**.
2. Click in the document below the rectangle.
3. Choose **Insert→Text→WordArt** 🄰.

4. Choose **Fill – Black, Text 1, Outline – Background 1, Hard Shadow – Accent1** from the menu that appears and then type **The Ergonomically Challenged Office**.

5. Place the mouse pointer on the border of the WordArt object and then drag to position it about 1" below the rectangle.

   Don't worry about centering it below the shape; you will center-align the objects in the next steps.

6. With the WordArt object still selected, hold down Shift and click the rounded rectangle above it that you created earlier.

   Both objects should be selected—handles appear on both.

7. Choose **Drawing Tools→Format→Arrange→Align** 🖫 **→Align Center**.

   This center-aligns the objects with each other.

8. If necessary, drag the selected objects so they are centered between the margins.

Insert a Picture

9. Scroll down and position the insertion point in the left cell of the table.

10. Choose **Insert→Illustrations→Pictures** 🖾.

11. Navigate to your **Word Chapter 3** folder and double-click **ErgoChair.jpg** to insert it.

12. Hold the Shift and resize the picture using a corner handle until it matches the height of the text on the right.

    This picture has a white background. Later, you will add background color to your brochure and the picture's white background won't blend with the background color. Your chair would look like this when the background color is applied. Therefore, you will make it transparent, allowing the brochure's background color to show through.

What: Luncheon Seminar
Where: The Bakery Café
When: September 27th at noon

13. With the chair image selected, choose **Picture Tools→Format→Adjust→Color** .

14. Choose **Set Transparent Color** at the bottom of the menu.

15. Click in the white background of the image.

    This makes the white background transparent, so when you add the page color to the brochure, the color will show through the picture's transparent background.

16. Click anywhere to deselect the image. Then position the mouse pointer on the line between the two cells and double-click to resize the cell.

What: Luncheon Seminar
Where: The Bakery Café
When: September 27th at noon

17. Select the table using the move handle and then choose **Home→Paragraph→Center** ▤.

18. With the table still selected, choose **Home→Paragraph→Borders** ⊞ **menu button** ▾.

19. Choose **No Border** to complete the page.

20. If gridlines appear in the table (although they won't print), follow these steps to remove them:
  - Make sure the table is selected.
  - Choose **Table Tools→Layout→Table→View Gridlines** .

21. Save your file.

Using Text Boxes and Page Setup Options

A text box is a special type of shape designed for inserting text or graphics. You may wonder how inserting a text box is different from drawing a shape and adding text inside it. It's because of the formatting. All documents are based on a theme, which contains a set of theme colors and theme fonts. The default theme for a new blank document is Office. When you originally created the rounded rectangles, they used a blue fill color that was the default fill color for *shapes*. Text boxes do not contain those formatting characteristics. You can format all of the text by selecting the text box itself or format only a portion of the text by selecting the part you want to change. The techniques for rotating, sizing, and moving are the same for text boxes as for other graphics.

 Insert→Illustrations→Shapes →Text Box | Insert→Text→Text Box

View the video "Creating a Text Box."

Page Setup Options

Commonly used page setup options include page breaks, margins, page orientation, and paper size. All of these are located in the Page Setup group on the Layout tab. Some page setup options also appear in the Print screen in Backstage view.

Layout→Page Setup

Tip! *You can use* Ctrl + Enter *to quickly insert a manual page break.*

View the video "Page Setup Options."

DEVELOP YOUR SKILLS: W3-D4

In this exercise, you will insert a text box, align it with other objects, and format the text box border and the text within it. Then you will insert a page break to create a second page for your brochure.

1. Save your file as **W3-D4-BrochureRevised**.

2. Choose **Insert→Illustrations→Shapes** and then choose **Text Box** from the Basic Shapes category in the Shapes gallery.

3. Position the mouse pointer below the WordArt object you created previously and then drag to draw a text box about **2" wide** and **½" tall**.

4. Type this text and size the box so the text wrapping is the same as shown:

> Email EOS@Yahoo.com or call
> 712-555-0123 to register.

5. If the email address appears as a hyperlink, right-click it and choose **Remove Hyperlink**.

6. Make sure the text box is selected and then choose **Home→Paragraph→Center** ▤.

7. Choose **Drawing Tools→Format→Shape Styles→Shape Outline** ◩ **menu button** ▾ and choose **Blue, Accent 1, Lighter 40%**.

8. With the text box still selected, hold down Shift and select the two objects above it.

9. Choose **Drawing Tools→Format→Arrange→Align** 🖫 and choose **Align Center**.

10. Click to deselect. If necessary, move the text box so it is well balanced on the page.

   Your brochure will be two pages in length, so you will now insert a page break to create a second page.

11. Position the insertion point at the bottom of the page.

12. Choose **Layout→Page Setup→Breaks** ⊟**→Page**.

   Notice the other Page Setup options, including Margins, Orientation, and Size.

13. If necessary, display formatting marks and notice the page break symbol and the new second page.

   Now you will delete the page break and use keystrokes to re-insert a page break.

14. Position the insertion point in front of the page break symbol and tap Delete.

15. Press Ctrl + Enter to insert another page break.

16. Save your file.

Working with SmartArt

It is often easier to grasp concepts if information is presented graphically rather than textually. The SmartArt gallery provides a large variety of graphics that you can add to documents. They make it easy to combine predesigned graphics with text to create sophisticated figures. SmartArt images are divided into the following categories.

Category	Purpose
▤ List	Shows nonsequential data
⋯ Process	Use to show a progression, a timeline, or sequential steps in a task, process, or workflow.
♻ Cycle	Shows a continual process
🗄 Hierarchy	Creates a hierarchical structure or shows a decision tree
▣ Relationship	Illustrates associations
✦ Matrix	Shows how parts relate to a whole
◮ Pyramid	Shows proportional relationships
◩ Picture	Used when you want to convey your message with or without explanatory text, or when you want to use pictures to complement a list or process

≡ Insert→Illustrations→SmartArt 🖾

Inserting SmartArt Text and Modifying an Image

You can use the SmartArt text pane to add text to your image. Text placeholders in the image are replaced with text as you enter in the SmartArt text pane. The font size adjusts based on the amount of information you type. If you prefer, you can type directly in the text placeholders in the image.

If you cannot find the exact image you want, you can modify, add, and delete shapes within the graphic. SmartArt objects are formatted the same way as other graphic shapes.

 View the video "SmartArt Text and Bullets."

 View the video "Modifying SmartArt."

DEVELOP YOUR SKILLS: W3-D5

In this exercise, you will create two SmartArt graphics: one to list the seminar topics and one to list ergonomic products. Then, you will customize and resize the graphics.

1. Save your file as **W3-D5-BrochureRevised**.
2. If necessary, move the insertion point to the top of page 2.
3. Choose **Home→Paragraph→Center** ≡.

   This will center the SmartArt image that will be inserted next on the page.
4. Choose **Insert→Illustrations→SmartArt** 📷.
5. Follow these steps to insert a SmartArt graphic:

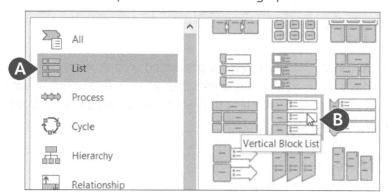

   Ⓐ Choose the **List** category.

   Ⓑ Scroll down and choose **Vertical Block List**.
6. Read the description in the bottom-right corner of the dialog box and then click **OK**.
7. If the text pane is not visible, click the tab.

Customize the Image

This image has three major text objects, but you will use only one.

8. Position the mouse pointer to the left of the first major bullet and then drag down to select the first six bullets.

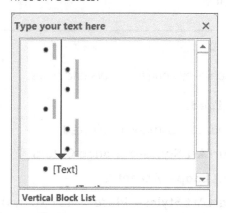

9. Tap Delete to remove the bullets.

10. Follow these steps to begin entering the seminar topics:

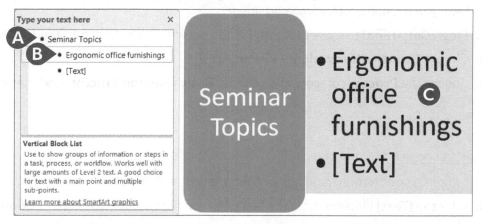

Ⓐ Position the insertion point to the right of the first bullet and type **Seminar Topics**.

Ⓑ Tap ↓ and type **Ergonomic office furnishings**.

Ⓒ Notice that the text appears in the graphic as you type.

11. Tap ↓ to go to the next line and type **Mobile workstations**.

12. Tap Enter to generate the next bullet and then type **Technology support**.

13. Tap Enter as needed and then type the following items to complete the list:
    • **Personal lighting options**
    • **Q&A**

14. Click **Close** × in the upper-right corner of the text pane.

15. Click the outside border frame to make sure the *entire* SmartArt image is selected.

    You will resize the SmartArt object next. If an object within the main frame is selected, you could accidentally resize only a part of the SmartArt object. Clicking the outside border frame prevents that.

16. Drag the bottom-center sizing handle up until the image is approximately half as tall as the original image.

17. Save your file.

Changing a SmartArt Style

The SmartArt Styles gallery allows you to apply interesting variations of the original graphic. Live Preview lets you sample the effect of the various styles without actually applying them.

≡ SmartArt Tools→Design→SmartArt Styles

DEVELOP YOUR SKILLS: W3-D6

In this exercise, you will customize SmartArt graphics by applying colors and styles.

1. Save your file as **W3-D6-BrochureRevised**.
2. Make sure the outside border of the seminar topics image is selected.
3. Choose **SmartArt Tools→Design→SmartArt Styles→Change Colors** 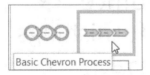.
4. In the Accent 1 category, choose **Gradient Loop – Accent 1**.
5. Choose **SmartArt Tools→Design→SmartArt Styles→More** ⊡ to display the SmartArt Styles gallery.
6. In the 3-D category, choose **Metallic Scene**.

   Next, you will add another SmartArt image.

7. Press Ctrl + End to move to the end of the document and then tap Enter twice.
8. Choose **Insert→Illustrations→SmartArt** 🖼.
9. Choose the **Process** category, then choose **Basic Chevron Process**, and then click **OK**.

   You can type directly in the image without opening the text pane.

10. Click the **[Text]** placeholder in the first arrow on the left and type **Our Products**.
11. Click in each **[Text]** placeholder and enter the text as shown:

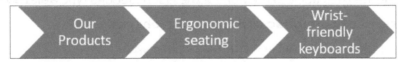

12. Click the outside border of the image and then follow these steps to add an arrow to the graphic:

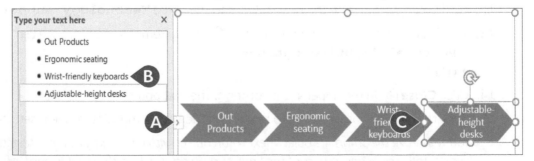

   Ⓐ Click the tab to open the text pane.
   Ⓑ Position the insertion point after the word *keyboards* and tap Enter.
   Ⓒ Type **Adjustable-height desks** in the new arrow.
13. **Close** ☒ the text pane.

Format the Image

14. Click the outside border of the shape.

15. Choose **SmartArt Tools→Design→SmartArt Styles→Change Colors** ⬚.

16. Choose the fourth item in the Accent 1 category, **Gradient Loop — Accent 1**.

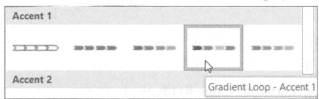

17. Click the **More** ⬚ button on the SmartArt Styles gallery, and in the 3-D category, choose **Cartoon**.

18. Choose **SmartArt Tools→Format→Align→Align Center** ⬚ **→Align Center**.

19. Save your file.

Formatting the Page Background

Page background formats add color and visual variety to your documents. Page colors and borders provide the finishing touches that add professional polish. For example, you can add colors from a gallery specifically designed to blend with a document's theme. Border colors are also designed to tastefully complement page colors.

Adding Page Colors and Page Borders

The Page Colors gallery is similar to other galleries you have worked with. The colors that appear in the Theme Colors section of the gallery, as the name implies, are based on the theme currently in effect in the document.

Page borders surround the outer edges of the entire page. You can adjust the color (again, based on the current theme), line thickness, and other features of the border.

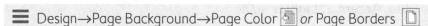

≡ Design→Page Background→Page Color ⬚ or Page Borders ⬚

DEVELOP YOUR SKILLS: W3-D7

In this exercise, you will sample background colors using Live Preview. Then you will add a background color to your brochure and a border surrounding the pages.

1. Save your file as **W3-D7-BrochureRevised**.

2. Choose **Design→Page Background→Page Color** ⬚.

3. Hover the mouse pointer over several colors in the Theme Colors area of the gallery.

Live Preview displays the effects of the different colors.

4. Choose **Dark Blue, Text 2, Lighter 40%**.

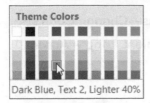

Now you'll add a page border.

5. Choose **Design→Page Background→Page Borders** .

6. Choose **Box** from the Setting area in the left-hand panel.

7. Follow these steps to format the page border:

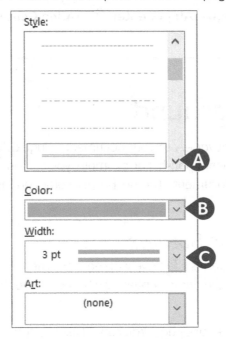

Ⓐ Choose the **double-line** Style.

Ⓑ Choose **Blue, Accent 1, Lighter 40%**.

Ⓒ Choose a Width of **3 pt** and then click **OK**.

8. Save and then close your file; exit Word.

Self-Assessment

Check your knowledge of this chapter's key concepts and skills using the Self-Assessment in your ebook or eLab course.

Reinforce Your Skills

Create a Flyer Recognizing an Outstanding Volunteer

Kids for Change has a volunteer program, and the person who volunteers the most hours in a quarter is recognized for his or her service. In this exercise, you will create a flyer announcing Janisha Robinson as the winner for this quarter. You will work with shapes, WordArt, pictures, and text boxes.

1. Start Word and create a new file based on the **Blank Document** template. Save it as **W3-R1-JanishaFlyer**.

2. Display formatting marks and tap Enter 20 times.

   It can be easier to work with graphics if some spacing is already set up.

3. If necessary, choose **View→Show→Ruler** to display the ruler.

4. Choose **Insert→Illustrations→Shapes**, and in the Stars and Banners category, choose **Down Ribbon**.

5. Position the crosshair mouse pointer next to the paragraph symbol at the top of the page.

6. Press and hold the mouse button and drag until the image is about **6½" wide** and **1½" tall**.

7. Type **Outstanding Member** in the image, then click the border to select the entire shape.

8. Choose **Home→Font→Font menu button** ▼ →**Comic Sans MS** and then apply **28 pt**, **Bold** B.

9. Choose **Home→Font→Font Color** A **menu button** ▼ and choose **Red** in the Standard Colors category.

Insert and Crop a Picture

10. Position the insertion point a little below the graphic.

11. Choose **Insert→Illustrations→Pictures**, navigate to your **Word Chapter 3** folder, and double-click **Janisha.jpg**.

    Now you will resize the picture.

12. Press and hold Shift and then position the mouse pointer on the handle in the upper-right corner of the picture.

13. Drag diagonally toward the center until the picture is about **3" wide**.

    Next you will crop off the left side of the picture.

14. Make sure the picture is selected and then choose **Picture Tools→Format→Size→Crop**.

WORD

15. Follow these steps to crop the picture:

Ⓐ Position the mouse pointer on the left-center cropping handle.

Ⓑ Drag to the right to Janisha's right hand and then click in the document to deselect.

Next you will place a border on the picture to give it a finished look.

16. Select the picture, then choose **Picture Tools→Format→Picture Styles→Picture Border** ☑ **menu button** ▾ and pick a shade of blue that you think will blend well.

Now you will choose a layout option that will allow you to freely move the picture on the page.

17. Click the **Layout Options** 🖼 smart tag at the upper-right side of the picture and choose **In Front of Text** (bottom-right).

18. Drag the picture to the center of the page.

Use WordArt

19. Position the insertion point a little below the picture.

20. Choose **Insert→Text→WordArt** 𝐴 and choose **Fill — Blue, Accent 1, Outline — Background 1, Hard Shadow — Accent 1**.

21. Type **Janisha Robinson** in the image and then click the outside border to select the entire image.

22. Choose **Drawing Tools→Format→WordArt Styles→Text Effects** 𝔸 **→Transform**.

23. In the Warp category, choose **Chevron Down**.

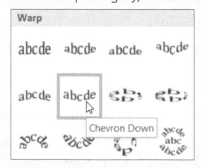

24. Center the WordArt on the page.

Add a Text Box

25. Choose **Insert→Illustrations→Shapes** 🔷 **→Text Box**.

26. Below Janisha's name, draw a text box that is approximately **4" wide** and **2½" tall** and then type the following text:

Kids Helping Communities

• After-school tutor

- `Schoolyard cleanup`
- `Meals for shut-ins`
- `Emergency relief food collection`

27. Click the border of the text box, choose **Home→Font→Font menu button ▾→Comic Sans MS**, and apply **20 pt** font size; resize the text box if needed.

28. Hold down ⟦Shift⟧ and select all the images.

29. Choose **Drawing Tools→Format→Arrange→Align 🖺→Align Center**.

    This center-aligns the images with each other.

30. Use the zoom control in the bottom-right corner of the screen to zoom out until you see the entire page.

31. If necessary, adjust the position of the images so they are well balanced on the page and then zoom back to **100%**.

32. Save and close the file.

REINFORCE YOUR SKILLS: W3-R2

Create a Flyer for Charity

Kids for Change is partnering with a local charity to collect clothing and household products for people with developmental disabilities. You have been asked to create a flyer to help in the collection process. In this exercise, you will change page orientation, work with graphic images, and add page color and a page border to the flyer.

1. Start a new document based on the **Blank Document** template and save it as **W3-R2-DonationsFlyer**.

2. If necessary, choose **View→Show→Ruler**.

3. Choose **Layout→Page Setup→Orientation 🖺→Landscape**.

4. Tap ⟦Enter⟧ 15 times to set up some spacing in advance and then position the insertion point at the top of the page.

5. Choose **Insert→Illustrations→Pictures 🖼** and then navigate to your **Word Chapter 3** folder and double-click **Donations.png**.

    Now you will use a text-wrapping layout option so you can easily move the image.

6. Make sure the image is selected, then click the **Layout Options 🖻** smart tag at the upper-right corner of the image and choose **In Front of Text** (bottom-right).

7. Drag the image to center it between the margins.

8. Position the insertion point below the picture.

Add WordArt and SmartArt

9. Choose **Insert→Text→WordArt 🄰** and choose **Fill – Gray – 50%, Accent 3, Sharp Bevel**.

10. Type the following text in the WordArt image:
    We need clothing, furniture, appliances, and household items.

11. Click outside the image to deselect.

12. Position the insertion point below the WordArt image.

13. Choose **Insert→Illustrations→SmartArt** 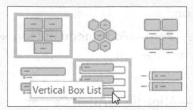; then click the **List** category, choose **Vertical Box List**, and click **OK**.

Now you will resize the SmartArt image so it fits on the first page.

14. Press and hold [Shift] and then position the mouse pointer on the handle in the upper-right corner of the image.

15. Drag diagonally toward the center of the image until it is about **3" wide**.

It should now be positioned on the first page.

16. Click the **Layout Options** ⊞ smart tag to the right of the image and choose **In Front of Text**.

Now you can move the image freely on the page.

17. Center the image between the margins.

Recolor the Image

18. Click the outside border to select the entire image.

19. Choose **SmartArt Tools→Design→Change Colors** ⠿ and choose **Colored Fill – Accent 3**.

20. Type the following in the three **[Text]** areas:

    Place boxes or bags by 8 a.m.

    Donations will be picked up by dark.

    Thank you for your contributions!

21. Click outside the image to deselect.

Change the Page Color and Add a Page Border

22. Choose **Design→Page Background→Page Color** 🖾 and then choose **White, Background 1, Darker 25%**.

Instead of using lines for the border, you will use an art border.

23. Choose **Design→Page Background→Page Borders** 🗋.

24. Click the drop-down arrow in the **Art** field at the bottom of the dialog box and choose the **hot air balloons**.

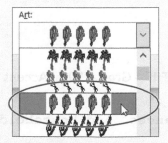

25. Click **OK** and turn off formatting marks.

26. Use the zoom controls at the bottom right of the screen to zoom out and see the entire page.

27. If necessary, adjust the position of the images so they are well balanced on the page and then zoom back to **100%**.

28. Save and close the file.

Create a Recycling Flyer

Kids for Change held a recycling campaign last month. Your cousin, Ingrid, is enjoying a semester studying at the Sorbonne in Paris. She saw the flyer you created, and she would like to implement a recycling program at the university. She asks that you create a copy of your flyer on standard European-size paper, A4. In this exercise, you will recreate the flyer using graphic images, a picture, a text box, as well as a page background and border.

1. Start a new document using the **Blank Document** template; save it as **W3-R3-RecycleFlyer**.

2. Choose **Layout→Page Setup→Size** ⬚ **→A4**.

3. Display the formatting marks and ruler, if necessary.

4. Tap Enter about twenty-five times to set up spacing in your flyer and then position the insertion point at the top of the page.

5. Choose **Insert→Text→WordArt** 𝐴 and choose **Fill – Gray – 25%, Background 2, Inner Shadow**.

6. Type **Reduce, Reuse, Recycle** in the WordArt image and then click the outside border.

7. Choose **Drawing Tools→Format→WordArt Styles→Text Fill** ⬚ **menu button** ▾**→Green, Accent 6**.

8. Choose **Drawing Tools→Format→Shape Styles→Shape Effects** ⬚ **→Shadow**.

9. In the Outer category, choose **Offset Diagonal Top Left**.

10. Choose **Drawing Tools→Format→WordArt Styles→Text Effects** ⬚ **→Transform**.

11. In the Warp category, choose **Chevron Up**.

12. If necessary, drag the WordArt to center it between the margins, then position the insertion point a little below it.

Add a Picture to the Flyer

13. Choose **Insert→Illustrations→Pictures** ⬚, navigate to your **Word Chapter 3** folder, and double-click **World.jpg**.

14. Hold down Shift and resize the picture until it's about **3" wide**.

15. Click the **Layout Options** smart tag and choose **In Front of Text** and then drag the picture to center it on the page.

Now you will place a border on the picture.

16. With the picture selected, choose **Picture Tools→Format→Picture Styles→Picture Border** ⬚ **menu button** ▾**→Weight→3 pt**.

17. Choose **Picture Tools→Format→Picture Styles→Picture Border menu button** ▾**→Green, Accent 6, Darker 25%**.

Add a Text Box

18. Choose **Insert→Illustrations→Shapes** 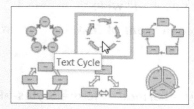→**Text Box**.

19. Draw a text box a little below the picture about **3½" wide** and **2" tall** and then type the following text in the text box:

    • **Separate your trash**
    • **Always look for recycle bins**
    • **Reuse shopping bags**
    • **If it's broken, fix it**
    • **Buy recycled products**

20. Click the border of the text box and choose **Home→Font→18 pt**.

21. Resize your text box if needed; don't allow the text to wrap.

22. Click the border to select the object.

23. Choose **Drawing Tools→Format→Shape Styles→Shape Outline** menu button ▼→**No Outline**.

24. Choose **Drawing Tools→Format→Shape Styles→Shape Fill** menu button ▼ and choose **Green, Accent 6, Lighter 60%**.

Use a Shape

25. Choose **Insert→Illustrations→Shapes**, and in the Stars and Banners category, choose **6-Point Star**.

26. While holding down [Shift], draw a star about **2½" wide** below the text box and on the left side of the page.

27. Choose **Drawing Tools→Format→Shape Styles** and from the Shape Styles gallery choose **Colored Fill – Green, Accent 6**.

28. Type the following in the star:

    Be a star!

    Do your part!

Insert SmartArt

29. Position the insertion point a little below the text box.

30. Choose **Insert→Illustrations→SmartArt**; then click the **Cycle** category, choose **Text Cycle**, and click **OK**.

31. Type the following items in the **[Text]** boxes in any order:

    Paper

    Metal

    Plastic

    Hazardous Waste

    Glass

32. Hold down [Shift] and resize the image until it's about **3½" wide**, then click the **Layout Options** smart tag and choose **In Front of Text**.

33. Arrange the star and SmartArt as needed so the star is on the left below the text box and the SmartArt is on the right below the text box.

34. Click the outside border of the SmartArt.

    This image has an inside frame and an outside frame.

35. Click one of the arrows in the image, and you'll see both frames.

36. With both frames selected, choose **SmartArt Tools→Format→Shape Styles**; in the Shape Styles gallery, choose **Colored Fill — Green, Accent 6**.

    This recolors that arrow that you originally clicked to display both frames. Also, notice that the Shape Styles gallery is now displaying the color you chose.

37. Click the next arrow (you won't see handles on the arrow) and click the green color that's visible in the gallery.

38. Continue until all arrows are recolored and then deselect the image.

39. Use the zoom controls to zoom out until you see the entire page.

40. If needed, rearrange the objects so they are balanced on the page to your satisfaction and zoom back to **100%**.

Add Page Color and a Page Border

41. Choose **Design→Page Background→Page Color** 🎨 **→Green, Accent 6, Lighter 60%**.

42. Choose **Design→Page Background→Page Borders** 🗔 and choose a line style, color, and width of your choice; click **OK**.

43. Save and close the file.

WORD

📎 Apply Your Skills

APPLY YOUR SKILLS: W3-A1

Create a Services Flyer

The Universal Corporate Events marketing manager asked you to create a flyer highlighting services that Universal Corporate Events offers. You will use a picture and graphics to add zing to your flyer.

1. Start a new document using the **Blank Document** template and save it as **W3-A1-Services**.
2. Tap Enter enough times to position the insertion point close to the bottom margin and then move the insertion point to the top of the page.
3. Insert the **Horizontal Scroll** shape from the Stars and Banners category.
4. Drag in the document until the scroll is about **6½" wide** and **1" tall**.
5. Type **Take Off with Universal Corporate Events** and then change the font size to **24 pt**.
6. Resize the shape, if necessary, and then position the insertion point a bit below the shape.
7. Insert the **Plane.jpg** picture located in your **Word Chapter 3** folder.
8. Click the **Layout Options** smart tag and choose **In Front of Text**.
9. While maintaining the height/width proportions, resize the picture to about **3" wide**, then position the picture just below the Shapes image and center it between the margins.

   Now you'll add a border to the picture.

10. Choose **Picture Tools→Format→Picture Styles→Picture Border menu button ▾→ Weight →3 pt**.
11. Change the picture border color to **Blue, Accent 1, Darker 25%**.

Add WordArt and a Text Box

12. Position the insertion point below the picture and insert a WordArt graphic using **Fill − Blue, Accent 1, Shadow**.
13. Type **Services We Offer**; center the graphic on the page.
14. Format the WordArt image by using the **Text Effects, Bevel** category, and choosing the **Circle**.
15. Then in the Text Effects, Transform category, choose **Arch Up** (first form in the Follow Path category).
16. Insert a text box shape below the WordArt image that is about **4" wide** and **1½" tall**.
17. Enter the following in the text box:
    - **Online itinerary**
    - **Online flight tracking**
    - **Travel insurance**
    - **Visa and passport services**
18. Remove the outline border from the text box.
19. Change the text to **22 pt** and then resize the text box if needed.

Align Images

20. Hold the Shift key and select all four images.

21. Use the **Align** feature to center-align the images with each other.

22. If necessary, drag the selected images to center them between the margins.

23. Zoom out to **Full Page View** and adjust the placement of the images as you deem necessary for the flyer to appear well balanced; then zoom back to **100%**.

24. Save and close the file.

APPLY YOUR SKILLS: W3-A2

Create a European Tours Flyer

A Universal Corporate Events sales rep has asked you to create a flyer for a corporate client who is planning an employee rewards plan. The client will be choosing among three options for the reward tour. In this exercise, you will change the page orientation, format the page background, and use SmartArt to highlight the details of the recommended tours.

1. Start a new file based on the **Blank Document** template and save it as **W3-A2-CorpTours**.

2. Use landscape orientation for the flyer, tap Enter until the insertion point is close to the bottom margin and then position the insertion point at the top of the page.

3. Apply the Page Color **Gold, Accent 4, Lighter 60%**.

4. Add a page border, making the formatting choices as shown. (Color is Gold, Accent 4, Darker 25%).

5. Use a WordArt image of your choice to add a **Universal Corporate Events** heading to the flyer; use a Text Fill color that blends well with the background color and a Text Effect of your choice.

6. Position the insertion point about 1" below the heading and insert the SmartArt graphic **Vertical Chevron List**, which is in the Process category.

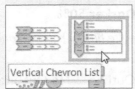

7. Resize the graphic, maintaining its proportions, to about **3" wide** and **3½" tall**.

8. Click the **Layout Options** smart tag and choose **In Front of Text**.

9. In the first blue *[Text]* box, type **London**; type **Berlin** and **Rome** in the next two blue *[Text]* boxes.

10. In the bulleted list to the right of *London*, enter **Stonehenge**, **Windsor Castle**, and **Tate Gallery**.

11. Enter **Dresden**, **Potsdam**, and **Rothenburg** for Berlin and **Pompeii**, **Tuscany**, and **Capri** for Rome.

Format the WordArt Graphic

12. Change the SmartArt color using the first color option in the Colorful category.

13. Select the white rectangle next to *London* and change the **Shape Fill** color to a color that you feel complements the London object.

14. Use the same technique to color the *Berlin* and *Rome* rectangles.

15. Arrange and size the objects in a balanced manner on the page.

16. Save and close the file.

APPLY YOUR SKILLS: W3-A3

Create a Mileage Awards Flyer

Universal Corporate Events provides car rentals for travelers, and the company is currently offering mileage awards. In this exercise, you will create a flyer highlighting the award offerings. You will use graphics for interest and format the flyer background for a polished, professional look.

1. Start a new document using the **Blank Document** template and name it **W3-A3-CarRental**.

2. Tap Enter until the insertion point is close to the bottom margin and then move the insertion point to the top of the page.

   Next you will use WordArt to create a heading for the flyer.

3. Insert a new **WordArt** image, using the design in the third row, fifth column.

4. Enter the following text: **Universal Corporate Events**.

Add a Text Box and a Picture

5. Insert a text box below the WordArt about **3½" wide** and **1" tall** and then type the following lines in the text box.

   Get behind the wheel!

   Get more reward travel!

6. Change the font size to **22 pt**; resize the text box if necessary.

7. Change the font color to **Gray — 25%, Background 2, Darker 50%**.

   Later you will add page color, and removing the text box's white fill background and its outline will make the text box blend in better.

8. Change the Shape Fill to **No Fill** and change the Shape Outline to **No Outline**.

9. Position the insertion point a bit below the text box; then, insert the **Driver.jpg** file from your **Word Chapter 3** folder.

10. While maintaining the picture's proportions, resize the picture to about **2½" wide**.

11. Click the **Layout Options** smart tag and choose **In Front of Text**. Then center the picture between the margins.

12. With the picture selected, insert the **Center Shadow Rectangle** from the Picture Styles gallery.

13. Position the insertion point just below the picture and insert **Wave** in the Stars and Banners category of the Shapes gallery.

14. Draw the shape about **4½" wide** and **1" tall**, type Book Now! in the shape, and change the font size to **36 pt**.

15. With the shape selected, choose **Drawing Tools→Format→Shape Styles→Shape Fill→Gray – 25%, Background 2, Darker 25%**.

16. Change the shape outline to **white**.

17. Position the insertion point a bit below the shape.

18. Choose **Insert→Illustrations→SmartArt**, and in the List category, choose **Vertical Box List**.

19. While maintaining its proportions, resize the shape to about **3" wide**.

20. Click the **Layout Options** smart tag, choose **In Front of Text** and then select all three **blue shapes**.

21. Choose **SmartArt Tools→Format→Shape Styles→Shape Fill** and then choose **Gray – 25%, Background 2, Darker 25%**.

22. Select all three white rectangles and then choose the same color for the **Shape Outline** ☑.

23. Center the SmartArt between the margins at the bottom of the page and then type the following in the three **[Text]** areas:

```
100 award miles per day
125 bonus miles per day
150 miles for booking with us
```

24. Click to deselect, then zoom out to a full page view and, if needed, arrange the objects so they are well balanced on the page and then zoom back to **100%**.

Add a Page Color and a Page Border

25. Add the page color **Gray – 25%, Background 2, Darker 10%**.

26. Choose **Design→Page Background→Page Borders** and choose a line style that you prefer; then apply a **white** color and **3 pt** width.

    There is more white in the bottom half of the flyer. It may look better if the SmartArt heading were white.

27. Change the SmartArt Text Fill to **white**.

28. Save and close the file; exit Word.

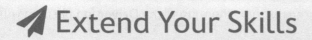 Extend Your Skills

These exercises challenge you to think critically and apply your new skills. You will be evaluated on your ability to follow directions, completeness, creativity, and the use of proper grammar and mechanics. Save files to your chapter folder. Submit assignments as directed.

W3-E1   That's the Way I See It

You just completed your training as a dietician, and now you are ready to advertise your services by distributing a brochure throughout the area. Start a new document and save it as **W3-E1-GoodDiet**. Design a brochure using WordArt, a picture, and a text box and use page color and a page border to give your brochure a polished look. Create a tagline for your business and explain the services you offer and the benefits of eating well. Also include a suggestion that the reader schedule an appointment today.

W3-E2   Be Your Own Boss

As the owner of Blue Jean Landscaping, a Georgia company, you hope to increase sales as your customers get ready to spruce up their gardens with spring plants. Start a new document and save it as **W3-E2-Spring**. Create a flyer using landscape orientation and include graphics of your choice and a picture. Describe the services you provide and use upbeat verbiage about spring gardening in Georgia. Suggest plants that are appropriate for Georgia's climate. If needed, conduct an Internet search for information about plants that grow well in Georgia in the spring. Give your flyer a finished look by adding page color and a page border.

W3-E3   Demonstrate Proficiency

Stormy BBQ is expanding to include a catering department! You have been asked to create a brochure announcing this new venture. Start a new document and save it as **W3-E3-Catering**. Include pictures of food that would normally be found in a BBQ restaurant, formatting and cropping them as necessary. Use a SmartArt graphic to list the types of events that you provide catering for and format the image to blend well with the pictures you have chosen. Use one or more text boxes containing testimonials from test customers who have already enjoyed your catering services. Add page color and a page border to your brochure.

4 | Creating Reports

In this chapter, you will create a simple report. Reports are important documents often used in business and education to distribute information, communicate ideas, and share viewpoints and plans on a variety of topics. You will format your report using tabs, indents, margin changes, and headers and footers. You will also learn about research papers, a requirement for nearly every college student as well as professionally employed individuals. Your paper will include footnotes, citations, a bibliography, and a table of figures. Finally, you will explore Track Changes, a feature that allows for collaborative editing of a document.

LEARNING OBJECTIVES

▸ Work with columns and set margins

▸ Apply styles

▸ Insert headers and footers

▸ Add footnotes and endnotes

▸ Insert citations and a bibliography

▸ Incorporate captions and a table of figures

▸ Insert comments and explore Track Changes

📁 Project: Researching Social Media and Internet Commerce

My Virtual Campus is a social networking technology company. It sells web applications to colleges and universities. Your marketing manager, José Morales, has asked you to look into the latest trends in social media in schools. It is important to understand how the "always connected" generation is using technology in the pursuit of education. Your manager also wants you to download an online article regarding social media in education that he can distribute in the next staff meeting. And he wants you to make the article's dense text more readable by using heading styles, headers and footers, and white space.

You are also working on your masters in marketing, and your professor wants you to write a research paper about the origins and evolution of Internet commerce. You will use many sophisticated features, such as headers and footers, footnotes, citations, and bibliographies in creating this research paper.

Creating a Business Report

When writing a business report, you want it to be easy to read. Dense blocks of text are difficult to read, so break up your report with lists, headings/subheadings, and white space. Use a clear, easy-to-read font, such as Calibri (Word's default font), Arial, or Times New Roman. Here are some principles of communication you may want to keep in mind when writing a report:

- ▸ Plan before you write.
- ▸ Know your audience.
- ▸ Use active voice.
- ▸ Avoid wordiness.
- ▸ Use plain language; avoid overblown words.

- ▸ Don't use clichés.
- ▸ Use parallel structure.
- ▸ Edit out anything that doesn't add to your meaning.
- ▸ Chunk your writing into short sections.

Setting Margins

Margins determine the amount of white space around the edges of the page. You can set margins for the entire document, a section, or selected text. The default margins in the Blank Document and Single Spaced (Blank) templates, as well as many others, are one inch all around. You can choose from a gallery of preset margins, or you can set your own custom margins.

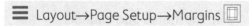 ☰ Layout→Page Setup→Margins ▦

Indenting Text

Indents offset text from the margins. You can set indents by using the buttons on the Ribbon or by adjusting the indent markers on the ruler. The Increase and Decrease Indent buttons adjust the indent of an entire paragraph (or one or more selected paragraphs) and affect the left indent only. They adjust the indent based on the default tab stops, which are set at every half inch.

You can set custom indents by dragging the indent markers on the horizontal ruler.

First line indent

Hanging indent

Left indent

Right indent

 View the video "Indent Markers."

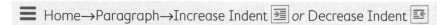 Home→Paragraph→Increase Indent 🔲 or Decrease Indent 🔲

DEVELOP YOUR SKILLS: W4-D1

In this exercise, you will increase the margins in a report to provide a little more white space. You will use the Increase Indent button on the Ribbon to offset quotes in the report, and you will create your own custom indents using the indent markers on the ruler.

1. Open **W4-D1-SocMediaRpt** from your **Word Chapter 4** folder and save it as **W4-D1-SocMediaRptRevised**.

2. If necessary, choose **View→Show→Ruler**.

    Now you will increase the margin width to add more white space to the report.

3. Choose **Layout→Page Setup→Margins** 🔲 and notice the preset margin settings.

    You want a 1.5" left and right margin, and that is not available in the preset list, so you will customize your own settings.

4. Choose **Custom Margins** at the bottom of the menu.

5. On the Margins tab of the Page Setup dialog box, change the left and right margins to **1.5"** and then click **OK**.

Margins			
Top:	1"	Bottom:	1"
Left:	1.5"	Right:	1.5"

Notice the gray margin areas at the ends of the ruler; they have increased to 1.5".

Now you will use the Increase Indent button to offset quotes in the report.

6. Below *The Net Generation* heading, select the second and third paragraphs, which are inside quotation marks.

7. Choose **Home→Paragraph→Increase Indent** 🔲.

    The paragraphs indent from the left a half inch based on the default tab settings; however, you want to indent the paragraphs from both the right and the left. So, now you will use the indent markers on the ruler to complete the job.

8. Follow these steps to adjust the left and right indents:

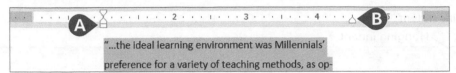

(A) Position the mouse pointer on the Left Indent marker (bottom rectangle) and drag to the **1"** mark.

(B) Drag the **Right Indent** marker to the **4½"** mark.

9. Save the report.

Setting Custom Tab Stops

Default tab stops are set every half inch, so the insertion point moves a half inch whenever you tap Tab. You can customize tab stops if you want other settings.

 Never use the Spacebar *key to line up columns. Even if it looks right on the screen, it most likely will not print correctly.*

Using the Ruler to Set Custom Tabs

Word has four types of custom tab stops: left, right, center, and decimal. You can set all four types using the horizontal ruler. It is critical that you position the insertion point in the line where you plan to set tabs. Tab settings are carried inside the paragraph symbol to the next paragraph when you tap Enter.

Use the Tabs box to choose the tab type. (ToolTips describe the symbols.)

You indicate the tab placement by clicking in the desired location on the ruler.

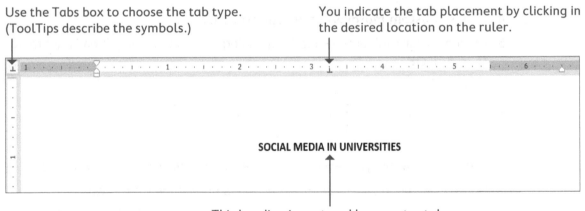

SOCIAL MEDIA IN UNIVERSITIES

This heading is centered by a center tab.

 You can delete a custom tab by dragging it off the ruler with your mouse. When you release the mouse button, the tab disappears.

Using the Tabs Dialog Box to Set Custom Tabs

You can also set custom tab stops in the Tabs dialog box. You can specify precise positions for tabs, choose the type of tab (alignment), clear custom tab stops, and set dot leader tabs. A leader tab generates a row of dots when you tap Tab. You often see dot leaders in a table of contents separating a topic from its page number.

You can change the default tab stops here.

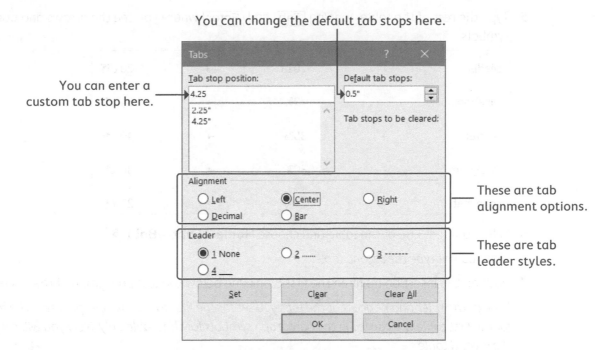

You can enter a custom tab stop here.

These are tab alignment options.

These are tab leader styles.

≡ Home→Paragraph→dialog box launcher 🔲→Tabs

DEVELOP YOUR SKILLS: W4-D2

In this exercise, you will set custom tabs and create two tabbed tables.

1. Save your report as **W4-D2-SocMediaRptRevised**.
2. If necessary, display formatting marks.
3. Position the insertion point on the blank line below the section titled *Rapid Increase in the Use of Social Media*.
4. Follow these steps to set tabs for the first table:

 If you accidentally click the tab in the wrong place, you can drag it to a new location with the mouse pointer, or you can drag it off the ruler and try again.

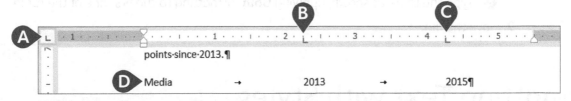

Ⓐ Verify that the Tabs box at the left of the ruler is set to a Left Tab. If not, click the box until it rotates around to Left Tab. (ToolTips describe the tab type.)

Ⓑ Click the ruler at the **2¼"** mark to set a tab.

Ⓒ Click the ruler at the **4¼"** mark for the second tab.

Ⓓ Type **Media** in the blank line and then type the next two entries, tapping Tab where you see the arrows and tapping Enter at the end of the line.

5. Type the rest of the table, tapping ⌈Tab⌉ and ⌈Enter⌉ where you see the arrows and paragraph symbols:

Media		2013		2015¶
Facebook	→	79%	→	84%¶
Twitter	→	35%	→	40%¶
Instagram	→	30%	→	36%¶
Snapchat	→	16%	→	23%¶

6. Select the first line of the table and choose **Home→Font→Bold** B .

Now you will type the second table.

7. Position the insertion point on the first blank line below the last paragraph of the document.

Look at the ruler and notice that the tabs you set for the first table have disappeared. The tab settings for the first table are carried in the paragraph symbols for that table only. Now you will set tabs for the second table.

8. Follow these steps to set the tabs and type the table:

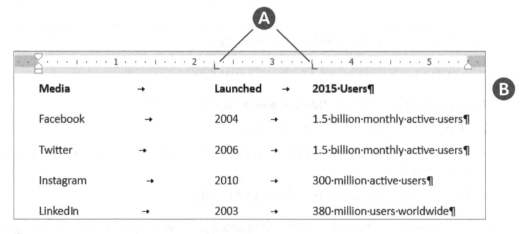

Ⓐ Set left tabs at the **2¼"** mark and the **3½"** mark.

Ⓑ Type the table as shown, applying **Bold** formatting to the first line of the table.

9. Save the file.

Formatting Text with Styles

A style is one of the most powerful formatting tools. It is a *group of formats* enabling you to apply multiple formats to a block of text all at once. Styles are based on the current template's theme, which is a set of colors, fonts, and graphic effects. There are styles for document elements, such as headings, titles, and special character formats, providing consistent formatting throughout a document.

Types of Styles

There are many built-in styles, and you are always working within a style. There are two basic types of styles: character and paragraph.

▶ Character styles: Character styles are applied to the word the insertion point is in or a selected group of words. Character styles contain only character formats, not paragraph formats. You can apply character styles *within* a paragraph that is formatted with a paragraph style.

▶ Paragraph styles: Paragraph styles are applied to all text in selected paragraphs or to the paragraph containing the insertion point. You can use any character or paragraph formats in a paragraph style. For example, you may want to format a heading with a large, bold font (character formatting) and apply paragraph spacing before and after the heading (paragraph formatting).

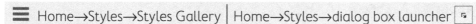 Home→Styles→Styles Gallery | Home→Styles→dialog box launcher

Collapsing Heading Topics

When you apply a heading style and the insertion point is in the heading, a small triangle marker appears at the left (whether formatting marks are displayed or not). You can click the marker to collapse and expand the text below it. In the following illustration, the text below *The Net Generation* is collapsed, allowing you to focus on certain parts of a document.

The·Net·Generation¶

■ Rapid·Increase·in·the·Use·of·Social·Media¶

A·study·conducted·by·Harvard's·Institute·of·Politics·(iop.harvard.edu)·reports·use·of·

In this illustration, *The Net Generation* content is expanded.

■ The·Net·Generation¶

In·her·article·appearing·in·The·Teaching·Professor,·August/September·2009,·Dalton·State·

College·psychology·professor·Christy·Price·makes·the·following·observations:¶

"...the·ideal·learning·environment·was·Millennials'·

preference·for·a·variety·of·teaching·methods,·as·

opposed·to·a·"lecture·only"·format."¶

"Respondents·thought·professors·who·involved·them·in·

class·with·a·variety·of·methods·(not·just·lecture)·as·

 View the video "Using the Styles Gallery and the Styles Task Pane."

In this exercise, you will use Live Preview in the Styles gallery to find styles that will give your report a professional, polished look. You will apply the Title style to the report's main heading and the Heading 1 style to the headings within the report.

1. Save your file as **W4-D3-SocMediaRptRevised**.

2. Click anywhere in the report's main heading, *SOCIAL MEDIA IN UNIVERSITIES,* at the top of page 1.

3. Choose **Home→Styles** and then click the **More** button to open the Styles gallery.

4. Hover the mouse pointer over the Title style to see its effect on the heading and then click to apply the style.

   Now you'll open the Styles task pane. It includes all the styles that are in the Styles gallery.

5. Click the **dialog box launcher** in the bottom-right corner of the Styles group.

   Next you'll apply the Heading 1 style to the headings in the body of the report.

6. Position the insertion point in *The Net Generation* heading and then click the **Heading 1** style in the task pane to apply that style to the heading.

7. Use the same technique to apply the Heading 1 style to the remaining headings: *Rapid Increase in the Use of Social Media* and *University Recruiting Through Social Networking.*

8. Close the Styles task pane.

   Now you will collapse and expand the text below The Net Generation heading.

9. Scroll up and position the insertion point in *The Net Generation* heading to display the triangle marker to the left of the heading.

10. Click the **marker** to collapse the text below the heading.

    Collapsing parts of a document allows you to center your focus on the remaining parts.

11. Click the **marker** again to expand the text.

12. Save the report.

Inserting Headers/Footers and Comments

Headers and footers appear at the top and bottom of every page in a document, respectively, above and below the margins. You can place text, page numbers, dates, and other items in the header and footer areas. When you enter information in these areas, it is repeated on every page of the document. There is a variety of built-in header and footer formatting styles, or you can create your own.

The Comment feature is a great collaboration tool. It allows reviewers and originators to communicate about a document by posting comments to each other.

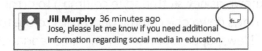

Clicking the reply button in the comments balloon allows threaded conversations between the originator and reviewers.

≡ Insert→Header & Footer→Header 🗋 or Footer 🗋 or Page Number 🗋

≡ Insert→Comments→Comment 💬

DEVELOP YOUR SKILLS: W4-D4

In this exercise, you will add headers and page numbers to the report using the built-in formats. Then you will add a comment to your report.

1. Save your file as **W4-D4-SocMediaRptRevised**.
2. Choose **Insert→Header & Footer→Header** 🗋 and choose the **Sideline** format from the gallery.
3. Click **Document Title** and type **My Virtual Campus** in its place.
4. Double-click in the document to close the header.
5. Choose **Insert→Header & Footer→Page Number** 🗋 and slide the mouse pointer down the menu to **Bottom of Page**.
6. Scroll down in the gallery and choose **Large Color 3**.
7. Double-click in the document to close the page number footer.

    You can open the header/footer area by double-clicking anywhere in either the header or footer area.

8. Double-click the footer area to open it and then double-click in the document again to close it.
9. Scroll through the report and observe the headers and page numbers.

    It would look better to have at least two lines of the first table at the top of the second page.

10. Position the insertion point in front of *Instagram* in the first table and press ⎡Ctrl⎤+⎡Enter⎤ to insert a page break.

Add a Comment

Now you will add a comment for your marketing manager. He will see it when he reads your report.

11. Scroll to the top of the document and select the word *Universities* (the anchor point for the comment) in the title.
12. Choose **Insert→Comments→Comment** 💬 and type the following in the comment balloon on the right:

    Jose, please let me know if you need additional information regarding social media in education.

13. Save and then close the report.

WORD

Arranging Text in Multiple Columns

You can use newspaper-style columns (also known as newsletter-style columns) to arrange text in multiple columns. In newspaper layout, text flows down one column and wraps to the top of the next column, as in a newspaper or magazine. Newspaper columns can enhance readability because shorter lines are easier to read, as the eye doesn't have to travel far across the page before reading the next line, and they break up dense text with random gaps. Columns are automatically reformatted as you add or delete text during editing cycles.

You can quickly set your text in columns with the Columns button on the Ribbon, or you can open the Columns dialog box where you can set up more sophisticated column layouts. For example, you can insert a line between columns and specify the width of each column.

These are commonly used column styles.

You can check this option if you want a line between columns.

You can preview your column setup here.

You can customize column widths and between-column spacing here.

≡ Layout→Page Setup→Columns 📄

≡ Layout→Page Setup→Columns 📄→More Columns

Column Breaks and Section Breaks

You can manually force a column to end by inserting a column break, thus moving the text at the break point to the top of the next column. This technique is often used to place headings at the top of columns and to balance columns on the last page of a multicolumn document.

Whenever you make a document-level formatting change that doesn't apply to the entire document, you need one or more section breaks to define the portion of the document affected by the change. For example, in a columnar magazine article, you may see a title line that extends across the page and then the body of the article is formatted in two columns. You need a section break to separate the one-column title from the two-column body of the article.

TYPES OF SECTION BREAKS

Section Break	Purpose
Next Page	Inserts a section break and starts the new section on the next page
Continuous	Inserts a section break and starts the new section on the same page
Odd Page	Inserts a section break and starts the new section on the next odd-numbered page; a blank page may be inserted to force the odd page section break
Even Page	Inserts a section break and starts the new section on the next even-numbered page; a blank page may be inserted to force the even-page section break

The following illustration shows the use of continuous section breaks that are sectioning off the two-column portion of a document.

The section above this break has one-column formatting, and the section below it has two-column formatting.

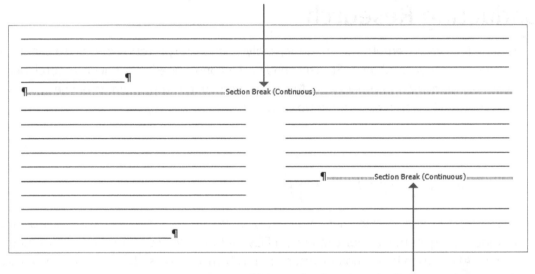

This section break ends the two-column section.

≡ Layout→Page Setup→Breaks ⊞→Page Breaks→Column

≡ Layout→Page Setup→Breaks ⊞→Page Breaks and then choose a Section Break type

DEVELOP YOUR SKILLS: W4-D5

Because the article your marketing manager wants to distribute at the next staff meeting consists of dense text, he wants you to set the article in newspaper columns to enhance readability. In this exercise, you will insert a section break after the introduction, and then you will layout the second section of the document in two columns.

1. Open **W4-D5-SocMedForStaff** from your **Word Chapter 4** folder and save it as **W4-D5-SocMedForStaffRevised**.

2. If necessary, display formatting marks.

   You want the introductory paragraph to span the page, so you will insert a section break before the social media article and then set the rest of the article in columns.

3. Position the insertion point in the second blank line following the first paragraph.

4. Choose **Layout→Page Setup→Breaks** **→Continuous**.

   This starts a new section on the same page.

5. Delete the blank line at the top of the second section.

6. Position the insertion point in the second section.

7. Choose **Layout→Page Setup→Columns** ▥**→Two**.

8. Scroll to page 2, and you'll see that the columns are not well balanced.

9. Position the insertion point at the beginning of the last paragraph in the left column beginning with *In the real world*.

10. Choose **Layout→Page Setup→Breaks** **→Column**.

11. Save and close the file.

📖 Conducting Research

Research is the systematic investigation, analysis, and interpretation of data to confirm facts, answer questions, or solve problems. Students and professionals need to conduct research and effectively document findings and conclusions. Much is written on this topic, and an online search yields many results. Try this search phrase: *how to conduct research for a paper*.

Writing a Research Paper

There are a number of documentation styles for research papers, each with their own specific formatting requirements. For example, IEEE standards are used for research in computers and electronics; APA is used in psychology research; Turabian style is used for research in literature, history, and the arts; and MLA is primarily used for research in the humanities.

The Modern Language Association publishes the *MLA Handbook for Writers of Research Papers*. The MLA style has specific formatting requirements, *some* of which are already defaults within Word. For example, the default margins of one inch comply with the MLA requirement. However, Word does not comply with *all* MLA guidelines by default.

Warning! *This chapter does not presume to be a resource for MLA guidelines. Refer to the MLA handbook or the MLA website (http://mla.org) for guidance in complying with MLA requirements.*

Working with Footnotes, Endnotes, and Citations

Footnotes, endnotes, and citations are important elements of most research papers. You use them to comment on, or cite a reference to, a designated part of the text. Footnotes appear at the bottom of pages on which they are inserted; endnotes, as the name implies, appear at the end of a document or section; and citations appear on a separate Works Cited page at the end of the document. Works Cited is another name for a Bibliography. You can enter the source information when you create the citation or insert a placeholder and add the source data later.

View the video "Inserting Footnotes."

 View the video "Inserting Citations."

≡ References→Footnotes→Insert Footnote AB¹ *or* Insert Endnote 🖼

≡ References→Citations & Bibliography→Insert Citation ⤵

DEVELOP YOUR SKILLS: W4-D6

In this exercise, you will begin the research paper that your marketing professor requested. You will use footnotes and endnotes to clarify information and citations to support your premise.

1. Open **W4-D6-Internet** from your **Word Chapter 4** folder and save it as **W4-D6-InternetRevised**.

2. If necessary, choose **View→Views→Print Layout** 📄.

   Footnotes may differ in appearance depending on the view you are using.

3. Position the insertion point at the top of the document and type the following four lines of text above the title, tapping [Enter] after each line, except the last:

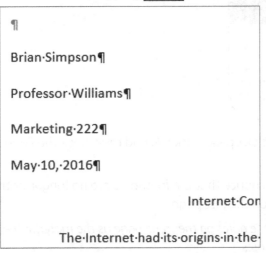

   Notice the paragraph text is double-spaced and the extra space after the paragraphs has been removed per MLA requirements. Now you will insert footnotes.

4. Position the insertion point to the right of the period at the end of the first paragraph.

5. Choose **References→Footnotes→Insert Footnote** AB¹.

   The footnote reference mark appears at the insertion point, and a corresponding footnote appears at the bottom of the page.

6. Follow these steps to complete the footnote:

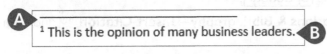

   Ⓐ Find a separator line and the footnote number.

   Ⓑ Type this text in the footnote area.

7. Use the same process to insert the footnote reference marks and the associated footnotes shown here.

The commercial potential of the Internet stems from the fact that it is a global network with inexpensive access.[2] The Internet is also available 24x7. The multimedia capability to the Internet is important for marketing and advertising. Quick product delivery, automated order-taking, and low overhead are several more factors that are driving Internet commerce.[3]

---

[1] This is the opinion of many business leaders.
[2] Some nations still have high rates due to limited competition among Internet service providers.
[3] These factors depend upon the capabilities of individual companies.

The default formatting of footnotes in Word does not adhere to MLA requirements. The text should use the same formatting as the body of the document (double-spaced, first line indented). You will format the footnotes later.

Now you will convert your footnotes to endnotes.

8. Choose **References→Footnotes→dialog box launcher** 🔲 and click **Convert**.

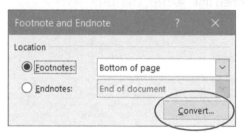

9. When the Convert Notes dialog box opens, click **OK** and then close the Footnote and Endnote dialog box.

10. Scroll through the document and notice that the footnotes are no longer at the bottom of page 1; they now appear as endnotes on the last page.

You decide that you prefer having the notes on the same page as the material they refer to, so you will convert the endnotes back to footnotes.

11. Choose **References→Footnotes→dialog box launcher** 🔲 and click **Convert**.

12. Click **OK** in the Convert Notes dialog box and then close the Footnote and Endnote dialog box.

Now you will choose the bibliography style for your paper and insert a citation.

13. Choose **References→Citations & Bibliography→Style ▾→MLA Seventh Edition**.

A citation should be placed inside the period at the end of a sentence.

14. At the end of the first paragraph on page 2, position the insertion point between the word *online* and the period and then tap Spacebar .

15. Choose **References→Citations & Bibliography→Insert Citation** 🔲 and then choose **Add New Source**.

16. Follow these steps to create the new source to insert as the citation:

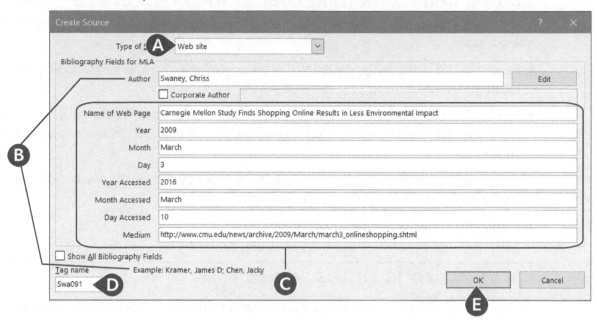

(A) If necessary, choose **Web Site**.

(B) Type the author's name as shown. Example text appears at the bottom of the window for each field.

(C) Enter the remaining information.

(D) The system uses tags internally to uniquely identify a source. The Tab Name you see may vary from this one.

(E) Click **OK**.

 Remember, Word does not follow all MLA guidelines. Refer to the MLA Handbook or website when writing academic papers.

Insert Citation Placeholders

17. On page 2, position the insertion point at the end of the third bullet point between *themselves* and the period and tap [Spacebar].

18. Choose **References→Citations & Bibliography→Insert Citation** and then choose **Add New Placeholder**.

19. Type **Fowler** in the Placeholder Name box and then click **OK**.

20. Position the insertion point at the end of the document between *years* and the period and tap [Spacebar].

21. Choose **References→Citations & Bibliography→Insert Citation** and then choose **Add New Placeholder**.

22. Type **Mogg** in the Placeholder Name box and then click **OK**.

23. Save the file.

Editing and Formatting Footnotes and Citations

You can edit footnote text directly in the footnote area. In addition to editing the text of a footnote, you can also:

▶ Reposition: You can change the position of a footnote reference mark by dragging it to another location in the document.

▶ Format: You can change various formatting features of footnotes. For example, you can change the numbering scheme, change the starting number, or even replace a footnote number with a special character.

You can add source information to a citation placeholder by clicking the placeholder drop-down arrow and choosing the option to edit the source.

 View the video "Editing Footnotes and Citations."

DEVELOP YOUR SKILLS: W4-D7

In this exercise, you will format, edit, and delete footnotes and edit citation placeholders and sources.

1. Save your file as **W4-D7-InternetRevised**.

2. Position the insertion point at the beginning of the second paragraph on page 1 and scroll, if necessary, to see the three footnote reference marks and the footnotes at the bottom of the page.

3. Choose **References→Footnotes→dialog box launcher** ⌐ to display the Footnote and Endnote dialog box.

4. If necessary, at the top of the dialog box, choose **Footnotes**.

5. In the Number Format field, click the drop-down arrow and choose **A, B, C …** and then click **Apply**.

   The footnote numbers change to alphabetic characters. You use the same technique to change the format of endnotes.

6. Choose **References→Footnotes→dialog box launcher** ⌐; change the Number Format back to the first option, numbers; and then click **Apply**.

7. If necessary, choose **View→Show→Ruler**.

8. Select the three footnotes at the bottom of the page and then follow these steps to format them:
   • Change line spacing to **double-space**.
   • Change the font size to **11 pt**.
   • On the ruler, drag the **First Line Indent** marker (top triangle) to the ½" mark.

Delete and Edit Footnotes and Edit Citation Placeholders

9. Select the reference mark following *marketplace* in the body of the document and tap ⎡Delete⎤.

   The reference mark and the footnote are removed, and the remaining footnotes renumber.

10. Click **Undo** ↺ to reinsert the footnote.

11. Position the insertion point between the last word and the period of the first footnote, tap ⎡Spacebar⎤, and type **and economists**.

12. Scroll to the *Fowler* citation at the end of the third bullet on page 2.

13. Follow these steps to open the Edit Source dialog box:

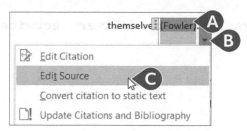

(A) Click the *Fowler* citation placeholder.

(B) Click this drop-down arrow.

(C) Choose **Edit Source**.

14. Enter the following information in the Edit Source dialog box in the order shown:
- Type of Source: **Web Site**
- Author: **Fowler, Geoffrey**
- Name of Web Page: **The Green Side of Online Shopping**
- Year: **2009**
- Month: **March**
- Day: **3**
- Year Accessed: **2016**
- Month Accessed: **March**
- Day Accessed: **14**
- Medium: **http://blogs.wsj.com/digits/2009/03/03/the-green-side-of -online-shopping/tab/article/**

15. Click **OK**.

16. Click **Yes** if a message appears asking if you want to update the master list and current document.

The citation may have picked up the name of the web page (title). If so, continue with step 17; otherwise, skip to step 18.

17. If necessary, click the drop-down arrow to the right of the Fowler citation and choose **Edit Citation**; then, check the **Title** box to suppress the title and click **OK**.

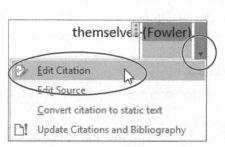

Now you will edit the Mogg placeholder.

18. Click the *Mogg* citation placeholder at the end of the document.

19. Click the drop-down arrow and choose **Edit Source**.

20. Enter the following information in the dialog box in the order shown:
  - Type of Source: **Web Site**
  - Author: **Mogg, Trevor**
  - Name of Web Page: **Google says its drone delivery service could take flight in 2017**
  - Year: **2015**
  - Month: **November**
  - Day: **3**
  - Year accessed: **2016**
  - Month Accessed: **March**
  - Day Accessed: **14**
  - Medium: **http://www.channelsellernews.com/shipping-tips-for -ecommerce/google-says-its-drone-delivery-service-could-take -flight-in-2017/**

21. Click **OK** and then save the file.

Working with Bibliographies

A bibliography is a list of the sources cited in the preparation of a document. Bibliographies are automatically generated based on the source information that you provide in the Create Source dialog box. The bibliography picks up the correct punctuation; however, certain formatting requirements are not defaults and must be addressed separately.

 The bibliography options may not format references as needed. Use the Insert Bibliography command to create citations more precisely.

 View the video "Bibliography Options."

≡ References→Citations & Bibliography→Bibliography 📑

DEVELOP YOUR SKILLS: W4-D8

In this exercise, you will create a bibliography for the citations in your paper. You will title the page as Works Cited, as this chapter is following the MLA documentation style. Finally, you will edit an existing citation, update the bibliography, and format the paragraphs with double spacing.

1. Save your file as **W4-D8-InternetRevised**.

2. Position the insertion point at the end of the document and then press ⌐Ctrl¬+⌐Enter¬ to insert a new page for the bibliography.

3. Choose **Home→Paragraph→Center** ≡ and then type **Works Cited** and tap ⌐Enter¬.

Insert and Update the Bibliography

4. Choose **References→Citations & Bibliography→Bibliography** 📑.

5. Choose **Insert Bibliography** at the bottom of the menu.

6. Scroll up to the second page, click the *Fowler* citation, and then click the **drop-down arrow**.

7. Choose **Edit Source** to open the dialog box.

8. Change the Day Accessed to **10** and click **OK**.

9. If the citation picked up the name of the web page, click the **drop-down arrow**, choose **Edit Citation**, check the **Title** checkbox, and click **OK**.

10. Scroll down to the Works Cited page and notice the date has not changed yet in the list.

11. Right-click anywhere in the list and choose **Update Field** from the menu that appears.

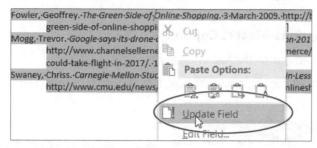

Notice the date accessed for the Fowler citation changed to 10 March 2016. Now you will format the list.

12. Select the bibliography list, but not the *Works Cited* title.

 If you click the list, it highlights in light gray. You must drag with the mouse to select the list, which then highlights in a darker gray.

13. Choose **Home→Paragraph→Line and Paragraph Spacing** and then choose **2.0**.

14. Save the file.

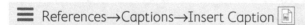

Inserting Captions and a Table of Figures

You use captions to insert text associated with figures in a paper. The captions then become entries in the table of figures. Later, if you alter some of the captions, they will be updated when you regenerate the table of figures.

≡ References→Captions→Insert Caption 📄

⚠ View the video "Inserting Captions."

DEVELOP YOUR SKILLS: W4-D9

In this exercise, you will insert a file that contains PowerPoint slides from a presentation. You will add captions to the slides in preparation for creating a table of figures.

1. Save your file as **W4-D9-InternetRevised**.

2. Position the insertion point after the third footnote reference mark in the body of the document (not the footnote area) toward the bottom of the first page.

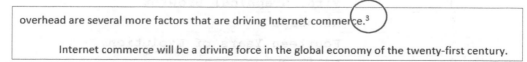

3. Tap [Enter] and then press [Ctrl]+[Enter] to insert a page break.

4. Choose **Insert→Text→Object** ☐ **menu button ▾→Text from File**.

5. In the Insert File dialog box, navigate to your **Word Chapter 4** folder, choose **W4-D9-Evolution**, and click **Insert**.

6. If necessary, display formatting marks and then position the insertion point in the first blank line below the first slide.

7. Choose **References→Captions→Insert Caption** 🖻.

The Caption dialog box should match the following illustration.

8. If *Figure 1* does not appear in the Caption text box, follow these steps; otherwise, go to the next step.

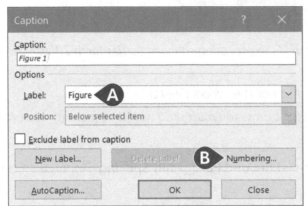
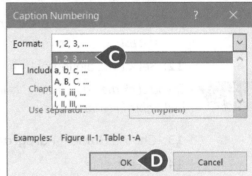

Ⓐ Click the **Label menu** button ▾ and choose **Figure**.

Ⓑ Click **Numbering** to open the Caption Numbering dialog box.

Ⓒ Click the **Format menu** button ▾ and then choose the **1,2,3, …** format.

Ⓓ Click **OK**.

9. If necessary, position the insertion point to the right of *Figure 1* in the Caption text box.

10. Tap [Spacebar], type **DOD and ARPANET**, and click **OK** to insert the caption.

The caption is placed at the left margin.

11. Choose **Home→Paragraph→Center** ☰.

12. Position the insertion point in the first blank line below the second slide.

13. Choose **References→Captions→Insert Caption** 🖻.

14. Tap [Spacebar], type **NSF**, and click **OK**.

15. Center ☰ the caption.

16. Add these captions and center them:

Slide Number	Caption Text
3	MILNET and TCP/IP
4	First Graphical Browser
5	Netscape
6	Fourteen Years of Evolution
7	Delivery Drones?

Now you will edit a caption.

17. Return to **slide 2**, select *NSF*, and type `National Science Foundation` in its place.

18. Save the file.

Inserting a Table of Figures

Academic papers often include a table of figures at the front, which guides the reader to illustrations, charts, tables, and other figures. This is particularly helpful in long documents. The table entries conveniently function as hyperlinks if you are reading the document online.

≡ References→Captions→Insert Table of Figures 🖹

DEVELOP YOUR SKILLS: W4-D10

In this exercise, you will generate a table of figures from the captions you inserted earlier.

1. Save your file as `W4-D10-InternetRevised`.

2. Move the insertion point to the top of the document and press Ctrl + Enter to insert a page break.

3. Press Ctrl + Home to position the insertion point at the top of the new page and then type `Table of Figures` and tap Enter twice.

4. Format the heading you just typed with **Center**, **Bold**, **16 pt**.

5. Place the insertion point in the blank line below the heading.

6. Choose **References→Captions→Insert Table of Figures** 🖹.

7. Follow these steps to complete the table:

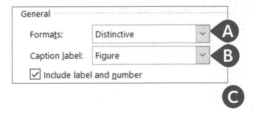

Ⓐ Choose **Distinctive** as the format.

Ⓑ If necessary, choose **Figure** as the caption label.

Ⓒ Click **OK**.

8. Save and then close the file.

Using Track Changes

The Track Changes feature is a useful tool when working with team members to collaborate on a report or other documents. You can electronically distribute copies to different members, and with Track Changes, the changes they make are marked. You can merge the changes from all copies into a single document, and then you can review each change and accept or reject it.

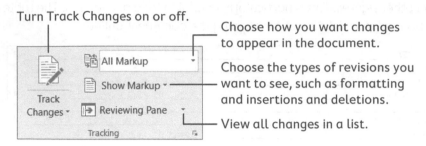

Turn Track Changes on or off.

Choose how you want changes to appear in the document.

Choose the types of revisions you want to see, such as formatting and insertions and deletions.

View all changes in a list.

Reviewing Tracked Changes

It's easy to find and review changes to a document. When you review changes, you can jump from one change to the next, giving you the opportunity to accept or reject each change in order. You can also accept or reject all changes at once. After you accept or reject a change, the revision marks are removed.

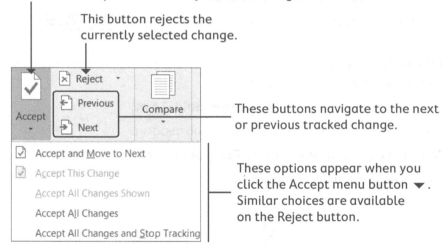

This button accepts the currently selected change.

This button rejects the currently selected change.

These buttons navigate to the next or previous tracked change.

These options appear when you click the Accept menu button ▼. Similar choices are available on the Reject button.

Self-Assessment

Check your knowledge of this chapter's key concepts and skills using the Self-Assessment in your ebook or eLab course.

Reinforce Your Skills

REINFORCE YOUR SKILLS: W4-R1

Format a Recycling Report

Kids for Change is planning a recycling fair, and you are creating a recycling report to be distributed during the fair. In this exercise, you will work with margins, indents, tabs, styles, and footers, and then you will format the body of the report into two columns. Finally, you will add a comment to the report.

1. Open **W4-R1-Recyc** from your **Word Chapter 4** folder and save it as **W4-R1-RecycRevised**.

   The document could use a little more white space in the left and right margins.

2. Choose **Layout→Page Setup→Margins** ▯ **→Normal**.

   This widens the left and right margins to 1". Now you'll indent the quote from the EPA to make it stand out on the page.

3. If necessary, choose **View→Show→Ruler**.

4. Position the insertion point in the **third paragraph**.

5. Place the mouse pointer on the **Left Indent** marker (the rectangle) and drag it to the **½"** mark and then place the mouse pointer on the **Right Indent** marker and drag it to the **6"** mark.

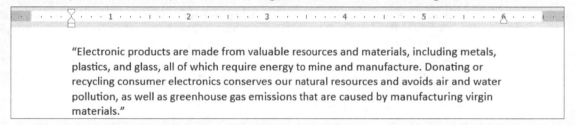

"Electronic products are made from valuable resources and materials, including metals, plastics, and glass, all of which require energy to mine and manufacture. Donating or recycling consumer electronics conserves our natural resources and avoids air and water pollution, as well as greenhouse gas emissions that are caused by manufacturing virgin materials."

Now you will set tabs for a table indicating where people can drop off electronics they want to recycle.

6. Position the insertion point at the bottom of the document.

7. Type the following heading line using the default tab grid, tapping [Tab] where you see the arrows and tapping [Enter] at the end of the line:

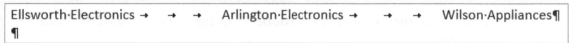

Ellsworth·Electronics → → → Arlington·Electronics → → → Wilson·Appliances¶
¶

8. Select the heading line and choose **Home→Font→Bold** [B].

9. Position the insertion point in the blank line below the heading line where you will set custom tabs.

10. Click the **tabs** box as many times as necessary to display the **Center Tab**. (It looks like an upside-down T.)

11. Perform these actions to set the following tab stops:
    - Click the **ruler** one tick mark to the right of **½"**.
    - Click one tick mark to the right of the **3"** mark.
    - Click at the **5½"** mark.

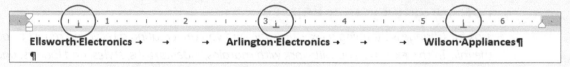

The center tab will cause the text to center around the tabs.

12. Type the following table, tapping [Tab] where you see the arrows and [Enter] where you see paragraph symbols.

Ellsworth·Electronics →	→	→	Arlington·Electronics →	→	→	Wilson·Appliances¶
→ Audio	→		Mobile·phones		→	Stoves¶
→ Car·&·GPS	→		Computers		→	Refrigerators¶
→ Mobile·phones	→		Digital·cameras		→	Freezers¶
→ Video·games	→		MP3·players		→	Washing·machines¶

Now you will adjust the last tab stop so it is better centered.

13. Select all lines to which the tab stop applies and drag the tab one tick mark to the right of **5½"**.

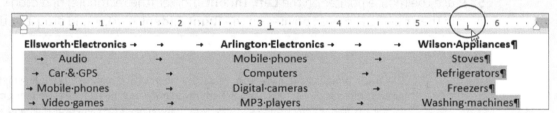

Now you will apply a style to the Report heading.

14. Position the insertion point in the heading line at the top of the page.

15. Choose **Home→Styles** and then click the **More** ▼ button to open the Styles gallery.

16. Choose **Title** from the gallery.

Add a Footer and a Comment

17. Choose **Insert→Header & Footer→Footer** 🗋 and choose **Edit Footer** at the bottom of the menu.

18. Type **Kids for Change** at the left side of the footer.

    Look at the ruler and notice that there are two custom tab stops: a center tab at 3¼" and a right tab at 6½".

19. Tap [Tab] twice.

    The insertion point is now aligned at a Right Tab.

20. Type **January, 2016** and then double-click in the body of the document to close the footer area.

Set the Document in Two Columns and Add a Comment

21. Select the body of the document from the first paragraph through the last bullet point.

22. Choose **Layout→Page Setup→Columns** ▦**→Two**.

    It might look better to keep the EPA quote together.

23. Position the insertion point in front of the line starting *The EPA provides*.

24. Choose **Layout→Page Setup→Breaks** ⊟**→Column**.

    Now you will insert a comment.

25. Move to the top of the document and select *Recycling* in the heading.

26. Choose **Insert→Comments→Comment** 🗩 and type the following in the comment balloon:

    `Jordan, please review and add any comments. I'll start on the`
    `Plastics Recycling section next.`

27. Save and close the file.

REINFORCE YOUR SKILLS: W4-R2

Create a Research Report

A Kids for Change volunteer has asked you to create another handout for the fair with an emphasis on acting locally. In this exercise, you will prepare the handout by inserting endnotes, footnotes, citations, a bibliography, and a table of figures.

1. Open **W4-R2-GlobalLocal** from your **Word Chapter 4** folder and save it as
   W4-R2-GlobalLocalRevised.

2. Position the insertion point after the period following *sales* in the second paragraph.

   > Kids for Change is a non-profit organization that helps minors in their
   >
   > social/community service within the mindset of "Think Globally, Act Locally."
   >
   > fundraisers, such as car washes, bake sales, and rain barrel sales. The kids are

3. Choose **References→Footnotes→Insert Endnote** 🔖.

   The insertion point jumps to the end of the document.

4. Type the following endnote text:

   `Proceeds go to organizations such as the local pantry.`

5. Position the insertion point after the comma following *construction* in the second to last line of the second paragraph.

   > fundraisers, such as car washes, bake sales, and rain barrel sales.
   >
   > community recycling drives, researching green construction, and
   >
   > garden program.

6. Choose **References→Footnotes→Insert Endnote** 🔖 and type the following endnote text:

   `Kids for Change successfully encouraged a local businessman to use`
   `green construction in a building addition.`

   You noticed a word is missing in the first endnote, so you will make that change now.

7. In the first endnote, position the insertion point to the left of *pantry*, type **food**, and tap Spacebar .

You've decided to convert the endnotes to footnotes so they will appear on the same page as the text they refer to.

8. Choose **References→Footnotes→dialog box launcher** 🔲 and then click the **Convert** button.

9. When the Convert Notes message appears, click **OK**; close the Footnote and Endnote dialog box.

Insert Citations

10. Choose **References→Citations & Bibliography** and then choose **MLA Seventh Edition** from the Style menu.

11. At the end of the fourth paragraph that begins with *The slogan*, position the insertion point between the word *activists* and the period and then tap Spacebar .

> practices – like environmental stewardship –
>
> of reference for some far-thinking activists|

12. Choose **References→Citations & Bibliography→Insert Citation** 🔲 and then choose **Add New Source**.

13. Enter the following information in the Create Source dialog box and then click **OK** when finished:
    - Type of Source: **Web Site**
    - Author: **Sathian, Sanjena**
    - Name of Page: **Think Locally, Act Globally**
    - Year: **2011**
    - Month: **July**
    - Day: **11**
    - Year Accessed: **2016**
    - Month Accessed: **September**
    - Day: **15**
    - Medium: **http://tyglobalist.org/onlinecontent/blogs /think-locally-act-globally/**

14. Position the insertion point following *Fluids* at the end of the fourth bullet point in the Jennifer King citation and then tap Spacebar .

> - Vehicle Fluids|

15. Choose **References→Citations & Bibliography→Insert Citation** 🔲 and then choose **Add New Source**.

16. Enter the following information in the Create Source dialog box and then click **OK** when finished:
    - Type of Source: **Web Site**
    - Author: **King, Jennifer**
    - Name of Page: **How Does Car Pollution Affect the Environment & Ozone Layer?**
    - Year: (Leave blank.)
    - Month: (Leave blank.)
    - Day: (Leave blank.)

- Year Accessed: **2016**
- Month Accessed: **September**
- Day: **15**
- Medium: `http://homeguides.sfgate.com/car-pollution-affect-environment-ozone-layer-79358.html`

17. Position the insertion point at the end of the document between *Nations* and the period and then tap ⎡Spacebar⎤.

> ns (CFCs). **And a treaty banning**
>
> United Nations │.

18. Choose **References→Citations & Bibliography→Insert Citation** ⬚ and then choose **Add New Source**.

19. Enter the following information in the Create Source dialog box and then click **OK** when finished:
- Type of Source: **Web Site**
- Author: **Trex, Ethan**
- Name of Page: **Whatever Happened to the Hole in the Ozone Layer?**
- Year: **2012**
- Month: **May**
- Day: **23**
- Year Accessed: **2016**
- Month Accessed: **September**
- Day: **15**
- Medium: `http://mentalfloss.com/article/30733/whatever-happened-hole-ozone-layer`

20. Position the insertion point at the end of the document, tap ⎡Enter⎤ twice, and then press ⎡Ctrl⎤+⎡Enter⎤ to insert a new page for the bibliography.

21. Choose **Home→Paragraph→Center** ⬚, type **Works Cited**, and then tap ⎡Enter⎤.

22. Choose **References→Citations & Bibliography→Bibliography** ⬚.

23. Choose **Insert Bibliography** at the bottom of the menu.

Insert Captions

Now you will insert a document that contains slides from a PowerPoint presentation, and you will add captions to the slides.

24. If necessary, display the formatting marks and then position the insertion point on the blank line before the page break at the end of page 2 and tap ⎡Enter⎤.

25. Choose **Insert→Text→Object** ⬚ **menu button** ▾**→Text from File**.

26. In the Insert File dialog box, navigate to your **Word Chapter 4** folder and double-click **W4-R2-YouCanHelp** to insert the file in your document.

27. Position the insertion point in the first blank line below the first slide.

28. Choose **References→Captions→Insert Caption** ⬚.

29. If *Figure 1* does not appear in the Caption text box, follow these steps; otherwise, go to the next step.
    - Click the **Label menu** button ▼ and choose **Figure**.
    - Click the **Numbering** button to open the Caption Numbering dialog box.
    - Click the **Format menu** button ▼ and then choose the **1,2,3, ...** format.
    - Click **OK**.

30. If necessary, position the insertion point to the right of *Figure 1* in the Caption text box, tap Spacebar , type **Conduct a Home Survey**, and then click **OK**.

    Now you will center the caption.

31. Choose **Home→Paragraph→Center** ≡ and then position the insertion point in the first blank line below the second slide.

32. Choose **References→Captions→Insert Caption** 📄.

33. Tap Spacebar , type **Reduce Car Use**, and click **OK**.

34. **Center** ≡ the caption.

35. Add the following captions and center them:
    - Slide 3: **Use Used**
    - Slide 4: **Think Before You Toss**

Insert a Table of Figures

36. Move the insertion point to the top of the document and insert a page break.

37. Move the insertion point to the top of the new page and type **Table of Figures** and tap Enter twice.

38. Format the heading with **Center**, **Bold**, **16 pt**.

39. Place the insertion point in the blank line below the heading.

40. Choose **References→Captions→Insert Table of Figures** 📄.

41. In the bottom-left of the Table of Figures dialog box, if necessary, change the format to **Distinctive**, ensure that the Caption Label says **Figure**, and then click **OK**.

42. Save and close the file.

REINFORCE YOUR SKILLS: W4-R3

Create an Organic Gardening Report

Kids for Change will host an organic gardening exhibition in the spring, and the planning is under way. You have already started a report about organic gardening for the exhibition. In this exercise, you will format the layout; apply styles; add a footer; and insert footnotes, endnotes, and citations. Then you will assign gardening duties to volunteers who will work in the Kids' garden starting in the spring. You will also create tabular columns and insert a comment.

1. Open **W4-R3-OrganicFood** from your **Word Chapter 4** folder and save it as **W4-R3-OrganicFoodRevised**.

    The left and right margins are a bit too wide in this document.

2. Choose **Layout→Page Setup→Margins** ▥→**Normal**.

    Now you will apply Styles to the title and report headings.

3. Choose **Home→Styles→dialog box launcher** ⌐ to open the Styles task pane.

4. Apply the **Title** style to the document title and then apply the **Heading 1** style to the other two headings: *Plant Production* and *Support Organic Food*.

5. Close the Styles task pane.

   Next, you will format the first two main paragraphs in columns.

6. Select the text from the first paragraph through the *Plant Production* heading and its following paragraph.

7. If necessary, display the formatting marks.

8. Choose **Layout→Page Setup→Columns** ▦ **→Two**.

   When you select text and then apply columns, the section breaks are inserted automatically.

Insert Captions and a Table of Figures

9. Position the insertion point on the first blank line below the first picture.

10. Choose **References→Captions→Insert Caption** ▤.

11. Make sure **Figure** is in the Label field and the numbering format is **1,2,3, …**.

12. If necessary, position the insertion point to the right of *Figure 1* in the Caption text box.

13. Tap Spacebar, type **Build Healthy Soil**, click **OK**, and then center ≡ the caption.

14. Position the insertion point in the first blank line below the second picture.

15. Choose **References→Captions→Insert Caption** ▤.

16. Tap Spacebar, type **Keep Chemicals Out of the Air, Water, Soil, and Our Bodies**, click **OK**, and then center ≡ the caption.

17. Follow the same process to place a caption titled **Taste Better and Truer Flavor** below the third picture.

18. Position the insertion point at the top of the document, press Ctrl + Enter to insert a page break, and then position the insertion point at the top of the new first page.

19. Type **Table of Figures**, tap Enter twice, and then apply **Center**, **Bold**, **16 pt** to the heading.

20. Position the insertion point on the blank line below the heading.

21. Choose **References→Captions→Insert Table of Figures** ▤.

22. In the dialog box, make sure **Distinctive** is the format style, ensure that the caption label is **Figure**, and click **OK**.

Add Footnotes and Citations

23. Position the insertion point to the right of the colon at the end of the first line below the *Support Organic Food* heading.

24. Choose **References→Footnotes→Insert Footnote** AB¹ and type the following text in the footnote area:

    See Sustainable Plant Agriculture for details on growing organic plants.

    Now you will choose the style for citations.

25. Choose **References→Citations & Bibliography→Style menu button** ▾ and choose **MLA Seventh Edition**.

26. Position the insertion point between the period and the word *bay* at the end of the second paragraph following the *Plant Production* heading, and tap [Spacebar].

> may conduct more sophisticated crop rotations and spread mulch or manure to keep weeds at bay.

27. Choose **References→Citations & Bibliography→Insert Citation** 📄 and then choose **Add New Source**.

28. Enter the following information and then click **OK** when finished:

- Type of Source: **Web Site**
- Author: **Mayo Clinic, Staff**
- Name of Web Page: **Nutrition and healthy eating**
- Year: (Leave blank.)
- Month: (Leave blank.)
- Day: (Leave blank.)
- Year accessed: **2016**
- Month Accessed: **October**
- Day Accessed: **15**
- Medium: **http://www.mayoclinic.org/healthy-lifestyle /nutrition-and-healthy-eating/in-depth/organic-food/art-20043880**

29. Position the insertion point at the end of the third bullet point below the *Support Organic Food* heading and tap [Spacebar].

30. Choose **References→Citations & Bibliography→Insert Citation** 📄 and then choose **Add New Source**.

31. Enter the following information and then click **OK** when finished:

- Type of Source: **Web Site**
- Author: **Greene, Alan, Scowcroft, Bob, Tawse, Sylvia**
- Name of Web Page: **Top 10 Reasons to Support Organic in the 21st Century**
- Year: (Leave blank.)
- Month: (Leave blank.)
- Day: (Leave blank.)
- Year Accessed: **2016**
- Month Accessed: **October**
- Day Accessed: **15**
- Medium: **http://www.organic.org/articles/showarticle/article-206**

Insert a Bibliography and Add a Footer

32. Position the insertion point at the end of the document and press [Ctrl]+[Enter] to insert a page break.

33. Choose **Home→Paragraph→Center** ≡ and then type **Works Cited** and tap [Enter].

34. Choose **References→Citations & Bibliography→Bibliography** 📑→ and then choose **Insert Bibliography**.

35. Choose **Insert→Header & Footer→Footer** and then scroll down and choose **Retrospect**.

36. Type **Kids for Change** in the author object (you may have to delete default text; print is automatically sets in all caps) and notice that the page number appears on the right side of the footer.

37. Double-click in the document to close the footer area.

38. Save and close the file.

    Now you will finish creating the document for assigning gardening project duties.

39. Open **W4-R3-GardenProj** from your **Word Chapter 4** folder and save it as **W4-R3-GardenProjRevised**.

40. Position the insertion point at the end of the document and then type the following heading line, tapping Tab wherever you see an arrow and tapping Enter at the end of the line:

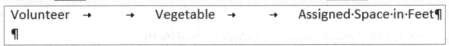

41. Format the heading line with **Bold** B .

    Now you will set center tabs for the body of the table.

42. Position the insertion point on the blank line below the heading line.

43. Click the **tabs** box to display the **Center Tab** if necessary.

44. Place tabs in the following locations:

    - Between the second and third tick marks from the left margin
    - Between the second and third tick marks to the right of 1½"
    - The first tick mark right of 3½"

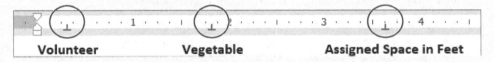

    Remember, if you click a tab in the wrong position, you can drag it to the correct position or drag it down and off the ruler and try again.

45. Type the body of the table as shown, tapping Tab wherever you see an arrow and tapping Enter at the end of each line:

Volunteer →	→	Vegetable →	→	Assigned·Space·in·Feet¶
→ Kirk	→	corn	→	10·x·8¶
→Rachael	→	peas	→	8·x·4¶
→ Lena	→	green·beans	→	8·x·3¶
→ Bly	→	tomatoes	→	10·x·8¶
→Trevor	→	cauliflower	→	8·x·4¶
→ Neil	→	carrots	→	6·x·4¶

    Now you will insert a comment.

46. Select the word *Change* in the heading, then choose **Insert→Comments→Comment** and type the following in the comment balloon: **Jeremy, please check the assigned spaces and make sure they are accurate.**

47. Save and close the file.

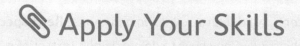 Apply Your Skills

APPLY YOUR SKILLS W4-A1

Complete a Trip Report on Belize

You went on a familiarization trip to Belize for Universal Corporate Events and have written a trip report about the country. In this exercise, you will format the layout of the document, apply styles to headings, and insert footers and a comment.

1. Open **W4-A1-Belize** from your **Word Chapter 4** folder and save it as **W4-A1-BelizeRevised**.

   The text is pretty dense on this page. It needs to be lightened up to make it more readable. You will start by widening the margin areas.

2. Choose **Layout→Page Setup→Margins** ▦ **→Normal**.

   Headings allow the reader to scan a document for high-level concepts, adding to the document's readability. You will apply styles to the document's headings.

3. Apply the **Heading 2** style to the heading at the top of the document and then apply the **Intense Reference** style to the remaining headings: *Overview, Diving and Snorkeling, Ruins,* and *Artists.*

   Offsetting the text from the headings will also add to the document's readability.

4. Position the insertion point in the paragraph following the *Overview* heading.

5. Choose **Home→Paragraph→Increase Indent** ▦.

6. Use the same technique to indent the remaining paragraphs. (If you select all the paragraphs following the *Ruins* heading, you can indent them all at once.)

   Next you will set the document in columns. Shorter lines are easier to read because the eye doesn't have to travel far across the page before reading the next line.

7. Select the text starting with the *Overview* heading through the last paragraph following the *Ruins* heading. (Do not include the *Artists* paragraph.)

8. Format the selected text in a two-column layout.

   The Ruins *heading is at the bottom of the left-hand column. It would look better at the top of the right-hand column.*

9. Position the insertion point in front of the *Ruins* heading and insert a column break to move the heading to the top of the next column.

Insert a Footer

10. Add a footer using the **Ion (Dark)** option.

    You will use the objects in the footer for a different purpose than the labels specify.

11. Type **Universal Corporate Events** in the Document Title object and type **August, 2016** in the Author object. (The text will automatically convert to all upper case.)

12. Close the footer area.

Set Custom Tabs

Now you will add information about some of the talented local artists.

13. If necessary, turn on the ruler and display formatting marks.

14. Position the insertion point in the second blank line at the end of the document.

15. Type the following heading row, using the formatting marks as a guide; be sure to tap Enter at the end of the heading line:

16. **Bold** the heading row.

17. Position the insertion point in the line below the heading row and set custom **Center Tabs**.

18. Type the rest of the table, using the formatting marks as a guide:

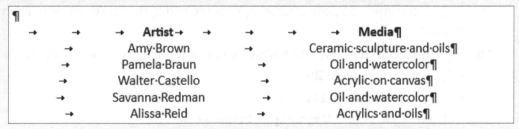

Now you'll add a comment to the document.

19. Select *Belize* in the document heading, insert a comment, and add the following text to the comment balloon:

Arrielle, since this is my first trip report, would you please check it out and add any comments you may have?

20. Save and close the file.

APPLY YOUR SKILLS W4-A2

Report on Italian Tourist Sites

Because you used to live in Italy, Universal Corporate Events has asked you to create a report detailing some Italian tourist sites and providing tips on train travel in Italy. In this exercise, you will insert footnotes and citations and generate a bibliography for your report. Then you will add captions to pictures and create a table of figures.

1. Open **W4-A2-Italy** from your **Word Chapter 4** folder and save it as **W4-A2-ItalyRevised**.

2. Position the insertion point at the end of the first paragraph, after the period following *each*.

3. Insert this footnote: **Other major attractions are listed on this website**.

4. In the paragraph beginning *In the article,* position the insertion point after the period following the word *choices*.

5. Insert this footnote: **This article also offers advice on train schedules, buying tickets, and boarding your train.**

Enter Citations and a Bibliography

6. Set the report style to **MLA Seventh Edition** if necessary. (Hint: Go to the References tab.)

7. Position the insertion point after the *Colosseum* bullet point near the top of the document.

8. Tap `Spacebar` and enter the following source information:
   - Type of Source: **Web Site**
   - Author: `Rome Travel, Guide`
   - Name of Web Page: `Rome Italy travel guide`
   - Year: (Leave blank.)
   - Month: (Leave blank.)
   - Day: (Leave blank.)
   - Year Accessed: **2016**
   - Month Accessed: **May**
   - Day Accessed: **23**
   - Medium: `http://www.rome.info/`

9. Position the insertion point after *Pompeii* at the end of the fourth bullet point under the *Day Trips* heading.

10. Tap `Spacebar` and insert a citation with the following source information:
    - Type of Source: **Web Site**
    - Author: `Casura, Lily`
    - Name of Web Page: `Daytrips from Rome`
    - Year: (Leave blank.)
    - Month: (Leave blank.)
    - Day: (Leave blank.)
    - Year Accessed: **2016**
    - Month Accessed: **May**
    - Day Accessed: **23**
    - Medium: `https://www.tripadvisor.com.au/Guide-g187791-1296`
      `-Rome _ Lazio.html`

11. Position the insertion point between *more* and the period at the end of the last paragraph.

12. Tap `Spacebar` and insert a citation with the following source information:
    - Type of Source: **Web Site**
    - Author: `Bakerjian, Martha`
    - Name of Web Page: `Italy Train Travel`
    - Year: (Leave blank.)
    - Month: (Leave blank.)
    - Day: (Leave blank.)
    - Year Accessed: **2016**
    - Month Accessed: **May**
    - Day Accessed: **23**
    - Medium: `http://goitaly.about.com/od/italytrainsportation/a`
      `/trains.html`

13. Position the insertion point at the end of the document, tap [Enter] twice, and insert a page break.

14. Type **Works Cited** as the heading and tap [Enter] twice.

15. Center the heading and then position the insertion point on the second blank line below the heading.

16. Insert a bibliography on the new page using the **Insert Bibliography** command.

17. Scroll to the top of the document, position the insertion point at the end of the *Colosseum* bullet point, and then tap [Enter] twice.

    Next, you will insert pictures of Rome's major attractions.

18. Choose **Insert→Text→Object** ▢ **menu button** ▾**→Text from File**.

19. Navigate to your **Word Chapter 4** folder and insert **W4-A2-RomePics**.

20. Positioning the insertion point on the first blank line below each picture, insert and center the following captions using the **1,2,3, ...** number format and the **Figure** label:
    - Picture 1 caption: **Trevi Fountain**
    - Picture 2 caption: **St. Peter's Square**
    - Picture 3 caption: **Spanish Steps**
    - Picture 4 caption: **Colosseum**

21. Insert a page break at the top of the document, and at the top of the new page, type **Table of Figures** and tap [Enter] twice.

22. Format the heading with **Center**, **Bold**, **16 pt**.

23. Position the insertion point on the blank line below the heading and generate the table of figures using the **Formal** format and **Figure** as the caption label.

24. Save and close the file.

APPLY YOUR SKILLS: W4-A3

Create Travel Reports

Universal Corporate Events is planning a Bangkok getaway for one of its clients, and you've been asked to research travel within Bangkok and interesting sites to see. In this exercise, you will format the layout of your report and add footnotes, citations, a bibliography, captions, and a table of figures. You have also been asked to write a sales report listing Universal Corporate Events' pending deals. You will work with margins and custom tabs, add header text, and insert a comment.

1. Open **W4-A3-Bangkok** from your **Word Chapter 4** folder and save it as **W4-A3-BangkokRevised**.

    The document needs some formatting to make it more readable. First you will add some styles to the document.

2. Select the title at the top of the document and apply the **Heading 1** style.

3. At the bottom of the page, apply the **Subtle Reference** style to the bulleted items.

4. If necessary, display the ruler and then position the insertion point in the second paragraph.

5. Position the mouse pointer on the Left Indent marker (the rectangle) on the ruler and drag it to the **½"** mark.

6. Drag the **Right Indent** marker to the **6"** mark.

7. Select text beginning with *Bangkok's Chao Praya Express Boats* down through *Myanmar* and then set the text in two columns.

   Next, you will insert pictures, add captions, and generate a table of figures.

8. Insert the **W4-A3-BNKPics** file at the end of the document.

9. Positioning the insertion point on the blank line below each picture and then insert and center the following captions using the **1,2,3, ...** number format and the **Figure** label:
   - Picture 1 caption: `Chatuchak Market`
   - Picture 2 caption: `Pak Klong Talat`
   - Picture 3 caption: `Bangkok Farmers Market`
   - Picture 4 caption: `Pratunam Market`

10. Insert a page break at the top of the document, and at the top of the new page, type **Table of Figures** and tap Enter twice.

11. **Center** and **Bold** the heading and then generate the table of figures on the blank line below the heading using the **Formal** format and **Figure** as the caption label.

Insert Footnotes and Citations

12. Position the insertion point in the first line of the first paragraph on page 2, to the right of *markets,* and insert this footnote:

    ---
    [1] Floating markets piled high with tropical fruits and vegetables provide an exciting shopping adventure.

13. Position the insertion point in the same line, this time to the right of *temples,* and insert this footnote:

    [2] Don't miss Wat Traimit's Golden Buddha or Wat Po's famous Reclining Buddha.

14. Choose the **MLA Seventh Edition** style for citations.

15. Insert a citation at the end of the indented paragraph at the top of the document and add the following source information:
    - Type of Source: **Web Site**
    - Author: **Thyberg, David**
    - Name of Web Page: **Bangkok Travel Tips**
    - Year: (Leave blank.)
    - Month: (Leave blank.)
    - Day: (Leave blank.)
    - Year Accessed: **2016**
    - Month Accessed: **September**
    - Day Accessed: **20**
    - Medium: **http://getawaytips.azcentral.com/bangkok-travel-tips -1945.html**

16. Insert a citation at the end of the second column next to *Myanmar* and add the following source information:
    - Type of Source: **Web Site**
    - Author: **Rowthorn, Chris**
    - Name of Web Page: **Take the boat out of Bangkok**
    - Year: **2012**
    - Month: **April**
    - Day: **13**
    - Year Accessed: **2016**
    - Month Accessed: **September**
    - Day Accessed: **20**
    - Medium: **http://www.bbc.com/travel/story/20120413
      -take-the-boat-out-of-bangkok**

17. Insert a citation at the end of the fourth bullet point at the end of page 2, and add the following source information:
    - Type of Source: **Web Site**
    - Author: **Hauglann, Maria Wulff**
    - Name of Web Page: **6 Markets in Bangkok You Should Not Miss**
    - Year: **2014**
    - Month: **July**
    - Day: **15**
    - Year Accessed: **2016**
    - Month Accessed: **September**
    - Day Accessed: **20**
    - Medium: **http://nerdnomads.com/6-markets-in-bangkok-you-should
      -not-miss**

    Now you will generate a Bibliography.

18. Insert a page break at the end of the document, type the title, **Works Cited**, center it on the page, and then tap [Enter] twice.

19. Generate the Bibliography on the first blank line below the title using the **Insert Bibliography** command.

20. Save and close the file.

Create a Sales Report

21. Open **W4-A3-SalesRpt** from your **Word Chapter 4** folder and save it as **W4-A3-SalesRptRevised**.

22. Change the margins to the preset **Normal** style.

23. Apply the **Title** style to *Sales Report* heading.

24. Position the insertion point on the second blank line at the end of the text, type **Pending Deals**, and format it with the **Heading 1** style.

25. Position the insertion point on the blank line below the *Pending Deals* heading and tap Enter.

26. Use the ruler to set **Left** tabs at **2½"** and **4½"** and then type the following table, bolding the heading line:

Company	→	Destination	→	Dates¶
Rogers·Electronics	→	Hawaii	→	Oct·2·through·7¶
Wilson·Construction	→	Miami	→	Oct·11·through·17¶
Milltown·Mortgage	→	New·York·City	→	Oct·20·through·27¶

27. Select the entire table and move the 2½" tab to **2¼"** and the 4½" tab to **4¾"**.

Insert a Header and a Comment

28. Insert a header using the **Blank** style and type **Universal Corporate Events** as the header.

29. Select **Report** in the heading line and insert the following comment:

Emma, do you have any prospects to add to the list?

30. Save and close the file.

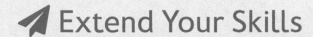 # Extend Your Skills

These exercises challenge you to think critically and apply your new skills. You will be evaluated on your ability to follow directions, completeness, creativity, and the use of proper grammar and mechanics. Save files to your chapter folder. Submit assignments as directed.

W4-E1   That's the Way I See It

You are an intern working in the corporate offices of a major grocery store chain. Your manager has asked you to research the pros and cons of reusable shopping bags compared to plastic bags. Start a new document and name it **W4-E1-ShopBags**.

Type a creative title and an original introductory paragraph for the paper and include two footnote comments in the paragraph. Using an Internet search, find two sources who favor reusable shopping bags and two sources who do not. Pull information from these sources and compare the two sides of the issue using a two-column tabular table listing the pros and cons. Insert citations at the end of each source and generate a bibliography from the citations. Add a page number in the footer area. Insert two pictures you find on the Internet representing reusable bags and plastic bags. Add captions to the pictures and create a table of figures. Use styles and indenting, and widen the left and right margins to make your report more readable. Save the file.

W4-E2   Be Your Own Boss

As the owner of Blue Jean Landscaping, you plan to hold a rose-pruning seminar for your customers. Research pruning techniques and create a report of your research results to hand out to customers at the event. Start a new document and name it **W4-E2-RoseSeminar**. Type a creative title and an original introductory paragraph and include a footnote comment in the paragraph. Cite three different sources in your report and generate a bibliography of your citations. Insert a header that includes your company name. Use styles and indents, and increase the margin width to add to the paper's readability. Set the body of the report in a two-column format and insert a column break, if necessary, to balance the columns. Include a comment at the top of the document asking your partner to review the document and make any suggestions she likes. Save the file.

W4-E3   Demonstrate Proficiency

The owner of Stormy BBQ is proud to serve free-range beef. He wants his employees to understand the benefits of using natural, grass-fed beef so they can discuss the idea with customers. He has asked you to prepare a report that he can distribute to all employees. Start a new document and name it **W4-E3-GrassFed**.

Conduct online research on the benefits of using free-range, natural beef. Type a creative title and an original introductory paragraph that includes two commentary footnotes. Cite three sources who favor free-range beef. Generate a bibliography for the citations. Use indents and styles, and adjust the margins to make your paper more readable. Add a footer that includes the company name and page numbers.

Insert **W4-E3-Cattle** as a Text from File object into your report. Copy and paste the pictures into your report, insert creative captions for the pictures, and generate a table of figures. Create a two-column tabular table listing the disadvantages of feedlot cattle (fossil fuel–intensive, for example) versus the advantages of grass-fed cattle (higher in omega-3 fatty acids, for example). Include at least five rows in the table. Insert a comment at the top of the document asking your admin to look it over for spelling and grammar errors. Save the file.

5 | Using Mail Merge

In this chapter, you will use the Mail Merge feature to turn boilerplate letters into personalized correspondence. The data source (list of variable information, such as the recipients' addresses) and the main document (form letter) only need to be set up and proofed once. Then you can generate hundreds of letters without checking each one. And you can use Mail Merge for more than letters. You can generate envelopes, labels, legal documents, or just about any fixed-text document that requires variable information. A data source can be a Word document, an Excel worksheet, an Access database, or an Outlook contact list.

LEARNING OBJECTIVES

▸ Build data sources

▸ Create main documents

▸ Perform a mail merge

▸ Deal with merge problems

▸ Generate envelopes and labels

Project: Promoting Exercise Classes

Raritan Clinic East is a pediatric medical practice. The practice serves patients ranging in ages from newborn to eighteen years. As the administrator who oversees the STAYFIT exercise classes at the clinic, once a week you receive the contact information for all new patients who would benefit from these classes. You will send a letter to the patients explaining the program. Once you set up the main document, you will be able to use it over and over for new patients. And once you design a flexible data source, you can use that same source layout for the exercise letters as well as other communications. Mail Merge is a real timesaver.

Introducing Mail Merge

Mail Merge is most often used for generating personalized documents, such as Word letters, mailing labels, and envelopes. But Mail Merge is a versatile tool that can be used with any type of document that combines boilerplate text with variable information, such as email, standard contracts, and legal verbiage. Mail Merge can be a big time-saver and is valuable for managing large mailings.

Components of Mail Merge

Merging creates a document that combines information from two files. They are known as the main document and the data source.

▸ **Main document:** This document controls the merge. It is a Word document that contains the fixed information and merge codes into which the variable information is merged. A typical form letter, for instance, has a different inside address and greeting line in each letter, while the rest of the text is the same for everyone receiving the letter.

▸ **Data source:** The data source can be another Word document, a spreadsheet, a database file, or contact list in Outlook. The data source contains field names that correspond with the merge codes in the main document.

▸ **Merged document:** This document is the result of the merge. It contains all of the letters addressed to each individual in your data source.

You can merge an existing main document with an existing data source, or you can create the main document and data source while stepping through the merge process.

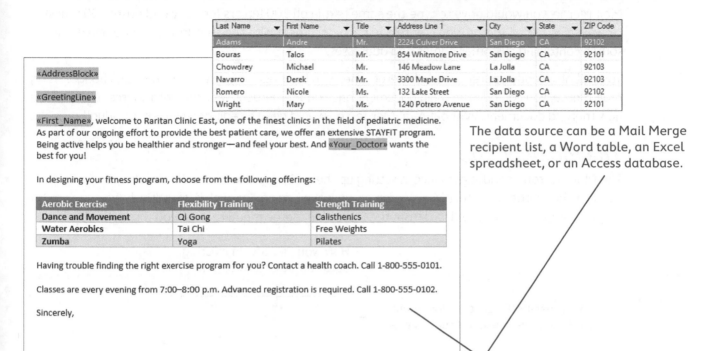

«AddressBlock»

«GreetingLine»

«First_Name», welcome to Raritan Clinic East, one of the finest clinics in the field of pediatric medicine. As part of our ongoing effort to provide the best patient care, we offer an extensive STAYFIT program. Being active helps you be healthier and stronger—and feel your best. And «Your_Doctor» wants the best for you!

In designing your fitness program, choose from the following offerings:

Aerobic Exercise	Flexibility Training	Strength Training
Dance and Movement	Qi Gong	Calisthenics
Water Aerobics	Tai Chi	Free Weights
Zumba	Yoga	Pilates

Having trouble finding the right exercise program for you? Contact a health coach. Call 1-800-555-0101.

Classes are every evening from 7:00–8:00 p.m. Advanced registration is required. Call 1-800-555-0102.

Sincerely,

Molly Lincoln
STAYFIT Coordinator

The data source can be a Mail Merge recipient list, a Word table, an Excel spreadsheet, or an Access database.

The main document contains standard text and merge codes where variables from the data source will be merged.

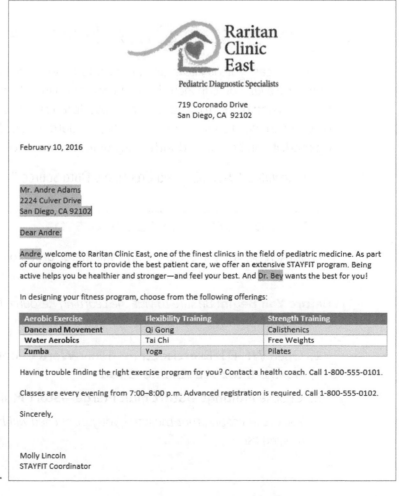

Here is a completed merge document with the variables from the data source.

The Benefits of Mail Merge

Mail Merge saves a lot of time. Imagine you want to send a letter to 100 customers. Without Mail Merge, you would have to type the same text in all 100 letters (or copy and paste 100 times). However, with Mail Merge, you create one main document with the standard text and one data source containing customer names and addresses.

You will also really appreciate Mail Merge when you later decide you want to make a change. Using Mail Merge, you can edit the main document once and remerge it with the data source to produce a new merged document. Without Mail Merge, you would need to edit each letter individually.

The Mailings Tab

The Mailings tab provides guidance in setting up the main document and data source, and it helps you conduct the merge. The Start Mail Merge group is the beginning point. Alternatively, you can use the Step-by-Step Mail Merge Wizard from the Start Mail Merge menu to walk you through the process.

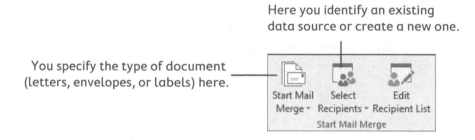

Here you identify an existing data source or create a new one.

You specify the type of document (letters, envelopes, or labels) here.

Working with the Data Source

Data sources typically contain names, addresses, telephone numbers, and other contact information. However, you can include any information in a data source. For example, you could include part numbers and prices to create a parts catalog. You can create a data source in Word, or you can use an external data source, such as an Access database or Excel spreadsheet. Once a data source is created, it can be merged with many different main documents.

 View the video "Designing and Creating a Data Source."

DEVELOP YOUR SKILLS: W5-D1

In this exercise, you will use the Start Mail Merge group on the Ribbon to specify a letter as your main document. Then you will customize the data source columns and enter data.

Before You Begin: *Be sure to visit the Learning Resource Center at labyrinthelab.com/lrc to retrieve the exercise files for this course before beginning this exercise.*

1. Open **W5-D1-ExerciseLtr** from your **Word Chapter 5** folder and save it as **W5-D1-ExerciseLtrRevised**.

2. Choose **Mailings→Start Mail Merge→Start Mail Merge** 📄 **→Letters**.

   You are indicating that the letter you just opened will be the main document. Now you will create your mailing list.

3. Choose **Mailings→Start Mail Merge→Select Recipients** 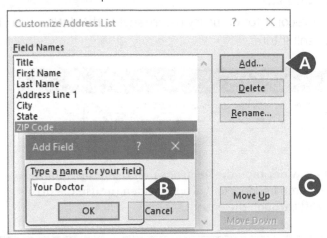→**Type a New List**.

   The New Address List dialog box opens. Now you will remove unnecessary fields and add a new field.

4. Click **Customize Columns** to open the Customize Address List dialog box.

5. Choose **Company Name** and click **Delete**; click **Yes** to verify the deletion.

6. Delete **Address Line 2**, **Country or Region**, **Home Phone**, **Work Phone**, and **E-mail Address**.

7. Follow these steps to add a field:

- Ⓐ Click **Add**.
- Ⓑ Type **Your Doctor** and click **OK**.
- Ⓒ Click **OK** to close the Customize Address List dialog box.

Enter Records

8. Follow these steps to begin the first record:

   The insertion point should be in the Title field.

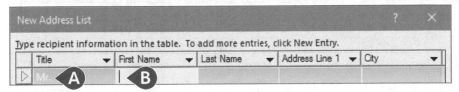

- Ⓐ Type **Mr.** in the Title field.
- Ⓑ Tap Tab to move to the next field.

 Don't type spaces after entering information in a field; Word will take care of it. You can click a field and make editing changes if necessary.

9. Type **Talos** and tap Tab to move to the next field.

10. Finish entering the Talos Bouras data shown, tapping Tab between fields. The list of fields will scroll as you Tab and type.

Mr. Talos Bouras	Ms. Nicole Romero	Mr. Michael Chowdrey
854 Whitmore Drive	132 Lake Street	900 C Street
San Diego CA 92101	San Diego CA 92102	La Jolla CA 92103
Dr. Gonzalez	Dr. Mansee	Dr. Kelly

11. When you complete the first record, click **New Entry** or tap Tab to generate a new row for the next record; then enter the two remaining records shown.

12. Leave the New Address List dialog box open.

Reviewing Your Records

It's a good idea to review your records for accuracy before saving the data source. However, if you miss an error, you can always edit it later.

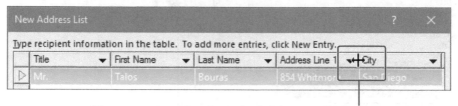

If an entry is wider than the field, position the mouse pointer between column headers and drag to widen (or use the arrow keys to scroll through the entry).

DEVELOP YOUR SKILLS: W5-D2

In this exercise, you will examine your records for accuracy and save your data source.

1. Position the mouse pointer on the scroll bar at the bottom of the dialog box and drag right and left to view all the fields.

2. Follow these steps to review your records:

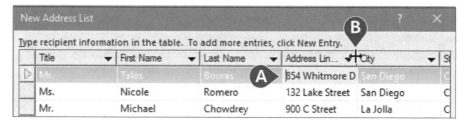

Ⓐ Position the insertion point here and use the arrow keys to move through the entry.

Ⓑ Position the mouse pointer here and drag to the right to display the entire entry.

3. Review your entry and correct any typos and then click **OK** to open the Save Address List dialog box.

4. Save the data source file as **W5-D2-ExerciseLtrData** in your **Word Chapter 5** folder.

Your data source is now connected to the main document.

Managing the Address List

The Mail Merge Recipients dialog box lets you sort and filter address lists, choose records to include in the mail merge, and edit the data source. If you used a Word table, Excel spreadsheet, or other file for your data source, you can edit directly in that data source file.

 View the video "Working with the Address List."

In this exercise, you will work with the Mail Merge Recipients dialog box, where you can sort, filter, and edit your mailing list.

1. Choose **Mailings→Start Mail Merge→Select Recipients** 📇**→Use an Existing List**.
2. Navigate to your **Word Chapter 5** folder and double-click **W5-D2-ExerciseLtrData**.
3. Choose **Mailings→Start Mail Merge→Edit Recipient List** 📇.
4. Follow these steps to sort and filter the list and open the Edit Source dialog box:

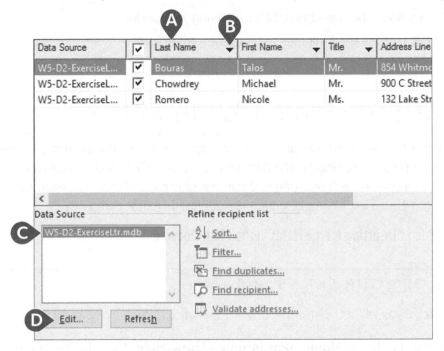

Ⓐ Click this field header to sort the list in ascending order by Last Name.

Ⓑ Click the drop-down arrow and choose **Chowdrey** to filter out other entries. Click the arrow again and choose **(All)** to redisplay all records.

Ⓒ Click the data source to activate the Edit button.

Ⓓ Click **Edit** to open the Edit Data Source dialog box.

The Edit Data Source dialog box looks and operates like the New Address List dialog box. The entries appear in the order in which they were originally entered.

5. Follow these steps to edit a record:

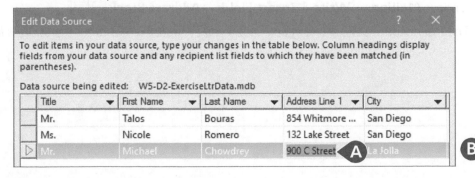

Ⓐ Click this address to select it.

Ⓑ Type **146 Meadow Lane** in its place.

6. Follow these guidelines to enter the three records in the following illustration:
   - Click the **New Entry** button or tap ⎡Tab⎤ at the end of the row for each new record.
   - Tap ⎡Tab⎤ to move from one field to the next.
   - If you accidentally tap ⎡Tab⎤ after the last record, use Delete Entry to remove the blank record.

Ms. Mary Wright	Mr. Derek Navarro	Mr. Andre Adams
1240 Potrero Avenue	3300 Maple Drive	2224 Culver Drive
San Diego CA 92101	La Jolla CA 92103	San Diego CA 92102
Dr. Gonzalez	Dr. Storm	Dr. Bey

7. Review the entries for accuracy and then click **OK** to close the dialog box.

8. Click **Yes** when the message appears verifying your update.

9. Click **OK** to close the Mail Merge Recipients dialog box.

Working with the Main Document

You accomplish a merge by combining a main document with a data source. Merge fields in a main document correspond to fields in the data source. Some merge codes, such as the Address Block code, are composite codes consisting of a number of grouped fields. For example, the Address Block code includes Title, First Name, Last Name, Address, City, State, and Zip.

 View the video "Inserting Merge Fields in the Main Document."

DEVELOP YOUR SKILLS: W5-D4

In this exercise, you will set up a form letter. The exercise letter main document should still be open.

1. If necessary, choose **Home→Paragraph→Show/Hide** ¶ to display formatting characters.

2. Select the **Today's Date** line and tap ⎡Delete⎤.

3. Choose **Insert→Text→Date & Time** 📅.

4. Choose the third date format, check **Update Automatically**, and click **OK**.

   Checking the Update Automatically option means the date in your letter will always be the current date, which is a convenient option for form letters that you want to use again.

5. Tap ⎡Enter⎤ four times after inserting the date.

   Now you will insert the Address Block code.

6. Choose **Mailings→Write & Insert Fields→Address Block** 📄.

   The Insert Address Block dialog box allows you to choose a format for the address block.

7. Follow these steps to insert an Address Block code:

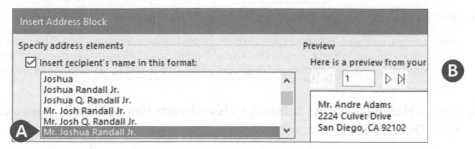

> ⒶChoose different formats and view the preview on the right; then choose **Mr. Joshua Randall Jr.**

> ⒷLeave the remaining options as shown and click **OK**.

The <<AddressBlock>> code appears in the letter. During the merge, the information from the data source will be inserted at the Address Block code location.

8. Tap Enter twice.

Now you will insert the Greeting Line code.

9. Choose **Mailings→Write & Insert Fields→Greeting Line** 📄.

10. Follow these steps to modify and insert the Greeting Line code:

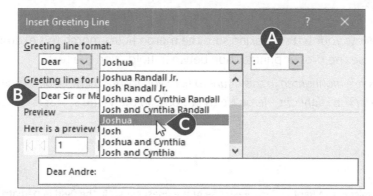

> ⒶChange this option to a **colon (:)**.

> ⒷNote the generic greeting that will be used for data records if they are missing last names.

> ⒸChoose **Joshua** from the list and then click **OK**.

11. Tap Enter twice.

12. Follow these steps to insert the First Name code into the letter:

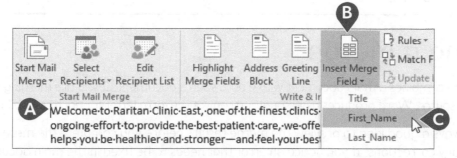

> ⒶIf necessary, position the insertion point to the left of *Welcome*.

> ⒷClick the **Insert Merge Field menu** button ▾.

> ⒸChoose **First_Name**.

13. Type a comma and tap Spacebar , then delete the uppercase *W* and replace it with a lowercase *w*.

14. Position the insertion point to the left of *wants* as shown.

«First_Name», welcome to Raritan Clinic East, one of the finest clinics in the field of pediatric medicine. As part of our ongoing effort to provide the best patient care, we offer an extensive STAYFIT program. Being active helps you be healthier and stronger—and feel your best. And wants the best for you!¶

15. Choose **Mailings→Write & Insert Fields→Insert Merge Field** 🖼 **menu button** ▾, choose **Your_Doctor**, and then tap Spacebar .

16. Take time to review your letter, making sure the merge fields match this example. In particular, make sure you use the proper punctuation between fields and the text.

The merge fields are highlighted in this figure to help you locate them; your merge fields do not need to be highlighted. (The Highlight Merge Fields button is in the Write & Insert Fields group.)

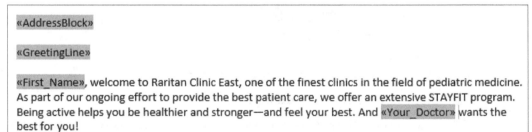

«AddressBlock»

«GreetingLine»

«First_Name», welcome to Raritan Clinic East, one of the finest clinics in the field of pediatric medicine. As part of our ongoing effort to provide the best patient care, we offer an extensive STAYFIT program. Being active helps you be healthier and stronger—and feel your best. And «Your_Doctor» wants the best for you!

 Any punctuation or spacing errors that occur in your main document will appear in every merged letter.

17. Choose **Home→Paragraph→Show/Hide** ¶ to turn off formatting marks.

18. Save your file.

Conducting a Merge

Merging combines a main document with a data source document. If you are merging a form letter with a data source, Word produces a personalized copy of the form letter for each record in the data source.

It's always a good idea to preview the merge results before you complete the merge so you can make any corrections. If you notice an error that needs to be fixed in the main document, simply click Preview Results again to return to the main document.

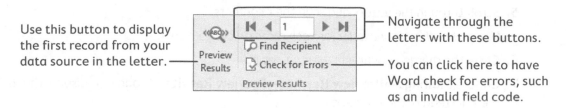

Use this button to display the first record from your data source in the letter.

Navigate through the letters with these buttons.

You can click here to have Word check for errors, such as an invalid field code.

When you feel confident that your letter and data source are accurate, you are ready to complete the merge.

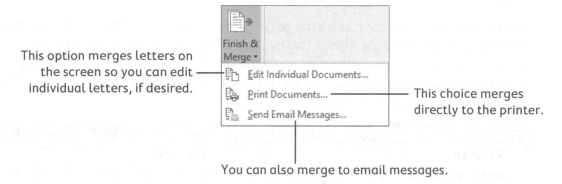

This option merges letters on the screen so you can edit individual letters, if desired.

This choice merges directly to the printer.

You can also merge to email messages.

To Save or Not to Save?

Merged documents are rarely saved because they can easily be reconstructed by merging the main document with the data source. Instead, merged documents are usually previewed, printed, and closed without saving. But you can certainly save the merged document if you wish to have a record of it. If a merged document contains errors, you can close it without saving, edit the main document or data source, and conduct the merge again.

DEVELOP YOUR SKILLS: W5-D5

In this exercise, you will use the Preview Results command to review your letters then you will complete the merge on the screen.

1. If necessary, switch to the **Mailings** tab.
2. Follow these steps to preview the merge:

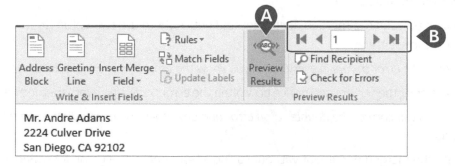

Ⓐ Click **Preview Results** to display the first inside address.

Ⓑ Use the navigation buttons to scroll through all of your merged documents.

3. Choose **Mailings→Finish→Finish & Merge** 📄→**Edit Individual Documents**.
4. Click **OK** to merge all records.

5. Scroll through the letters and scan their contents.

Notice that there is one letter for each record in the data source.

6. Close the merged document without saving.

7. Choose **Mailings→Preview Results→Preview Results** 🔍 again to display the main document instead of the previews.

Working with Merge Problems

Several common errors can cause a merge to produce incorrect results. The merged document (or preview) will usually provide clues as to why a merge fails to produce the intended results. Once you identify an error in the merged document, such as leaving out a comma or space before or after a merge field, you can then conduct the merge again to determine if the error was fixed. Repeat this process until the merge works as intended.

COMMON MERGE PROBLEMS

Problem	Solution
The same error appears in every merge letter.	The problem is in the main document. Correct the error and perform the merge again.
Some letters are missing data.	Some records in the data source are missing data. Add data and perform the merge again.
Some letters have incorrect data.	Some records in the data source are incorrect. Correct the errors and perform the merge again.

DEVELOP YOUR SKILLS: W5-D6

In this exercise, you will examine your document for merge problems. This exercise does not address all possible merge problems; it does, however, address one specific error that you will make intentionally. You will insert a colon after the Greeting Line code.

1. Position the insertion point after *<<GreetingLine>>* and type a colon.

2. Choose **Mailings→Finish→Finish & Merge** 📄→**Edit Individual Documents**.

3. Click **OK** to merge all records.

4. Browse through the merged document and notice there are two colons following the greeting line in every letter.

Because the error occurs in every letter, you know the error is in the main document.

5. Locate any other errors and notice how often the errors occur (in every merged letter or just one).

Next you will correct the double colon error and any other errors you discovered that occurred in all letters.

6. Close the merged document without saving; then remove the colon following *<<GreetingLine>>* and save the main document.

7. Follow these guidelines if you find a data error in just one letter.
   - Choose **Mailings→Start Mail Merge→Edit Recipient List** ⬚.
   - In the Mail Merge Recipients dialog box, highlight the data source in the bottom-left corner and click **Edit**.
   - Fix any errors and click **OK**; click **Yes** to update the data.
   - Click **OK** to close the dialog box.
8. When you have corrected any errors, execute the merge again.
9. Close the merged document without saving it and then save and close the exercise letter main document.

Merging Envelopes and Labels

When you begin a mail merge, you are presented with options for the type of main document you can create. In addition to form letters, you can choose envelopes, labels, and other types of documents. You can use the same data source for various main documents. For example, you can use the same data source for envelopes and mailing labels that you used for the form letter.

Generating Envelopes with Mail Merge

Mail Merge lets you choose the envelope size and formats. The standard business (Size 10) envelope is the default. Check your printer manual for instructions on loading envelopes.

Various envelope sizes are available.

Here you can choose the font and positions of the delivery and return addresses.

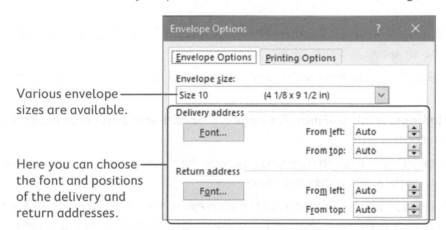

DEVELOP YOUR SKILLS: W5-D7

In this exercise, you will choose an envelope as the main document and connect the exercise letter data file to the envelope.

1. Start a new, blank document.
2. Choose **Mailings→Start Mail Merge→Start Mail Merge** ⬚**→Envelopes**.
3. In the Envelope Options dialog box, if necessary, choose **Size 10** as the envelope size and click **OK**.
   Now you will attach the same data source that you used for your letter.
4. Choose **Mailings→Start Mail Merge→Select Recipients** ⬚**→Use an Existing List**.
5. In the Select Data Source dialog box, navigate to your **Word Chapter 5** folder and open **W5-D2-ExerciseLtrData**.

Arranging the Envelope

You can insert an Address Block code in the envelope main document just as you do for form letter main documents. If you are not using envelopes with preprinted return addresses, you can type your return address. You save an envelope main document like any other main document.

DEVELOP YOUR SKILLS: W5-D8

In this exercise, you will place the return address and the Address Block code on the envelope. Then you will merge the envelope main document with the data source.

1. If necessary, display formatting marks.
2. Type this return address, starting at the first paragraph symbol in the upper-left corner of the envelope:

   Raritan Clinic East
   719 Coronado Drive
   San Diego, CA   92102

3. Position the insertion point next to the paragraph symbol toward the center of the envelope.
4. Choose **Mailings→Write & Insert Fields→Address Block** .
5. Click **OK** to accept the default address block settings.

   The address information from the data source will appear in this location. Now you will preview the merge.

6. Choose **Mailings→Preview Results→Preview Results** to display a record from the data source in the envelope.
7. Use the navigation buttons in the Preview Results group to scroll through all of your merged envelopes.
8. Choose **Mailings→Finish→Finish & Merge →Edit Individual Documents** and click **OK** to merge all records.
9. Turn off formatting marks and then scroll through the envelopes and notice that there is one envelope for each record in the data source.

   You could use the envelopes for mailing the letters created in the previous exercises. Each letter would have a corresponding envelope because they are generated from the same data source.

10. If necessary, fix any problems with the mail merge and merge the envelopes again.
11. Close the merged document without saving it.
12. Choose **Mailings→Preview Results→Preview Results** to turn off the preview.
13. Save the main document envelope as **W5-D8-ExerciseLtrEnv** in your **Word Chapter 5** folder and then close it.

Generating Labels with Mail Merge

You can use Mail Merge to generate mailing labels for each record in a data source. Mail Merge lets you choose the label format, sheet size, and other specifications. It also lets you insert an Address Block code and other codes in the main document. Like other main documents, a label main document can be saved for future use.

 View the video "Using Label Options."

In this exercise, you will set up a labels main document and merge it with the data source used in the previous exercises.

1. Start a new, blank document and, if necessary, display formatting marks.

2. Choose **Mailings→Start Mail Merge→Start Mail Merge** 🖹**→Labels**.

3. Follow these steps to choose a printer option and a label:

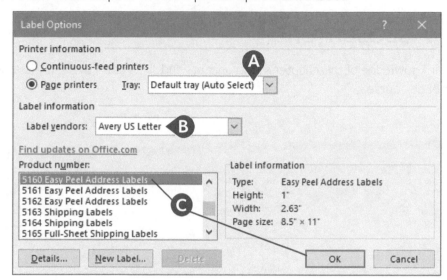

Ⓐ Choose **Default Tray**. The text in parentheses may vary based on the printer model.

Ⓑ Choose **Avery US Letter**.

Ⓒ Choose **5160 Easy Peel Address Labels** and click **OK**.

The labels main document appears in the window. Labels are contained in a Word table, but don't worry. You don't have to be a table expert to create labels.

Connect the Data Source

4. Choose **Mailings→Start Mail Merge→Select Recipients** 🖼**→Use an Existing List**.

5. In the Select Data Source dialog box, navigate to your **Word Chapter 5** folder and open **W5-D2-ExerciseLtrData**.

6. Make sure the insertion point is next to the paragraph symbol in the first address label.

   Notice that the space for the first label is blank and all the rest have a Next Record code in them. Now you will add the Address Block code.

7. Choose **Mailings→Write & Insert Fields→Address Block** 🖹 and click **OK**.

8. Choose **Mailings→Write & Insert Fields→Update Labels** 🖺 to place the Address Block code in all labels.

   Your address will fit the labels better if you remove the additional spacing.

9. Select the table and choose **Layout→Paragraph**; then type **0** in the **Before** field and tap ⌨Enter.

10. Choose **Mailings→Preview Results→Preview Results** 🔍 to see how the labels will look when you print them.

11. Turn off Preview Results when you are finished.

Conduct the Merge

12. Choose **Mailings→Finish→Finish & Merge** **→Edit Individual Documents**.

13. Click **OK** to merge all the records.

14. Close your merged document without saving it.

15. Save the labels main document in your **Word Chapter 5** folder as **W5-D9-MergeLabels**.

16. Close the document and then exit Word.

Self-Assessment

Check your knowledge of this chapter's key concepts and skills using the Self-Assessment in your ebook or eLab course.

Reinforce Your Skills

Create a Data Source and Main Document

In this exercise, you will create a data source and main document for a Kids for Change mailing. The kids are holding a fund-raiser for a microlending project that focuses on providing economic opportunities for entrepreneurs in India. They will conduct a mailing to announce the upcoming project and canvass their neighborhoods for donations.

1. Start Word, open **W5-R1-Fundraiser** from your **Word Chapter 5** folder, and save it as **W5-R1-FundraiserRevised**.

2. Choose **Mailings→Start Mail Merge→Start Mail Merge** 📄**→Letters** to identify the fund-raising letter as the main document.

3. Choose **Mailings→Start Mail Merge→Select Recipients→Type a New List**.

4. Click **Customize Columns**.

5. Click **Address Line 2** and click **Delete**; click **Yes** to confirm the deletion.

6. Also delete the following fields:
   - Country or Region
   - Home Phone
   - Work Phone
   - E-mail Address

7. Click **Add**, type **Member First Name**, and then click **OK**.

8. Also add a field called **Member Last Name** and then click **OK** twice.

9. With the insertion point in the **Title** field, type **Ms.** and tap ⌨Tab.

10. Follow these guidelines to complete the data source list:
    - Continue typing and tabbing to complete the first record shown.
    - Be sure to include the member first name, Eric, and last name, Speck, in the first record.
    - Tap ⌨Tab to begin a new record and then continue typing and tabbing to enter the next three records.
    - Note that there is no company information for the third record; ⌨Tab through that field.
    - If you accidentally tap ⌨Tab following the last record, use the **Delete Entry** button to remove the blank record.

Ms. Loretta Morales	Mr. Tony D'Agusto	Mr. Allan Morgan	Ms. Margarita Elizondo
Morales Super Market	Tony's Trattoria	951 4th Street	Elan Fashions
311 Ocean Street	675 Miller Ave.	Miami FL 33136	307 Dolphin Way
Miami FL 33130	Miami FL 33129		Miami FL 33136
Member: Eric Speck	**Member:** Wendy Chang	**Member:** Stella Hopkins	**Member:** Diego Cantero

11. Review your records for accuracy; click **OK** when you are satisfied with your work.

12. Save the data source in your **Word Chapter 5** folder as **W5-R1-FundraiserData**.

WORD

Set Up the Main Document

13. In the fundraiser letter, select **[Inside Address]** (but not the paragraph symbol at the end of the line) and tap `Delete`.

14. Choose **Mailings→Write & Insert Fields→Address Block** 📄 and then click **OK** to accept the default address block settings.

15. Delete **[Name]** in the greeting line but not the paragraph symbol at the end of the line.

16. Choose **Mailings→Write & Insert Fields→Greeting Line**.

17. Choose **Joshua** and **colon** in the Greeting Line Format area as shown and click **OK**.

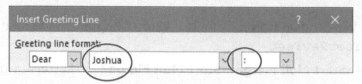

18. In the last sentence of the first paragraph, delete **[Member Name]**.

19. Choose **Mailings→Write & Insert Fields→Insert Merge Field menu button** ▼→ **Member_First_Name**.

20. Tap `Spacebar` and insert the **Member_Last_Name** field.

21. Save and close the letter.

REINFORCE YOUR SKILLS: W5-R2

Merge a Letter, Envelopes, and Labels

Kids for Change is starting an after-school tutoring program. The tutoring supervisor will send form letters to parents announcing the program. In this exercise, you will merge a data source with a letter. You will also merge the data source with envelopes and labels.

1. Open **W5-R2-ParentLtr** from your **Word Chapter 5** folder and save it as **W5-R2-ParentLtrRevised**.

   Notice the merge fields in the letter, including four merge fields in the body of the letter, and that <<Child_Name>> appears twice.

2. Choose **Mailings→Start Mail Merge→Start Mail Merge** 📄→**Letters**.

3. Choose **Mailings→Start Mail Merge→Select Recipients→Use an Existing List**.

4. Navigate to your **Word Chapter 5** folder and open **W5-R2-ParentData**.

5. Choose **Mailings→Preview Results→Preview Results**.

6. Scroll through the letters and then turn off **Preview Results**.

7. Choose **Mailings→Finish→Finish & Merge** 📄→**Edit Individual Documents** and then click **OK** to merge all records.

8. Scroll through the merged letters; close the file without saving it.

9. Save and close the parent letter main document.

Generate Envelopes

10. Start a new, blank document.

11. Choose **Mailings→Start Mail Merge→Start Mail Merge→Envelopes**.

12. Click **OK** to accept the envelope defaults.

13. Choose **Mailings→Start Mail Merge→Select Recipients→Use an Existing List**.

14. Navigate to your **Word Chapter 5** folder and open **W5-R2-ParentData** to attach the data source to the envelope.

15. If necessary, display formatting marks; then type this return address at the first paragraph symbol in the upper-left corner of the envelope:

```
Kids for Change
726 Throckmorton Ave.
Sacramento, CA  95613
```

16. Position the insertion point next to the paragraph symbol toward the center of the envelope.

17. Choose **Mailings→Write & Insert Fields→Address Block**; click **OK** to accept the address block defaults.

18. Choose **Mailings→Preview Results→Preview Results**.

19. Navigate through the records and then turn off **Preview Results**.

20. Save the envelope as **W5-R2-ParentEnv**; close the envelope file.

Generate Mailing Labels

21. Start a new, blank document.

22. Choose **Mailings→Start Mail Merge→Start Mail Merge→Labels**.

23. If necessary, choose **Avery US Letter** as the Label Vendor and **5160 Easy Peel Address Labels** as the Product Number and then click **OK**.

24. Choose **Mailings→Start Mail Merge→Select Recipients→Use an Existing List**.

25. Navigate to your **Word Chapter 5** folder and open **W5-R2-Parent Data**.

26. Display formatting marks, if necessary, and then make sure the insertion point is next to the paragraph symbol in the first label.

27. Choose **Mailings→Write & Insert Fields→Address Block**; click **OK** to accept the address block defaults.

28. Choose **Mailings→Write & Insert Fields→Update Labels** 🔄 to insert the Address Block code on all labels.

29. Choose **Mailings→Preview Results→Preview Results** to verify all labels will print correctly.

Because the addresses are three lines, they fit on the Avery 5160 labels without removing extra spacing.

30. Turn off **Preview Results** to return to the labels main document.

31. Save the labels file as **W5-R2-ParentLabels** in your **Word Chapter 5** folder.

32. Close the file.

Merge Letters and Envelopes

Kids for Change is sponsoring a walkathon fund-raiser to buy musical instruments for the local elementary school. The walkathon supervisor will be contacting Kids for Change members and encouraging their participation. In this exercise, you will designate a letter as the main document and create a data source. Then you will preview the results and correct any merge problems before conducting the merge. Finally, you will generate envelopes for the letters.

1. Open **W5-R3-Walkers** from your **Word Lesson 5** folder and save it as **W5-R3-WalkersRevised**.

2. Choose **Mailings→Start Mail Merge→Start Mail Merge→Letters** to designate the Walkers letter as the main document.

3. Choose **Mailings→Start Mail Merge→Select Recipients→Type a New List**.

   Now you will customize the data source columns.

4. Click **Customize Columns** to display the Customize Address List dialog box.

5. Click **Company Name** and click **Delete**; click **Yes** to confirm the deletion.

6. Delete the following fields and then click **OK**:
   - Address Line 2
   - Country or Region
   - Work Phone
   - E-mail Address

7. Place the insertion point in the **Title** field, type **Mr.**, and tap ⬚Tab to move to the next field.

8. Type **Sean** in the **First Name** field, tap ⬚Tab, and type **Corn** in the **Last Name** field.

9. Continue tabbing and typing to complete the Sean Corn record as shown, tap ⬚Tab to begin the next record, and then enter the remaining records.

Mr. Sean Corn 308 Alhambra Avenue Monterey CA 93940 831-555-0134	Mr. Craig Dostie 31200 Erwin Street Monterey CA 93940 831-555-0167	Ms. Alexia Lopez 2134 Harbor Blvd. Monterey CA 93942 831-555-0132
Ms. Margaret Wong 1308 West Ramona Blvd. Monterey CA 93940 831-555-0198	Ms. Phyllis Coen 4745 Buffin Avenue Monterey CA 93943 831-555-0178	Mr. Winston Boey 263 East Howard Street Monterey CA 93944 831-555-0196

10. Review your records for accuracy and make any necessary corrections.

    Now you will sort your list by Last Name.

11. Click the **Last Name** column header to sort the list alphabetically in ascending order and then click **OK**.

12. Navigate to your **Word Chapter 5** folder and save the file as **W5-R3-WalkersData**.

Set Up the Main Document and Correct Merge Problems

13. Follow these guidelines to insert the merge codes:
- Replace *INSIDE ADRESS* with the **Address Block** code using the default formats.
- Replace *GREETING LINE* with the **Greeting Line** code, changing the Greeting Line Format name to **Joshua**.
- In the last paragraph, replace *HOME PHONE* with the **Home_Phone** code.

14. Use the **Preview Results** feature to review your letters, correct any errors in the main document, and then turn off Preview Results.

Phyllis Cohen's name is misspelled in the data source. You will make that correction now.

15. Choose **Mailings→Start Mail Merge→Edit Recipient List** 📇.

16. Click the data source in the bottom-left corner and click **Edit**.

17. Change the spelling from *Coen* to **Cohen** and then click **OK**.

18. Click **Yes** to verify the update and then click **OK** to close the Mail Merge Recipients dialog box.

19. Use the navigation buttons in the Preview Results group to verify the change to the data source and any changes you made to the main document, and then turn off **Preview Results**.

20. Choose **Mailings→Finish→Finish & Merge** 📄→**Edit Individual Documents** and then click **OK**.

21. Scroll through your letters and then close the merged document without saving it; save and close the main document letter.

Merge Envelopes

22. Start a new, blank document.

23. Choose **Mailings→Start Mail Merge→Start Mail Merge→Envelopes**.

24. Make sure the envelope is **Size 10** and click **OK**.

Now you will attach the data source to your envelope.

25. Choose **Mailings→Start Mail Merge→Select Recipients** 📇→**Use an Existing List**.

26. Navigate to your **Word Chapter 5** folder and open **W5-R3-WalkersData**.

27. If necessary, turn on formatting marks; then type this return address at the top paragraph symbol in the upper-left corner of the envelope:

```
Kids for Change
456 Bayside Road
Monterey, CA   93943
```

28. Position the insertion point next to the paragraph symbol toward the middle of the envelope.

29. Choose **Mailings→Write & Insert Fields→Address Block** and then click **OK**.

30. Choose **Mailings→Preview Results→Preview Results**.

31. Use the navigation buttons to view all envelopes and then turn off the preview.

32. Choose **Mailings→Finish→Finish & Merge→Edit Individual Documents** and then click **OK**.

33. Scroll through the envelopes and then close the file without saving it.

34. Save the envelope main document as **W5-R3-WalkersEnv** in your **Word Chapter 5** folder; close the document.

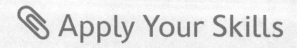

Apply Your Skills

Create a Data Source and Main Document

Universal Corporate Events is announcing a new affordable and flexible program for its small-business clients. In this exercise, you will create a small-business client data source, and you will review the records and sort the list. Then you will specify a letter as a main document and insert merge fields in the letter.

1. Open **W5-A1-SmallBiz** from your **Word Chapter 5** folder and save it as **W5-A1-SmallBizRevised**.

2. Specify the Small Biz letter as the main document.

   Now you will customize the columns for your new data source.

3. Delete and add columns as needed to create the following fields in your data source:

   - Title
   - First Name
   - Last Name
   - Company Name
   - Address Line 1
   - City
   - State
   - Zip Code
   - Agent Name

4. Add these records to your data source:

Mr. Tony Simpson	Mr. Jason Jones	Ms. Debbie Thomas
Bigger Time Video Distributors	Move It Distribution	Barker Books
312 York Lane	2233 Crystal Street	497 Tennessee Street
Richmond CA 94804	San Mateo CA 94403	Richmond CA 94804
Agent Name: David Roth	**Agent Name:** Tammy Nelson	**Agent Name:** Jacob Williams

5. Sort the data source in ascending alphabetic order by **Company Name**.

6. Save the data source as **W5-A1-SmallBizData** in your **Word Chapter 5** folder.

7. Delete the *Today's Date* placeholder, choose **Insert→Text→Date & Time** 📅, choose the third date format, and make sure **Update Automatically** is checked.

8. Follow these guidelines for inserting merge codes in the main document:

   - Replace *INSIDE ADDRESS* with the **Address Block** code using the default formats.
   - Replace *GREETING LINE* with the **Greeting Line** code and change the ending punctuation to a colon.
   - In the last paragraph, replace *AGENT NAME* with the **Agent_Name** code.

9. Preview the letters and check that the spacing is correct and then turn off the preview and make any needed changes.

10. Save and close the letter.

Complete a Merge

Universal Corporate Events is conducting a seminar on visa requirements for United States citizens. It is sending a form letter invitation to its clients' in-house travel agents. In this exercise, you will merge letters, envelopes, and labels. You will also correct merge problems.

1. Open **W5-A2-VisaLtr** from your **Word Chapter 5** folder and save it as **W5-A2-VisaLtrRevised**.
2. Designate the letter as the main document and **W5-A2-VisaData** from your **Word Chapter 5** folder as the data source.
3. Preview the merge and notice that there is an error in the greeting line.
4. Close the preview and then edit the main document and preview the letters again, checking that the greeting line is correct.
5. Close the preview; save and close the main document.

Merge Envelopes and Labels

6. Start a new, blank document and create a **Size 10** envelope as the main document with this return address:
   Suzanne Frost, Sales Manager
   Universal Corporate Events
   129 Potter Road
   Middlefield, CT 06455
7. Attach **W5-A2-VisaData** as the data source for the envelopes.
8. Insert an **Address Block** code in the middle of the envelope using the default formats.
9. Preview the envelopes.
10. Save the envelope main document in your **Word Chapter 5** folder as **W5-A2-VisaEnv** and then close it.
11. Start a new, blank document and create a label main document using **Avery US Letter** as the Label Vendor and **5160 Easy Peel Address Labels** as the Product Number.
12. Attach **W5-A2-VisaData** as the data source.
13. Insert the **Address Block** code in the first label using the default formats and use the **Update Labels** command to replicate the Address Block code on all labels.
14. Preview the results and notice that the addresses don't fit well on the labels.
15. Close the preview, select the labels table, and remove Word's extra spacing by entering **0** in the **Before** field.
    Hint: The Before field is at Layout→Paragraph.
16. Preview the results again to ensure that the labels fit correctly.
17. Close the preview and save the labels main document in your **Word Chapter 5** folder as **W5-A2-VisaLabels**.
18. Close the labels main document.

Create a Mail Merge for Trip Winners

A Universal Corporate Events client is rewarding its top sales performers with a trip to Tokyo. It will send an itinerary letter to the company's winners. In this exercise, you will create a data source using customized columns and add merge codes to main documents. You will preview and merge the main documents with the data source, make an editing change to a record, and sort the data source.

1. Open **W5-A3-TokyoLtr** from your **Word Chapter 5** folder and save it as **W5-A3-TokyoLtrRevised**.

2. Specify the letter as the main document and then start a new data source list.

3. Customize the columns by deleting some fields and keeping the fields shown here:
   - Title
   - First Name
   - Last Name
   - Company Name
   - Address Line 1
   - City
   - State
   - Zip Code

4. Create the data source using these three records and save it as **W5-A3-TokyoData**.

Ms. Jasleen Mahal	Mr. George Iverson	Mr. Anthony Waldek
Superior Storage Devices	Superior Storage Devices	Superior Storage Devices
951 Industrial Way	951 Industrial Way	951 Industrial Way
Trenton NJ 08601	Trenton NJ 08601	Trenton NJ 08601

5. Follow these guidelines to insert merge codes in the letter:
   - Replace *INSIDE ADDRESS* with **Address Block** code using the default formats.
   - Replace *GREETING LINE* with **Greeting Line** code using the default formats.
   - In the first paragraph, replace *COMPANY NAME* with the **Company_Name** code.
   - In the last paragraph, replace *FIRST NAME* with the **First_Name** code.

Preview the Merge Results

6. Preview the merge, make sure the spacing is correct, and then close the preview.

7. Modify the spacing in the main document if necessary.

   You want the greeting line to be less formal, so you will change the format to the recipient's first name.

8. Right-click the **Greeting Line** code and choose **Edit Greeting Line** from the menu.

9. In the Greeting Line Format area, click the drop-down arrow next to Mr. Randall, choose **Joshua** from the list, and click **OK**.

10. Preview the letters again to ensure the change was made and then turn off the preview.

11. Merge the letter with the data source, choosing **Edit Individual Documents**, and then scroll through the letters.

12. Close the merged document without saving it; save and close the main document.

Merge Envelopes and Labels

13. Start a new, blank document, designate it as a mail merge envelope, and use a **Size 10** envelope.

14. Insert this return address on the envelope:

    ```
    Ms. Tasha Reynolds
    Universal Corporate Events
    456 Riverview Road
    Trenton, NJ  08601
    ```

15. Attach the Tokyo data source to the envelope and insert the **Address Block** code using defaults.

16. Merge the envelopes and check them for accuracy; if necessary, correct any errors and conduct the merge again.

17. Close the merge document without saving it.

18. Save the envelope main document as **W5-A3-TokyoEnv** and then close it.

19. Start a new, blank document and designate it as **Labels**.

20. Choose **Avery US Letter** as the Label Vendor and **5160** as the Product Number.

21. Attach the Tokyo data source, insert the **Address Block** code in the first label, and update the labels to replicate the **Address Block** code in all labels.

22. Preview the labels and notice the addresses don't fit well because of Word's extra spacing.

23. Close the preview, select the labels table, and remove the extra spacing.

24. Preview the labels again to verify the change in spacing and then close the preview.

25. Save the labels main document as **W5-A3-TokyoLabels** and then close it.

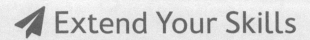 # Extend Your Skills

These exercises challenge you to think critically and apply your new skills. You will be evaluated on your ability to follow directions, completeness, creativity, and the use of proper grammar and mechanics. Save files to your chapter folder. Submit assignments as directed.

W5-E1 That's the Way I See It

You are planning a field trip for the fifth grade class you teach. Create a permission letter informing parents of the trip and how it relates to students' school work (e.g., visiting an aquarium after studying about ocean life). Include a request for parents to sign and return the letter. Save the letter as **W5-E1-FieldTripLtr**.

Create a three-record data source of parent names and addresses and any other variables you choose. Customize the data source with only the column headings you need. Save the data source as **W5-E1-FieldTripData**. Insert merge codes in the form letter and merge the main document and data source. Save the merged document as **W5-E1-FieldTripLtrMerged**. Create an envelope main document with your return address, merge it with your data file, and save it as **W5-E1-FieldTripEnvMerged**.

W5-E2 Be Your Own Boss

You are introducing a rewards program for Blue Jean Landscaping customers. Create a form letter of two to three paragraphs describing how customers can accumulate points toward purchases. Mention three other benefits (make them up) for program members. Save the letter as **W5-E2-RewardsLtr**.

Create a data source of three customers' names and addresses and any other fields you want to use. Customize the data source for only those columns needed and save it as **W5-E2-RewardsData**. Insert merge field codes in the letter and conduct the merge, saving the merged document as **W5-E2-RewardsLtrMerged**. Finally, create a labels document named **W5-E2-RewardsLabels** and merge it with the data source. Save the merged labels as **W5-E2-RewardsLabelsMerged**.

W5-E3 Demonstrate Proficiency

Stormy BBQ has added brisket of beef to its menu! They offered a free beef brisket meal and a $20 gift certificate to the first five customers who visited their restaurant on New Year's Day. They plan to mail the certificates to the qualifying customers. As a Stormy BBQ employee, you have been asked to compose a congratulatory letter to go with the certificates.

Compose an appropriate letter of two or three paragraphs saved as **W5-E3-CertLtr**. Create a name and address data source for five winners. Customize the data source by adding any fields you want to use in your letter; delete any fields you don't intend to use. Save the data source as **W5-E3-CertData**. Merge the letter and the data source and save the merge document as **W5-E3-CertLtrMerged**. Finally, create an envelope main document to go with the mailing and include Stormy BBQ's return address and the Address Block code on a Size 10 envelope. Save the envelope main document as **W5-E3-CertEnv**. Preview the envelopes to verify that they will print correctly. Make corrections if necessary, merge the envelope with your data source, and then save the merged document as **W5-E3-CertEnvMerged**.

A newsletter should be an essential part of every organization's communication plan. It's a great way to rally support for new programs or products and to maintain an ongoing relationship with your clients. In this chapter, you will create engaging newsletters using graphics and special text effects to add eye appeal. Finally, you will add a cover page to give a professional touch to your newsletter.

LEARNING OBJECTIVES

▸ Add graphic effects

▸ Use section breaks and columns

▸ Wrap text around a graphic image

▸ Insert a cover page

▸ Print part of a full document

📂 Project: Creating a Client Newsletter

As a leading pediatric facility, Raritan Clinic East stays ahead of the curve by updating its protocols with the latest discoveries. It stays in regular contact with its patient population through a monthly newsletter. As an administrator for the clinic, you have been asked to publish this month's newsletter, which describes meningitis, its symptoms, where outbreaks are likely to occur, and its treatment. You will add interest to your newsletter by using graphics and special text formatting.

📖 Six Tips for an Effective Newsletter

A newsletter is an effective way to keep in touch with clients. It adds a personal touch that can create a bond between your organization and the reader.

▸ Know your audience.

▸ Have a compelling opening line.

▸ Use a clean, simple layout with plenty of white space.

▸ Be informative and educational and provide true value.

▸ Use graphics but don't overdo it.

▸ Insert headings and subheadings to chunk your information into easy-to-read segments.

Adding Special Effects to Text

To add interest and dimension to newsletters, you can use graphic effects. For example, you can add WordArt for flair. You can create WordArt by adding your own text to a WordArt object, or you can apply a WordArt object to existing text. Either way, you have a full array of WordArt formatting tools available on the contextual Drawing Tools Format tab.

Font effects are interesting, special treatments of text. Options include strikethrough, superscript/subscript, small caps, and all caps.

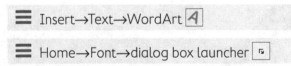

☰ Insert→Text→WordArt 𝐴

☰ Home→Font→dialog box launcher ⌐

In this exercise, you will begin creating the newsletter for Raritan Clinic East. You will start with a WordArt heading, which you will format with a new fill color, font color, and text effects. Then you will use the Font dialog box to adjust the font style and size, and then you will add font effects.

1. Start Word; open a new, blank document; and save it to your **Word Chapter 6** folder as **W6-D1-RaritanNewsltr**.

2. Display formatting marks and then type these heading lines at the top of the document:

   Raritan Clinic East
   The Children's Clinic
   November, 2016

3. Tap [Enter] three times.

4. Select *Raritan Clinic East* but do not select the paragraph mark at the end of the line.

5. Choose **Insert→Text→WordArt** 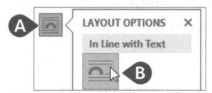 and then choose **Fill – Blue, Accent 1, Shadow**.

6. With the WordArt object selected, follow these steps to place it in line with the text:

   Ⓐ Click the **Layout Options** smart tag.

   Ⓑ Choose **In Line with Text** and then click in the document to close the gallery.

7. Click the border of the WordArt to select the entire object.

8. Choose **Drawing Tools→Format→Shape Styles→Shape Fill menu button** ▾ and then choose **Blue, Accent 5, Lighter 40%** from the gallery.

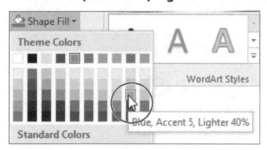

9. Choose **Drawing Tools→Format→WordArt Styles→Text Fill menu button** ▾ and then choose **White, Background 1**.

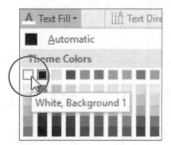

WORD

10. With the object selected, choose **Drawing Tools→Format→WordArt Styles→Text Effects** .

11. Drag the mouse pointer down to the Transform category and then choose **Chevron Down**.

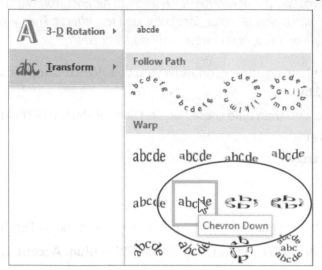

Now you will center all headings and format one of the headings.

12. Position the mouse pointer in the left margin area next to the WordArt object and then click and drag down to select the WordArt and the other two headings.

13. Choose **Home→Paragraph→Center** ≡.

14. Select *The Children's Clinic* and then choose **Home→Font→dialog box launcher** 🗗 to display the Font dialog box.

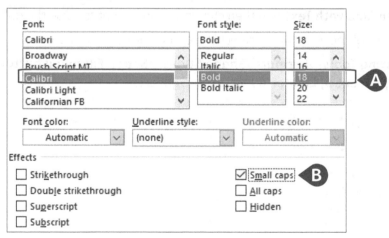

(Ⓐ) Choose **Calibri**, **Bold**, **18 pt**.

(Ⓑ) In the Effects area, check **Small Caps**.

(Ⓒ) Click **OK**.

15. Save the file.

Inserting a Picture and Using Picture Effects

Including pictures in your documents can make them rich and colorful and enhance your message. In addition to accessing pictures online, you can also insert pictures directly from files. For example, you can insert a scanned picture or a picture taken with a digital camera and stored on your computer.

And Word has great picture effects that you can add to your images, such as shadows, reflections, glows, soft edges, bevels, and 3-D rotations.

☰ Insert→Illustrations→Pictures 🖾

☰ Picture Tools→Format→Picture Styles→Picture Effects ◢

DEVELOP YOUR SKILLS: W6-D2

In this exercise, you will insert and crop a graphic image. Then you will add a picture effect to the image.

1. Save your file as **W6-D2-RaritanNewsltr**.
2. Position the insertion point on the blank line below the date.
3. Choose **Insert→Illustrations→Pictures** 🖾.
4. Navigate to your **Word Chapter 6** folder and double-click the **W6-D2-RaritanClinic.png** graphics file to insert it.

   Next you will crop the words off of the image.

5. With the picture selected, choose **Picture Tools→Format→Size→Crop** 🖾.
6. Position the mouse pointer on the right-center cropping handle and drag left to crop off the words *Raritan Clinic East*.
7. Position the mouse pointer on the bottom-center cropping handle and drag up to remove the words at the bottom of the image, and then click in the document to finish cropping.
8. If necessary, choose **View→Show→Ruler** and then resize the image from a corner sizing handle, making it approximately **1½" wide**.
9. With the image selected, choose **Picture Tools→Format→Picture Styles→Picture Effects** ◢.
10. Drag the mouse pointer to the **Shadow** category, and in the Outer category choose **Offset Diagonal Bottom Right**.
11. Choose **Home→Paragraph→Center** ☰.
12. Save the file.

Inserting a Section Break and Setting Up Columns

Whenever you have a page-oriented formatting change that affects only part of a document, such as margins, page orientation, or columns, you need to set off that part with a section break. You use a Continuous break to start a new section within a page. You use a Next Page section break to start a new section on a new page, or, if your document is laid out in a book-like format, you can specify that the section break should start on an Even Page or Odd Page.

When you set a document or a section of a document in columns, you can choose preset formats or set up your own column width and spacing.

☰ Layout→Page Setup→Breaks ⊟

☰ Layout→Page Setup→Columns ▦

In this exercise, you will insert a section break and lay out the newsletter in columns. Then you will customize the column layout.

1. Save your file as **W6-D3-RaritanNewsltr**.
2. Position the insertion point on the second blank line below the picture object.
3. Choose **Layout→Page Setup→Breaks** 🗒→**Continuous**.
4. Position the insertion point anywhere above the section break.
5. Choose **Layout→Page Setup→Columns** 🔲 and notice that one column is highlighted.

   Whenever text or images span the width of the page between the margins, it is considered one column.

6. Position the insertion point below the section break.

Add Newsletter Text and Customize Columns

7. Choose **Insert→Text→Object** 🔲 **menu button** ▾→**Text from File**.
8. Navigate to your **Word Chapter 6** folder and double-click **W6-D3-NewsltrTxt**.
9. Choose **Layout→Page Setup→Columns** 🔲 and then choose **More Columns** to open the Columns dialog box.
10. Follow these steps to customize the columns:

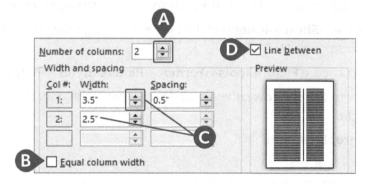

A Use the spin box to change the number of columns to **2**.
B Remove the checkmark from this checkbox.
C Use the spin box to change the width of column 1 to **3.5"** and notice that column 2 resizes automatically.
D Place a checkmark in the **Line Between** box to add a line between your columns.

11. Click **OK** and then scroll through the document to see the effect.

    The columns don't really look good this way. While you could click Undo, if you were to change your mind at a later time, there is still a quick way to return the columns back to equal size.

12. Choose **Layout→Page Setup→Columns** 🔲→**More Columns**.
13. Click the **Equal Column Width** checkbox and click **OK**.
14. Scroll through the document to see how it looks.
15. Save the file.

Artistic Effects and Wrapping Text Around a Picture

There are many tools on the contextual Format tab that allow you to customize images. Artistic effects can take your image styling to the next level. Some effects represent the image in pencil, paint, and various textures.

≡ Picture Tools→Format→Adjust→Artistic Effects 🖼

DEVELOP YOUR SKILLS: W6-D4

In this exercise, you will insert a picture and apply an artistic effect as well as a picture style to it. Then you will use the Layout Options smart tag to wrap text around the picture and you will balance the columns at the end of the newsletter.

1. Save your file as **W6-D4-RaritanNewsltr**.
2. Position the insertion point on page 2 to the left of the heading *The New Vaccine*.
3. Choose **Insert→Illustrations→Pictures 🖼**.
4. Navigate to your **Word Chapter 6** folder and double-click **W6-D4-VaccinePic.jpg** to insert the picture in the newsletter.
5. Resize the picture using a corner handle until it is about **1½" wide**.

Apply an Artistic Effect and a Picture Style

6. With the picture selected, choose **Picture Tools→Format→Adjust→Artistic Effects 🖼** and then choose **Crisscross Etching**.
7. Choose **Picture Tools→Format→Picture Styles→More ▾** button on the Picture Styles gallery.
8. Use Live Preview to sample various styles and then choose **Simple Frame, Black**.

Wrap Text Around a Picture

9. With the picture selected, click the **Layout Options** smart tag and choose the **Tight** text wrapping option.

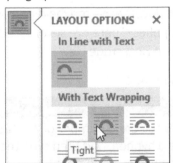

10. Click in the document to close the Layout Options gallery.

    Now you will balance the columns on page 2.

    You don't have to insert column breaks and move text around to balance columns. Inserting a Continuous section break at the end of the columns you want to balance is a quick trick for accomplishing the task.

11. Position the insertion point after the period following *disease* at the end of page 2.
12. Choose **Layout→Page Setup→Breaks ⊟→Continuous**.
13. Save your file.

Inserting Cover Pages

A cover page catches a reader's eye as the first dynamic part of your document. You can easily add professional polish to a document by using a built-in cover page. There are a number of predesigned cover pages for you to choose from. And, if desired, you can modify the color and other design elements to achieve a cover page that best suits your needs.

≡ Insert→Pages→Cover Page 📄

DEVELOP YOUR SKILLS: W6-D5

In this exercise, you will add a cover page to your newsletter. Then you will add text to two text controls and delete text controls that you do not need.

1. Save your file as **W6-D5-RaritanNewsltr**.
2. Choose **Insert→Pages→Cover Page** 📄, scroll through the gallery of available options, and choose **Banded**.
3. Click the **Document Title** control and type **Raritan Clinic East Newsletter**.

   The text wraps automatically within the control.

   Now you will repurpose one of the controls and delete controls you don't need.
4. Scroll to the bottom of the page, click the **Author** control (it may contain a person's name), and type **November, 2016**.
5. Click the **COMPANY NAME** control, click the **Company** tab at the top to select the entire control, and then tap Delete.
6. Use the same technique to delete the **Company Address** control.
7. Save the file.

Printing Part of a Document

Sometimes you may want to print only part of a longer document—maybe a page or two or even just a couple of paragraphs. This can save both time and supplies. There are several techniques that make this an easy task, and they are found in the Print screen in Backstage view.

Custom Print options allow you to stipulate specific pages to print.

CUSTOM PRINT OPTIONS	
Print Consecutive Pages	Enter the page number of the first page to print, type a hyphen, and then type the page number of the last page to print.
Print Non-Consecutive Pages and Ranges	Enter the page numbers you want to print separated by commas (for example: 3,5,7,10-15).
Print a block of text	Select the text to print. Navigate to the Print screen in Backstage view. Choose Print Selection from the drop-down list.

≡ File→Print

DEVELOP YOUR SKILLS: W6-D6

In this exercise, you will explore options for printing part of a document. You will see how to print consecutive and nonconsecutive pages as well as a block of selected text.

1. Choose **File→Print** to display the Print screen in Backstage view.

    In the Settings part of the screen, notice that Print All Pages is the default.

2. Click the drop-down arrow next to Print All Pages.

3. Follow these steps to review the printing options:

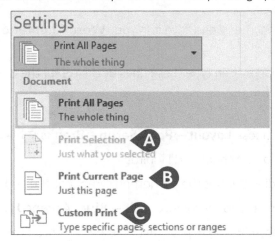

   - Ⓐ This option is available only when you select text prior to accessing the Print screen.
   - Ⓑ This choice prints the page where the insertion point is located.
   - Ⓒ This option allows you to specify printing only certain pages.

4. Click the drop-down arrow to close the menu.

You can specify which custom pages to print in the Pages field without opening the menu. When you begin entering page numbers, the setting automatically switches to Custom Print.

5. If you want to stay green and not print, click the **Back** ⬅ button or print to PDF (you can make that choice in the Printer drop-down list).

6. Save the file and exit Word.

Self-Assessment

Check your knowledge of this chapter's key concepts and skills using the Self-Assessment in your ebook or eLab course.

Reinforce Your Skills

Publish a Schoolyard Habitat Newsletter

Children who live in cities often miss out on the joys of the countryside. Kids for Change is seeking volunteers to help set up schoolyard habitats where children can experience firsthand the fun of creating their own gardens. In this exercise, you will create a newsletter with a section break and columns, and you will work with graphic images.

1. Start Word; create a new, blank document; and save it in your **Word Chapter 6** folder as **W6-R1-SchoolHabitat**.

2. If necessary, display formatting marks; then type these lines at the top of the document:
   Schoolyard Habitat
   Kids for Change

3. Tap ⌷Enter⌷ three times and then choose **Layout→Page Setup→Breaks** ⊞ **→Continuous**.
   Next you will apply a WordArt format to Schoolyard Habitat.

4. Select the *Schoolyard Habitat* heading but not the paragraph symbol at the end of the line.

5. Choose **Insert→Text→WordArt** ▢ and then choose **Fill – Blue, Accent 1, Shadow**.
   Next you will use the Layout Options smart tag to position the second line below the WordArt image.

6. With the WordArt object selected, click the smart tag and choose **In Line with Text**.

7. If necessary, click the border of the image to select the entire image.

8. Choose **Drawing Tools→Format→WordArt Styles→Text Effects** ▢ and then slide the mouse pointer down to **Glow**.

9. In the Glow Variations section, choose **Green, 11 pt Glow, Accent Color 6**.

10. Choose **Drawing Tools→Format→WordArt Styles→Text Fill menu button** ▾ and then choose **Green, Accent 6, Darker 25%**.

11. Position the mouse pointer in the margin area to the left of the WordArt image and drag down to select it and the *Kids for Change* line.

12. Choose **Home→Paragraph→Center**.

13. Format the text *Kids for Change* with **Comic Sans MS, Bold, 16 pt** font.

14. Position the insertion point on the paragraph symbol below the section break.

15. Choose **Insert→Text→Object** ▢ **menu button** ▾ and choose **Text from File**.

16. Navigate to your **Word Chapter 6** folder and insert **W6-R1-HabitatContent**.

17. Position the insertion point on the second blank line below the text you just inserted.

18. Choose **Layout→Page Setup→Breaks→Continuous**.

19. Position the insertion point on the second blank line below the second section break.

Insert, Size, and Format a Picture

20. If necessary, choose **View→Show→Ruler**.

21. Choose **Insert→Illustrations→Pictures** and double-click the **W6-R1-Butterfly.jpg** picture to insert it.

22. With the picture selected, position the mouse pointer on the upper-right sizing handle and resize the picture to approximately **1" wide**.

23. Choose **Picture Tools→Format→Picture Styles**, click the **More** ⊡ button on the Picture Styles gallery, and then choose **Reflected Rounded Rectangle**.

24. Choose **Home→Paragraph→Center**.

Apply Columns

25. Position the insertion point anywhere in section 2.

26. Choose **Layout→Page Setup→Columns→More Columns**.

27. Choose **Two** in the Presets area, place a checkmark in the **Line Between** checkbox, and click **OK**.

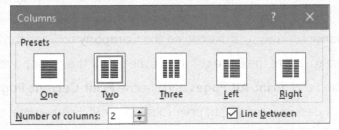

The Habitat Team *heading should be moved to the top of the second column.*

28. Position the insertion point in front of the heading at the bottom of the first column.

29. Choose **Layout→Page Setup→Breaks→Column**.

30. Choose **File→Print** to preview the document and then click the **Back** ⟵ button to return to the Word screen.

31. Save and close the file.

REINFORCE YOUR SKILLS: W6-R2

Add Pizazz to a Wetlands Protection Newsletter

Kids for Change is starting a wetlands protection project. It is sending out a newsletter discussing the importance of wetlands and is seeking volunteers to become part of the project. In this exercise, you will insert a picture in the newsletter, apply artistic effects, and wrap text around the picture. You will add a cover page and print part of the newsletter.

1. Open **W6-R2-Wetlands** from your **Word Chapter 6** folder and save it as **W6-R2-WetlandsRevised**.

2. In the *Wetlands Are Busy Places* paragraph, position the insertion point at the beginning of the third sentence (begins with Wetlands).

3. Choose **Insert→Illustrations→Pictures** 🖼, navigate to your **Word Chapter 6** folder, and double-click **W6-R2-WetlandsPic.png**.

4. If necessary, turn on the ruler; then resize the picture from a corner handle until it is about **2" wide**.

5. Click the **Layout Options** smart tag, choose **Tight**, and then click in the document to close the gallery.

6. Click the picture border and choose **Picture Tools→Format→Adjust→Artistic Effects** 🖼→ **Plastic Wrap**.

    Next, you will balance the columns.

7. Position the insertion point at the end of the right-hand column.

8. Choose **Layout→Page Setup→Breaks→Continuous**.

    Now you will add a cover page to the newsletter and you will print only the second page of the document.

9. Choose **Insert→Pages→Cover Page** 📄**→Whisp**.

10. Click the **Document Title** control and type `Wetlands`.

11. If necessary, click the **Document Subtitle** control and type `Why They Are Important`.

12. Scroll to the bottom of the cover page, click the **Author Name** control, and type `Roger Washington`.

13. Click the **Company Name** control, click directly on the **Company** tab, and tap `Delete`.

14. Use the same technique to delete the **Date** control at the top of the cover page.

15. Choose **File→Print**; then click **Print All Pages** and choose **Print Current Page**.

16. Click the **Print** button, if desired, choosing to print to paper or PDF; otherwise, click the **Back** ⬅ button to return to the Word window.

17. Save and close the file.

REINFORCE YOUR SKILLS: W6-R3

Create a Newsletter to Fight Water Pollution

Kids for Change is starting a Protect Our Waterways project to fight water pollution. The supervisor for the project is using a newsletter as a means of getting the word out. In this exercise, you will set a document in newsletter columns and work with graphics.

1. Open **W6-R3-WaterPollution** from your **Word Chapter 6** folder and save it as **W6-R3-WaterPollutionRevised**.

2. If necessary, display formatting marks; then position the insertion point on the second paragraph symbol below the heading at the top of the document.

3. Choose **Layout→Page Setup→Breaks→Continuous**.

4. Select the heading at the top of the document but not the paragraph symbol at the end of the line.

5. Choose **Insert→Text→WordArt** 🅰 and then choose **Fill – Blue, Accent 5, Outline – Background 1, Hard Shadow – Accent 5**.

6. With the WordArt object selected, click the **Layout Options** smart tag and choose the **Top and Bottom** layout.

7. Click in the document to close the gallery and then click the border of the WordArt object.

8. Choose **Drawing Tools→Format→WordArt Styles→Text Effects** 🅰 and slide the mouse pointer down to **Transform**.

9. Choose **Square** in the Warp category.

10. Position the insertion point on the WordArt border and drag to the right to center the object between the margins.

Use Font Effects and Insert a Picture

11. Select the *Water Pollution* heading in the body of the document.

12. Choose **Home→Font→dialog box launcher** 🔲 and then check **Small Caps** in the Effects section and click **OK**.

13. Choose **Home→Clipboard** and double-click **Format Painter**.

    Double-click the Format Painter when you want to copy a format to multiple text blocks.

14. Use the **Format Painter** to apply **Small Caps** to the other headings.

15. Click the **Format Painter** again to turn it off.

16. Position the insertion point on the second blank line below the last paragraph.

17. Choose **Insert→Illustrations→Pictures**, navigate to your **Word Chapter 6** folder, and double-click **W6-R3-FishingPic.jpg**.

18. If necessary, turn on the ruler; then resize the picture from a corner handle until it is about **2½" wide**.

19. Choose **Picture Tools→Format→Picture Effects** 🔲 **→Soft Edges** and then choose **10 Point**.

Apply and Balance Columns

20. Click the insertion point in the body of the document.

21. Choose **Layout→Page Setup→Columns** 🔲 **→More Columns**.

22. Choose **Two** in the Presets area, check the **Line Between** checkbox, and then click **OK**.

23. Delete the paragraph symbol at the top of the left-hand column.

24. Position the insertion point on the last paragraph symbol at the bottom of the right-hand column.

25. Choose **Layout→Page Setup→Breaks→Continuous**.

26. Select the picture and choose **Home→Paragraph→Center**.

Add a Cover Page

27. Choose **Insert→Pages→Cover Page** and choose **Grid**.

28. Click the **Document Title** control and type **Let's Fight Water Pollution**, and the text will automatically wrap.

29. Delete the other text controls on the page.

30. Save and close the file.

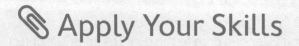

Apply Your Skills

Publish a Travel Newsletter

Universal Corporate Events keeps its clients informed about the latest travel industry news by publishing a monthly newsletter. In this exercise, you will create a newsletter in column format and with graphic images.

1. Open **W6-A1-CorpTravel** from your **Word Chapter 6** folder and save it as **W6-A1-CorpTravelRevised**.

2. If necessary, display formatting marks; then position the insertion point on the second blank line below the *Meeting and Event Planning Services* heading and insert a **Continuous** section break.

3. Select the first heading (Universal Corporate Events) but not the paragraph symbol at the end of the line.

4. Apply **WordArt** to the first line heading using **Fill – Gray-50%, Accent 3, Sharp Bevel**.

5. Use the **Layout Options** smart tag to apply **Top and Bottom** text wrapping.

6. Apply the **Square** text effect in the Warp section of the **Transform** category to the WordArt object.

7. Choose **Drawing Tools→Format→WordArt Styles→Text Fill menu button ▾** and then choose **Blue, Accent 5, Lighter 40%**.

8. Format the second heading line, *Meeting and Event Planning Services*, with **Tahoma 14 pt** font.

9. Center both heading lines. (Drag the WordArt object to center it.)

10. Position the insertion point at the beginning of the first subheading.

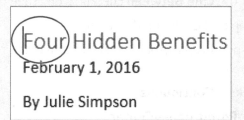

11. Tap [Enter] and then position the insertion point on the blank line.

Insert and Format Pictures

12. Insert the **W6-A1-HappyPic.png** and resize it to **1" wide**.

13. With the image selected, choose **Picture Tools→Format→Picture Styles→Picture Effects→Glow** and then choose **Gold, 8 pt glow, Accent color 4**.

14. Position the insertion point at the beginning of the *Avis Budget Reports* heading on page 2.

15. Tap [Enter] and then position the insertion point on the blank line.

16. Insert **W6-A1-RentalPic.jpg** and resize it to **2" wide**.

17. Open the **Picture Styles** gallery and choose **Soft Edge Oval**.

18. Position the insertion point in the body of the document; format the document in an equal-width, two-column layout, with a line between the columns.

The Better Direction heading at the bottom of the right-hand column on page 1 would look better at the top of the next column.

19. Position the insertion point in front of the *4* and then choose **Layout→Page Setup→Breaks→ Column**.

There are two lines flowing onto the last page, and it would look better if they were on page 2. Resizing the rental picture might solve the issue.

20. Resize the picture to **1½"** or the size needed to make the lines flow to page 2.

21. Save and close the file.

APPLY YOUR SKILLS: W6-A2

Create a Bleisure Newsletter

This month's Universal Corporate Events newsletter focuses on the latest "bleisure" (a blend of business and leisure) travel trend. In this exercise, you will create a two-column newsletter, with a cover page and images, that is designed to keep clients' travel agents updated with the latest developments in the travel industry.

1. Open **W6-A2-BleisureTravel** from your **Word Chapter 6** folder and save it as **W6-A2-BleisureTravelRevised**.

2. If necessary, display formatting marks; then position the insertion point at the end of the heading, *The Bleisure Trend,* and tap ⏎ Enter twice.

3. With the insertion point on the second blank line, insert a **Continuous** section break.

4. Select the heading, *The Bleisure Trend,* but not the paragraph symbol and apply the WordArt style **Fill — Blue, Accent 1, Shadow**.

5. Open the **Layout Options** smart tag and apply **Top and Bottom** wrapping.

6. Select the WordArt object, choose **Drawing Tools→Format→WordArt Styles→Text Effects→Shadow**, and from the Outer category, apply the **Offset Diagonal Top Right** style.

7. Drag the WordArt to the right to center it between the margins.

8. Using the Font dialog box, format the *Introduction* heading with **14 pt** font size and **Small Caps**.

9. Use the **Format Painter** to apply the same format to the other headings in the document.

10. With the insertion point in the body of the document, format the section with two equal-width columns and a line between the columns.

Add a Picture and a Cover Page

11. Position the insertion point in front of the paragraph beginning, *In fact*, on page 1.

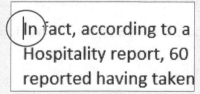

12. Insert the picture file **W6-A2-BleisurePic.jpg** and then resize it to **1½" wide**.

13. Click the **Layout Options** smart tag and choose **Tight** wrapping.

14. Delete the extra paragraph symbol at the top of the left-hand column.

    There are just a few lines flowing onto the second page. Next, you will narrow the margins to make the document fit on one page.

15. Choose **Layout→Page Setup→Margins** and then choose the preset **Narrow** option.

    Now you will finish off the newsletter with a cover page.

16. Insert a cover page using the **Slice (Dark)** option.

17. Click the **Document Title** control and type `Universal Corporate Events`.

18. Click the **Document Subtitle** and type `Bleisure Travel`.

19. Save and close the file.

APPLY YOUR SKILLS: W6-A3

Create a Travel Tips Newsletter

Universal Corporate Events shares travel tips with its clients' travel agents in this month's newsletter. In this exercise, you will publish a two-column travel tips newsletter incorporating WordArt, a picture, and a cover page.

1. Open **W6-A3-TravelTips** from your **Word Chapter 6** folder and save it as **W6-A3-TravelTipsRevised**.

2. Select *Universal Corporate Events* at the top of the document but not the paragraph symbol at the end of the line.

3. Apply the WordArt style **Fill, White – Outline – Accent 1, Glow – Accent 1**.

4. Choose **Drawing Tools→Format→WordArt Styles→Text Effects**, and in the **Reflection** category, choose **Tight Reflection, Touching**.

5. Open the **Layout Options** smart tag, choose **Top and Bottom**, and then drag the WordArt object to the right to center it between the margins.

6. Position the insertion point on the second paragraph symbol below the WordArt heading and insert a **Continuous** section break.

7. Position the insertion point in the body of the document and format the text in two columns.

8. Delete the paragraph symbol at the top of the left-hand column.

9. Position the insertion point at the end of the right-hand column, tap [Enter], and insert the picture **W6-A3-AirportPic.png**.

10. Resize the picture so it is even with the bottom of the left-hand column.

11. Choose **Picture Tools→Format→Picture Styles→Picture Border menu button ▾** and then choose **Blue, Accent 5, Lighter 40%**.

12. Click the **Picture Border menu button ▾** again, choose **3 pt** from the **Weight** menu, and then center the image within the column.

13. Insert the **Slice (Light)** cover page.

14. Edit the controls as indicated:
- Document Title control: **Travel Tips**
- Document Subtitle control: **Universal Corporate Events**

15. Click the **School** control at the bottom of the page and notice the School and Course Title controls are inside a rectangle shape.

16. Click the border of the rectangle to select everything inside it and tap [Delete].

17. Save and close the file; exit Word.

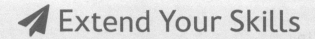 Extend Your Skills

These exercises challenge you to think critically and apply your new skills. You will be evaluated on your ability to follow directions, completeness, creativity, and the use of proper grammar and mechanics. Save files to your chapter folder. Submit assignments as directed.

W6-E1 That's the Way I See It

As a small-business owner, you want to keep your customers interested in what you're doing, so you decide to send out monthly newsletters. Determine the type of business you own and then place a WordArt object with your company's name at the top of a new document. The object should span the margins (one column). Conduct online research related to your type of business to find information you think will be of interest to your customers. Pull the information into your document, remembering to cite your sources. Lay out the document in newsletter-style columns. Insert an image that relates to the content and use a style from the Picture Styles gallery to enhance the image. Place headings within the newsletter and format them with Small Caps along with a font and font size of your choice. Add a cover page that blends well with your newsletter. Save your newsletter as **W6-E1-MyBiz**.

W6-E2 Be Your Own Boss

As the owner of Blue Jean Landscaping, you decide to keep in touch with customers by distributing a newsletter. Start a new document and save it as **W6-E2-Landscape**.

Place the company name at the top of the newsletter using a WordArt style. Insert a continuous section break after the WordArt. Search online for decorative plants and shrubs that can be used for landscaping. Pull in the results of your research as the primary content for the newsletter, ensuring you cite your sources. Format the text in newsletter-style columns. Insert a picture that reflects the newsletter content and apply a Picture Effect. Then insert headings in the document body and apply Small Caps and the font and point size of your choice. Add a cover page of your choice.

W6-E3 Demonstrate Proficiency

Stormy BBQ keeps its customers engaged through a monthly newsletter. This month's newsletter will describe the benefits of local farm-raised pork and beef. Conduct online research to gather the primary content for your newsletter, ensuring you cite your sources. Place the name of the business at the top of the newsletter formatting it with WordArt and then apply the Text Fill of your choice. Insert a section break to separate the WordArt from the main article. Format the newsletter in columns with a line between. Insert at least two pictures that enhance your message. Add headings within the newsletter, add the text effect of Small Caps or All Caps, and then apply the font and font size of your choice. Add a cover page that blends well with the newsletter. Save your file as **W6-E3-FarmRaised**.

7 Working with Long Documents

L ong documents are important in both academia and business and range in type from dissertations to research reports. In this chapter, you will use styles to provide consistent heading formatting, which leads the reader's eye through the document. You will customize styles and other features to suit your needs, and you will use several techniques to quickly navigate long documents. Finally, you will work with long tables to make them easy to read and to find information.

LEARNING OBJECTIVES

▸ Format with styles

▸ Create and manage custom styles

▸ Use themes and style sets

▸ Customize bullets and numbering

▸ Navigate long documents

▸ Format long tables

Project: Reporting on Common Childhood Illnesses

Raritan Clinic East periodically hosts seminars for parents of young children to discuss common childhood illnesses. As a certified nursing assistant, you have been asked to research these illnesses and compile a report that the clinic will use as a handout for the seminars. You will use styles, themes, and other formatting features to make your report engaging to the reader. Then you will create a table to keep track of the attendees.

Formatting Text with Styles

A style is a collection of formats that you can apply to text. When you type a document, you are automatically using a style. This is typically the Normal style, which includes Calibri font, 11 pt, left-justified, and so forth. Or, you might be using a custom template that is set up with a different default style. Styles are based on the current template's theme, which is a set of colors, fonts, and graphic effects. Styles help you provide consistent formatting throughout a document.

The Styles gallery on the Ribbon is limited to frequently used styles. For a more in-depth approach and access to more styles, you must open the Styles task pane.

 View the video "The Styles Gallery and the Styles Task Pane."

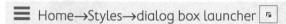 Home→Styles→dialog box launcher 🔲

Custom Styles

Thus far, you have used Word's built-in styles. However, there may be situations in which the built-in styles do not meet your needs. For example, Raritan Clinic East has formatting standards set for different types of documents. You can create custom styles to meet those standards.

There are two approaches you can take to create custom styles. The method you choose is a matter of personal preference; both are equally effective.

▸ **Style by definition:** Choose all formats from the Create New Style from Formatting dialog box.

▸ **Style by example:** Format a block of text with the formats you wish to include in your style. The Create New Style from Formatting dialog box can copy the formats from your formatted text.

 View the video "Create a Style by Definition and a Style by Example."

DEVELOP YOUR SKILLS: W7-D1

In this exercise, you will create custom styles. You'll begin by opening the Styles task pane and creating a new style by example for the document heading. Then you will create a style by definition.

1. Start Word, open **W7-D1-SickKids** from your **Word Chapter 7** folder, and save it as **W7-D1-SickKidsRevised**.

2. Select the *Raritan Clinic East* heading at the top of the document.

   Now you will apply the example formatting.

3. Choose **Home→Font→Font menu button** ▾ and then choose **Tahoma** from the menu.

4. Click the **Font Size menu** button ▾ and choose **24 pt**.

5. Choose **Home→Paragraph→Center** ≡.

6. Choose **Home→Styles→dialog box launcher** ⌐ to display the Styles task pane.

7. At the bottom of the task pane, click the **New Style** ⊞ button to open the Create New Style from Formatting dialog box.

8. Follow these steps to complete the new style:

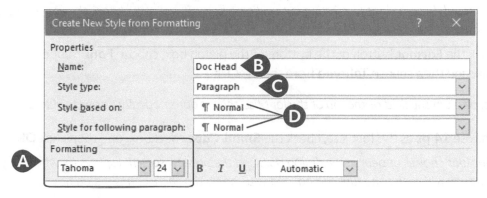

Ⓐ Notice the example formatting that you applied earlier.

Ⓑ Name the style **Doc Head**.

Ⓒ Make sure the Style Type is **Paragraph**.

Ⓓ If necessary, set the new style to be based on the **Normal** style and the formatting for the following paragraph to **Normal**.

9. At the bottom of the dialog box, make sure the **Add to the Styles Gallery** box is checked and then click **OK**.

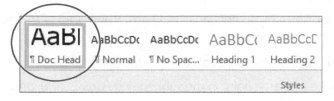

When the text that has the style applied is selected or the insertion point is in the text, your new style is highlighted in the Styles gallery on the Ribbon and in the Styles task pane.

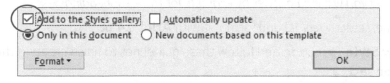

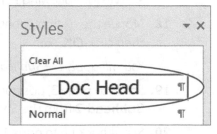

Create Styles by Definition

Now you'll create a style by definition for the subheading at the top of the document.

10. Click in the *Childhood Diseases Seminar* subheading.

11. Click the **New Style** button at the bottom of the Styles task pane.

12. Set up the top portion of the dialog box as shown.

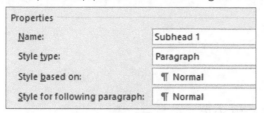

You could do some font formatting in this dialog box, but you will choose the Format button instead because it provides more font options.

13. Click the **Format** button at the bottom of the dialog box, choose **Font** to open the Font dialog box, and then choose **Tahoma** from the Font list.

 If you type a t in the field at the top of the font list, the list automatically scrolls to the Ts.

14. Choose **14 pt** as the font size, check the **Small Caps** checkbox, and then click **OK**.

Your font choices appear in the dialog box, and the preview screen displays the effect of your choices. Next you will center the subheading, and you can do that here in this dialog box.

15. Click the **Center** button in the paragraph alignment group and then click **OK**.

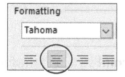

The new style appears in the Styles gallery on the Ribbon and in the Styles task pane.

Now you will create styles for the subheadings in the body of the document. You will have two levels of subheadings, and you will create styles by example for these subheadings.

16. In the next line, select *WebMD* and format it with **Arial**, **14 pt**.

17. Click the **New Style** button and follow these guidelines to finish creating the style:
- Name: **Subhead 2**
- Style Type: **Paragraph**
- Style Based On: **Normal**
- Style for Following Paragraph: **Normal**

18. Notice the example font formatting you applied in the Formatting area of the dialog box and then click **OK**.

You will apply the Subhead 2 style to another subheading in the document.

19. Scroll to page 3, position the insertion point in the subheading *Parents.com*, and choose **Subhead 2** from the Styles gallery.

20. Scroll back up to page 1, position the insertion point in the *RSV* subheading, and choose **Home→Font**.

21. Choose the **Arial** font and the **12 pt** font size.

22. Click the **New Style** button and follow these guidelines to finish creating the style:
    - Name: **Subhead 3**
    - Style Type: **Paragraph**
    - Style Based On: **Normal**
    - Style for Following Paragraph: **Normal**

23. Notice the example settings in the Formatting area and then click **OK**.

    Now you will apply Subhead 3 to the rest of the subheadings in the document.

24. Click in the *Ear Infection* subheading and choose **Subhead 3** from the Styles task pane.

25. Use the same technique to apply Subhead 3 to the remaining subheadings:
    - Glue Ear
    - Croup
    - Hand-Foot-and-Mouth Disease
    - Pinkeye
    - Fifth Disease
    - Common Cold
    - Strep Throat
    - Influenza
    - Symptoms You Should Never Ignore

26. Save the file.

Modifying Styles and Clearing All Formatting

You can modify a built-in style as well as styles that you create. Modifying styles can help you maintain consistency when you make formatting changes and can speed up that process. You can make global formatting changes by modifying a style. When you change a style, the change is applied to all the text in the current document that is formatted with the style. This eliminates the need to modify each text block individually—a big time saver.

There may be times when it is easier to reformat text from the beginning rather than trying to figure out which formats were used. This can be particularly helpful if you've inherited a heavily formatted document. The Clear All command in the Styles task pane is a quick way to remove styles and all other unwanted formatting from a document or a selected block of text.

DEVELOP YOUR SKILLS: W7-D2

In this exercise, you will modify the Subhead 3 style. When you do, you will see how it impacts all text formatted with that style. Then you will use the Clear All feature to remove formatting from a heading.

1. Save your file as **W7-D2-SickKidsRevised**.

2. Hover the mouse pointer over **Subhead 3** in the Styles task pane and click the drop-down arrow.

3. Choose **Modify** from the menu to open the Modify Style dialog box.

    This dialog box contains the same elements as the Create New Style from Formatting dialog box.

4. Click the **Italic** button to add that format to the Subhead 3 style and then click **OK**.

5. Scroll through the document and notice that all the subheadings with the Subhead 3 style are now italicized.

    You've decided to reformat the heading at the top of the document. Because this style is used only once in the document, you will clear all the formatting and apply direct formatting to the heading.

6. Select the *Raritan Clinic East* heading at the top of the document, scroll to the top of the Styles task pane, and choose **Clear All**.

7. Click the **Font group dialog box launcher** 🔲 and then choose **Tahoma**, **22 pt**, **Small Caps** and click **OK**.

8. Choose **Home→Paragraph→Center** ≣.

    Notice that the Normal style is highlighted in the task pane. You applied direct formatting to text that is formatted with the Normal style.

9. Save the file.

Removing and Deleting Styles

You can remove a style from the Styles gallery on the Ribbon without removing it from the Styles task pane. Because the Styles gallery on the Ribbon is a quick way to get to styles, you should save it for just the styles you use frequently and not clutter it with styles that you don't often use or don't plan to use at all. You can leave the style in the task pane for future use, or, if you prefer, you can delete it from the task pane. Completely deleting a style removes its formatting from the document.

DEVELOP YOUR SKILLS: W7-D3

In this exercise, you will remove the Doc Head style from the Styles gallery and then delete it from the task pane.

1. Save your file as **W7-D3-SickKidsRevised**.

2. If the Doc Head style is not visible in the Styles gallery on the Ribbon, click the **More** 🔽 button to open the gallery and then locate the Doc Head style.

3. Right-click on the style name and choose **Remove from Styles Gallery**.

    Notice that Doc Head is still visible in the Styles task pane. You'll delete it next.

4. Hover the mouse pointer over Doc Head in the Styles task pane, click the drop-down arrow, and choose **Delete Doc Head**.

5. When the message appears verifying the deletion, click **Yes**.

    The style is deleted from the task pane.

6. Save and close your document.

Using Themes and Style Sets

Themes and style sets are document-level formatting features that can instantly add color and visual variety to your entire document. A theme is a combination of colors, fonts, and graphic elements that you can apply to any document. Style sets change font and paragraph properties. Themes and style sets create the biggest impact when you use built-in styles.

≣ Design→Document Formatting→Themes 🅰

≣ Design→Document Formatting→Style Sets gallery

Customizing a Theme

You can customize any theme to match your creative side. Changing a theme font changes any text formatted with fonts that have (Headings) or (Body) next to their names in the font list. Calibri Light (Heading) and Calibri (Body) are the theme fonts for the default Office theme. When you change the theme, the associated theme fonts change. You can also customize the theme color. Changing a theme color or font does not permanently change the built-in theme; it modifies only your current document.

DEVELOP YOUR SKILLS: W7-D4

In this exercise, you will use a different version of the Childhood Diseases Seminar handout. This version uses Word's built-in styles, and a cover page has been added. You will use Live Preview to examine a variety of themes and style sets, and you will also apply a new theme and style set to your report.

1. Open **W7-D4-SickKids** from your **Word Chapter 7** folder and save it as **W7-D4-SickKidsRevised**.

2. Scroll to page 1 of the main document and position the insertion point in the *Raritan Clinic East* heading.

   Notice that the built-in Title style is highlighted in the Styles task pane.

3. Position the insertion point in the *Childhood Diseases Seminar* subheading and see that the built-in Heading 1 style is active in the Styles task pane.

4. Examine the other headings, and you can see that built-in styles have been applied.

   Remember, themes and style sets are most effective when using the built-in styles.

5. Scroll up to the cover page and choose **Design→Document Formatting→Themes** [Aa] to display the Themes gallery.

6. Hover the mouse pointer over several different themes and observe the changes in your document.

7. Choose the **Frame** theme.

8. Scroll through the document to see the impact of the new theme.

   The built-in headings in the body of the document respond to a change in the theme.

Change the Theme Color and Font

9. Scroll so that the bottom of the cover page and the top of page 1 are both visible.

10. Choose **Design→Document Formatting→Colors** ▦.

11. Use **Live Preview** to examine the different color schemes to see their effects and then choose **Blue Warm**.

12. Choose **Design→Document Formatting→Fonts** [>].

13. Use **Live Preview** to examine the font options and then choose **Franklin Gothic**.

Change the Style Set

14. Choose **Design→Document Formatting** and then click the **More** [▼] button to open the Style Sets gallery.

15. Use Live Preview to examine the different Style Sets and then choose **Centered**.

16. Scroll through the document to see the changes and then close the Styles task pane.

17. Save the file.

Customizing Bullet and Number Formats

The Bullets and Numbering libraries enable you to choose a different style for your bulleted or numbered list. You can also define your own custom formats. When working with long documents, you may want to adjust the formatting for certain lists as a visual cue that certain lists go together or should be considered separately.

 Remember that too much formatting can distract from your message. Less is more.

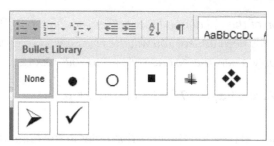

Bullet Library

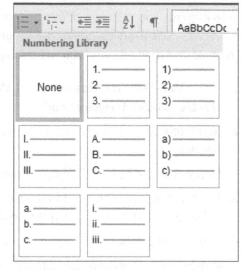

Numbering Library

You can customize bullet styles by defining a symbol, picture, font, or alignment. You can customize the numbering style, font, format, and alignment.

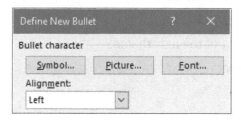

Customize Bullet Format

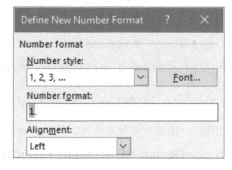

Customize Number Format

≡ Home→Paragraph→Bullets

≡ Home→Paragraph→Numbering

DEVELOP YOUR SKILLS: W7-D5

In this exercise, you will choose a different bullet style from the Bullet Library. Then you will create a custom bullet using a symbol as the new bullet style.

1. Save your file as **W7-D5-SickKidsRevised**.

2. Scroll to page 4 and position the insertion point in the *Symptom #1* line.

3. Choose **Home→Paragraph→Bullets** :≡ **menu button** ▾ and choose the square bullet (location may vary).

Notice that all the bullets in the list were updated. Next you will create a custom bullet.

4. Choose **Home→Paragraph→Bullets** :≡ **menu button** ▾ and choose **Define New Bullet**.

5. Follow these steps to define a symbol as a new bullet:

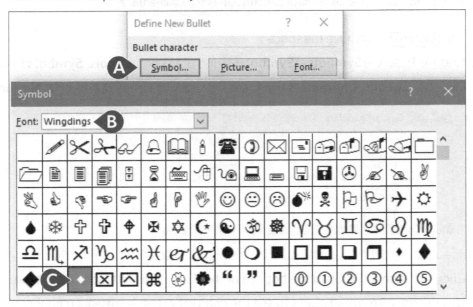

Ⓐ Click the **Symbol** button to open the Symbol dialog box.

Ⓑ Choose the **Wingdings** font.

Ⓒ Make sure the scroll box is at the top of the scroll bar, choose this symbol (location may vary), and then click **OK** twice.

Again, all of the bullets have changed to the custom bullet.

6. Choose **Home→Paragraph→Bullets** :≡ **menu button** ▾ to display the Bullet library.

The new bullet was added to the library. Now you'll remove the bullet so the next student who uses your computer will have the same experience.

7. Right-click the new bullet in the Bullet library area and choose **Remove**.

8. Display the Bullet Library again and notice that the new bullet was removed; close the menu.

9. Save your file.

Using Special Characters

Special characters appear in the Symbol dialog box. There is a variety of special characters, including nonbreaking hyphens or spaces. These characters allow you to keep terms together that should remain together on one line, such as dates, phone numbers, and names.

≡ Insert→Symbols→Symbol Ω→Special Characters

DEVELOP YOUR SKILLS: W7-D6

In this exercise, you will insert nonbreaking spaces in doctors' names that appear in the document. This will correct doctors' names that split across two lines, and it's also a safety measure in the event that future edits would cause the name to split across two lines.

1. Save your file as **W7-D6-SickKidsRevised**.

2. Scroll to page 3, locate the fifth line in the *Common Cold* paragraph, and position the insertion point after *Fred*.

> might lead to an overdose," says pediatrician Fred|Hirschenfang, M.D.,

3. Tap ⏎ **Delete** to remove the space.

4. Choose **Insert→Symbols→Symbol** Ω and then choose **More Symbols** from the menu.

5. Click the **Special Characters** tab in the Symbol dialog box and choose **Nonbreaking Space**.

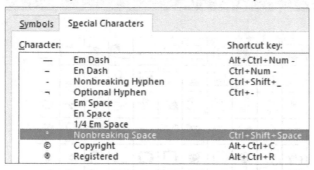

6. Click the **Insert** button at the bottom of the dialog box and then click **Close**.

7. Display the formatting marks to see the character that represents a nonbreaking space.

8. Position the insertion point after the comma following the last name and ⏎ **Delete** the space.

9. Choose **Insert→Symbols→Symbol** Ω**→More Symbols**, click the **Special Characters** tab, and choose **Nonbreaking Space**.

   Notice the shortcut keystrokes for a nonbreaking space: ⏎ Ctrl + ⏎ Shift + ⏎ Space . You can use the keystrokes for the remaining two names.

10. Click the **Insert** button and then click **Close**.

11. Scroll down to the sixth line in the next paragraph and notice the doctor's name that starts at the end of the line.

12. Position the insertion point after the *y* in *Jay* and tap ⏎ **Delete** .

13. Press ⏎ Ctrl + ⏎ Shift + ⏎ Space to insert a nonbreaking space.

14. Use the same technique to replace the space following the comma after the last name with a nonbreaking space.

15. Locate *Dr. Hirschenfang's* name starting at the end of the sixth line in the *Influenza* paragraph and replace the space between *Dr.* and his last name with a nonbreaking space.

16. Save the file.

Navigating Long Documents

A long, complex document can be difficult to navigate. Fortunately, there are a number of helpful tools that make it easier. The Navigation pane provides several ways to move around a document, and bookmarks are useful if you frequently need to return to the same location in a document. If you want to compare two separate parts of the same document, using the Split Window feature is a great way to do so.

The Navigation Pane

The Navigation pane provides three primary methods for locating a search term in a document: headings, pages, and results.

The Pages option displays thumbnails of pages where the search term appears; clicking a thumbnail jumps the document to that page.

The Results option displays the search term in context; clicking one of the results jumps the document to that page.

Search terms are entered here.

The Headings option will list any heading styles in your document. If the search term appears within a heading, it will be highlighted. Click a heading to jump to that part of the document.

The arrows allow you to search up and down the document.

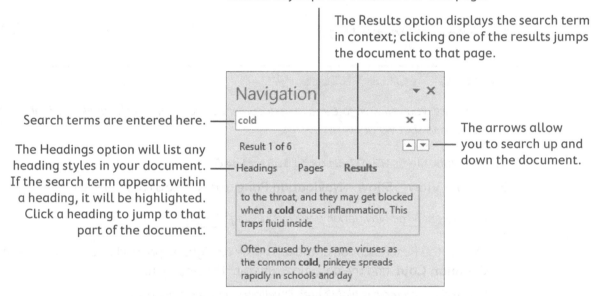

☰ View→Show→Navigation Pane | Ctrl + F

Navigating with Bookmarks

You can assign a bookmark name to text or other objects in a document. Once a bookmark is set up, you can easily navigate to it by choosing the desired bookmark name from the Bookmark dialog box.

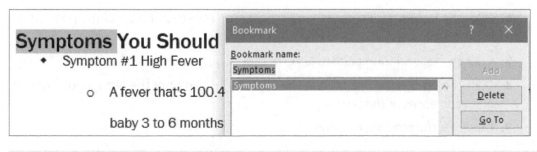

☰ Insert→Links→Bookmark

Splitting the Window

Imagine you want to check whether the executive summary of a report accurately reflects the report's content. Splitting the window is the answer. You can view the executive summary in one window and scroll through the rest of the document in the other window.

Childhood Diseases Seminar

WebMD

Split bar — Despite vaccines that have made many childhood diseases rare, many common illnesses continue to plague children. Following are descriptions of a few of these illnesses taken from the WebMD website.

cold-like symptoms before the rash is seen. Once the rash appears, the child is usually no longer contagious. Up to 20% of kids get it by age 5, and up to 60% have had it by age 19. The rash usually

 View→Window→Split

DEVELOP YOUR SKILLS: W7-D7

In this exercise, you will navigate in a long document using several techniques: Navigation pane, bookmarks, and split window.

1. Save your file as **W7-D7-SickKidsRevised**.
2. Choose **View→Show→Navigation Pane** and enter **cold** as your search term.

 You can also open the Navigation pane by pressing Ctrl + F.

3. Choose the Results option at the top of the Navigation pane, click the fourth result, **Common Cold**, and the document jumps to that location.

   Notice that the term is highlighted in yellow wherever it appears.
4. Click the **Headings** option at the top of the Navigation pane.

   If the document contains heading styles, they are listed here. The headings where the search term appears are highlighted in yellow.
5. Click the *Ear Infection* heading to jump to that part of the document and, again, the search term is highlighted in yellow.
6. Click the **Pages** option at the top of the pane to see thumbnails of the pages that contain the search term.
7. Click the second thumbnail to jump to that page.
8. Click the up and down arrows in the upper-right corner of the Navigation pane to scroll through all occurrences of the term.
9. Close ⊠ the Navigation pane.

Use Bookmarks

10. Scroll to page 4 and select *Symptoms* in the heading titled *Symptoms You Should Never Ignore*.
11. Choose **Insert→Links→Bookmark** 🔖 and then type **Symptoms** in the Bookmark Name field and click **Add**.

Tip! *A bookmark name can be up to 40 characters, including letters and numbers, but it must begin with a letter and cannot contain spaces or symbols.*

12. Press Ctrl + Home or scroll up to move to the top of the document.

13. Choose **Insert→Links→Bookmark** 🔖.

14. *Symptoms* is already selected, so click **Go To** to jump to the bookmarked text and then click **Close**.

Split the Window

15. Choose **View→Window→Split** ⬚.

    A split bar appears across the window. Notice on the right-hand side of the screen that there are two scroll bars, one for the top window and one for the bottom window.

16. In the top window, scroll to the top of page 1 and, in the bottom window, scroll to the top of page 3.

    You can also split the window into different proportions, allowing more text to show on one side.

17. Position the mouse pointer on the split bar.

18. When the mouse pointer changes to a double-headed arrow, drag the split bar up about an inch.

19. Double-click the split bar to return to one window.

20. Save and close the file.

Large Tables

If you're working with large tables, making them user-friendly is important. It should be easy for the reader to scan a table and get information. If possible, columns should be wide enough to prevent text from wrapping within the cells. Adding white space within the table makes the text appear less dense. Repeating column headers from one page to the next is essential for the reader to understand the meaning of the data. Sizing a table to best fit the page adds to its readability.

≡ Table Tools→Layout→Cell Size→dialog box launcher ⌐

≡ Table Tools→Layout→Alignment→Cell Margins ▣

DEVELOP YOUR SKILLS: W7-D8

In this exercise, you will modify a large table, making it easier to read by widening columns where text is wrapping, adding white space within cells, and repeating column headers from page to page. You'll also add a caption to the table.

1. Open **W7-D8-SeminarAttendees** from your **Word Chapter 7** folder and save it as **W7-D8-SeminarAttendeesRevised**.

    The text is wrapping in several columns, making it difficult to read. At the same time the table already spans the width of the page. Rotating this document to landscape (horizontal) orientation and changing the table width should solve the problem.

2. Choose **Layout→Page Setup→Orientation** 🔄 and choose **Landscape** from the menu.

3. Choose **Table Tools→Layout→Cell Size→dialog box launcher** ⌐.

4. In the Table Properties dialog box, if necessary, click the **Table** tab.

5. Change Preferred Width to **9"** and then click **OK**.

   Adding white space within the cells will certainly add to the table's readability.

6. Choose **Table Tools→Layout→Alignment→Cell Margins** 🔲.

7. In the Table Options dialog box, change the top and bottom cell margins to **0.05** and then click **OK**.

8. If necessary, position the insertion point in the first row of the table.

   This is the row that will repeat at the top of each page.

9. Choose **Table Tools→Layout→Cell Size→dialog box launcher** 🔲 and click the **Row** tab.

10. Place a checkmark in the **Repeat as Header Row at the Top of Each Page** checkbox and then click **OK**.

11. Scroll down to see the header row at the top of page 2.

    Now you will add a caption to the table.

12. Choose **References→Captions→Insert Caption** 🔲 and then click the **New Label** button toward the bottom of the dialog box.

13. In the New Label dialog box, type **Childhood Diseases Seminar Attendees** and click **OK**; click **OK** again to close the Caption dialog box.

14. Scroll to the bottom of the document to see the caption.

    Captions are typically numbered, but because this is the only table in the document, numbering is not necessary.

15. Position the insertion point at the end of the caption and then tap Backspace twice to delete the number.

16. Save and close the file; exit Word.

Self-Assessment

 Check your knowledge of this chapter's key concepts and skills using the Self-Assessment in your ebook or eLab course.

Reinforce Your Skills

Create a New Members Handout

Kids for Change wants new members to understand the importance of its motto, Think Globally, Act Locally. One of the members researched the origins of the phrase, and now you've been asked to format the document to make it more engaging. In this exercise, you will use styles, themes, and style sets to add appeal. You will begin by testing several different styles to see what you like best.

1. Start **Word**; open **W7-R1-GlobalLocal** from your **Word Chapter 7** folder and save it as **W7-R1-GlobalLocalRevised**.

2. Position the insertion point in *Introduction* at the top of page 1.

    You will apply a built-in style first.

3. Choose **Home→Styles** and in the Styles gallery on the Ribbon choose **Heading 1**.

    Now you will create a style by example.

4. Select the *Definition* heading for the next paragraph.

5. Choose **Home→Font→dialog box launcher** ⬜.

6. In the Font dialog box, choose **Arial Black**, **14 pt**, and **Small Caps**, and then click **OK**.

7. Choose **Home→Font→Font Color menu button** ▼ and choose **Orange, Accent 2, Darker 25%** from the color pallet.

8. Choose **Home→Styles→dialog box launcher** ⬜.

9. Click the **New Style** ⬜ button at bottom of the task pane.

10. Complete the information at the top of the dialog box as follows:
    *   Name: **MyStyle1**
    *   Style Type: **Paragraph**
    *   Style Based On: **Normal**
    *   Style for Following Paragraph: **Normal**

    Notice that your formatting has been copied into the Formatting area of the dialog box.

11. If necessary, click the **Add to the Styles Gallery** checkbox and click **OK**.

    The style name now appears in the Styles gallery on the Ribbon and in the Styles task pane. Next you will create a style by definition.

12. Scroll down and position the insertion point in the heading, *Origin in Town Planning*.

13. Click the **New Style** ⬜ button at the bottom of the task pane.

14. Complete the information at the top of the dialog box as follows:
    *   Name: **MyStyle2**
    *   Style Type: **Paragraph**
    *   Style Based On: **Normal**
    *   Style for Following Paragraph: **Normal**

15. In the Formatting area, choose **Century Schoolbook**, **14 pt**, and center alignment, and then click **OK**.

16. Scroll down and position the insertion point in the heading for the last paragraph, *Origins of the Phrase*, and apply the built-in **Heading 2** style.

Modify a Style

After scanning the different styles, you've decided to modify the Heading 1 style.

17. Position the insertion point in the *Introduction* heading at the top of page 1.

18. Hover the mouse pointer over the **Heading 1** style in the Styles task pane, click the drop-down arrow, and choose **Modify**.

19. Click the **Format** button at the bottom of the dialog box and choose **Font**.

20. Choose **Bold** in the Font Style field, click the drop-down arrow in the **Font Color** field, and choose **Green, Accent 6, Darker 25%**.

21. Check the **Small Caps** checkbox and then click **OK**.

22. In the Formatting area of the Modify Style dialog box, click the **Center** button and then click **OK**.

    Notice that the modifications you made are reflected in the style name in the Styles gallery. Now you need to decide on a style for the subheadings. You will modify the Heading 2 style.

23. Scroll to the last page and click in the heading, *Origins of the Phrase*. Hover the mouse pointer over **Heading 2** in the Styles task pane, click the drop-down arrow, and choose **Modify**.

24. In the Formatting area, click the **Bold** button, click the drop-down arrow in the color field and choose **Green, Accent 6, Darker 25%**, and then click **OK**.

    You are happy with the Heading 2 style, so now you'll apply it to the other subheadings.

25. Scroll up and position the insertion point in the heading, *Origin in Town Planning*, and then click the **Heading 2** style in the Styles task pane.

26. Scroll up and position the insertion point in the *Definition* heading and then apply the **Heading 2** style.

    Now you will investigate formats further using themes and style sets.

27. If necessary, scroll so the *Introduction* heading is at the top of the screen.

28. Choose **Design→Document Formatting→Themes** [Aa], use Live Preview to examine different Themes, and then choose **Slate** from the gallery.

29. Scroll up to the cover page to see the effect of the new theme.

30. Scroll back to page 1 and position the *Introduction* heading toward the middle of the screen.

31. Choose **Design→Document Formatting** and then click the **More** [▼] button from the Style Sets gallery.

32. Use Live Preview to view the effects of several Style Sets and then choose **Lines (Simple)**.

    Because you won't be using MyStyle1 and MyStyle2, you will delete them from the Styles task pane.

33. Hover the mouse pointer over **MyStyle1** in the task pane, click the drop-down arrow, and choose **Delete MyStyle1**.

34. When the message appears confirming the deletion, click **Yes**.

    The style was also removed from the Styles gallery on the Ribbon.

35. Use the same technique to delete **MyStyle2**.

36. Close the Styles task pane and then save and close the file.

Help Kids Cultivate Social and Emotional Skills

A number of educational organizations have developed training programs to help teachers work with kids in developing social and emotional skills. Kids for Change members are evaluating various programs to determine which program they would like to see implemented in their local schools. In this exercise, you will customize bullet and number formats, use navigation techniques that make it easy to quickly move around long documents, and format a large table to enhance its readability.

1. Open **W7-R2-SocLearningforKids** from your **Word Chapter 7** folder and save it as **W7-R2-SocLearningforKidsRevised**.

2. Scroll down and position the insertion point in the first bulleted list on page 1.

3. Choose **Home→Paragraph→Bullets** ☰ **menu button** ▾ and choose **Define New Bullet**.

4. Click the **Symbol** button.

5. Choose the **Webdings** font, scroll to the top of the gallery if necessary, choose the character shown (location may vary), and click **OK** twice.

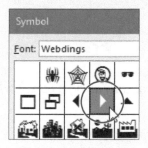

6. Position the insertion point in the next bulleted list that starts at the bottom of page 1.

7. Choose **Home→Paragraph→Bullets menu button** ▾ and choose the same bullet, which appears in both the Recently Used Bullets and Document Bullets categories.

8. Use the same technique to change the bullets in the last bulleted list at the bottom of page 3.

   Now you will remove the new bullet so the next student who uses your computer will have the same experience.

9. Choose **Home→Paragraph→Bullets menu button** ▾.

10. Right-click the new bullet in the Bullet Library area and choose **Remove**.

Apply Numbers to a List

11. Scroll up and select the list that appears below the heading *The 12 Tools* at the top of page 3 and choose **Home→Paragraph→Numbering** ☰.

    Now you'll choose a different number format for the list.

12. Choose **Home→Paragraph→Numbering menu button** ▾ and then choose the format shown. (Location may vary.)

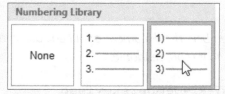

Notice that the last three numbers are left-aligned with the numbers above. They should be right-aligned.

13. Choose **Home→Paragraph→Numbering menu button** ▼ and then choose **Define New Number Format**.

14. Click the drop-down arrow in the Alignment field, choose **Right**, and then click **OK**.

    Notice how the numbers are now aligned.

Navigate in a Document

You know that you'll often have to navigate through this document as team members have questions about its contents, so you want to take some time to practice quick navigation techniques.

15. Press Ctrl + F to open the Navigation pane and type **toolbox** in the search field at the top of the Navigation pane.

16. Click the down-pointing arrow at the top of the Navigation pane several times to jump to the term.

17. Make sure the **Results** category at the top of the pane is active and then scroll down and click the last result in the list to jump to that location.

18. Click the **Headings** category at the top of the pane and click **Dovetail Learning** to jump to that location.

19. **Close** ✕ the Navigation pane.

Insert a Bookmark

If there is a section of the document that you will return to frequently, using a bookmark provides a way to locate it easily.

20. Double-click *Dovetail* in the heading line.

21. Choose **Insert→Links→Bookmark** 🔖 and then type **Dovetail** in the Bookmark Name field and click **Add**.

22. Press Ctrl + Home or scroll up to move to the top of the document.

23. Choose **Insert→Links→Bookmark**.

24. Click **Go To** in the Bookmark dialog box to jump to the bookmark and then click **Close**.

Split the Window

Now you will compare the mission statements for Wings for Kids and Dovetail Learning.

25. Choose **View→Window→Split** ⬚ and in the top window scroll to the top of page 1 until the mission statement is visible.

26. In the bottom window, scroll until the mission statement for Dovetail Learning is visible.

    This is an easy way to compare two different parts of a document.

27. Double-click the split bar in the middle of the window to return to one window.

28. Save and close the file.

Work with a Large Table

You will use the Members mailing list to send members the document about social learning. In preparation for that, you will now enhance the table by making it more readable.

29. Open **W7-R2-Members** and save it as **W7-R2-MembersRevised**.

30. Choose **Table Tools→Layout→Alignment→Cell Margins** ⊞, change the top and bottom cell margins to **0.08**, and click **OK**.

    The table is now spilling over to the next page. You will repeat the header row so it will also appear at the top of the next page.

31. If necessary, position the insertion point in the header row of the table.

32. Choose **Table Tools→Layout→Cell Size→dialog box launcher** ⌐ .

33. Click the **Row** tab, check the **Repeat as Header Row at the Top of Each Page**, and click **OK**.

34. Scroll down to see the header row at the top of the second page.

35. Save and close the file.

REINFORCE YOUR SKILLS: W7-R3

Format a Report on Childhood Obesity

Kids for Change is sponsoring a seminar on childhood obesity, presented by representatives from the World Health Organization and the Centers for Disease Control and Prevention. The organizations have already submitted background reading for the seminar. In this exercise, you will format the document to make the paragraphs and tables more engaging. You will also use techniques for navigating a long document.

1. Open **W7-R3-Obesity** from your **Word Chapter 7** folder and save it as **W7-R3-ObesityRevised**.

2. If the Styles task pane is not open, choose **Home→Styles→dialog box launcher** ⌐ to open it.

3. If necessary, position the insertion point in the heading at the top of the document and then choose the **Title** style from the task pane.

4. Scroll down to page 2, position the insertion point in the heading *CDC Introduction*, and apply the **Title** style.

5. Scroll back to the top of page 1 and position the insertion point in the first subtitle, which begins with *What can be done*.

6. Apply the **Subtitle** style from the Styles task pane and then apply **Subtitle** to the remaining headings:
   • General recommendations
   • Societal recommendations
   • What Needs to Be Done?
   • What Can Parents Do?

   You decide that the subtitles are not very appealing. Next, you will test a different theme to see if it improves the subtitles.

7. Choose **Design→Document Formatting→Themes** Aa and choose **Parcel** from the gallery.

   Applying the Theme didn't really help the subtitles, so you will modify the Subtitle style.

8. Position the insertion point in the **first subtitle** at the top of page 1.

9. Hover the mouse pointer over **Subtitle** in the Styles task pane, click the drop-down arrow, and choose **Modify** from the menu.

10. In the Formatting area of the dialog box, click the **Italic** button and change the font size to **16 pt**, and then click **OK**.

11. Scroll through the document and notice that the subtitles updated throughout the document.

12. Scroll to the bottom of page 2 and notice the subtitle at the bottom of the page.

    It should be moved to the top of the next page.

13. Position the insertion point in front of the subtitle and press Ctrl + Enter to insert a page break and move the subtitle to the top of the next page.

14. Close the Styles task pane.

Customize Bullet Formats

15. Click the first item in the bulleted list on page 1, choose **Home→Paragraph→Bullets** ☰ menu button ▾, and choose **Define New Bullet**.

16. Click the **Symbol** button in the Define New Bullet dialog box.

17. In the Symbol dialog box, choose the **Wingdings 2** font, scroll to about the middle of the list and choose the symbol shown, and then click **OK** twice.

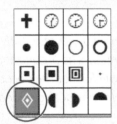

18. Scroll down to the next bulleted list and click in the first item.

19. Choose **Home→Paragraph→Bullets menu button** ▾ and choose the same button style from the Recently Used Bullets category.

20. Use the same technique to reformat the last bulleted list.

Navigate in a Long Document

21. Scroll to the top of page 2 and select *CDC* in the heading.

22. Choose **Insert→Links→Bookmark** 🔖.

23. Type **CDC** in the Bookmark Name field and click **Add**.

24. Press Ctrl + Home or scroll up to move to the top of the document.

25. Choose **Insert→Links→Bookmark**, click the **Go To** button to jump to the bookmark, and then close the dialog box.

26. Press Ctrl + F to open the Navigation pane and type **WHO** in the search field.

    The document scrolls to the first occurrence of WHO.

27. Click the insertion point in the page and then close the Navigation pane.

28. Choose **View→Window→Split** ▢ and scroll in the bottom pane until the *CDC Introduction* heading appears.

    This is a great way to compare different parts of the same document without opening a separate window.

29. Double-click the split bar to return to a single window.

30. Save and close the file.

Work with a Long Table

Kids for Change has scheduled its programs and seminar topics well in advance, so it has plenty of time to coordinate the events. However, the table is not easy to read and to locate data. You will format the table to make it easier to work with.

31. Open **W7-R3-Programs** from your **Word Chapter 7** folder and save it as **W7-R3-ProgramsRevised**.

32. Position the insertion point in the table and choose **Table Tools→Layout→Alignment→Cell Margins** 🔲.

33. Change the top and bottom margins to **0.08** and click **OK**.

The increased margins caused the table to flow to the next page. Next, you will set up the header row to repeat on every page.

34. Position the insertion point in the header row at the top of the table.

35. Choose **Table Tools→Layout→Cell Size→dialog box launcher** 🔲.

36. If necessary, click the **Row** tab, check **Repeat as Header Row at the Top of Each Page**, and then click **OK**.

37. Scroll to page 2 to see the repeating header row.

38. Save and close the file.

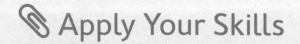

Apply Your Skills

Multitask with Styles

Universal Corporate Events representatives, when planning a corporate event for a client, are often challenged with a juggling act of details ranging from hundreds of hotel reservations and travel accommodations to organizing meals and side trips. Your manager asked you to research the concept of multitasking and prepare a report on your findings. Your content has been approved, and it is now time to format the document to make it appealing to the reader. In this exercise, you will enhance the document by formatting with styles, themes, and style sets.

1. Open **W7-A1-Multitasking** from your **Word Chapter 7** folder and save it as **W7-A1-MultitaskingRevised**.

   You will start by creating a style by example.

2. Select the *Introduction* heading at the top of the document, apply the **Stencil** font, **16 pt**, and center the heading.

3. Open the Styles task pane and click the **New Style** button.

4. Follow these guidelines to complete the top part of the dialog box:
   - Name: **IntroStyle**
   - Style Type: **Paragraph**
   - Style Base On: **Normal**
   - Style for Following Paragraph: **Normal**

5. If necessary, check the **Add to the Styles Gallery** checkbox at the bottom of the dialog box and click **OK**.

   Notice that the new style appears in the Styles gallery on the Ribbon and in the Styles task pane. Next, you will apply a built-in style and then modify it.

6. Position the insertion point in the next heading, *The multitasking myth*, and then apply the **Heading 2** style.

7. Hover the mouse pointer over the **Heading 2** style in the Styles task pane, click the drop-down arrow, and choose **Modify**.

8. Click the **Format** button at the bottom of the dialog box and choose **Font**.

9. In the Font dialog box, set the font to **Bold**, **14 pt**, and the color **Black**, **Text 1**.

10. Check the **Small Caps** checkbox and then click **OK** twice.

11. Apply the modified **Heading 2** style to the rest of the subtitles in the document:
    - You're not really multitasking
    - It's slowing you down
    - You're making mistakes
    - You're not actually good at it

    Next, you will work with themes and style sets to enhance your formatting.

12. Choose **Design**→**Document Formatting**→**Themes** and choose **Parallax**.

13. Choose **Design**→**Document Formatting** and then click the **More** button and apply the **Shaded** style set.

Next, you will modify the theme color.

14. Choose **Design**→**Document Formatting**→**Colors** and choose **Paper**.

You've decided to change the Introduction *heading to make it blend better with the subheadings.*

15. Position the insertion point in the *Introduction* heading and choose the **Title** style from the Styles task pane.

16. You don't plan to use the IntroStyle anymore, so using the Styles task pane, delete the style and then close the task pane.

17. Click the **Home** tab and notice that the IntroStyle has been removed from the Styles gallery on the Ribbon.

There is a heading at the bottom of page 1 that should be moved to the top of page 2.

18. Position the insertion point in front of the heading at the bottom of page 1 and press `Ctrl`+`Enter` to move it to the top of page 2.

19. Save and close the file.

APPLY YOUR SKILLS: W7-A2

Plan a Bicycle Trip in the Loire Valley

A client of Universal Corporate Events is planning a bicycling trip in the Loire Valley of France as a reward for Employee of the Year winners in each of its branch offices. Universal Corporate Events is providing a sample itinerary for the client to review. In this exercise, you will polish the sample itinerary for the trip. And the client has requested a list of châteaux in the Loire Valley, so you will prepare that in a table and format it for ease of reading.

1. Open **W7-A2-LoireTour** from your **Word Chapter 7** folder and save it as **W7-A2-LoireTourRevised**.

2. Position the insertion point in the first bulleted item.

3. Define a new bullet that uses the Wingdings 3 symbol shown here.

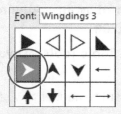

Now you'll apply the new bullet to the remaining bulleted items.

4. Position the insertion point in the next bulleted item and choose **Home**→**Paragraph**→ **Bullets menu button** ▾.

The new bullet appears in the Recently Used Bullets category.

5. Click the bullet, scroll through the document, and notice that the bullet was applied to the rest of the bulleted items.

Next, you will use nonbreaking spaces to keep a name together on a line.

6. Scroll to the second-to-last line in the *Day 3* paragraph, position the insertion point after *Leonardo* and delete the space.

7. Choose **Insert→Symbols→Symbol** and choose **More Symbols**.

8. Choose **Nonbreaking Space** in the Special Characters tab and then finish inserting the character. *Remember the keystrokes for a nonbreaking space:* `Ctrl`+`Shift`+`Space`.

9. Position the insertion point after *da*, delete the space, and then press `Ctrl`+`Shift`+`Space` to insert another nonbreaking space.

10. If necessary, display formatting marks and notice the symbol used for nonbreaking spaces.

Navigate in a Long Document

Next, you will insert a bookmark for navigating in the document.

11. Create a bookmark for the text *Day 6*, using **Day6** as the bookmark name.

12. Move to the top of the document and then use the Bookmark feature to jump to Day 6.

    Now you will locate a term in the document.

13. Open the Navigation pane, type **Day 1** in the search field, and then position the insertion point in the **Day 1** page.

14. Click the **Headings** button at the top of the Navigation pane, click the **Day 4** heading to jump to that location, and then close the **Navigation** pane.

    Next you will split the window so you can compare different parts of the document.

15. Choose **View→Window→Split** and then scroll the top window to **Day 1** and the bottom window to **Day 6**.

16. Double-click the split bar to return to one window.

17. Save and close the file.

Work with a Large Table

You will make some modifications to a table to improve its readability. You'll begin by increasing the cell margins and then repeat the header row for each page.

18. Open **W7-A2-Chateaux** from your **Word Chapter 7** folder and save it as **W7-A2-ChateauxRevised**.

19. Position the insertion point in the table, choose **Table Tools→Layout→Alignment→ Cell Margins**, and change the top and bottom margins to **0.08**.

20. With the insertion point in the first row of the table, choose **Table Tools→Layout→ Cell Size dialog box launcher**.

21. Use the **Row** tab in the Table Properties dialog box to repeat the header row on each page.

22. Scroll to the top of page 2 to see the repeated header row.

23. Save and close the file.

APPLY YOUR SKILLS: W7-A3

Prepare Cuban Travel Information for a Client

Universal Corporate Events has asked you to research information about travel to Cuba, and your research has been approved. In this exercise, you will format the document so it can be presented to clients.

1. Open **W7-A3-CubaTravel** from your **Word Chapter 7** folder and save it as **W7-A3-CubaTravelRevised**.

2. Apply the **Heading 1** style to the *Cuba Background* heading at the top of the document.

   Hint: If necessary, display the Styles task pane.

3. Apply the **Heading 2** style to the headings *U.S.–Cuba Relations*, *U.S. Assistance to Cuba*, and *Bilateral Economic Relations*.

4. Scroll down to the *Outdoor Activity* heading and apply the **Heading 1** style.

5. Scroll down to the *Top-Rated Cuban Tourist Attractions* heading and apply the **Heading 1** style.

   Next you will modify the theme and style set.

6. Apply the **Metropolitan** theme to the document and then open the Style Sets gallery and choose **Basic (Simple)**.

   Next, you will modify the heading styles.

7. Position the insertion point in the *Cuba Background* heading and then modify the **Heading 1** style by changing the font color to **Brown, Accent 3**.

8. Scroll to page 3 and notice that the other Heading 1 styles were updated.

9. Position the insertion point in the *U.S.-Cuba Relations* heading and then modify the **Heading 2** style to use the font color **Brown, Accent 3**.

10. Close the **Styles** task pane then scroll down to see that the other Heading 2 headings updated.

11. Scroll to page 3, position the insertion point in the first bulleted item, and define a new bullet using the symbol character shown from the **Wingdings** font.

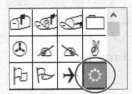

Format a Table for Readability

12. Scroll to the table and change the top and bottom cell margins to **0.08**.

13. Repeat the header row on all pages.

    Now you will add a caption to the table.

14. Scroll to the bottom of the table and position the insertion point on the first blank line below the table.

15. Insert **Excerpt from PlanetWare Website** as the table caption.

    Notice the number 1 appears at the end of the caption. Because there is only one table in the document, the number is not necessary.

16. Delete the number **1** at the end of the caption.

17. Save and close the file; exit Word.

⏴ Extend Your Skills

These exercises challenge you to think critically and apply your new skills. You will be evaluated on your ability to follow directions, completeness, creativity, and the use of proper grammar and mechanics. Save files to your chapter folder. Submit assignments as directed.

W7-E1 That's the Way I See It

You have just started your own personal training business and will advertise your business with an informative brochure (maximum two pages) to be distributed through local businesses in the community. Decide on a name for your business. Include a mission statement and a description of your background qualifications. Create a bulleted list of the services you offer and another bulleted list of the benefits your clients will enjoy. Customize the bullets using a symbol of your choice. Use Word's built-in heading styles to make your brochure professional-looking and easy to read. Customize the headings using themes and style sets and any other modifications you wish to make. Create a table listing classes you offer, short descriptions of the classes, and the days and times the classes will meet. Apply the table style of your choice and increase the cell margins to add white space. Don't forget your contact information. Feel free to use an Internet search to gather ideas to assist you with content. Save your file as **W7-E1-Exercise**.

W7-E2 Be Your Own Boss

You want to increase your customer base at Blue Jean Landscaping, so you will create a one- or two-page flyer advertising your business. Write an "About Us" paragraph describing the services you offer and include a mission statement. Also, write a paragraph or two about your background qualifications. Include another paragraph about the pesticide safety techniques you employ at your company. Blue Jean Landscaping saves customers money by having them provide the labor for their projects. Create a bulleted list of the physical tasks customers will accomplish to take advantage of your cost-cutting offer. Create a table listing classes you offer, such as "How to Plant Roses," to educate your customers in the skills they need to provide the labor for their gardens. Use built-in heading styles to section off the different parts of the flyer and modify the styles to suit your taste. Customize the bullets for your bulleted list, format the table with a table style, and add white space to the table by increasing cell margins. If necessary, search the Internet for information about landscaping companies to help you with the content. Save the file as **W7-E2-Landscape**.

W7-E3 Demonstrate Proficiency

As the owner of Stormy BBQ, you are proud of serving only locally grown, organic vegetables and free-range, farm-raised pork and beef. Create a two-page flyer to distribute to customers at the cash register. Include a mission statement and a paragraph or two describing the history of Stormy BBQ and include one or two customer testimonials. Create a bulleted list of the benefits of eating locally produced food. Insert a menu in the form of a table that spans two pages and add a caption to the table. Use custom styles that you create from scratch to section off the topics in your flyer and create custom bullets for your list. Apply a table style to your menu, add white space for ease of reading, and repeat the header row at the top of page 2. Conduct an Internet search if you need help with the menu or benefits of the healthy food you serve. Save the file as **W7-E3-BBQ.**

8 | Organizing Long Documents

P lowing through a long document can be challenging for the reader if it is not well-organized. Word offers several great tools for organizing documents. A table of contents and an index help readers locate specific topics and terms. Headers and footers display important information, such as page numbers and chapter names. In this chapter, you will work with these tools, organizing long documents and making them more accessible to the reader.

LEARNING OBJECTIVES

▸ Create a table of contents
▸ Work with multiple headers and footers
▸ Insert an index
▸ Keep text together
▸ Add a watermark

📂 Project: Organizing a Long Document

The Raritan Clinic East policies and procedures manual contains principles and guidelines adopted by the clinic to reach its long-term goals. It influences all major decisions and activities in day-to-day operations. You recently accepted a position in the human resources department at Raritan Clinic. You have been tasked with reviewing the current policies and procedures manual, and you have identified numerous "finishing" features that need to be added to the manual to make it easier to use. By adding a table of contents, index, and headers and footers, you believe the document will be more user-friendly.

Creating a Table of Contents

Readers appreciate a good table of contents. It outlines the document and adds a professional appearance. And if the document is electronic, the table of contents links provide Internet-like navigation.

The Table of Contents (TOC) feature automatically builds a table of contents by gathering up the headings that are formatted with heading styles. The headings in the TOC are organized in the sequence in which they appear in the document. In addition, TOC styles are applied that correspond to the heading levels. The styles then format the table entries. For example, Heading 2 entries are subordinate to Heading 1 entries. You can automatically update a table of contents created with the built-in heading styles.

You can apply a predesigned table of contents format from the Table of Contents gallery, or you can create a custom table of contents, which gives you more control over the formatting.

☰ References→Table of Contents→Table of Contents 📄

Creating a Page for the Table of Contents

In most documents, the table of contents appears either at the beginning of the document or just after the title page in documents containing a title page. Because the table of contents is often created after the document is complete, you may need to create a new page to hold the table.

When headers and footers or other page-level formatting such as page numbering appears in a document, it is better to create a page to hold the table of contents using a section break. This allows flexibility, such as numbering the table of contents page(s) with Roman numerals (i, ii, iii) and the rest of the document with Arabic numerals (1, 2, 3).

Table of Contents Links

A table of contents is inserted as a large field composed of various table entries. Each entry within the table functions as a hyperlink. You can quickly navigate in the document using the links.

In this exercise, you will open the Raritan Clinic East policies and procedures manual and review its heading styles. Then you will create a table of contents and navigate in the document using the links. Finally, you will remove the table of contents.

1. Start Word, open **W8-D1-RaritanP&P** from your **Word Chapter 8** folder, and save it as `W8-D1-RaritanP&PRevised`.

2. Choose **Home**→**Styles**→**dialog box launcher** 🔲 .

3. Scroll to the first page of the body of the document and position the insertion point in the heading *Mission Statement*.

   Notice that Heading 1 in the Styles task pane is highlighted, indicating that it is the style used to format the heading.

4. Position the insertion point in several additional headings on page 2.

   You will notice that both Heading 1 and Heading 2 styles are on the page.

5. Close the Styles task pane and then position the insertion point in front of the heading *Mission Statement*.

   Now you will insert a section break to create a blank page for the table of contents.

6. Choose **Layout**→**Page Setup**→**Breaks** 🔲 and then choose **Next Page**.

7. If necessary, display formatting marks; then scroll up and position the insertion point to the right of the paragraph symbol, just in front of the section break, and tap ⎵Enter⎵.

8. Choose **References**→**Table of Contents**→**Table of Contents** 🔲 and then choose **Automatic Table 2** from the gallery.

9. Scroll up and review the table of contents.

   You can see that the headings in the document are used as the table of contents entries.

Navigate Using Hyperlinks

10. Hover the mouse pointer over the *Initial Diagnostic Evaluation* entry in the table and notice the pop-up message.

11. Press ⎵Ctrl⎵ and click the link, and Word jumps to that heading in the document.

12. Scroll up to the top of the table of contents and then click the table to select it.

13. Click the **Table of Contents** 🔲 button in the upper-left corner and choose **Remove Table of Contents** at the bottom of the menu.

14. Save the file.

WORD

The Update Table Button

When you make changes to headings or move text in a document, you need to update the table of contents. There is an Update Table button that makes this task easy. Whenever the insertion point is anywhere in the table of contents, two buttons appear in the upper-left corner of the table.

The Table of Contents button displays the Table of Contents gallery, including a command to remove the table.

The Update Table button updates the table of contents with the latest changes.

When you click the Update Table button, a dialog box presents options for updating page numbers only or the entire table. Choose the page numbers option if you have been adding text but haven't changed any headings.

 You can right-click a table of contents and choose Update Field from the menu.

≡ References→Table of Contents→Update Table │ F9

The Table of Contents Dialog Box

The Table of Contents gallery provides the fastest method for creating a table of contents, but if you wish to have more control over the formatting of your table, you can use the Table of Contents dialog box. When you use the dialog box, you must also manually add the title that precedes the table. In addition, there are no Table of Contents or Update Table buttons at the top of the table as there are for a table generated from the Table of Contents gallery. To update a manual table of contents, you can use the F9 shortcut keystroke.

View the video "Creating a Custom Table of Contents."

DEVELOP YOUR SKILLS: W8-D2

In this exercise, you will insert a custom table of contents using the Table of Contents dialog box. Then you will edit a heading and update the table of contents.

1. Save your file as **W8-D2-RaritanP&PRevised** and, if necessary, display formatting marks.

   The insertion point should be just to the left of the section break at the top of the blank table of contents page.

2. Tap ⌷Enter⌷ to create a new, blank line.

   The blank line will hold the title. Next you will reformat its paragraph symbol with your desired title formatting.

3. Follow these steps to format and add the table title:

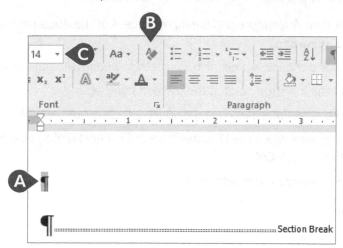

Ⓐ Select this paragraph symbol.

Ⓑ Choose **Home→Font→Clear All Formatting**.

Ⓒ Change the font size to **14 pt**.

4. Type `Table of Contents` and tap `Enter`.

5. Choose **References→Table of Contents→Table of Contents** 📄.

6. Choose **Custom Table of Contents** at the bottom of the gallery to open the Table of Contents dialog box.

7. Follow these steps to generate a table of contents:

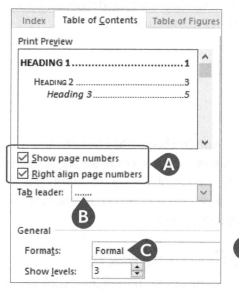

Ⓐ Make sure these checkboxes are checked.

Ⓑ Make sure that dots are chosen here.

Ⓒ Choose **Formal** as the format.

Ⓓ Click **OK**.

8. Scroll to the bottom of the table and delete the extra paragraph symbol.

WORD

Edit a Heading and Update the Table of Contents

9. Locate the heading *Patient Attendance and Billing* on page 4 of the document and change *Attendance* to **Appointments**.

Now that you have made a change in a heading, you need to update the table of contents.

10. Scroll up and position the insertion point in the table of contents.

Notice that there is no Update Table button in the upper-left corner of the table.

11. Tap F9 to begin the update; when the Update Table of Contents dialog box appears, choose **Update Entire Table** and click **OK**.

The word Attendance *changed to* Appointments.

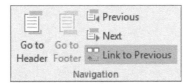

12. Save your file.

Multiple Headers and Footers

Initially, the header and footer content is the same throughout a document because the Link to Previous feature is turned on by default, as shown in this illustration.

When a document contains multiple sections, you can break the link between sections and thereby create a new header and footer for each document section. For example, suppose you want to number the front portion of a long document using small Roman numerals and the body of the document using Arabic numerals. Separating the document into sections is the first important step before creating multiple headers and footers within a document.

Restarting and Formatting Page Numbers

When you have more than one section in a document, you may wish to control the starting page number within a section. Typically, the body of a document should start at page 1 rather than continuing the Roman numerals from the front matter. You may also want to control the page number formats. The Page Number Format dialog box provides options to restart numbering and to modify the number format, such as changing from Roman numerals to Arabic numerals.

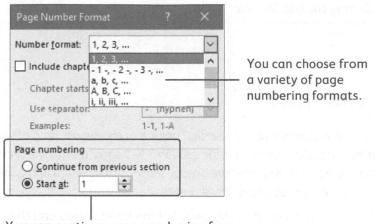

You can choose from a variety of page numbering formats.

You can continue page numbering from the previous section or restart numbering with a specific number.

Different First Page Header or Footer

There may be times when all you want to do is set up a different header or footer on the first page of a document. For example, suppose you want all pages of a document numbered in the footer area of each page except for the cover page. You can set a different first page header or footer simply by choosing the Different First Page option.

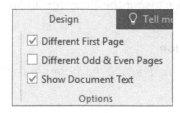

DEVELOP YOUR SKILLS: W8-D3

In this exercise, you will insert header text that will appear in both sections of the document. You will also break the connection between footers so you can have different footers in each section, and then you will change the starting page number on the second page of the document.

1. Save your file as **W8-D3-RaritanP&PRevised** and, if necessary, display formatting characters.

2. Position the insertion point in **section 2**, which begins with *Mission Statement*.

3. Choose **Insert→Header & Footer→Header** 📄 and then choose **Edit Header** at the bottom of the gallery.

4. Take a moment to observe the header area.

¶

Header -Section 2- **Mission·Statement**¶   Same as Previous

The Header -Section 2- tab indicates that the insertion point is in the header area of section 2; the Same as Previous tab indicates that text you type in section 2 will carry over to the previous section. In other words, the sections are linked. You want the header sections to be linked in this instance because the word DRAFT should appear on all pages. You'll add that next.

5. Tap ⌜Tab⌝ to position the insertion point at the center of the header area and then type **DRAFT**.

6. Format the header text with **bold**, **14 pt**, and then double-click in the body of the document to close the header area.

7. Scroll up to the table of contents.

Notice that the word DRAFT appears in the header. That's because the headers in both sections are linked. Now you will add a footer that appears in only one section.

8. Scroll down and position the insertion point in **section 2**.

9. Choose **Insert→Header & Footer→Footer** ⬚ and then choose **Edit Footer**.

Notice the Same as Previous tab in the footer area. You don't want the footer text to appear on the table of contents page, so you will break the link.

10. Choose **Header & Footer Tools→Design→Navigation**.

The Link to Previous button is highlighted, meaning it is turned on and the footers in sections 1 and 2 are linked.

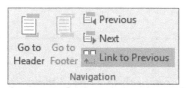

11. Click the **Link to Previous** ⬚ button to turn it off and break the link between the two sections.

The Same as Previous tab at the right side of the footer area disappeared.

12. Choose **Header & Footer Tools→Design→Header & Footer→Footer** ⬚ and then choose **Blank**.

13. Click **Type Here** and type **Policies & Procedures Manual**.

14. Tap ⌜Tab⌝ to position the insertion point in the center of the footer area and then type **Raritan Clinic East**.

15. Tap ⌜Tab⌝ to position the insertion point at the right side of the footer.

16. Choose **Header & Footer Tools→Design→Header & Footer→Page Number** ⬚.

17. Choose **Current Position** and then choose **Plain Number**.

Change the Starting Page Number

You want to start numbering with a 1 on the first page of the document body.

18. Choose **Header & Footer Tools→Design→Header & Footer→Page Number** ⬚.

19. Choose **Format Page Numbers** and then choose **Start At**.

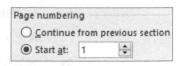

Page numbering
○ Continue from previous section
● Start at: 1

Number 1 is chosen automatically, but you could change it if you needed to.

20. Click **OK** to restart page numbering with a 1 and then double-click in the document body to close the header and footer areas.

21. Scroll up and notice that the footer does not appear on the table of contents page.

22. Scroll down and observe the footer text in the rest of the document.

Because the page numbering changed, you need to update the table of contents again.

23. Scroll to the table of contents and position the insertion point in the table of contents.

24. Tap F9, choose **Update Entire Table**, and then click **OK**.

25. Save your file.

Creating an Index

Adding an index to a document gives the reader an easy way to find important words. To create an index, you mark the entries and then generate the index. The entries you mark are sorted alphabetically and their page numbers are inserted.

Marking Index Entries

When entries and subentries are marked, it's important to note that marking index entries is a case-sensitive action. If you mark all occurrences of a word such as *Billing* for inclusion in the index, only those occurrences of the word where the *B* is capitalized are marked. So, it's important to consider which occurrences you want marked before selecting Mark All.

 View the video "Main Entries and Subentries."

≡ References→Index→Mark Entry

≡ References→Index→Insert Index

≡ References→Index→Update Index

DEVELOP YOUR SKILLS: W8-D4

In this exercise, you will mark index entries and subentries in preparation for generating an index.

1. Save your file as **W8-D4-RaritanP&PRevised**.

2. Go to the first page of the body of the manual and select the heading *Mission Statement*.

3. Choose **References→Index→Mark Entry** 📄.

Now you will edit the main entry text.

4. Type **Goals** in the Main Entry field to replace the text that was automatically inserted in the Mark Index Entry dialog box.

The text that was in the field came from the words you selected in the document. You can always replace or edit the suggested entries in this manner.

5. Click **Mark** at the bottom of the dialog box.

   Now you will examine an index code.

6. If necessary, drag the dialog box to the side and notice that the code { XE "Goals" } was inserted into the document.

   This code identifies Goals as a main index entry.

7. Select the word *specialties* at the end of the second line in the second paragraph under the *Mission Statement* heading.

8. Click the Mark Index Entry dialog box to activate it and then click **Mark** to use the proposed text as the main entry.

9. Select *General Medicine* in the first line of the third paragraph below Scope of Services, click the dialog box to activate it, and click **Mark**.

10. Scroll down and select *Patient* in the heading *Patient Appointments and Billing*, click the dialog box, and click **Mark**.

Mark All Entries

Depending on the nature of the document you are marking, there may be text you want to mark every time it appears.

11. Select *Billing* in the heading *Patient Appointments and Billing* and then click the dialog box.

12. Click **Mark All** to mark all occurrences of *Billing* for inclusion in the index.

    *Remember, it only marks **Billing** if it begins with a capital letter.*

13. Select *billing* toward the end of the first line in the third paragraph below *Patient Appointments and Billing*, click the dialog box, and click **Mark All**.

Mark Subentries

14. If necessary, scroll down to the *Patient Records* heading; then follow these steps to mark records as a subentry:

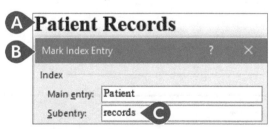

   Ⓐ Select *Patient* in the heading.

   Ⓑ Click the **Mark Index Entry** dialog box to activate it.

   Ⓒ Type **records** in the Subentry field and click **Mark**.

15. Navigate to the second paragraph below the *Patient Records* heading, select *files* in the first line, and click the dialog box to activate it.

16. Double-click *files* in the Main Entry field and then press [Ctrl]+[X].

17. Click the **Subentry** field and then press [Ctrl]+[V] to paste *files* into the field.

18. Type **Patient** in the Main Entry field and then click **Mark**.

19. Close the **Mark Index Entry** dialog box.

20. Save your file.

Generating Index Entries Using a Concordance

If a document is extremely long, marking index entries can be overwhelming. There is an automatic option for marking words and phrases to be included in an index. This option allows you to create a list of words and phrases you want to include and saves it as a separate file that acts as a concordance file.

When you use a concordance file to generate an index, it's important to know how it works. These guidelines will provide you with some basic information.

▸ The list of words and phrases to be included as main entries should be typed in one column straight down the left margin of the document or in the first column of a table.

▸ The document should contain only the words and phrases to be marked.

▸ To mark entries with subentries, create the concordance using a table layout. In the first column, type the words you want to mark as the main entry. In the second column, type the main entry followed by a colon, followed by the text for the subentry, without spaces.

| patient | patient:records |

▸ Entries can be listed in any order in the concordance. They will be sorted and grouped alphabetically when you generate the index. However, sorting the words helps identify duplicate words in the concordance.

DEVELOP YOUR SKILLS: W8-D5

In this exercise, you will mark index entries using a concordance document.

1. Save your file as **W8-D5-RaritanP&PRevised**.
2. Open **W8-D5-P&PConcordance** from your **Word Chapter 8** folder.
3. Scroll through the document, review its contents, and then close the document.
4. Position the insertion point anywhere on the title page at the top of the document.
5. Choose **References→Index→Insert Index** 📄.
6. Click **AutoMark** at the bottom of the dialog box to display the Open Index AutoMark File dialog box.
7. Navigate to your **Word Chapter 8** folder and double-click **W8-D5-P&PConcordance**.

   Although nothing appears to happen, the list of words and phrases in the concordance is compared with the manual. When a word is located, the entry is automatically marked in the manual.

8. Scroll through and review the document.

   Notice the numerous index marks that were added from the concordance in addition to the individual marked items from the previous exercise.

9. Turn off formatting marks.

   Because index codes can be quite lengthy, displaying them can cause text to roll onto other pages. Turning off formatting marks ensures that page numbers are accurate.

10. Save the file.

Inserting and Updating the Index

After all the index entries are marked, you can insert the index using the Index dialog box. You can choose the overall format for the index and select several other formatting options. You can update an index in the same manner as a table of contents.

≡ References→Table of Contents→Update Index | F9

There are several ways you can modify an index once you create it. You can:

▸ use the Index dialog box to change various formatting options.

▸ format the index directly.

▸ change the text of an entry by replacing it directly in the code that was originally created and then update the index.

▸ delete an entry by removing the code and updating the index.

 The format that's active in the Index dialog box will be reapplied if you update the index.

DEVELOP YOUR SKILLS: W8-D6

In this exercise, you will generate and format an index.

1. Save your file as **W8-D6-RaritanP&PRevised**.
2. Press Ctrl + End or scroll down to move to the end of the document.
   An index should begin on a blank page.
3. Type the heading **Index** and tap Enter.
4. Select the heading and format the text as **bold, 16 pt**.
5. Position the insertion point on the blank line below the Index heading.
6. Choose **References→Index→Insert Index** 📄.
7. Choose **Formal** from the Formats list at the bottom of the dialog box and then click **OK**.

Modify the Index Format

8. Click anywhere in the index and then choose **References→Index→Insert Index** 📄.
9. Choose **Modern** at the bottom of the dialog box and then choose **Run-In** at the top-right corner.
10. Click **OK**; click **OK** again when the message appears asking if you want to replace the index.
    The new index is inserted with the Run-In number style. Notice how the style affects the subentries. You've decided you like the previous indented subentries.
11. Click **Undo** ↺ to reverse the change.
12. Save the file.

Keeping Text Together

If you're working on a long document that goes through multiple revision cycles, controlling pagination can be a challenge. There are several options in the Paragraph dialog box that can be helpful.

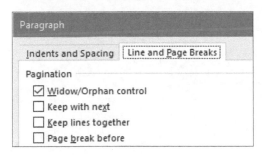

- **Widow/Orphan Control:** Places at least two lines of a paragraph at the top or bottom of a page; checked by default

- **Keep with Next:** Forces a paragraph to appear with the paragraph that follows it; often used to keep a heading with the following paragraph

- **Keep Lines Together:** Prevents a page break in the middle of a paragraph

- **Page Break Before:** Forces a page break before a specific paragraph

DEVELOP YOUR SKILLS: W8-D7

In this exercise, you will use the Keep with Next option to ensure that specified segments of text stay together when a document is automatically paginated.

1. Save your file as **W8-D7-RaritanP&PRevised**.
2. On the first page of the document body, select the *Patient Management Procedures* heading and the *Entry into Services* subheading.

   A heading should not appear alone at the page bottom. Although that is not the case now, further editing may split a heading from the paragraph that follows.

3. Choose **Home→Paragraph→dialog box launcher** .
4. If necessary, click the **Line and Page Breaks** tab, check **Keep with Next**, and click **OK**.

   This ensures that the heading, the subheading, and the paragraph following the subheading will "stick together" during future edits and automatic pagination.

5. Scroll down to the next page and select the *Patient Appointments and Billing* heading.
6. Choose **Home→Paragraph→dialog box launcher** , check **Keep with Next**, and click **OK**.
7. Save your file.

Watermarks

A watermark is text or a graphic placed behind text or other objects in a document; it is visible only in Print Layout or Read Mode view. Some common watermarks include a faint image of the word *Draft* or *Confidential* in the background.

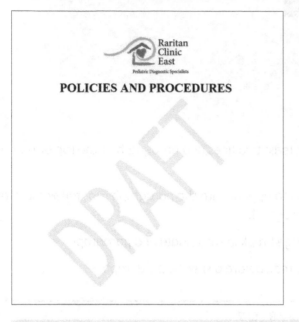

≡ Design→Page Background→Watermark

DEVELOP YOUR SKILLS: W8-D8

The changes made to the policies and procedures manual need to be approved by your manager. Although the word DRAFT appears in the header, you've decided that using the word as a watermark would be more effective. In this exercise, you will delete the term in the header and then add a watermark to the document.

1. Save your file as **W8-D8-RaritanP&PRevised**.
2. Position the insertion point at the top of the document and double-click the header area to open it.
3. Select the word *DRAFT* and tap Delete.
4. Double-click in the body of the document to close the header area.
5. Choose **Design→Page Background→Watermark** and then choose **Draft 1** from the gallery.
6. Scroll through a few pages to view the watermark.
7. Save and close the file; exit Word.

Self-Assessment

 Check your knowledge of this chapter's key concepts and skills using the Self-Assessment in your ebook or eLab course.

Reinforce Your Skills

REINFORCE YOUR SKILLS: W8-R1

Organize a Document with a TOC and Headers and Footers

Kids for Change is providing background reading for its next monthly meeting in which it'll brainstorm new ideas to help kids in the community thrive. You will add a table of contents and headers and footers to make the document more accessible to the readers.

1. Start Word, open **W8-R1-Organizations** from your **Word Chapter 8** folder, and save it as **W8-R1-OrganizationsRevised**.

2. If necessary, display formatting marks; then choose **Home→Styles→dialog box launcher** 🗔 to open the Styles task pane.

3. Starting on the first page of the main body of the document, position the insertion point in the headings and notice the heading styles in effect.

4. Close the Styles task pane.

5. On page 2, notice the section break at the top of the page.

6. Position the insertion point on the blank line above the section break.

7. Choose **References→Table of Contents→Table of Contents** 📄 and then choose **Automatic Table 1** from the gallery.

Modify a Heading

8. Scroll to page 3 and, in the first subheading below *Change for Kids*, select *Tutoring* and replace it with **Teaching**.

9. On page 2, position the insertion point in the table of contents and click **Update Table** 🗋 at the top of the table of contents border.

10. Choose **Update Entire Table** and click **OK**.

Create a Custom Table of Contents

11. Choose **References→Table of Contents→Table of Contents** and then choose **Custom Table of Contents**.

12. Make sure all three checkboxes are checked and then, if necessary, choose **Formal** from the Formats drop-down list.

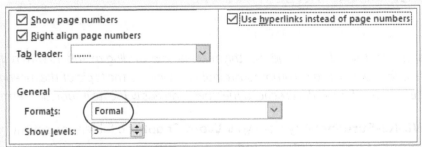

13. Click **OK**; when the message appears confirming the replacement, click **OK** again.

Add Multiple Headers and Footers

14. Position the insertion point in section 2 of the document, which begins with *Introduction*.

15. Choose **Insert→Header & Footer→Header** ▢ and then choose **Edit Header**.

Notice the Same as Previous tab at the right side of the header area. You will now break the link between sections 1 and 2.

16. Choose **Header & Footer Tools→Design→Navigation→Link to Previous** ▦.

Notice that the Same as Previous tab no longer appears at the right side of the header.

17. Tap ⌞Tab⌝ to position the insertion point in the center of the header and then type **Kids for Change**.

18. Double-click in the body of the document to close the header area.

19. Scroll up and notice that the header doesn't appear on pages 1 and 2; scroll down and observe the header on pages 3 and 4.

20. If necessary, position the insertion point in the page starting with *Introduction*, which is section 2.

21. Choose **Insert→Header & Footer→Footer** ▢ and then choose **Edit Footer**.

Notice the Same as Previous tab at the right side of the footer area.

22. Choose **Header & Footer Tools→Design→Navigation→Link to Previous** to break the link between sections 1 and 2.

23. Choose **Header & Footer Tools→Design→Header & Footer→Footer** and then choose **Austin**.

Notice that the Austin format placed a border around the page and that page numbering starts at page 2. You will now change the numbering to start on page 1.

24. Choose **Header & Footer Tools→Design→Header & Footer→Page Number** ▣ and then choose **Format Page Numbers**.

25. In the Page Number Format dialog box, choose **Start At** from the bottom of the dialog box.

The number defaults to 1, which is what you want.

26. Click **OK** and then double-click in the body of the document to close the footer area.

27. Scroll down and notice the numbering on the third and fourth pages; scroll up and notice that there are no footers on the first two pages.

28. Save and close the file.

REINFORCE YOUR SKILLS: W8-R2

Add an Index to a Document

The leader for the next Kids for Change monthly meeting is providing members with a document containing ideas for how kids can promote sustainability, which is the topic of the meeting. In this exercise, you will create an index for the document so members can easily locate important terms.

1. Open **W8-R2-Sustainability** from your **Word Chapter 8** folder and save it as **W8-R2-SustainabilityRevised**.

2. If necessary, display formatting marks; then select *wood products* in the first bullet point.

3. Choose **References→Index→Mark Entry** ▣.

That places wood products in the Main Entry field.

4. Type **salvaged** in the Subentry field and then click **Mark**.

   *Notice the colon between **wood products** and **salvaged** in the index code in the document. This indicates that **salvaged** is a subentry of **wood products**.*

5. Select *salvaged* in the Subentry field, type **recycled** in its place, and click **Mark**.

   This adds another subentry for wood products.

6. Select *light bulbs* in the third bullet point and then click the dialog box to activate it.

7. Type **fluorescent** in the Subentry field and then click **Mark**.

8. Now change the subentry text to **standard** and click **Mark**.

   This adds another subentry for light bulbs.

9. Select *paper products* in the fifth bullet point, click the dialog box, and click **Mark**.

10. Select *recycle* in the second line of the sixth bullet point and then click the dialog box.

11. Mark the following terms as subentries for *recycle*:
    - wood products
    - paper products
    - plastic containers
    - cell phones
    - electronics

12. Close the dialog box.

Insert an Index

13. Press ⎡Ctrl⎤+⎡End⎤ or scroll down to move to the end of the document and then press ⎡Ctrl⎤+⎡Enter⎤ to insert a page break.

14. Type **Index** and tap ⎡Enter⎤, format the heading with **bold**, **16 pt**, and then position the insertion point on the blank line below the heading.

15. Turn off formatting marks.

    Remember, displaying index codes can affect page numbering.

16. Choose **References→Index→Insert Index** 🖹.

17. Follow these guidelines to complete the index:
    - Choose **Classic** in the Formats list.
    - Check the **Right Align Page Numbers** checkbox.
    - Choose **dots** in the Tab Leader field.

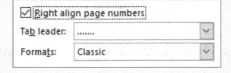

18. Click **OK**.

Modify an Entry and Update the Index

19. Scroll to the second-to-last bullet point and select *Computer Takeback Campaign*.

20. Choose **References→Index→Mark Entry**.

    This phrase will be a subentry under recycle, so you will cut the term and paste it into the Subentry field.

21. Press ⌐Ctrl¬+⌐X¬, position the insertion point in the **Subentry** field, and press ⌐Ctrl¬+⌐V¬.

22. Type **recycle** in the Main Entry field and then click **Mark**.

23. Close the dialog box and scroll down to the index.

24. Turn off formatting marks.

    Formatting marks were turned on when you marked the last entry.

25. Hover the mouse pointer over the index, right-click, and choose **Update Field**.

Finalize the Document

This document will go through some revisions, so you want to be sure the lines in the second-to-last bullet point don't split between pages if repagination takes place.

26. Scroll up and select the bullet point that begins with *Recycle old electronics*.

27. Choose **Home→Paragraph→dialog box launcher** ⌐🗔¬.

28. If necessary, click the **Line and Page Breaks** tab, check **Keep Lines Together**, and click **OK**.

    Now you will insert a DRAFT watermark so this document isn't mistaken for the final version.

29. Choose **Design→Page Background→Watermark** ⌐🗎¬ and choose **Draft 2** from the gallery.

30. Save and close the file.

REINFORCE YOUR SKILLS: W8-R3

Organize a Long Document

Kids for Change is planning a fair, Sustainability for the Twenty-First Century. One of the members has prepared a report of background information that will be used to kick off the planning session. You have been asked to organize the document to make it more accessible for the reader. In this exercise, you will create a table of contents and an index and insert headers and footers.

1. Open **W8-R3-WikiSustain** from your **Word Chapter 8** folder and save it as **W8-R3-WikiSustainRevised**.

2. If necessary, display formatting marks; then scroll through the document and observe the heading styles.

    Now you will insert a new page for the table of contents and then generate the table of contents.

3. On the second page, position the insertion point in front of *Introduction*.

4. Choose **Layout→Page Setup→Breaks** and insert a **Next Page** section break.

5. Scroll up and position the insertion point in front of the section break (to the right of the paragraph symbol) and then tap ⌐Enter¬.

6. Choose **References→Table of Contents→Table of Contents** ⌐🗎¬→**Automatic Table 2**.

Update the Table of Contents

7. Hover the mouse pointer over the *Energy* link in the table of contents and then press ⌐Ctrl¬ and click the link to jump to that heading in the document.

8. Position the insertion point at the end of the *Energy* heading, tap ⌐Spacebar¬, and then type **consumption**.

9. Now update the entire table of contents.

   Notice that the table of contents updated with the change. Now you'll change the table of contents format.

10. Choose **References→Table of Contents→Table of Contents→Custom Table of Contents**, choose the **Formal** format, click **OK**, and then choose **Yes** to replace the table of contents.

Add Headers and Footers

11. Scroll down and position the insertion point in **section 2**, which begins with *Introduction*.

12. Choose **Insert→Header & Footer→Header** 🗋 **→Edit Header** and break the link between sections 1 and 2.

13. Tap ⬜Tab twice to position the insertion point at the right side of the header area, type **Sustainability in the Twenty-First Century**, and close the header area.

    Notice that the header appears throughout section 2, but it does not appear in section 1.

14. Position the insertion point in **section 2**; choose **Insert→Header & Footer→Footer** 🗋**→ Edit Footer** and then break the link.

15. Choose **Header & Footer Tools→Design→Header & Footer→Footer** 🗋**→Austin**.

    Now you will set the page numbering to start at 1 in section 2.

16. Choose **Header & Footer Tools→Design→Header & Footer→Page Number** 🔢 and then choose **Format Page Numbers**.

17. Set the numbering to start at 1 and then close the footer area.

Create an Index

18. Select the *Atmosphere* heading toward the top of the new page 1 and mark it as an index entry.

19. Type **global warming** in the Subentry field and then click **Mark**.

20. Select the text in the Subentry field, type **carbon reduction** in its place, and click Mark.

21. Select the Subentry text, type **air pollution:nitrogen oxides** (no spaces surrounding the colon), and click **Mark**.

    Whether you're creating a concordance or marking entries in the Mark Index Entry dialog box, the word to the right of the colon is a subentry of the word on the left.

22. Now mark these items in the Subentry field:
    ```
    air pollution:sulfur oxides
    air pollution:photochemical smog
    air pollution:acid rain
    air pollution:sulfate aerosols
    ```

23. Click in the document, scroll down and select *Management of human consumption* toward the bottom of page 2, and then click the dialog box to activate it.

24. Type **Energy Consumption:increase in CO2** in the Subentry field and click **Mark**.

25. Mark these entries in the Subentry field:
    Energy Consumption:fossil fuel emissions
    Energy Consumption:climate change
    harvesting rainwater
    ethical consumerism
    local food production
    circular material flow
    renewable sources
    industrial ecology

26. Close the dialog box.

27. Position the insertion point at the end of the document, create a new page for the index, and then turn off formatting marks.

    Remember, the index codes can cause a change in pagination.

28. Type **Index** and tap ⌷Enter⌷, format the text with **bold**, **14 pt**, and then position the insertion point on the blank line below the text.

29. Insert an index using the Modern format, right-align page numbers, and use dots as the tab leader.

    Notice the subentries under air pollution *and* Energy Consumption. *Now you'll mark another entry and then update the index.*

30. Scroll to page 1, select the *Freshwater and oceans* heading, and mark it as an index entry.

31. Click in the document, select the *Land use* heading on page 2, mark it as an index entry, and then close the Mark Index Entry dialog box.

32. Turn off formatting marks.

    Word turned on formatting marks when you marked the new index entries.

33. Position the insertion point in the index and tap ⌷F9⌷.

Keep Text Together

If this document is revised, using some pagination features will simplify the process. In this example, you want the Management of human consumption *heading to always be at the top of a new page.*

34. Scroll to page 2 and position the insertion point in front of *Management of human consumption*.

35. Choose **Home→Paragraph→dialog box launcher** ⌷☞⌷ and, if necessary, click the **Line and Page Breaks** tab.

    Some pagination options are already in place for this text.

36. Check the **Page Break Before** checkbox and click **OK**.

    This ensures that this heading will always start on a new page. Because pagination has changed, it's a good idea to update the table of contents and the index.

37. Position the insertion point in the table of contents and update the entire table.

38. Position the insertion point in the index and tap ⌷F9⌷.

39. Save and close the document.

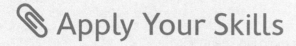

Apply Your Skills

APPLY YOUR SKILLS: W8-A1

Finalize a Report

Universal Corporate Events sent you to Munich on a familiarization trip. You have completed the content for your report and now will apply some formatting. In this exercise, you will create a table of contents to make it easy to locate specific topics in the report and also add a header and footer.

1. Open **W8-A1-Munich** from your **Word Chapter 8** folder and save it as **W8-A1-MunichRevised**.

2. Open the **Styles** task pane, scroll through the document to observe some of the heading styles in use, and then close the task pane.

3. Position the insertion point in front of *Introduction* on the first page of the body and insert a **Next Page** section break.

4. If necessary, display formatting marks, scroll up and position the insertion point in front of the section break, and tap [Enter].

5. Insert an **Automatic Table 1** table of contents and use the **Parks** hyperlink to jump to that heading.

6. Position the insertion point at the end of the heading, tap [Spacebar], and type **and recreation**.

7. Update the table of contents to reflect the change.

8. Open the Table of Contents dialog box, apply the **Classic** format, choose the **dots** from the Tab Leader drop-down list, and click **OK**.

9. When the message box appears confirming the replacement, click **OK**.

10. Position the insertion point in **section 2**, which begins with *Introduction*, edit the header, and break the link between sections 1 and 2.

11. Insert a header using the **Banded** style from the Header gallery; close the header area.

12. With the insertion point in section 2, edit the footer to break the link between sections 1 and 2, and then insert a footer using the Banded style.

13. Set up the page numbering to start at **1** in section 2.

14. Close the footer area and then save and close the document.

APPLY YOUR SKILLS: W8-A2

Create an Index and Use Pagination Options

Universal Corporate Events has asked you to do some research on Bangalore for a client. Now that you've completed the research, you will add an index making it easy for the client to locate important terms. In this exercise, you will mark entries and subentries and use a concordance to create the index. Then you will make additions to the index and update it.

1. Open **W8-A2-Bangalore** from your **Word Chapter 8** folder and save it as **W8-A2-BangaloreRevised**.

2. If necessary, display formatting marks; then mark the three main headings on page 1 (*Background*, *Climate*, and *Get in*) as main index entries.

3. Mark *By plane* as a subentry of *Get in*.

4. On page 6, mark *Landmarks* and *Temples* as main index entries.

5. Navigate to your **Word Chapter 8** folder and open **W8-A2-Concordance**, examine the file, and then close it.

6. Use the **AutoMark** button in the Index dialog box, together with **W8-A2-Concordance**, to mark additional index entries and then turn off formatting marks.

   Now you'll insert an index.

7. Scroll to the end of the document and insert a page break to create a blank page for your index.

8. Type **Index** at the top of the new, blank page and tap Enter.

9. Format *Index* with **bold, 14 pt**, position the insertion point on the blank line below the heading, and insert an index using the **Formal** format.

10. Scroll up to page 1 and select *Background*.

11. Choose **References→Index→Mark Entry**.

12. Mark these terms as subentries of Background:
    - population
    - Garden City of India
    - IT industry

13. Turn off formatting marks and update the index.

14. On page 1, select the *Background* heading.

15. Open the Paragraph dialog box and check **Keep with Next** on the Line and Page Breaks tab.

16. Select the *Climate* heading and apply the **Keep with Next** option.

17. Select the *Get in* and *By plane* headings and apply the **Keep with Next** option.

18. Save and close the file.

APPLY YOUR SKILLS: W8-A3

Organize a Long Document

A Universal Corporate Events agent wrote a report on Basque country. Now it's time to enhance the document's readability. In this exercise, you will create a table of contents and an index. You will work with headers and footers and set up a page break pagination option.

1. Open **W8-A3-Basque** from your **Word Chapter 8** folder and save it as
   W8-A3-BasqueRevised.

2. If necessary, display formatting marks; then open the **Styles** task pane.

3. Scroll through the document, observe the heading styles, and then close the task pane.

4. To create a new page for the table of contents, insert a **Next Page** section break just before the heading *The Basque Country* on page 2.

5. Scroll up, position the insertion point in front of the section break, tap Enter, and then insert an **Automatic Table 2** table of contents.

6. Use the **Climate** link in the table of contents to jump to the *Climate* heading; type **Basque** in front of *Climate* and then update the table of contents to reflect the change.

7. Create a custom table of contents by applying the **Distinctive** format.

8. Position the insertion point in section 2, which begins with *The Basque Country* heading; edit the header, break the link between sections 1 and 2, and insert a header using the **Blank style**.

9. Type **The Basque Country** in the Type Here area; close the header area.

10. With the insertion point in section 2, edit the footer and break the link between sections 1 and 2.

11. Insert a footer using the **Austin style** and format the starting page number to start at page 1; close the footer area.

Mark Entries and Create an Index

12. Mark index main entries and subentries using the headings indicated in this table.

Main Entry	Subentry
Features	Atlantic Basin Middle section Ebro Valley
Basque Climate	
Transport	Road Rail Airports Seaports

13. Turn off formatting marks, position the insertion point at the end of the document, and insert a page break.

14. Type **Index** and tap ⌷Enter⌶, format the text with **bold, 14 pt**, position the insertion point on the blank line below the heading, and insert a **Formal** index.

15. Mark the *Cuisine* heading (page 4) as a main entry, turn off formatting marks, and then update the index.

Keep Text Together

16. Position the insertion point in front of the *Transport* heading (page 2) and insert the **Page Break Before** pagination option.

17. Because you changed pagination, update the table of contents and the index.

18. Save and close the file.

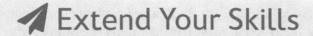 # Extend Your Skills

These exercises challenge you to think critically and apply your new skills. You will be evaluated on your ability to follow directions, completeness, creativity, and the use of proper grammar and mechanics. Save files to your chapter folder. Submit assignments as directed.

W8-E1   That's the Way I See It

As a small-business owner, you want to offer your customers a document that provides an in-depth, categorized overview of your products. If you were a bookstore owner, for example, you might categorize books by genre (e.g., history, biography, fiction). Start a new document and save it as **W8-E1-ProductDescriptions**. Decide on the type and name of your business. Type an introduction (3–4 sentences) for each main product category, providing longer content for the subcategories. Format main categories with Heading 1 and give each at least three subcategories (Heading 2). Your document should be at least seven pages, including a cover page, a table of contents, and index (ten main entries and at least three subentries). Be sure to insert a Next Page section break between the table of contents and the body of the document. Also include multiple footers (page numbering starting at page 1 in section 2, no footers in section 1) and the Keep Text Together option (keep heading lines together with the paragraph following headings; apply this feature at least twice). You may copy content from the Internet, but cite your sources.

W8-E2   Be Your Own Boss

As the owner of Blue Jean Landscaping, you want to provide your customers with in-depth information for their spring gardens, focusing on fruits, vegetables, and legumes. Start a new document and save it as **W8-E2-SpringPlanting**. Create an introduction (3–4 sentences). Do online research to create at least three subcategories for each category. Format the category headings with Heading 1 and the subcategories with Heading 2. Provide detailed information, such as the best growing conditions for a particular type of tomato. Your document should be at least seven pages, with a cover page, table of contents, and index. You may copy content from the Internet, but cite your sources. Insert a Next Page section break between the table of contents and the document body. Use page numbers in the section 2 footer, starting at page 1; use no footer in section 1. Your index should include twenty main entries and at least five subentries.

W8-E3   Demonstrate Proficiency

Stormy BBQ is planning to sell a book about BBQ cooking, and you have been asked to provide the research, which you will do online. You can feel free to copy content from online sources—just remember to cite your sources. Start a new document and save it as **W8-E3-BBQBook**. The book will include three main categories: BBQ Grills and Tools, BBQ Tips and Techniques, and BBQ Recipes. Each category heading should be formatted with the Heading 1 style. Create a short introduction (3–4 sentences) for each main category. Based on your research identify at least two subcategories for each category; format the subcategory headings with the Heading 2 style. Use a Next Page section break to designate a cover page and table of contents as section 1 and the rest of the document as section 2. Insert a header with the company name that appears only in section 2. Insert a page number footer that appears only in section 2 and that starts numbering at page 1. Create an index of at least fifteen terms of your choice, including main entries and at least five subentries.

9 | Collaborating in Word

The Internet makes it easy for project teams to collaborate on drafting documents. Team members can exchange documents across the country as easily as across the hall. There are several features that make collaboration activities more efficient. For example, you can track all of the changes made to a document by each team member and combine these changes into a single document for review. In this chapter, you will work with these collaboration tools.

LEARNING OBJECTIVES

▸ Use the highlighter tool

▸ Track your changes to a document

▸ Review tracked changes from others

▸ Send emails from Word

▸ Review changes from multiple reviewers

▸ Compare documents with no tracked changes

📂 Project: Collaborating on a Manual

As a member of the human resources department, you have been working to finalize the Raritan Clinic East Policies & Procedures Manual. It's now ready for review by personnel in the human resources department. As others review the manual, they will use collaboration tools to mark suggested changes. Some reviewers will insert comments to identify their recommendations, while others will use the Track Changes feature to mark suggested edits. Some will highlight text to identify wording that needs revising. Your task will be to review all suggested edits and comments and finalize the document for printing.

The Highlighter

The highlighter pen works just like its real-life counterpart (except that you can easily erase the highlighting). The pen applies a transparent color to the text background and offers a variety of highlighting colors. You can color-code the highlights you use in a document if you wish. For example, you might highlight a note to yourself in yellow and a "waiting for information" reminder in green.

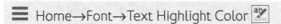 ☰ Home→Font→Text Highlight Color 🖊️

DEVELOP YOUR SKILLS: W9-D1

In this exercise, you will highlight a note to yourself and a reminder that you are waiting for additional information from the Finance department.

Before You Begin: *Be sure to visit the Learning Resource Center at labyrinthelab.com/lrc to retrieve the exercise files for this course before beginning this exercise.*

1. Start Word, open **W9-D1-PolicyManual** from your **Word Chapter 9** folder, and save it as **W9-D1-PolicyManualRevised**.
2. Make sure the insertion point is at the beginning of the document and then do a search for *Pediatric General Medicine*.
3. On page 2, position the insertion point in front of *Pediatric*.
4. Type this text and tap ⎵Spacebar after the period: **Chin has more information about these specialties.**
5. Choose **Home→Font→Text Highlight Color** 🖊️ **menu button** ▼ and then choose **Bright Green** from the gallery.

   When the mouse pointer is in the body of the document, it looks like a highlighter pen.
6. Drag the pen across the text you just added to highlight it.
7. Choose **Text Highlight Color** 🖊️ to turn off the pen.

   Notice that the color on the button face reflects the most recently used color.

 Tip! *Tapping* Esc *also turns off the pen.*

8. Press Ctrl + End or scroll down to move to the end of the document and then type this text: **Check with Finance to see if they have information to add.**

9. Select the sentence, choose **Text Highlight Color** **menu button** ▾, and then choose **Yellow**.

   This highlights the selected text and changes the button color to yellow.

10. Save the file and leave it open.

 Always leave your file open at the end of an exercise unless instructed to close it.

Tracking Changes to a Document

Track Changes is one of the most useful tools for collaborating with team members as you pass documents back and forth. Reviewers can track changes while they edit, and the originator can see who is making what changes in the document and either accept or reject the suggested changes.

Reviewers can also use the Comment feature to leave messages in a document as a means of collaborating with the originator. For example, reviewers may want to explain to the originator why they are making a particular change.

≡ Review→Tracking→Track Changes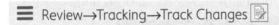

📖 Review and Collaboration

You will often have opportunities at school and work to collaborate with others on writing projects. In today's world, when requests for instant feedback are the norm, knowing the typical online reviewing process can ensure that you're well-prepared to be a valuable contributor. Reviewers use Track Changes to mark edits and add comments so reviewers and the originator can converse back and forth. It's important to use Track Changes so the originator can see all of the proposed edits. Files may be passed back and forth among team members via email, cloud storage, or other means. Then the originator can combine the edited documents, accepting and rejecting edits to create the final document.

Viewing Tracked Changes

You have options for viewing edits made to documents using Track Changes. The method you choose is a matter of personal preference.

▸ **Inline:** Edits are marked directly within sentences and paragraphs. Text that is deleted by the reviewer is colored and marked through with a line, and text that is added appears underlined and in a different color.

▸ **Balloons:** Comments and edits appear in balloons on the right side of the document called the markup area. Each balloon identifies the person who made the edit as well as the type of edit made—inserted text, deleted text, and so forth.

 The balloons method is the primary method used in this chapter.

 View the video "Display Options for Track Changes and Comments."

Setting the Username and Initials

Track Changes uses information set up in the Word Options dialog box to identify the username for edits made to a document. As a result, whenever you collaborate on a document in which Track Changes is used, it is important to make sure your username and initials are set correctly.

≡ Review→Tracking→dialog box launcher [▫]→Change User Name

WORD

Setting Reviewer Ink Colors

Track Changes can use different colors to distinguish the edits of each reviewer who works on the document. Each reviewer can specify colors for his or her comments and tracked changes. This makes it easier to rapidly identify changes submitted by a specific reviewer. It also allows you to keep a consistent color for a reviewer you work with frequently, rather than settling on colors that may be assigned automatically.

☰ Review→Tracking→dialog box launcher 🗔 →Advanced Options

DEVELOP YOUR SKILLS: W9-D2

In this exercise, you will turn on Track Changes, change the tracking colors, and set the user's name and initials for the revised Raritan Clinic East policy manual.

1. Choose **Review→Tracking→dialog box launcher** 🗔 and then click the **Advanced Options** button.

2. Follow these steps to choose options for your reviewer ink color settings:

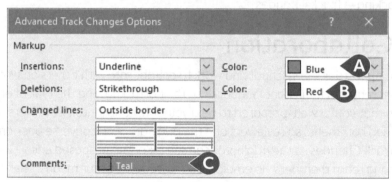

- Ⓐ Set the color for Insertions to **Blue**.
- Ⓑ Set the color for Deletions to **Red**.
- Ⓒ Set the color for Comments to **Teal**.

3. Click **OK**.

4. Click the **Change User Name** button at the bottom of the Track Changes Options dialog box and, if necessary, enter your username and initials.

5. If you want to override the settings from the current Microsoft Account, check the checkbox below the Initials field, Always Use These Values Regardless of Sign In to Office, and then click **OK** twice.

Adding Comments to a Track Changes Document

The Comment feature is a great collaboration tool to use in conjunction with Track Changes. The Reply button in the comment balloon allows reviewers and originators to communicate back and forth during the editing and reviewing process. For example, a reviewer might want to point out the reason for a deletion.

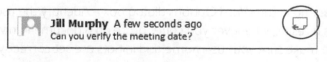

☰ Review→Comments→New Comment 🗨

In this exercise, you will choose the balloon display for tracking changes, and then you will insert a comment and make revisions to the document.

1. Save your file as **W9-D3-PolicyManualRevised**.

2. If necessary, choose **Review→Tracking→Display for Review** and then choose **All Markup** from the menu.

3. Choose **Review→Tracking→Track Changes** and, if necessary, display formatting marks.

4. Choose **Review→Tracking→Show Markup→Balloons** and, if necessary, choose **Show Revisions in Balloons**.

   Deleted text, comments, and formatting changes will appear in balloons in the Markup Area. Added text will be underlined in the body.

5. Scroll to page 2. In the last paragraph on the page, select *Referral* at the beginning of the paragraph.

6. Choose **Review→Comments→New Comment**.

7. Type this text in the comment balloon: **Indent to match other paragraphs.**

8. In the same paragraph, locate and select the text *(see Appendix A)* in the next line and then delete it.

   The deleted text appears in a balloon in the Markup Area, and a gray change bar appears in the left margin to help reviewers locate changes.

9. Follow these guidelines to continue with deletions:
   - Search for the word *see* to locate each additional cross-reference to an appendix.
   - Delete the cross-reference for Appendices B–K.
   - Delete extra spaces between words where appropriate.

10. Search for *Patient Management Procedures* and then position the insertion point at the end of the heading.

11. Follow these steps to insert introductory text for the heading:

Patient·Management·Procedures¶

→ It·is·important·that·standard·management·procedures·be·used·to·maintain·the·standards·of· treatment·that·each·patient·deserves.··These·procedures·are·described·in·the·following·pages.¶

   A Tap [Enter].
   B Tap [Tab] and then type the text shown here.
   C Notice the gray change bar in the left margin that helps locate changes.

   Notice the formatting balloons in the Markup Area. Although the font is the same for the other body text, the style is different from the heading; therefore, the difference is noted.

12. Close the Navigation pane and save the file.

WORD

Reviewing Tracked Changes

Reviewers' tracked changes are only suggestions that don't become permanent unless the originator accepts them. If the originator doesn't agree with a reviewer's suggestion, it can be rejected.

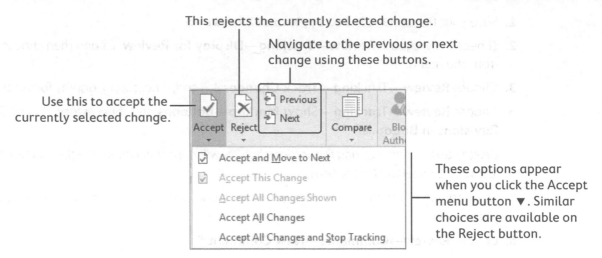

This rejects the currently selected change.

Navigate to the previous or next change using these buttons.

Use this to accept the currently selected change.

These options appear when you click the Accept menu button ▼. Similar choices are available on the Reject button.

 Tip! *You can right-click a proposed change and choose an Accept or Reject command from the pop-up menu.*

Displaying Tracked Changes

You can display tracked changes in four distinctive views. Depending on the type of detail you want to focus on, each view offers specific advantages.

VIEWS FOR TRACKED CHANGES	
Markup	**Description**
Simple Markup	This shows where a change occurred with a red change bar in the margin. Clicking the change bar displays the markup details.
All Markup	This option shows all markups.
No Markup	This hides all markups and displays a final document appearance with the proposed changes.
Original	Select this to show the original document and hide all markups.

≡ Review→Changes→Accept ☑ or Reject ☒

≡ Review→Tracking→Display for Review 🗎

DEVELOP YOUR SKILLS: W9-D4

In this exercise, you will display the document using different markup views. Then you will review tracked changes to the document, accepting some changes and rejecting others.

1. Save your file as **W9-D4-PolicyManualRevised**.

2. Choose **Review→Tracking→Display for Review** 🗎→**Original** and then scroll through the document.

   The document now appears as it did before changes were made.

3. Choose **Display for Review** 🔲→**All Markup** and then scroll through the document.

   Notice the balloons in the Markup Area on the right. Deleted text, comments, and formatting changes appear in balloons, while inserted text is underlined in the body.

4. Choose **Display for Review** 🔲→**Simple Markup** and then scroll through the document.

   Red change bars appear in the margin where changes occurred. Clicking the change bar displays all of the changes in detail; clicking it again hides the details. This is a good view for a document with lots of changes.

5. Choose **Display for Review** 🔲→**No Markup** and then scroll through the document.

   This view helps you see what the final document will look like.

Accept and Reject Changes

6. Position the insertion point at the top of the document.

7. Choose **Review**→**Changes**→**Next** 🔲.

   This turns on All Markup view and then jumps to and highlights the text you added to the document. This is a good addition, so you will accept it.

8. Choose **Accept** 🔲.

   The change marks are removed from the new paragraph, and the focus moves to the next change— the formatting balloon associated with the change you just accepted.

9. Choose **Accept** 🔲.

10. Choose **Accept** 🔲.

11. Choose **Next** 🔲 to skip the comment and move to the next change, the deleted reference to *Appendix A*.

12. Choose **Reject** 🔲.

    The deleted text is restored and you move to the next tracked change.

13. Reject each deleted reference to an appendix.

    The insertion point returns to your comment.

14. Choose **Review**→**Comments**→**Delete** 🔲.

15. Choose **Review**→**Tracking**→**Track Changes** 🔲 to turn off the feature.

16. Position the insertion point at the beginning of the paragraph starting with *Referral* (bottom of page 2) and tap ⎵Tab⎵ to indent the first line.

17. Save the file.

Saving and Sending Files

Before reviewers can do their jobs, you must get the document to them. You can use the Internet to share your document in several ways, including the following:

▸ Email

▸ Microsoft OneDrive

▸ Network drive

This chapter uses email as the method for sharing files.

Experience shows that it works best to name each copy of a document sent for review with the reviewer's name. Then, as the documents are returned from review, it's easy to track which reviewer sent each one. It's also a good idea to save all reviewer copies in a single folder to keep them together.

≡ File→Share→Email 🗩

DEVELOP YOUR SKILLS: W9-D5

In this exercise, you will send an email with a copy of the policy manual document attached. For this example, you will send the attachment to your own email address.

1. Choose **Review→Tracking→Track Changes** 📝.

   Turning on the feature helps ensure that the reviewers will use Track Changes.

2. Choose **File→Share→Email** 📧 and then choose **Send as Attachment**.

3. Follow these steps to complete the email form:

   If your user ID was not set up as a user with an Outlook account, you will see a message saying that no profiles have been created. If so, just dismiss the message, turn off Track Changes, and read through the rest of the exercise.

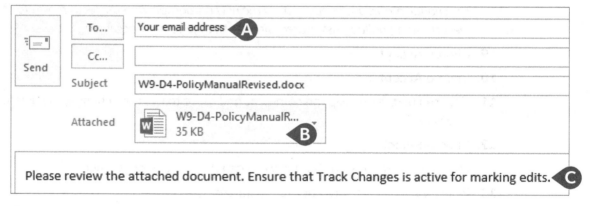

- Ⓐ Enter your actual email address here (don't type the text shown).
- Ⓑ Verify that the attachment appears here.
- Ⓒ Add this message for the reviewers.

4. Send the email.

5. Choose **Review→Tracking→Track Changes** 📝 to turn off Track Changes.

Reviewing Changes from Multiple Reviewers

If you set up a document to track changes, you can send copies of the document for review by others. As the reviewers make revisions, their changes are tracked. When the reviewers send you their edited copies, you can combine the tracked changes into a single document. Each reviewer's changes are marked in a different color so you can recognize input from different reviewers. After the changes are merged, you can navigate through the combined document and accept or reject edits from all users at one time. In fact, by seeing the edits from all reviewers in one document, you will be able to identify the trouble spots in the document because different reviewers may try to modify the same area of the document.

≡ Review→Compare→Compare 📑→Combine

Displaying Specific Markups and Reviewers

There are numerous options for displaying tracked changes for combined documents. For example, you may want to look at only the insertions and deletions suggested by reviewers. If you don't need to keep track of formatting changes, you may wish to turn off the Formatting option so you won't be prompted for formatting changes.

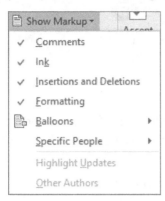

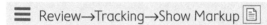
Review→Tracking→Show Markup 📄

If you combine two reviewer documents with the original, you can choose to see changes from both at once, or, at times, you may wish to focus on just one reviewer. You can do that by removing the checkmark in front of the other reviewer's name.

DEVELOP YOUR SKILLS: W9-D6

In this exercise, you will combine proposed changes from two reviewers with the original document. You will also explore additional features used for working with combined documents.

1. Save your file as **W9-D6-PolicyManualRevised**.
2. Choose **Review→Compare→Compare** 📄 and then choose **Combine**.
3. Follow these steps to begin combining documents:

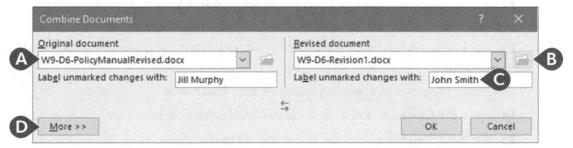

- Ⓐ Choose **W9-D6-PolicyManualRevised** here.
- Ⓑ Click **Browse** and open **W9-D6-Revision1** from your **Word Chapter 9** folder.
- Ⓒ Although there may be another name in this field, type **John Smith** here so you'll know who suggested any unmarked changes.
- Ⓓ Click **More > >** to expand the dialog box.

Note! *If Track Changes is not turned on, the reviewer's name does not appear with the change. Normally changes are tracked, and the name does not need to be entered in the dialog box.*

4. Follow these steps to control document display:

> **Show changes**
>
> Show changes at:
> ○ Character level
> ⓐ ● Word level
>
> Show changes in:
> ● Original document ⓑ
> ○ Revised document
> ○ New document

ⓐ Ensure that **Word Level** is active.

ⓑ Choose **Original Document**.

The Word Level option causes the entire word to be highlighted, even if only one character or punctuation mark changes. This makes it easier to spot small edits. Now John Smith's proposed edits are embedded in the original document, ready for review.

5. Click the **< < Less** button to collapse the dialog box; click **OK**.

Hide Source Documents

6. Click **Compare** 📑, slide the mouse pointer to **Show Source Documents**, and then, if necessary, choose **Hide Source Documents**.

This provides more room on the screen.

7. Choose **Compare** 📑 and then choose **Combine**.

8. In the Original Document field, choose **W9-D6-PolicyManualRevised**.

9. Click the **Browse** button next to the Revised Document field and open **W9-D6-Revision2** from your **Word Chapter 9** folder.

10. Type **Brett Reynolds** in the Label Unmarked Changes With field and click **OK**.

Brett Reynolds' edits are now displayed with the original and John Smith's edits.

Turn On the Reviewing Pane

11. If necessary, choose **Review→Tracking→Reviewing Pane** 📄 **menu button** ▼ and then choose **Reviewing Pane Vertical**.

The Reviewing Pane (labeled Revisions *at the top) summarizes the proposed changes from both reviewers.*

12. Scroll down the Reviewing Pane to the suggested change by Brett Reynolds, where he deleted *attending*.

13. Click *attending* in the Reviewing Pane and notice that the document scrolls to the location of that change.

Notice the Deleted: attending *balloon in the Markup Area.*

14. Click the **Close** ⊠ button at the top of the reviewing pane.

15. Press ⌈Ctrl⌉+⌈Home⌉ to move to the top of the document.

16. Review all changes to the document:
- Delete all comments and accept all formatting changes.
- Accept all edits by John and Brett with one exception: On page 3, John deleted a space between *(see Appendix B)* and *Children*. Reject that change.

17. Save the file as **W9-D6-Combined** and then close it.

Comparing Documents

Sometimes documents that are sent for review are returned with no visible edits. Reviewers might turn off Track Changes so that the edits they make are not immediately evident. To determine whether edits have been made, you can use the Compare feature. It enables you to merge two documents into one file; then the documents are examined and automatically marked up using Track Changes so you can locate edits.

To Combine or Compare?

The basic procedures are the same for comparing and combining documents, but each command has a different use.

The Combine command allows you to combine the tracked changes from one or multiple reviewers in one document, and then you can go through the single document to accept or reject the changes.

The Compare command is designed for comparing two documents: one edited version of a document, in which the reviewer did not use Track Changes, and the original. If you attempt to use the Compare feature to add a second reviewer's document, you will be advised that it will automatically accept the first person's changes before comparing the second edited document. Thus, you won't have the option of accepting or rejecting changes from the first reviewer.

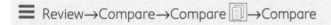 Review→Compare→Compare 🗐→Compare

---

DEVELOP YOUR SKILLS: W9-D7

In this exercise, you will compare an original document with a document received from a reviewer that appears to have no changes in it.

1. Open **W9-D6-PolicyManualRevised** from your **Word Chapter 9** folder and save it as **W9-D7-PolicyManualRevised**.

2. Choose **Review→Compare→Compare** 🗐 and then choose **Compare** from the menu.

3. Follow these steps to compare this file with another document:

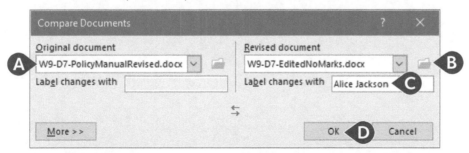

Ⓐ Choose **W9-D7-PolicyManualRevised** as the original document.

Ⓑ Click the **Browse** button for the revised document, navigate to your **Word Chapter 9** folder, and choose **W9-D7-EditedNoMarks**.

Ⓒ Type **Alice Jackson** here to identify the reviewer.

Ⓓ Click **OK** and then click **Yes** if you're asked if you want to continue with the comparison.

4. Scroll through the document and observe Alice's edits.

You won't accept and reject changes in this example.

5. Save the file as **W9-D7-AliceEdits** and exit Word.

Self-Assessment

 Check your knowledge of this chapter's key concepts and skills using the Self-Assessment in your ebook or eLab course.

Reinforce Your Skills

Encourage Good Bugs with Companion Planting

Kids for Change is sponsoring a Master Gardener's seminar, and you have researched companion planting. In this exercise, you will use the highlighter to place reminders in your document, add comments, and track and review changes. You will also email your document as an attachment.

1. Start Word, open **W9-R1-CompanionPlant** from your **Word Chapter 9** folder, and save it as **W9-R1-CompanionPlantRevised**.

2. If necessary, display formatting marks; then position the insertion point at the end of the first paragraph and tap Enter.

3. Type this text: **Make copies on 3-hole punched paper.**

4. Choose **Home→Font→Text Highlight Color** menu button ▾ →**Turquoise**.

5. Drag the mouse pointer, which now appears as a highlighter pen, across the sentence you just typed.

6. Choose **Text Highlight Color** to turn off the highlighter and then position the insertion point at the end of the document.

7. Type this text: **Reminder: Check with Ilsa to see if lupine and savory attract lady bugs.**

8. Select the sentence and then choose **Home→Font→Text Highlight Color menu button** ▾ → **Bright Green**.

Customize Your Track Changes

9. Choose **Review→Tracking→dialog box launcher** ◰ and then click **Change User Name**.

10. If necessary, enter your username and initials, click **OK**, and then click the **Advanced Options** button.

11. Choose the following colors and then click **OK** twice.
    - Insertions: **Pink**
    - Deletions: **Dark Blue**
    - Comments: **Violet**

Work with Comments and Track Changes

12. Move to the top of the document and select the word *March* in the third line of the first paragraph.

13. Choose **Review→Comments→New Comment** 🗩 and then type this text: **Do we have a specific date yet?**

14. Scroll down to the *Tomatoes + Cabbage* combination and select the last word, *leaves*.

15. Click the **New Comment** button and type this text: **Did Ilsa verify that this combination really works?**

    Now you'll turn on Track Changes and make some editing changes.

16. Choose **Review→Tracking→Track Changes**.

17. In the first sentence below the *Companion Planting* heading on page 1, select *makes for* and type **produces** in its place.

18. In the fifth line of the same paragraph, select *mate* and type **pair** in its place.

19. In the first line of the *Radishes + Spinach* section on page 2, select *yor* and type **your** in its place.

20. Scroll down to the *Collards + Catnip* section, position the insertion point at the end of the sentence, tap [Spacebar], and type this text: **And it will make your cat very happy!**

21. Position the insertion point at the end of the *Marigolds and Melons* section and tap [Enter].

22. Type this text: **Asparagus + Basil: Seems to encourage lady bugs**.

23. Bold the text *Asparagus + Basil:*.

Now you'll review the tracked changes.

24. Choose **Review→Tracking→Display for Review** ▤ **menu button** ▼ →**Original** and scroll through the document.

The document now appears as it was before tracking changes.

25. Use the same technique to experiment with **Simple Markup**, **No Markup**, and **All Markup**, leaving it set at **All Markup**.

Now you will respond to comments and accept and reject the changes as you are playing the role of the reviewer.

26. Position the insertion point at the top of the document.

27. Choose **Review→Changes→Next** ▣.

The insertion point moves to the first comment.

28. Click **Reply** ▭ in the upper-right corner of the comment balloon and type this text: **I'll check with Ilsa.**

29. Choose **Next** ▣.

The insertion point moves to the tracked deleted words makes *for.*

30. Choose **Accept** ▣.

The focus moves to the added word produces.

31. Choose **Accept** ▣.

32. Accept the deletion of *mate* and the addition of *pair*.

The insertion point moves to the added Asparagus + Basil *information.*

33. Choose **Reject** ▣.

The insertion point moves to the next comment.

34. Click **Reply** ▭ in the upper-right corner of the comment balloon and then type this: **I'll check with her.**

35. Choose **Next** ▣ and accept the deletion of *yor*, the addition of *your*, and accept the *"And it will make your cat very happy!"* addition.

Send a Document for Review

36. Make sure Track Changes is still on.

Remember, you want to ensure that reviewers use Track Changes.

37. Choose **File→Share→Email** ▣ and then choose **Send as Attachment**.

If your user ID was not set up as a user with an Outlook account, you will see a message saying that no profiles have been created. If so, just dismiss the message, turn off Track Changes, and read through the rest of this exercise.

38. In the email form, enter your email address in the To field and then change the **Subject** to **Companion planting document attached for review**.

   Notice that the document is already attached.

39. Type this text in the body of the email: **Please be sure Track Changes is turned on when you review the document.**

40. Click **Send** and then choose **Review→Tracking→Track Changes** 📝 to turn it off.

41. Save and close the file.

REINFORCE YOUR SKILLS: W9-R2

Combine and Compare Tracked Changes

Kids for Change is planning to participate in California Coastal Cleanup Day. You've researched some information on why this is important, and now your document has been reviewed by two other members. In this exercise, you will analyze the reviewers' edits and comments to finalize your document.

1. Open **W9-R2-CleanCoast** from your **Word Chapter 9** folder and save it as **W9-R2-CleanCoastRevised**.

2. If necessary, choose **Review→Tracking→Display for Review** 📖→**All Markup**.

3. Choose **Show Markup** 📄 and then slide the mouse pointer to **Balloons** and, if necessary, choose **Show Only Comments and Formatting in Balloons**.

4. Choose **Review→Compare→Compare** 🔲→**Combine**.

5. Choose **W9-R2-CleanCoastRevised** from the **Original Document** drop-down list.

6. Click **Browse** on the right side of the dialog box, navigate to your **Word Chapter 9** folder, and open **W9-R2-CleanCoastElla**.

7. Click the **More** button to expand the dialog box and make sure **Word Level** and **Original Document** are chosen, click the **Less** button to collapse the dialog box, and then click **OK**.

8. Choose **Compare** 🔲 and then slide the mouse pointer down to **Show Source Documents** and, if necessary, choose **Hide Source Documents**.

9. Combine the second document, **W9-R2-CleanCoastNed**, with **W9-R2-CleanCoastRevised** and then click **OK**.

10. Position the insertion point at the top of the document and then follow these guidelines to review the changes:
    - Accept all additions and deletions made by Ella and Ned.
    - Reply to Ned's first comment with: **I'll contact one of the Park School teachers.**
    - Reply to Ella's comment with: **We should incorporate that in the report.**
    - Reply to Ned's second comment with: **Are you willing to follow up on this?**

11. Save the file as **W9-R2-CoastEllaNed** and then close it.

Compare Docs

12. Open **W9-R2-Pups** from your **Word Chapter 9** folder and save it as **W9-R2-PupsRevised**.

13. Choose **Review→Compare→Compare** 🔲→**Compare**.

14. Choose **W9-R2-PupsRevised** from the **Original Document** drop-down list.

15. Click the **Browse** button on the right side of the dialog box and open **W9-R2-PupsArthur** from your **Word Chapter 9** folder.

16. Type `Arthur Menendez` in the Label Changes With field on the right and click **OK**.

17. Make sure the insertion point is at the top of the document.

18. Choose **Next** 🖹.

    The first change is a little difficult to see—a comma was added following donors.

19. Accept the change and then continue through the document accepting each addition and deletion.

20. Click **OK** when the message appears indicating there are no more changes.

21. Save the file as **W9-R2-PupsCompare** and then close it.

REINFORCE YOUR SKILLS: W9-R3

Collaborate in Word

Kids for Change will have a booth at a local farmer's market next month where the group will talk about the importance of buying locally grown food. It is preparing a handout that discusses the significance of buying local, and now the document will be reviewed by two members. In this exercise, you will share the file with reviewers using Word's email and then combine tracked changes from two reviewers. Then you will compare another document with a reviewer who forgot to use Track Changes.

1. Open **W9-R3-BuyLocal** from your **Word Chapter 9** folder and save it as **W9-R3-BuyLocalRevised**.

   First, you will turn on Track Changes to ensure that the reviewers use it, and then you will email the document.

2. Choose **Review→Tracking→Track Changes** 📝.

3. Choose **File→Share→Email** 🖼️→**Send as Attachment**.

   In this example, you will send the email to yourself. If your user ID was not set up as a user with an Outlook account, you will see a message saying that no profiles have been created. If so, just dismiss the message, turn off Track Changes, and read through the rest of the email portion of the exercise.

4. In the email form, enter your email address in the **To** field and change the **Subject** to `Global research attached`.

   Notice that the document is already attached.

5. Type the following text in the body of the email and then click **Send**:

   `Please review and propose any changes you would like.`

Combine Tracked Changes from Two Reviewers

6. Choose **Review→Compare→Compare** 📄→**Combine** and in the Original Document field choose **W9-R3-BuyLocalRevised**.

7. On the right side of the dialog box, click the **Browse** button, open **W9-R3-BuyLocalMarjorie**, and then click **OK**.

8. Choose **Compare** 📄→**Combine**.

9. In the Original Document field, choose **W9-R3-BuyLocalRevised**.

10. On the right side of the dialog box, browse for and open **W9-R3-BuyLocalSerge** and then click **OK**.

11. If necessary, position the insertion point at the top of the document.

12. Use **Next** 🔁 and **Accept** ☑ to review and accept all proposed changes.

13. Reply to Serge's comment about the number of copies with this text: **I'll check to see how many we made last year.**

14. Reply to Marjorie's comment with this text: **I know she is looking into it. I don't think she has heard back from them yet.**

15. Save the document as **W9-R3-BuyLocalCombined** and then close it.

Compare Documents

Kids for Change will participate in Community Health Week and has prepared a research document on childhood obesity. The document was sent out for review, but the reviewer forgot to use Track Changes, so you will use the Compare feature to locate the changes.

16. Open **W9-R3-Obesity** and save it as **W9-R3-ObesityRevised**.

17. Choose **Review→Compare→Compare** 🗐 **→Compare**.

18. In the Original Document field, choose **W9-R3-ObesityRevised** and, on the right side of the dialog box, browse for **W9-R3-ObesityMargo**.

19. Type **Margo Meyers** in the Label Changes With field and then click **OK**.

20. Scroll through the document and observe Margo's edits.

You agree with all of the changes, so you'll accept them all at once.

21. Choose **Accept** ☑ **menu button** ▾ **→Accept All Changes**.

22. Save the file as **W9-R3-MargoEdits** and then close it.

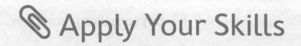 Apply Your Skills

APPLY YOUR SKILLS: W9-A1

Create a Report on Crete

Universal Corporate Events is adding Crete to its Mediterranean tour offerings. You've prepared a report about Crete, and now you're asking a colleague to review it. In this exercise, you will use the highlighter and Track Changes to edit the document, and then you'll send it on for further review.

1. Open **W9-A1-Crete** from your **Word Chapter 9** folder and save it as **W9-A1-CreteRevised**.

2. Position the insertion point at the end of the paragraph that is below the Crete heading.

3. Tap `Spacebar` and then type this text: **The Roman and Turkish remnants are worth adding to the tour.**

4. Highlight the sentence with pink.

5. Open the **Track Changes Options dialog box**, click **Change User Name**, and, if necessary, enter your username and initials.

6. Click the **Advanced Options** button in the same dialog box and choose these colors:
   - Insertions: **Green**
   - Deletions: **Red**
   - Comments: **Turquoise**

7. Select the city name, *Heraklion*, in the first bullet point.

8. Use the **New Comment** button to insert this comment: **A quick stop in Heraklion to see Knossos would be nice.**

9. Select the city name, *Elounda*, at the beginning of the fifth bullet point and insert this comment: **A good spot for celebrity watching.**

10. Turn on **Track Changes** and, in the fourth line of the paragraph below the *Crete* heading, replace *was* with **were**.

11. In the next line, replace *place* with **island**.

12. In the second line of the second bullet point, replace *Brits* with **British**.

13. Scroll to page 2 and locate the second-from-the-last bullet point about the city of Rethymno.

14. Position the insertion point after the space at the end of the paragraph and type this text: **There is a daily ferry from Athens**.

15. Ensure that **All Markup** is active in the Display for Review field and then position the insertion point at the top of the document.

    Now you'll play the role of the reviewer.

16. Use **Next** and **Accept** to find and accept all editing changes.

17. Create an email using these guidelines:
    - Use Word's Email feature to send the file as an attachment.
    - Insert your email address in the To field.

      If your user ID was not set up as a user with an Outlook account, you will see a message saying that no profiles have been created. If so, just dismiss the message, turn off Track Changes, and read through the rest of this exercise.

    - Change the subject to **Crete Review**.
    - Add this message in the body of the email: **I hope my comments are helpful.**
    - Send the email.

18. Save and close the file.

APPLY YOUR SKILLS: W9-A2

Prepare a Report on Whistler Blackcomb

Universal Corporate Events has a client who wants to reward outstanding employees with a ski vacation, and you've been researching Whistler Blackcomb. In this exercise, you will combine the documents from two reviewers into your original document. Then you will use the Compare feature with a document that was reviewed without Track Changes.

1. Open **W9-A2-Whistler** from your **Word Chapter 9** folder and save it as **W9-A2-WhistlerRevised**.

2. Ensure that the Display for Review feature is set to **All Markup**.

3. Choose **Show Markup→Balloons** and, if necessary, choose **Show Revisions in Balloons**.

4. Combine your original document with Colleen's revised document, **W9-A2-WhistlerColleen**, and enter **Colleen Chase** in the Label Unmarked Changes With field.

5. Combine your original document with Anthony's revised document, **W9-A2-WhistlerAnthony**, and enter **Anthony Nichols** in the Label Unmarked Changes With field.

6. Choose **Compare→Compare**, slide the mouse pointer to **Show Source Documents**, and, if necessary, choose **Hide Source Documents**.

7. Position the insertion point at the top of the document.

8. Accept all changes made by Colleen, Anthony, and Jill, except the change in the first paragraph of the article where Colleen changed kilometers to miles; reject both the deletion and the addition.

9. Save the file as **W9-A2-WhistlerColleenAnthony** and then close it.

   You have researched information about San Diego for a Universal Corporate Events representative, and it has been reviewed by a colleague, Mel. However, Mel did not use Track Changes, so you will use the Compare feature to highlight the changes.

10. Open **W9-A2-SanDiego** from your **Word Chapter 9** folder and save it as **W9-A2-SanDiegoRevised**.

11. Compare **W9-A2-SanDiegoRevised** in the Original Document field with **W9-A2-SanDiegoMel** and type Mel Johnson in the Label Changes With field.

12. Scroll through the document and check the changes.

13. All the changes look good, so accept them all at once.

14. Save the file as **W9-A2-SDCompared** and then close it.

APPLY YOUR SKILLS: W9-A3

Collaborate on a Cabo San Lucas Brochure

Universal Corporate Events has asked you to conduct research for a marketing brochure on Cabo San Lucas. In this exercise, you will make changes to your original document and send it to reviewers. Then you will combine and compare the reviewed documents.

1. Open **W9-A3-Cabo** from your **Word Chapter 9** folder and save it as **W9-A3-CaboRevised**.

2. Make sure **Show Revisions in Balloons** is selected on the Balloons submenu in the Show Markup drop-down list.

3. Open the **Track Changes Options** dialog box and make sure your username and initials appear in the Word Options dialog box.

4. Change the colors in the Advanced Track Changes Options dialog box as follows:
   • Insertions: **Bright Green**
   • Deletions: **Turquoise**
   • Comments: **Dark Red**

5. Turn on **Track Changes**.

6. Below the *See* heading, replace the last word in the first paragraph *abundant* with **plentiful**.

7. In the fourth line of the first bullet point, replace *allows for* with **provides**.

8. In the second line of the next bullet point, enter a comma after *old* and delete the word *and*.

   Now you will review your changes.

9. Position the insertion point at the top of the document and then use the **Next** button to move to and reject the *abundant* deletion and the *plentiful* addition.

10. Accept the rest of the changes.

11. Select *Submarine* in the second bullet point below the heading, *Scuba Diving & Watersports*, and then add this comment: **This looks like a fun activity. Let's check it out.**

12. Save the file.

Check Track Changes Options and Email Files

13. Check that Display for Review is set to **All Markup**.

14. Use the **Email** feature and the **Send as Attachment** option to send the document for review following these guidelines:

   If your user ID was not set up as a user with an Outlook account, you will see a message saying that no profiles have been created. If so, dismiss the message and go to the next step.
   • Enter your own email address in the To field.
   • Change the Subject to **Cabo Review**.
   • Enter this text in the body of the email: **Please make sure Track Changes is turned on**
   • Send the email.

Combine Tracked Changes and Compare Documents

15. Use the combine feature to combine the following documents:
- The original document is **W9-A3-CaboRevised**.
- The first revised document is **W9-A3-CaboAudrey**. (Enter **Audrey Ellis** in the Label Unmarked Changes With field.)
- The second revised document is **W9-A3-CaboJose**. (Enter **Jose Santos** in the Label Unmarked Changes With field.)

16. Accept all changes by Audrey, Jose, and Jill at once.

17. Save the file as **W9-A3-CaboCombo** and then close it.

You recently completed a report on Singapore, which was reviewed by your colleague Ellen. However, she forgot to use Track Changes, so you will use the Compare feature to assess her changes.

18. Open **W9-A3-Singapore** and save it as **W9-A3-SingaporeRevised**.

19. Compare this file with **W9-A3-SingaporeEllen**.

20. Enter **Ellen Pledger** in the **Label Changes With** field.

21. Review the changes and then accept them all.

22. Save the file as **W9-A3-SingCompared** and then close it.

◢ Extend Your Skills

These exercises challenge you to think critically and apply your new skills. You will be evaluated on your ability to follow directions, completeness, creativity, and the use of proper grammar and mechanics. Save files to your chapter folder. Submit assignments as directed.

W9-E1 | That's the Way I See It

Your business professor has assigned you to prepare a report on the best business opportunities for the coming year. To begin, choose a business that appeals to you. Then create a short introduction (4–5 sentences) summarizing your reasons for choosing the business. Search the Internet and copy content of one to two pages on business prospects, citing your sources. Save the file as **W9-E1-Biz**.

Create two copies of the file (**W9-E1-BizJohn** and **W9-E1-BizJorge**). Turn on Track Changes and revise the document using your own ideas. Do the same for the "Jorge" document, making different revisions than you did for John. Combine the revised files with your original file. Note that, because you created the John and Jorge files yourself, your name will appear as the reviewer in all cases. Accept and reject revisions as you see fit and then save and close the file.

W9-E2 | Be Your Own Boss

As the owner of Blue Jean Landscaping, you are researching recent articles on business opportunities in landscaping to determine future growth potential. Create a report of one or two pages using online content (citing your sources). Provide a short introductory paragraph (4–5 sentences) summarizing the outlook for the landscaping business. Save your file as **W9-E2-Landscape** and then make a copy, naming it **W9-E2-LandscapeArt**.

Begin to share the document with Art via email from within Word. Fill out the email form. Make up Art's email address and a subject. When complete, tap PrtScn and paste the screenshot into a new Word document saved as **W9-E2-Email**. Close the email form without sending. For the "Art" document, revise the document without Track Changes. Insert at least one comment and then save the document. Compare your original with the "Art" file. Note that, because you created the "Art" file yourself, your name will appear as the reviewer. Display the Reviewing Pane in a vertical alignment and then tap PrtScn. Add the screenshot to your "Email" document. Accept and reject revisions as you see fit and include a reply to Art's comment. Save and close the file.

W9-E3 | Demonstrate Proficiency

Stormy BBQ plans to hold a BBQ Festival. You've been asked to conduct online research to gather ideas for the festival. Using your own ideas and content from online articles, create a report of one or two pages (citing your sources). Provide an introductory paragraph of (4–5 sentences) summarizing the purpose of the festival. Save the report as **W9-E3-Festival** and then make a copy, naming it **W9-E3-FestivalCarla**. Change the reviewer ink setting for insertions, deletions, and comments to red. Tap PrtScn and then paste the screenshot of the Advanced Track Changes Options dialog box in a new document saved as **W9-E3-Ink**.

Make revisions to the "Carla" file, including at least one comment and then save it. Combine the "Carla" file with your original. Note that, because you created the "Carla" file yourself, your name will appear as the reviewer. Accept and reject changes as you see fit and insert a reply to the comment. Highlight one sentence with bright green and then save the file.

10 | Sharing and Securing Content

I n this chapter, you will work in Backstage view to control document access. Online storage, such as OneDrive, allows people to store and retrieve documents from any computer with Internet access, and virtual collaboration means that your documents are often in others' hands. There are features that help you control document content and security and guard your personal information.

LEARNING OBJECTIVES

▸ Use file compatibility features

▸ Check documents with the Document Inspector

▸ Restrict formatting and editing in a document

▸ Mark a document as final

▸ Secure documents with passwords and digital signatures

Project: Securing Confidential Information

At Raritan Clinic East, privacy and security of patient records are vitally important. As a Raritan employee, you will explore features that ensure that documents sent outside the clinic remain confidential and contain no information that could enable those receiving the documents to learn more about patients than they have a need to know. You will use Backstage view and identify some of the security features you can use.

Preparing Documents for Sharing

There are a number of things to think about when sharing documents with colleagues or clients. Compatibility issues between the current and earlier versions of Word should be considered. Additionally, documents can contain hidden or personal information about your organization or about the document that you do not want to share publicly. The Document Inspector can help you deal with these matters.

Compatibility Issues

The most recent versions of Word (2007–2016) use the *.docx* file format. Versions of Word prior to 2007 used a *.doc* file format. Benefits of the latter format include smaller file size, improved damaged-file recovery, and more control of personal information. It's important to understand how the current version of Word behaves with documents created in earlier versions. Likewise, you need to make sure your documents can be read by those using earlier versions. There are several things to think about in dealing with compatibility issues.

▶ The latest versions, Word 2016 and Word 2013, are compatible.

▶ Word 2007, 2010, and 2013 can open *.docx* files created with Word 2016.

▶ Opening a document in Word 2016 that was created in Word 2010 or earlier opens in Compatibility Mode. The features in Word 2016 are downgraded to be compatible with the older versions. The term *[Compatibility Mode]* appears in the title bar.

▶ To open a Word 2016 document in Word 2010 or earlier, you can install the Compatibility Pack for Word, which you can download for free from the Microsoft website.

▶ You can convert documents to Word 2016 that were created in versions prior to Word 2013.

▶ You can save a Word 2016 document as a Word 97-2003 document so it can be opened by users of those versions. Some features of the current version either won't be available or will be modified in a manner more compatible with older versions.

In this exercise, you will open a Word 2003 document in Word 2016 Compatibility Mode. You will then try to insert a Word 2016 SmartArt graphic (a new feature) in the 2003 document and see how Compatibility Mode deals with this feature.

1. Start Word, open **W10-D1-2003ProcMan** from your **Word Chapter 10** folder, and save it as **W10-D1-2003ProcManRevised**.

   Notice the term [Compatibility Mode] *in the title bar at the top of the screen.*

   W10-D1-2003ProcManRevised.doc [Compatibility Mode] - Word

   Now you will attempt to add a Word 2016 SmartArt graphic to the Word 2003 Compatibility Mode document.

2. If necessary, display formatting marks and then position the insertion point in front of the paragraph mark at the top of page 2.

3. Choose **Insert→Illustrations→SmartArt** .

   Note that Word opens the Word 2003 Diagram Gallery, rather than the Word 2016 SmartArt gallery, because the Compatibility Mode document cannot work with Word 2016's SmartArt feature.

4. Click **Cancel** to close the Diagram Gallery.

   Next you will observe how Word saves the Compatibility Mode document.

5. Choose **File→Save As** and navigate to your **Word Chapter 10** folder.

   Notice that Word 2016 defaults to the Word 97–2003 format in the Save As Type field. Word 2016 defaults to the older format unless you purposely convert the document to a .docx format or save it as a Word Document (*.docx) via the Save As Type drop-down list.

6. Click **Back** in the upper-left corner to return to the document.

7. Leave the file open.

To Convert or Not to Convert?

If most of the people you share documents with are using pre-2007 versions of Word, it's a good idea to keep their documents in Compatibility Mode. This ensures that documents will look the same in Word 2016 as they do in the older version. It also ensures that the features available in Word 2016 will be limited to, or similar to, the features available in older versions.

Choosing a Conversion Method

If you are working with a Compatibility Mode document that would benefit from the full functionality of Word 2016 features that are currently disabled or limited, you have a candidate for conversion. When you convert the document, Word 2016 turns on the new and enhanced features.

There are two ways to convert an older version (*.doc*) document to a Word 2007-2016 (*.docx*) document:

▶ **Convert:** The Convert command appears on the Info screen in Backstage view when a document is open in Compatibility Mode. Using the command performs a conversion that overwrites the original document. As a result, the older version document is no longer available.

▶ **Save As:** When you resave and rename a document using the Save As command, you are actually making a *copy* of the document. When you perform a Save As with a Compatibility Mode document, you still have the original *.doc* file, and you create a new second file, a *.docx* file.

☰ File→Info→Convert

☰ File→Save As

Consider the User

Always keep the person who sent you the document or the person to whom you are sending a document in mind before converting. If you are editing a document that needs to be returned to someone who is using an earlier version of Word, leave the document in its original format rather than converting it.

The Office Compatibility Pack

People who have earlier versions of Word and who need to work with Word 2016 documents can download a free compatibility pack from the Microsoft website to open, edit, and save Word 2016 documents. However, some features will still not be available.

DEVELOP YOUR SKILLS: W10-D2

In this exercise, you will convert a Word 2003 document to the .docx format and then add a Word 2016 SmartArt graphic.

1. Save your file as **W10-D2-2003ProcManRevised**.
2. Choose **File→Info→Convert**.

   A message appears indicting that conversion may cause some minor layout changes. For example, in this document, the pagination is altered slightly when converted.

3. Click **OK** to acknowledge the message.

   Notice that the term [Compatibility Mode] *has disappeared from the title bar.*

4. Position the insertion point on page 2 at the beginning of the first paragraph below the *Scope of Services* heading and make sure the insertion point is to the left of the tab that begins that paragraph.

5. Tap [Enter] and then position the insertion point next to the paragraph mark for the blank line you just created.

6. Choose **Insert→Illustrations→SmartArt** 📧.

   Because you converted the document, the SmartArt gallery is now available.

7. Follow these steps to insert a SmartArt graphic:

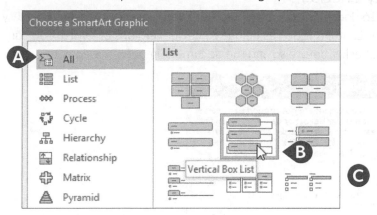

Ⓐ Choose **All** from the category list.

Ⓑ Choose the **Vertical Box List** graphic.

Ⓒ Click **OK**.

8. If necessary, click the tab at the left side of the graphic to open the Type Your Text Here pane.

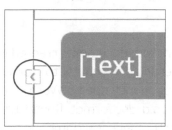

9. Type the text shown:

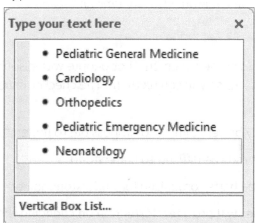

10. Close ☒ the Type Your Text Here pane.

11. Save the document.

Preparing Backward-Compatible Documents

If you know that you'll be working with people who have older versions of Word, and if it's important that all features are compatible among the versions, you might start your new document by saving it as a Word 97–2003 document. That way, you avoid using features unavailable in older versions.

The Compatibility Checker

If you save a Word 2016 document down to an older Word version, the Compatibility Checker notifies you if the document contains features unique to newer versions of Word. You can also manually run the Compatibility Checker before saving the document in older versions.

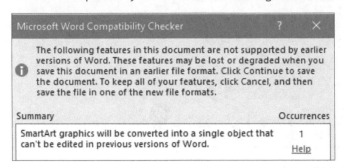

The Compatibility Checker alerts you to how Word 2016 features will be handled if you save a document to an earlier version of Word.

≡ File→Info→Check for Issues→Check Compatibility

Round-Tripping Documents

Round-tripping is a term that you may hear as you work with documents created in various versions of Word. Round-tripping refers to the practice of converting a document to a different format and then saving it back to the original format. For example, you may open a Word *.doc* file, convert it to a *.docx* file, and then decide to save your changes back to a *.doc* format. Round-tripping can create issues with the document that corrupt it so that it acts strangely or is damaged beyond repair.

 Avoid round-tripping your document to prevent unwanted loss of time and data.

The Accessibility Checker

The Accessibility Checker checks elements of the document that people with disabilities may find difficult to read and informs you of the issues so you can fix them. The checker issues errors, warnings, and tips.

▸ **Errors:** Elements of the document may be very difficult or impossible to understand.

▸ **Warnings:** Elements of the document may be difficult to understand.

▸ **Tips:** Elements of the document may be better organized for understandability.

Clicking an item in one of these categories will provide information on changing the content to make it more accessible. There is also a link to Help text that describes in detail what you can do to make documents more accessible.

≡ File→ Info→Check for Issues→Check Accessibility

DEVELOP YOUR SKILLS: W10-D3

In this exercise, you will begin the process to save a Word 2016 document to a Word 97–2003 format version for people who have not yet upgraded. Then you will check for accessibility issues.

1. Choose **File→Save As** and navigate to your **Word Chapter 10** folder.

2. Click the **Save as Type** drop-down list, choose **Word 97–2003 Document**, and click **Save**.

   Word displays the Compatibility Checker with a message indicating that you will not be able to edit the SmartArt graphic, so you've decided not to complete the conversion.

3. Click **Cancel**.

4. Choose **File→Info→Check for Issues→Check Accessibility** to open the Accessibility Checker task pane.

   Notice the two categories: Errors and Tips. There are no warnings for this document.

5. Click the **Read More About Making Documents Accessible** link at the bottom of the task pane to display the Help window.

6. Click the **Creating Accessible Word Documents** link to view the content and then close the Help window and the task pane.

Document Properties and the Document Inspector

Valuable information about a document appears in the Properties panel in Backstage view. Among the data Word stores within a document are the author's name, dates for file creation and editing, and the file storage location. Sending this data along with a document can inadvertently reveal to recipients some data that you would rather protect.

If you intend to share a document with colleagues or clients, you may use the Document Inspector to ensure that it contains no hidden or personal information either in the document itself or in the document properties. For example, a document could contain comments and tracked changes that are hidden from view. Document properties could contain information such as the author's name and the company name.

The Document Inspector will display a list of issues found in a document. The only option for removing data for a category is to remove all data within that category. Sometimes you may want to manually review information before deciding which data to remove.

 Before using the automatic Remove All option for a category, make a copy of the document, run the Document Inspector on the copy, and remove all issues to see the effect. This will help prevent unwanted data loss.

≡ File→Info→Properties

≡ File→Info→Check for Issues→Inspect Document

DEVELOP YOUR SKILLS: W10-D4

In this exercise, you will view document properties and run the Document Inspector. You will remove all personal data from the document.

1. Save your file as **W10-D4-2003ProcManRevised**.

2. Choose **File→Info** and review the properties information in the panel on the right.

   Notice that names appear in the Related People area. You can remove the author's name if desired.

3. Right-click the author's name and choose **Remove Person**.

4. In the Info window, click **Check for Issues** and then choose **Inspect Document**.

5. If prompted to save changes, click **Yes**.

   The Document Inspector dialog box opens. You can remove the checkmark from any items you don't want inspected. In this example, you will leave all checkboxes checked.

6. Click **Inspect** at the bottom of the dialog box and review the results.

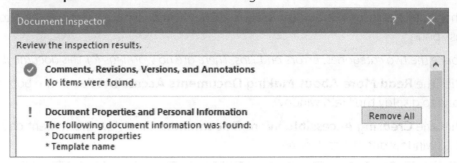

The inspector found document properties.

7. Click **Remove All** to the right of Document Properties and Personal Information and then click **Close**.

8. Choose **File→Info** and notice that, in the Properties panel, all names associated with the document have been removed.

9. Click **Back** ← and save the file.

Controlling Document Access

When you share documents with colleagues and clients, it can be helpful to control the changes that others can make. There are several features to assist you with protecting documents. For example, you can restrict the kinds of formatting and editing changes a reviewer can make. You can add a password to a document, and you can mark a document as final, thereby discouraging changes to it.

Restrict Editing

The Restrict Editing feature enables you to limit editing changes reviewers can make. You also have the option to further limit access with a password.

▸ **Restrict for Tracked Changes:** This setting protects a document from having Track Changes disabled. Every change to the document will be noted. In addition, no one can accept or reject changes while the document is protected.

▸ **Restrict for Comments:** This setting permits reviewers to insert and edit comments in the document but not to edit the document itself.

▸ **Restrict for Filling in Forms:** This setting permits users to insert data only in unrestricted areas of a form.

≡ File→Info→Protect Document→Restrict Editing

DEVELOP YOUR SKILLS: W10-D5

In this exercise, you will set editing restrictions to allow tracked changes, thus preventing reviewers from disabling the feature.

1. Save the file as **W10-D5-2003ProcManRevised**.

2. Choose **File→Info→Protect Document→Restrict Editing** to open the Restrict Editing task pane.

3. Follow these steps to turn on document protection for Tracked Changes:

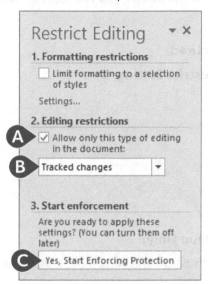

Ⓐ Ensure this checkbox is checked.

Ⓑ Ensure **Tracked Changes** is chosen here.

Ⓒ Click **Yes, Start Enforcing Protection**.

Word displays the Start Enforcing Protection dialog box. At this point, you can either click OK to restrict editing without a password or enter the desired password.

4. Click **OK** to dismiss the password dialog box.

5. On page 2, delete *of Services* in the *Scope of Services* heading.

The change is marked with Track Changes. No one can alter the document without changes being tracked.

6. Click **Stop Protection** at the bottom of the Restrict Editing task pane.

7. Click **Close** ✕ in the upper-right corner of the Restrict Editing task pane.

8. Choose **Review→Changes→Next** 🗒 and then **Accept** ☑ the change.

9. Click **OK** when the message appears.

10. Save the file.

WORD

Allow Changes to Part of a Document

If you choose No Changes (Read Only) in the Editing Restrictions list, the Exceptions option appears where you can specify certain areas of the document that a person can edit freely. For example, if a document is in its final version except for one section, you can exempt the incomplete section of the document so that it can be edited. You can also choose the people you want to allow to edit.

DEVELOP YOUR SKILLS: W10-D6

In this exercise, you will specify the document as read-only; however, you will apply an exception to three paragraphs so reviewers can make changes to them.

1. Save your file as **W10-D6-2003ProcManRevised**.
2. Choose **File→Info→Protect Document→Restrict Editing**.
3. Follow these steps to restrict editing:

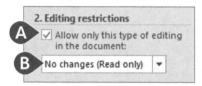

   Ⓐ Make sure a checkmark appears here.

   Ⓑ Set the restriction level to **No Changes (Read Only)**.

4. Scroll to page 3 and select the three paragraphs below the *Entry into Services* heading.
5. Place a checkmark in the **Everyone** checkbox under Exceptions (Optional).

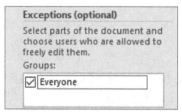

   This specifies that all reviewers will be able to edit these paragraphs.

6. Click **Yes, Start Enforcing Protection** at the bottom of the task pane.
7. Click **OK** to bypass setting a password.
8. Click to deselect the paragraphs.

   The editable paragraphs are shaded to make them easily visible to reviewers.

Attempt to Edit in a Restricted Area

9. Select a word anywhere there is no shading and tap ⌈Delete⌉.

   Nothing happens because you are restricted to editing only the shaded paragraphs.

10. Delete the third paragraph in the shaded area.

    The deletion is allowed because it is in the area that was specified as an exception.

11. Click **Stop Protection** at the bottom of the task pane.

12. Select the two remaining shaded paragraphs and then remove the checkmark from the **Everyone** checkbox in the task pane.

13. Click in the document and notice the shading has been removed.

14. Save the file.

Restrict Formatting

When you share a document with multiple reviewers, it's easy to imagine a jumble of formats if there are no restrictions. You can restrict reviewers to applying only the Word styles you choose. Formatting is restricted to a list of specified styles, thus providing formatting consistency and preventing anyone from indiscriminately formatting the document.

DEVELOP YOUR SKILLS: W10-D7

In this exercise, you will use the Restrict Editing task pane to apply formatting restrictions.

1. Save your file as **W10-D7-2003ProcManRevised**.

2. Choose **File→Info→Protect Document→Restrict Editing**.

3. Follow these steps to open the Formatting Restrictions dialog box:

Ⓐ Place a checkmark here.

Ⓑ Click the **Settings** link.

4. Follow these steps to set specific restrictions:

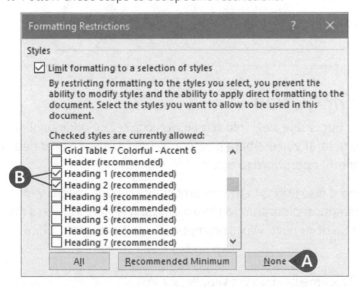

Ⓐ Click **None** to uncheck all of the checkboxes at once.

Ⓑ Scroll down and place checkmarks in the **Heading 1** and **Heading 2** checkboxes.

The only formatting change a reviewer can make is to add Heading 1 or Heading 2 formatting.

5. Click **OK**, and when Word displays a message asking if you want to remove other styles, click **No**.

Removing other styles from the document would reformat the entire document, possibly with unexpected results.

6. In section 2 of the Restrict Editing task pane, remove the checkmark next to **Allow Only This Type of Editing in the Document**.

7. Click **Yes, Start Enforcing Protection** in the Restrict Editing task pane.

In this example, you will not add a password.

8. Click **OK** to dismiss the password dialog box.

Notice that the task pane now contains a link to Available Styles.

9. Click the **Available Styles** link to display the Styles task pane.

In addition to the Normal style, the only styles available are Heading 1 and Heading 2.

10. Scroll to the top of page 2 and apply the **Heading 1** style to Our Mission.

11. Close the Styles task pane and then display the **Home** tab.

Notice that all of the Font and Paragraph formats are grayed out in the Ribbon because formatting is restricted to two heading styles.

12. Click **Stop Protection** at the bottom of the Restrict Editing task pane and then close the task pane.

Notice that the Font and Paragraph formats are restored on the Ribbon.

13. Save the file.

Passwords and Encryption

By using commands on the Backstage view Info screen, you can set an additional password that is required to open the document. If you use both passwords, the reviewer would need a password to open the document and another password to edit it.

Adding a document password also encrypts the document. Encryption means Word alters information using a code or mathematical algorithm so the information is inaccessible to unauthorized readers. When you encrypt a document, Word prompts you for a password. Note that passwords are case-sensitive.

≡ File→Info→Protect Document→Encrypt with Password

In this exercise, you will set a document password and then remove it.

1. Choose **File→Info→Protect Document→Encrypt with Password**.
2. Type **pass** in the Encrypt Document dialog box and click **OK**.
3. Type **pass** in the Confirm Password dialog box and click **OK**.

   Notice that the security setting is displayed in the Info screen.

4. Click **Back** ⊖ and then save and close the document.

   Depending on the security settings on your computer, you may receive a message asking whether you would like to increase the security. Respond by clicking No.

   Now you'll open the document with a password.

5. Choose **File→Open** and click **W10-D7-2003ProcManRevised** at the top of the Recent Document list.

   In some classrooms, the Recent Documents list may be cleared upon rebooting the computer. If so, navigate to your Word Chapter 10 folder to open the document.

6. Type **pass** in the password box and click **OK**.

   Now you will remove the password.

7. Choose **File→Info→Protect Document→Encrypt with Password**.
8. Select the characters in the password field, tap Delete, and then click **OK**.
9. Click **Back** ⊖ to return to the document and then save the file.

Marking a Document as Final

Another way to control edits and access to content is to mark the document as "final." Using the Mark as Final command makes a document read-only. As a result, readers and reviewers will know that this document appears as it did when it went to a client, was filed electronically, or was in some other way beyond the point where edits would be useful. Marking as final also prevents accidental altering of the document. When a document is marked as final, the following message appears in the Info tab in Backstage view.

Editing Documents Marked as Final

When the Marked as Final feature is turned on, a yellow bar appears at the top of the document. The message in the bar lets you know that the document has been marked as final to discourage editing, and the Ribbon is hidden. Note that the feature only *discourages* editing. It is not as secure as a password would be. The button in the message bar enables you to edit the document anyway.

≡ File→Info→Protect Document→Mark as Final

DEVELOP YOUR SKILLS: W10-D9

In this exercise, you will mark a document as final and then remove the designation to re-enable editing.

1. Choose **File→Info→Protect Document→Mark as Final**.
2. When Word displays a message that the document will be marked as final and saved, click **OK**.

   Word displays additional information about this setting.
3. Take a moment to read the information and then click **OK**.

   The security setting is displayed on the Info screen.
4. Click **Back** ⬅ to return to the document.

   Notice the Marked as Final *bar at the top of the screen.*
5. Select the heading *Our Mission* on page 2.
6. Tap Delete and see that the text is not deleted.
7. Choose **File→Info→Protect Document→Mark as Final** to turn off the feature.
8. Click **Back** ⬅ and notice that the Marked as Final bar at the top of the screen has disappeared.
9. Save the file.

Attaching Digital Signatures

With the capability to rapidly pass documents globally, security concerns may arise. For example, how can a client know for certain that a critical document originated in your office? A digital signature is a secure means of stamping a document as authentic and originating only from you. Other people cannot modify a signed document without removing the digital signature or marking it as invalid.

You may use a digital signature when passing documents to others as an email attachment, as a downloadable file on your organization's intranet, from a website, or on a flash drive. You add a digital signature to a file by first attaching a digital certificate.

Digital Certificates

Digital certificates may be obtained from third-party vendors, who check identification before issuing a certificate. If you post documents on an intranet or the Internet, your network administrator will usually provide you with an authentic digital certificate.

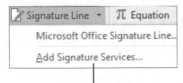

This option on the Signature Line
menu links to a Microsoft website,
where you can choose a third-party vendor.

You may also create your own digital certificate, although its use is limited. Self-made certificates are not verified by any outside agency; therefore, they're not necessarily a reliable measure, but they are the most convenient.

DEVELOP YOUR SKILLS: W10-D10

In this exercise, you will create a temporary digital certificate on your local computer. You will start by locating the SELFCERT application on your computer, which is installed as part of the Microsoft Office 2016 package.

1. Open **File Explorer** and navigate to the **SELFCERT** application through a path such as C:\Program Files (x86)\Microsoft Office\root\Office16.

Note! *You may need to seek assistance to determine the correct file path for this application on your computer. And note that you may not have user permission to create a digital certificate on computers that are for general use by multiple people.*

2. Scroll to locate the **SELFCERT** application. 🏅 SELFCERT.EXE

3. Double-click the file. When the Create Digital Certification dialog box opens, type **James Elliott** in the **Your Certificate's Name** field.

4. Click **OK**; when a message appears indicating that a certificate was successfully created for James Elliott, click **OK** again.

   You have now created a digital certificate that can be used to apply a digital signature to your files.

5. Close the File Explorer window and then save the file.

Digital Signatures

There are two ways to add a digital signature to a document:

▸ You can add a visible signature line to a document and then capture the digital signature when the document is signed.

▸ If a visible signature line is not necessary, you can add an invisible digital signature. A signature button appears on the status bar at the bottom of the screen, so the recipient can verify that the document has a digital signature.

≡ Insert→Text→Signature Line

DEVELOP YOUR SKILLS: W10-D11

In this exercise, you will add a signature line to a document and add a digital signature. You will then attempt to modify the signed document. Finally, you will remove the visible signature and add an invisible digital signature.

1. Save your file as **W10-D11-2003ProcManRevised**.
2. Press `Ctrl`+`End` to move to the end of the document and then tap `Enter` twice.
3. Choose **Insert→Text→Signature Line** 🖉 to display the Signature Setup dialog box.
4. Complete the information as shown:

The Instructions to the Signer *text is provided by default. You can modify it if necessary. In this exercise, you'll leave the text as it is.*

5. Click **OK** to complete the signature setup.

A signature line appears with the signer's name and title below. Now you'll sign the document.

6. Right-click the signature line and choose **Sign**.

7. Follow these steps to sign the document:

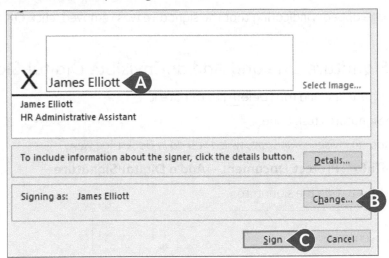

- **A** Type **James Elliott** here.
- **B** If the Signing As name isn't James Elliott, click **Change**, choose **James Elliott**, and click **OK**. Click **Yes** when the message appears to use the certificate.
- **C** Click **Sign**.

If you didn't change the Signing As name, a message appears indicating the certificate cannot be verified and asking whether you want to use this certificate. Remember, a self-created certificate is not verified by a third-party agency.

8. If necessary, click **Yes** to use the certificate.

9. When a message appears indicating your signature has been saved, click **OK**.

A yellow bar appears at the top of the document indicating that the document is marked as final. The Recoverable Signature note above the signature is notifying you that the signature is not verified by an outside agency. A signature button appears on the status bar indicating that there is a digital signature in the document.

10. Attempt to delete a word in the paragraph above the signature line.

A message briefly appears on the status bar indicating that you can't make a change because the selection is locked.

Now you will remove the signature so you can add an invisible signature. Remember, you can use an invisible signature when a visible signature is not required; however, a signature button will still appear on the status bar.

11. Click the signature button on the status bar to display the Signatures task pane.

You may notice the term Recoverable Error at the top of the task pane. This is because you are using a self-created certificate.

12. Right-click the **James Elliott** signature in the task pane and choose **Remove Signature**.

A message appears verifying that you want to remove the signature.

13. Click **Yes** to remove the signature.

14. When a message appears indicating that the signature was removed, click **OK** to dismiss the message.

Remove the Signature Line and Add an Invisible Digital Signature

15. Select the signature line and tap ⌷Delete⌷ to remove it.

16. **Close** ⌷×⌷ the Signatures task pane.

    Now you will add an invisible signature, which you do in Backstage view.

17. Choose **File→Info→Protect Document→Add a Digital Signature**.

18. Follow these steps to add the signature:

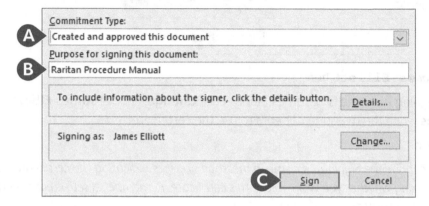

   Ⓐ Choose **Created and Approved This Document**.

   Ⓑ Type **Raritan Procedure Manual** here.

   Ⓒ Click **Sign**.

    A message appears indicating the certificate cannot be verified. Again, a self-created certificate is not verified by a third-party agency.

19. Click **Yes** to use the certificate.

20. When a message appears indicating the signature has been saved with the document, click **OK**.

    Notice the Marked as Final note in the yellow bar at the top of the screen and the signature button on the status bar.

    Because you cannot edit a document after a signature has been attached, there is no option to save the document. When you close the document, the signature will still be attached.

21. Close the file and exit Word.

Self-Assessment

 Check your knowledge of this chapter's key concepts and skills using the Self-Assessment in your ebook or eLab course.

Reinforce Your Skills

REINFORCE YOUR SKILLS: W10-R1

Plan for Trout in the Classroom

Kids for Change hopes to get involved in the "Trout in the Classroom" project, in which kids raise fish from eggs until they are ready to be released in streams. A team member created a research report in Word 2003, but the rest of the team is using Word 2016. In this exercise, you will convert a Word 2003 document to the Word 2016 format, and you will work with backward compatibility, document properties, and the Document Inspector.

1. Start Word, open **W10-R1-Trout** from your **Word Chapter 10** folder, and save it as **W10-R1-TroutRevised**.

   Observe the term [Compatibility Mode] *in the title bar. Now you will attempt to add a SmartArt graphic to the document.*

2. Press ⌈Ctrl⌉+⌈End⌉ to position the insertion point at the end of the document.

3. Choose **Insert→Illustrations→SmartArt** 📲.

   The Word 2003 Diagram Gallery opens because a Word 2003 document is not compatible with the SmartArt feature.

4. Click **Cancel** to close the Diagram gallery.

   Now you will convert the document to the Word 2016 format.

5. Choose **File→Info→Convert** and click **OK** when the conversion message appears.

   Notice that [Compatibility Mode] *no longer appears in the title bar; the document is now in the Word 2016 format. Now you will insert a SmartArt graphic.*

6. Choose **Insert→Illustrations→SmartArt** 📲.

7. Choose the **Process** category on the left, choose **Continuous Block Process**, and click **OK**.

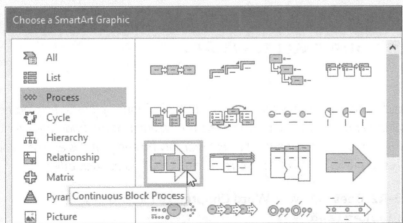

8. Click the tab to the left of the graphic and type the following in the Type Your Text Here pane; close the text pane when you're finished:

   • First bullet: **Hatch**

   • Second bullet: **Release**

9. Click the third text box in the graphic to select it and tap ⌈Delete⌉.

10. Position the mouse pointer on the graphic's upper-right corner sizing handle and then drag down diagonally toward the center of the image until it is about half its original size.

Prepare a Backward-Compatible Document

You want to make sure that the originator of the file will have access to it. You will format a Word 2016 document to be compatible with earlier versions.

11. Choose **File→Save As** and navigate to your **Word Chapter 10** folder.

12. Click the **Save As Type** drop-down list, choose **Word 97-2003 Document (*.doc)**, and click **Save**.

The Compatibility Checker opens, indicating that SmartArt graphics are not supported in earlier versions of Word. You will cancel the conversion so the SmartArt graphic will work as intended.

13. Click **Cancel**.

Inspect the Document

14. Choose **File→Info** and observe the Properties panel on the right.

Names appear in the Related People area.

15. In the Info screen, choose **Check for Issues→Inspect Document**.

A message appears indicating that you should save your changes because the Document Inspector may remove data that can't be restored.

16. Click **Yes** to save the file and open the Document Inspector.

In this example, you will leave all checkboxes checked.

17. Click **Inspect**.

The inspector found properties and personal information, which you will remove.

18. Click **Remove All** in the Document Inspector and then close the dialog box.

19. Choose **File→Info** and notice that the names were removed from the Related People area in the Properties panel.

20. Click **Back** ⊙ to return to the document.

21. Save and close the file.

REINFORCE YOUR SKILLS: W10-R2

Help in a Backyard Bee-Counting Project

There has been a decline in the bee population, and Kids for Change plans to help gather data by taking part in a bee-counting project. One of the members has researched methodologies for doing this. The research will be the basis of discussion for the next monthly meeting. In this exercise, you will use document protection features to prevent the document from being modified accidentally.

1. Open **W10-R2-Bees** from your **Word Chapter 10** folder and save it as **W10-R2-BeesRevised**.

2. Chose **File→Info→Protect Document→Restrict Editing** and place a checkmark in the check-box below the Editing Restrictions heading in the task pane.

3. Choose **Tracked Changes** from the drop-down list and then click **Yes, Start Enforcing Protection**.

4. When the dialog box opens, enter **pass** in both password fields and click **OK**.

5. Select *method* in the first line of the first paragraph below the *Counting the Vanishings Bees* heading and type **technique** in its place.

   The changes are marked because no one can modify the document without changes being tracked.

6. Click **Stop Protection**; when the Unprotect Document box appears, type **pass** in the Password field and click **OK**.

   Now you will accept the changes you made.

7. Choose **Review→Changes→Next** ⏭.

8. **Accept** ☑ both changes and then click **OK** when the message appears.

Apply Editing Restrictions

Now you will apply editing exceptions and specify only certain parts of the document that can be edited. You will, however, allow reviewers to add comments anywhere in the document.

9. Choose **Comments** from the drop-down list in the Editing Restrictions section of the task pane.

10. Select the first three paragraphs in the main article and then place a checkmark in the **Everyone** checkbox below the Exceptions (optional) heading in the task pane.

11. Click **Yes, Start Enforcing Protection** and then click **OK** to close the dialog box without setting a password.

12. Deselect the paragraphs and notice that the unprotected area is shaded, making it easy for reviewers to locate.

13. Select any word outside the shaded section and attempt to delete it.

    The deletion doesn't work because only the shaded area can be edited.

14. In the first line of the third shaded paragraph, select *decline in* and replace it with **waning**.

    The change is allowed because it is in the area specified as an exception. Now you will add a comments as comments were specifically permitted in the Restrict Editing task pane.

15. In the fifth paragraph of the article, select *$200 billion*.

16. Choose **Review→Comments→New Comment** 🗨.

    Comments are allowed, not only in the exceptions area, but anywhere in the document.

17. Type this text: **Can anyone verify this dollar amount?**

18. Click **Stop Protection**.

19. Select the shaded paragraphs; remove the checkmark from the **Everyone** checkbox in the task pane and then close the task pane.

20. Right-click the comment in the markup area and choose **Delete Comment**.

Set a Document Password and Mark a Document as Final

21. Choose **File→Info→Protect Document→Encrypt with Password**.

22. Type **pass** in the Encrypt Document dialog box and click **OK**.

23. Type **pass** in the Confirm Password dialog box, click **OK**, and then save and close the document.

 Depending on the security setting on your computer, you may receive a message asking if you would like to increase the security. Respond by clicking No.

24. Choose **File→Open** and click **W10-R2-BeesRevised** at the top of the Recent Documents list.

25. Type **pass** in the password box and click **OK**.

26. In the Backstage Info screen, choose **Protect Document** again and choose **Mark as Final**; when the message appears, click **OK**.

27. When additional information about this setting appears, click **OK**.

28. Click **Back** ⬅ to return to the document.

    Notice the Marked as Final bar at the top of the screen.

29. Select the first paragraph in the main article and tap Delete .

    The text is not deleted because the document is marked as final.

30. Choose **File→Info→Protect Document→Mark as Final** to turn off the feature.

31. Click **Back** ⬅.

    The Marked as Final bar at the top of the document has disappeared.

Create a Digital Certificate and Add a Digital Signature

Now you will generate a self-created digital certificate so you can apply a digital signature to your document. Remember, a self-created certificate is not verified by an outside agency.

32. Open **File Explorer** 📁 and navigate to the **SELFCERT** application through a path such as C:\Program Files (x86)\Microsoft Office\root\Office16.

 Note! *You may need to seek assistance to determine the correct file path for this application on your computer. And note that you may not have user permission to create a digital certificate on computers that are for general use by multiple people.*

33. Scroll to locate the **SELFCERT** application. 📜 SELFCERT.EXE

34. Double-click the file; when the Create Digital Certification dialog box opens, type **Charles Eng** in Your Certificate's Name field and click **OK**.

35. When the message appears indicating the certificate was successfully created, click **OK** and then close the File Explorer window.

36. Position the insertion point at the end of the document and choose **Insert→Text→ Signature Line** 📝.

37. Follow these guidelines to complete the information in the dialog box:
    - Suggested Signer: **Charles Eng**
    - Suggested Signer's Title: **Project Manager**
    - Suggested Signer's E-mail Address: **CharlesEng@Kids.com**.
    - Click **OK** to complete the setup.

38. Right-click the signature line and choose **Sign**; type **Charles Eng** next to the X in the Sign dialog box.

39. If the Signing As name at the bottom of the dialog box is not Charles Eng, follow these steps:
    - Click the **Change** button, choose **Charles Eng**, and click **OK** to close the dialog box.

      A message appears indicating the certificate cannot be verified because a self-created certificate is not verified by an outside agency.
    - Click **Yes** to use the certificate.

40. Click the **Sign** button to close the Sign dialog box; click **Yes** to acknowledge that the certificate cannot be verified.

41. Click **OK** when the next message appears.

42. Attempt to delete a word in the document.

The deletion does not work because you cannot edit a signed document.

43. Save and close the document.

REINFORCE YOUR SKILLS: W10-R3

Learn About 4-H

Kids for Change is thinking about partnering with the 4-H organization on a project. One of the members has researched the organization, and the research document will be the basis for discussion in the next monthly meeting. In this exercise, you will prepare a document for sharing by considering compatibility issues and controlling access to the document. Finally, you will apply a digital signature to the document.

1. Open **W10-R3-4H** from your **Word Chapter 10** folder and save it as **W10-R3-4HRevised**.

Notice the [Compatibility Mode] *term in the title bar. Next you will convert this Word 2003 document to a Word 2016 document.*

2. Choose **File→Info→Convert**.

3. When the message appears indicating the conversion may cause changes, click **OK**.

The term [Compatibility Mode] *no longer appears in the title bar. Now you will work with the Document Inspector.*

4. Choose **File→Info** and notice that names appear in the Related People area of the Properties panel.

5. In the Info screen, choose **Check for Issues→Inspect Document**.

6. When the message to save changes appears, click **Yes**.

7. When the Document Inspector opens, leave all checkboxes checked and then click **Inspect** and review the results.

The inspector found properties and personal information in the document.

8. Click **Remove All** and then close the Document Inspector.

9. Choose **File→Info** and notice that the names have been removed in the Related People area of the Properties pane.

Restrict Editing and Apply Editing Exceptions

10. In the Backstage Info screen, choose **Protect Document→Restrict Editing**.

11. If necessary, check the checkbox below the Editing Restrictions heading in the task pane and choose **Tracked Changes** from the drop-down list.

12. Click **Yes, Start Enforcing Protection** and then click **OK** to close the dialog box without setting a password.

13. In the first paragraph below the *About 4-H* heading, position the insertion point in front of *universities*, type **colleges and**, and tap Spacebar.

The changes are marked with Tracked Changes because that was chosen in the Restrict Editing task pane.

14. Click **Stop Protection** and then right-click the tracked change and choose **Accept Insertion**.

15. Choose **No Changes (Read Only)** from the drop-down list in the Editing Restrictions section of the task pane.

16. Select the three paragraphs below the *Cooperative Extension System* heading on page 1 and then check the **Everyone** checkbox in the task pane.

17. Click **Yes, Start Enforcing Protection** and click **OK** to bypass setting a password.

18. Click in the document to deselect the text and notice that the exceptions text is shaded.

19. If necessary, display formatting marks.

20. Position the insertion point next to the paragraph symbol at the end of the third line in the second paragraph.

21. Tap ⌞Delete⌟ twice to combine the paragraphs and then tap ⌞Spacebar⌟.

22. Click **Stop Protection**, select the shaded paragraphs, and then remove the checkmark from the **Everyone** checkbox.

23. Close the Restrict Editing task pane.

Mark the Document as Final

24. Choose **File→Info→Protect Document→Mark as Final**.

25. When a message appears indicating that the document will be marked as final and saved, click **OK**.

26. When the message appears with additional information about this setting, click **OK**.

27. Click **Back** ⊙ to return to the document and notice the Marked as Final bar at the top of the screen.

28. Close the document.

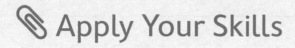

Apply Your Skills

APPLY YOUR SKILLS: W10-A1

Plan a Tour of Mexico City

Universal Corporate Events is planning a tour of Mexico City for a client. The initial research is complete, and now it's time for colleagues to review the article. In this exercise, you will work with compatibility issues, convert a document to different formats, and work with document properties and the Document Inspector.

1. Open **W10-A1-MexCity** from your **Word Chapter 10** folder and save it as **W10-A1-MexCityRevised**.

2. Position the insertion point at the end of the document.

3. Attempt to insert a SmartArt graphic and then use the **Convert** command in Backstage view to convert the document to a **Word 2016 format**.

   Notice that [Compatibility Mode] *does not appear in the title bar.*

4. Open the **SmartArt Graphic** dialog box, choose the **List** category, and then choose **Vertical Box List** (second graphic in the second row).

5. Open the **Type Your Text Here** pane and add this text at the bullet points:
   - **History**
   - **Economy**
   - **Climate**

6. Close the text pane and then resize the graphic to about half its original size.

7. Use the **Save As** command and navigate to your **Word Chapter 10** folder.

8. Choose **Word 97-2003 Document (*.doc)** from the Save as Type list and then click **Save**.

   When the Compatibility Checker opens, notice that the SmartArt graphic will be converted to an object that can't be edited. You may want to edit the object in the future, so you will prevent the conversion.

9. Click **Cancel**.

   Next, you will work with document properties and the Document Inspector.

10. Go to Backstage view and notice the names in the Related People area in the Properties panel.

11. Use the **Document Inspector** to inspect all categories listed in the dialog box.

12. Remove all document properties and personal information and then close the dialog box.

13. Go to Backstage view and notice that no names appear in the Related People area of the Properties panel.

14. Save and close the file.

Organize a San Francisco Tour

Universal Corporate Events is adding San Francisco to its West Coast tour options. A Universal Corporate Events rep has done some research, and now some other reps who are familiar with San Francisco will review the document. In this exercise, you will use features for securing the document so accidental changes are not made.

1. Open **W10-A2-SanFran** from your **Word Chapter 10** folder and save it as **W10-A2-SanFranRevised**.

2. Open the **Restrict Editing** task pane and restrict editing to **Tracked Changes**.

3. Enforce protection, using **pass** as the password.

   Notice the message in the task pane indicating that all changes will be tracked.

4. Make the following edits:
   - In the fourth line of the first paragraph of the main article, delete *road*.
   - Replace *Within* at the beginning of the second paragraph with **In**.
   - In the second line of the same paragraph, delete the comment in parentheses.

5. Stop protection, enter your password, and accept the changes you made.

   Now you will use formatting restrictions.

6. Apply formatting restrictions that limit formatting to the use of the **Heading 1** style; do not allow other styles to be removed.

7. Start enforcing protection and bypass using a password.

8. Display the available styles and apply the **Heading 1** style to the *Landmarks* and *Neighborhoods* headings.

9. Stop protection and then accept the formatting changes.

   Now you will apply an editing exception.

10. Restrict editing to **Comments** and then select the *Chinatown* paragraph (starts at the bottom of page 1).

11. Check the **Everyone** checkbox to make the paragraph editable by all reviewers.

12. Start enforcing protection and bypass adding a password.

13. Make the following edits:
    - In the first sentence of the *Chinatown* paragraph, delete the phrase *part tourist trap, part*.
    - Select the *Landmarks* heading on page 1 and add this comment:
      A trip to Muir Woods to see giant redwoods is a great side trip.

14. Stop protection, select the *Chinatown* paragraph, and remove the checkmark from the **Everyone** checkbox.

Create a Digital Certificate and Add a Signature

15. Open **File Explorer** and navigate to the **SELFCERT** application.

16. Double-click **SELFCERT** and then type **Ella Mae Chang** in the field at the bottom of the Create Digital Certificate dialog box.

17. Close the **File Explorer** window.

18. Position the insertion point at the end of the document and tap ⌈Enter⌉ twice.

19. Use the **Signature Line** command to open the Signature Setup dialog box.

20. Follow these guidelines to enter the information in the dialog box:
    - Suggested Signer: **Ella Mae Chang**
    - Suggested Signer's Title: **Project Manager**
    - Suggested Signer's E-mail Address: **EllaMae@uce.com**

21. Add **Ella Mae Chang** to the signature line.

    Remember, you may need to change the Signing As name.

22. Attempt to delete a word in the document.

    The deletion is not permitted because a signed document cannot be modified.

23. Delete the signature line in the document.

    Now you will add an invisible signature.

24. Use the **Info** screen in Backstage view to add a digital signature.

25. In the Sign dialog box, choose **Created This Document** from the Commitment Type list.

26. In the **Purpose for Signing This Document** field, type **San Francisco Itinerary**.

27. Click **Yes** to use the certificate; when the message appears indicating the signature has been saved, click **OK**.

28. Close the file.

APPLY YOUR SKILLS: W10-A3

Prepare a Cape Town Itinerary

A Universal Corporate Events rep has conducted some research for a Cape Town travel itinerary. Now some colleagues will review the document. In this exercise, you will prepare the document for sharing. You will consider compatibility issues, apply editing restrictions and exceptions, and add a digital signature.

1. Open **W10-A3-CapeTown** from your **Word Chapter 10** folder and save it as **W10-A3-CapeTownRevised**.

2. Choose **Design→Document Formatting ›Themes**.

    This feature is not available in a Word 2003 document. Now you will convert the document to the Word 2016 format.

3. Use the **Convert** command to convert the document to the Word 2016 format.

4. Choose **Design→Document Formatting** and notice that the Themes feature is now available.

    Now you will apply editing and formatting restrictions and formatting exceptions.

5. Apply the **Tracked Changes** editing restrictions, but don't add a password.

6. Make these edits:
    - In the first line of the first paragraph in the main article, replace *neighborhood* with **community**.
    - At the end of the same line, replace *inhabited* with **occupied**.

7. Stop protection and then accept the editing changes.

8. Apply formatting restrictions that limit formatting to the **Heading 1** and **Title** styles; don't allow any other formatting styles in the document to be removed.

9. Enforce protection, but don't set a password.

10. Display the available styles, apply the **Heading 1** style to the *What to See in Cape Town* heading, and then close the Styles task pane.

11. Stop protection and accept the formatting change you made.

    Now you will apply editing exceptions to specify an area of the document where reviewers can freely edit.

12. Restrict editing to **Comments**, select the *Kirstenbosch Botanical Gardens* paragraph at the bottom of page 1, and then check the **Everyone** checkbox.

13. Enforce protection and bypass setting a password.

14. In the fourth line of the editable paragraph, right-click *diverse*, slide the mouse pointer to **Synonyms**, and choose **varied**.

15. Select *Bo-Kaap* at the beginning of the article and add this comment: **I think we should definitely include this in the tour**.

16. Stop protection.

17. Select the exceptions paragraph, remove the checkmark from the **Everyone** checkbox, and then close the task pane.

Add a Digital Signature

18. Open **File Explorer** and navigate to the **SELFCERT** application.

19. Double-click **SELFCERT** and enter **Marty Zane** at the bottom of the Create Digital Certificate dialog box; close the **File Explorer**.

20. Position the insertion point at the end of the document.

21. Set up the signature line with the following information:
    - Suggested Signer: **Marty Zane**
    - Suggested Signer's Title: **Project Manager**
    - Suggested Signer's E-mail Address: **MartyZane@uce.com**

22. Sign the signature line by entering **Marty Zane** next to the X in the Sign dialog box.

23. If necessary, change the Signing As name.

24. Close the document and exit Word.

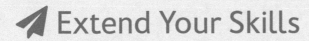# Extend Your Skills

These exercises challenge you to think critically and apply your new skills. You will be evaluated on your ability to follow directions, completeness, creativity, and the use of proper grammar and mechanics. Save files to your chapter folder. Submit assignments as directed.

W10-E1 That's the Way I See It

As the owner of a small business, you are considering adding a new product to your line. Decide on the type of business you are in and what the new product will be. Conduct online research of the new product.

Create a short introduction (3–5 sentences) describing why you think the new product will enhance your line. Copy content of one to two pages about the product, citing your sources. Include at least two headings. Save the file in Word 97-2003 Document (**.doc*) format as **W10-E1-NewProd**.

Convert the file to the current format. Insert a SmartArt graphic from the List category and list three benefits of your new product. Restrict formatting to Heading 1 and Heading 2 styles and then apply heading styles to all of the headings. Restrict editing to Comments. Select one paragraph and make it exception text that all reviewers may freely edit. Add a comment to text that is not part of the exception text.

W10-E2 Be Your Own Boss

As a member of the marketing team at Blue Jean Landscaping, you are researching online marketing articles specifically targeted to the landscaping business. After researching several articles, decide which marketing approach you will use and write a short introduction (5–6 sentences) describing the benefits of your chosen approach.

Copy the article as the basis for your research document, citing your source. Save the document as **W10-E2-Market**. Because you will be distributing this document to current and potential customers, you want to check it for personal information. Examine the document properties to determine whether your name is visible in the Properties panel. Use the Document Inspector to remove all personal information. Set a document password (**pass**). Finally, create a digital certificate in your name and apply a visible digital signature to the end of the document and sign it.

W10-E3 Demonstrate Proficiency

The owner of Stormy BBQ is considering expanding the business to include a BBQ food truck. Conduct online research regarding how to start a food truck business. Create a one- to two-page report, copying information from the Internet and citing your sources. Write a short introduction (four to five sentences) summarizing why you think a food truck is a good or bad addition to the business. Save the document as **W10-E3-FoodTruck**.

Because you will distribute this document for the Stormy BBQ marketing staff to review, you will prepare it for sharing. Examine your document's properties and use the Document Inspector to remove all personal information. Apply editing restrictions, making it read-only. Enforce protection and assign the password (**pass**). Select a paragraph in the document and apply the exception that makes the paragraph available to all reviewers to edit. Finally, create a digital certificate in your name and apply an invisible digital signature to the document.

11 | Personalizing Word

As a Word user, you can increase productivity by customizing the application to work the way you want it to work. You can modify Word options and document properties to meet your needs. You can also automate repetitive tasks by recording macros and adapting AutoCorrect to automatically insert text that you use frequently. In this chapter, you will work with Word options, AutoCorrect, document properties, and macros to enhance the way you work.

LEARNING OBJECTIVES

▸ Customize Word options

▸ Use AutoCorrect to insert customized text

▸ Modify document properties

▸ Create and run macros

📁 Project: Setting Up Word to Work the Way You Do

You have been working with Raritan Clinic East for several months. By examining the types of documents you have created during this time, you have some ideas for setting up Word to make it more efficient. You have learned that most documents are saved in folders in a specific location, and you want to set the default directory to access your main folder. You plan to pin documents you use all the time to the Recent Documents list so they are always at the top of the list, and you have discovered that using document properties can be helpful in searching for files located in a large group of files. You have also identified tasks that you perform repeatedly and terms that you type over and over that you will automate.

Setting Word Options

The Word Options dialog box contains numerous options that enable you to control the way Word acts. In the Proofing category, you can set up your own AutoCorrect terms to print. In the Save category, you can change the AutoRecover time interval and identify the default folder you want to use to store files. You can use the Advanced category to set the number of documents that appear in the Recent Documents list.

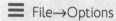 File→Options

Customizing AutoCorrect

In addition to correcting errors, AutoCorrect lets you automatically insert customized text and special characters. It's also useful for replacing abbreviations with full phrases. For example, you could set up AutoCorrect to insert the name of your company whenever you type an abbreviation for it. And you can delete entries that come with Word that may interfere with your writing; however, this is not recommended when working on public or shared computers, as in improving your own productivity, you may inadvertently complicate that of others.

 View the video "An Overview of the AutoCorrect Dialog Box."

 View the video "AutoCorrect Exceptions."

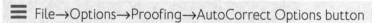 File→Options→Proofing→AutoCorrect Options button

DEVELOP YOUR SKILLS: W11-D1

In this exercise, you will create a custom AutoCorrect entry. You type Raritan Clinic East *over and over in your work, so it's an ideal candidate for an AutoCorrect shortcut.*

1. Start Word, open **W11-D1-DraftProc** from your **Word Chapter 11** folder, and save it as **W11-D1-DraftProcRevised**.

2. Choose **File→Options**, click the **Proofing** category in the left panel, and then click the **AutoCorrect Options** button to open the AutoCorrect dialog box.

3. Follow these steps to create an AutoCorrect shortcut:

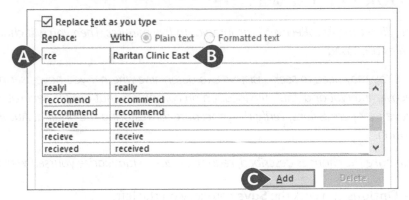

Ⓐ Type **rce** in the Replace field.

Ⓑ Type **Raritan Clinic East** in the With field.

Ⓒ Click **Add**.

4. Click **OK** twice.

5. Press ⎡Ctrl⎤+⎡End⎤ to move to the end of the document and then scroll to the top of the page.

6. In the first line of the first paragraph, position the insertion point in front of the word *share* and type **at** ⎡Spacebar⎤ **rce** ⎡Spacebar⎤.

7. In the first line of the second paragraph, delete *the Clinic*, type **rce** ⎡Spacebar⎤, and correct any spacing if necessary.

   Now you will delete the AutoCorrect term so that the next person who uses your computer will have the same experience.

8. Choose **File→Options**, click the **Proofing** category in the left panel, and then click the **AutoCorrect Options** button to open the AutoCorrect dialog box.

9. Type **rce** in the Replace field to scroll the list to that term.

10. Click **Delete** and then click **OK** twice.

11. Save the file.

Changing the AutoRecover Interval and Default File Location

If you are concerned about power failures or are working on an important document, you may wish to reduce the amount of time between automatic saves. Your documents are saved every ten minutes by default.

When Word and other Office programs are installed on a computer, default file locations are set up. The default save location is your OneDrive. If you want to save to a local computer, you can change the save location and reduce the time it takes to navigate to that location. The new save location applies to new, unsaved documents. A document that was previously saved will default to the folder in which it was originally saved.

☰ File→Options→Save→Save AutoRecover Information Every *x* Minutes

☰ File→Options→Save→Default Local File Location

 You may not have user permissions to change the AutoRecover interval or the default file location on a public or shared computer.

WORD

In this exercise, you will set the AutoRecover time interval to five minutes. Then you will change the default file location where files are saved.

Before You Begin: *You may need to seek assistance to determine whether you have user permission to change the AutoRecover interval or default file location on computers that are for general use by multiple people. If you do have user permissions, verify the procedure for restoring the original AutoRecover interval and default file location.*

If you are unable to make the changes described, read the steps to familiarize yourself with the process.

1. Choose **File→Options** and click the **Save** category on the left.

 As you make changes, first make a note of the current settings so you can reset them to the original state later in this chapter.

2. Follow these steps to change the AutoRecover interval:

  Ⓐ Locate the **Save Documents** section at the top of the dialog box.

  Ⓑ Write down the current AutoRecover interval so you can reset it later.

  Ⓒ Use the spin box controls to set the time to **5** minutes.

  Your documents will now automatically save every five minutes.

3. In the same section of the dialog box, check the **Save to Computer by Default** checkbox.

4. To specify a particular folder, click the **Browse** button to the right of the Default Local File Location field.

5. In the Modify Location dialog box, scroll in the left column to **Desktop** and then click **OK** twice.

   The Desktop is now your default save location. Next you will test the change.

6. Press Ctrl + N to start a new, blank document.

7. Choose **File→Save As** and notice that *This PC* is highlighted rather than OneDrive.

8. Click the **Browse** button at the bottom of the Save As panel on the left.

   The Save As dialog box opens with the Desktop as the target save location.

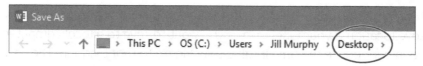

9. Click **Cancel** to close the Save As dialog box and then click **Close** in the left panel to close the blank document.

   If you made changes in this exercise, you will reset them to their original state later in this chapter.

Modifying the Recent Document List

The Open screen in Backstage view displays a list of recent documents accessed on the computer. By default, the Recent Documents list shows the last twenty-five documents opened on the computer. When a document appears in this list, you can open it by clicking the document name. You can turn off the feature so that no documents are listed or change the number of documents shown in the list.

If you move a document to a different folder using an application such as Windows Explorer, the link to the document in the Recent Documents list is broken. After moving a document, you need to re-navigate to the new location to open the file.

Changing the Number of Files in the Recent Documents List

When you work with only a few documents, the documents you need will always appear in the Recent Documents list. If you find that you primarily work with the last few documents before moving on to new documents, you may want to change the number of documents shown to reduce the number of documents you have to select from. Setting the number of documents to display in the list is controlled by settings in the Word Options dialog box. Settings range from zero to fifty.

 View the video "Set the Number of Recent Documents to Display."

≡ File→Options→Advanced→Show This Number of Recent Documents

Pinning a File to the Recent Documents List

Periodically, you may find yourself modifying a document over an extended period of time. To ensure that the document always appears in the Recent Documents list, you can pin it to the list. Pinned documents appear at the top of the list and remain in the list regardless of how many additional documents you access.

 View the video "How to Pin a File to the Recent Documents List."

Clearing the List of Recently Used Documents

Workers who perform tasks associated with specific projects might enjoy the ability to clear all unpinned items from the Recent Documents list, thus displaying only the documents they purposely pinned. In addition, if you are using a computer you share with others, you may want to clear the list so others won't have easy access the documents you used, especially if you work with confidential documents.

 View the video "Setting the Recently Used List to Zero."

 You may not have user permissions to change the Recent documents list on a public or shared computer.

In this exercise, you will change the number of documents that appear in the Recent Documents list. You will also pin a document to the list.

Before You Begin: *You may need to seek assistance to determine whether you have user permission to change the Recent Documents list. If you do have user permissions, verify the procedure for restoring the original Recent Document settings.*

If you are unable to make the changes described, read the steps to familiarize yourself with the process.

1. Choose **File→Options** and then follow these steps to change the number of documents shown in the Recent Documents list:

   Ⓐ Choose the **Advanced** category.

   Ⓑ Scroll down to the **Display** options.

   Ⓒ Write down the value in this box and then change the number of documents to **10**.

2. Click **OK** and then choose **File→Open** and note that a maximum of ten documents appear in the Recent Documents list. (Your list may have fewer than ten documents.)

3. Right-click any document in the list and notice (but don't click) the Clear Unpinned Documents command.

   Clicking this would clear all unpinned documents from the list.

4. Tap [Esc] to close the menu.

   Now you will pin, and then unpin, a document in the list.

5. Right-click any document in the list and choose **Pin to List**.

   The document moves to the Pinned category at the top of the list and a pushpin icon appears on the right.

6. Click the pushpin icon of the document you just pinned to unpin it.

7. Click **Back** Ⓔ to return to the document window.

Restoring Default Settings

Setting custom options for the way you work is a great practice for a computer that is assigned to you. However, when you are working on a computer you share with others, it is generally a good idea to restore the default settings you have changed.

DEVELOP YOUR SKILLS: W11-D4

In this exercise, you will restore the default settings in the Word Options dialog box. By restoring the options to their original state, you also will review the features just covered.

Before You Begin: *Retrieve the default settings you wrote down as you modified options earlier.*

1. Choose **File→Options** and then follow these steps to restore your AutoRecover interval:

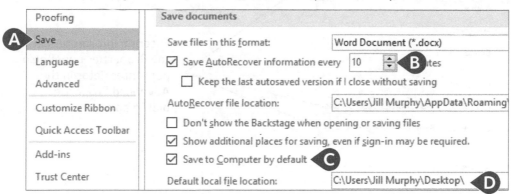

Ⓐ Choose the **Save** category.

Ⓑ Reset the AutoRecover duration to **10**, or enter the setting you wrote down when you made the change in this field.

Ⓒ Uncheck this box if it was previously unchecked.

Ⓓ Enter the file location path you wrote down earlier.

Leave the dialog box open.

2. Follow these steps to restore your Recent Documents list:

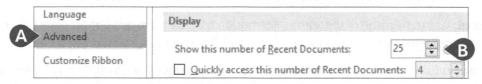

Ⓐ Choose the **Advanced** category.

Ⓑ In the Display section, reset the number of recent documents to **25**, or enter the original setting you wrote down when you made the change in this field.

3. Click **OK**.

Document Properties

Each time you create a new document, properties information is pulled from options set on your computer as well as information detected about the document. Properties information appears in the Properties panel of the Info screen in Backstage view. Information includes such items as the size of the file, the date on which it was created/modified, and the author's name. The Advanced Properties feature contains more data about your document, and this is where you can create custom properties.

The Advanced Properties dialog box contains the widest array of properties.

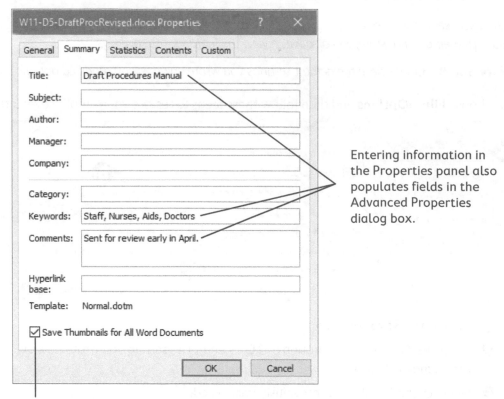

Entering information in the Properties panel also populates fields in the Advanced Properties dialog box.

Checking the "Thumbnails" checkbox fills in the Contents tab with headings (Heading 1 through Heading 3 styles) that appear in the document.

Following are descriptions of the tabs in the Advanced Properties dialog box:

▸ **General:** Contains some of the same information as the Properties panel in Backstage view, as well as additional information, including location and file attributes, such as Read Only

▸ **Summary:** Contains the same text boxes as the Properties panel, including Title, Keywords (Tags), and Comments; checking the Save Thumbnails for All Word Documents checkbox fills in the Contents tab with headings (Heading 1 through Heading 3 styles) that appear in the document

▸ **Statistics:** Contains many of the same statistics as the Properties panel in Backstage view as well as additional fields, such as Paragraphs, Lines, and Characters

▸ **Contents:** Contains the document headings (Heading 1 through Heading 3 styles) when the Save Thumbnails for All Word Documents checkbox is checked on the Summary tab

▸ **Custom:** Allows you to define additional fields, which can be useful when searching for a document in a large group of documents

---

DEVELOP YOUR SKILLS: W11-D5

In this exercise, you will add comments and keywords (tags) to the procedures manual.

1. Save your file as **W11-D5-DraftProcRevised**.
2. Choose **File→Info** and review the document properties in the Properties panel on the right side of the screen.

3. Enter the information shown in the **Title**, **Tags**, and **Comments** fields and then enter your name in the **Author** field.

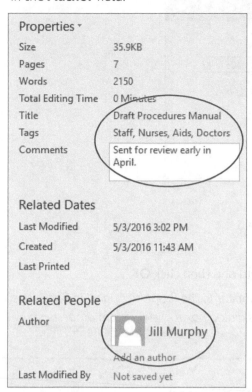

4. Click the **Properties** heading/button at the top of the Properties panel and then click **Advanced Properties**.

   Notice that the properties you entered in the Properties panel are replicated in the Summary tab.

5. Click **OK** and then click **Back** ⬅ to return to the document.

6. Save the file.

Creating a Custom Property

Though the available properties are sufficient for most documents, there may be times when you want to store additional properties. When there is no existing property to meet your needs, you can create a custom property and define the type of data you plan to place in the field, including Text, Date, and Number. A list of suggested names is provided for custom fields, but you can also define your own property names. For example, if you want to include a due date for a document, you can create a new Due Date property and assign Date as the data type. These custom properties don't appear in the Properties panel in the Backstage Info view. To view them, you need to refer to the Custom tab of the Advanced Properties dialog box.

DEVELOP YOUR SKILLS: W11-D6

In this exercise, you will create a custom property for the procedures manual to hold the due date for the final version of the document.

1. Save your file as **W11-D6-DraftProcRevised**.

2. Choose **File→Info**, click **Properties** at the top of the Properties panel, and choose **Advanced Properties**.

3. Follow these steps to create a new custom property:

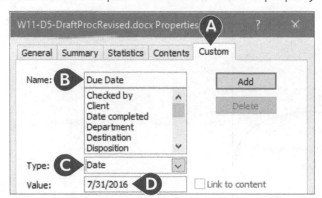

Ⓐ Click the **Custom** tab.

Ⓑ Type **Due Date** in the Name field.

Ⓒ Select **Date** from the Type list.

Ⓓ Type **7/31/2016** in the Value field and then click **OK**.

Remember, custom properties do not appear in the Properties panel in Backstage view. Refer to the Custom tab in the Advanced Properties dialog box to view custom properties.

4. Save and close the document.

Automating Tasks with Macros

Macros are useful for automating routine tasks, especially those that involve many steps. You can record a series of steps using the macro recorder, and then play them back automatically when needed. For example, you may need to switch to a color printer frequently. You can record the steps of the process in a macro, and, when it's time to switch printers, the macro can quickly perform the steps. Whenever you find yourself doing the same thing over and over, you have a candidate for a macro.

☰ View→Macros→Macros

Assign Macros to a Toolbar or a Keyboard Shortcut

If you intend to use a macro frequently, you can assign it to a keyboard shortcut or a button on the Quick Access toolbar for easy access. This is not required, though. You can always run a macro directly from the Macros dialog box.

Store Macros

Macros can be stored in documents or templates, including the Normal.dotm template, which is the default. The *m* in the *.dotm* file extension indicates the template can contain macros. Macros stored there are available to all documents on the system.

Macro names cannot contain spaces. ———

You can assign a macro to run from a Quick Access toolbar button or a keyboard shortcut. ———

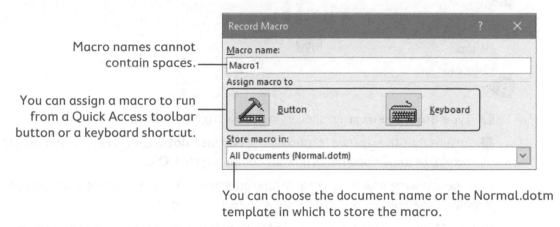

You can choose the document name or the Normal.dotm template in which to store the macro.

Recording Limitations

Certain mouse motions such as scrolling, selecting options from drop-down lists, and resizing windows cannot be recorded in macros. You may also find that certain commands are grayed out on the Ribbon or in the drop-down list during the macro recording. You can overcome these limitations by choosing alternative techniques. For example, if selecting an item from a drop-down list doesn't record in a macro, display the dialog box containing the feature and make the selection there. Instead of scrolling in a document, use arrow keys to position the insertion point (keystrokes are recorded). Likewise, when selecting text with the mouse fails to record, try [Shift] plus arrow keys or other keyboard shortcuts.

When you record a macro and change settings in a dialog box using arrow keys, the change normally sticks until you exit Word; this means the dialog box doesn't reset to its default state. As a result, running the macro again in the same session may change the setting to the *next* option in the dialog box.

 When necessary, reset the dialog box to the default state as part of the macro.

DEVELOP YOUR SKILLS: W11-D7

In this exercise, you will record a macro that sets up the orientation, margins, and page size for a survey form. The macro will also insert and format text.

1. Create a new, blank document.
2. Choose **View→Macros→Macros** ▦ **menu button** ▼→**Record Macro**.

3. Follow these steps to name the macro and begin the recording process:

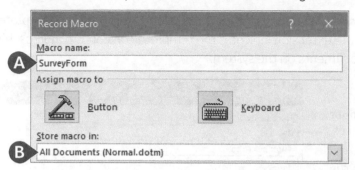

Ⓐ Type **SurveyForm** (no spaces) in the Macro Name field.

Ⓑ Ensure that the storage location is the **Normal.dotm** template, which makes the macro available to all documents on your computer; click **OK**.

The mouse pointer now has a cassette tape attached to it, indicating that your steps are being recorded. Now you will perform the steps you wish to record.

4. Choose **Home→Styles** and click the **No Spacing** style in the Quick Styles gallery.

This sets line spacing at 1.0 and removes the after-paragraph spacing.

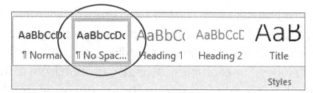

5. Choose **Home→Font→Bold** B .

6. Type **Raritan Clinic East Pediatric Diagnostic Specialties**.

7. Choose **Layout→Page Setup→Orientation** 📄 and then choose **Landscape**.

8. Choose **Layout→Page Setup→Margins** ▦ and then choose **Custom Margins** at the bottom of the gallery.

9. Set the top and bottom margins to **0.4"** and the left and right margins to **0.5"**.

10. Click the **Paper** tab at the top of the dialog box and set the width to **7"** and the height to **5"**.

11. Click **OK** to apply the settings.

Stop Recording and Run the Macro

12. Choose **View→Macros→Macros** 📑 **menu button** ▼→**Stop Recording**.

The macro is now ready for playback.

13. Close the document without saving it and then create a new, blank document.

14. Choose **View→Macros→Macros** 📑.

15. Follow these steps to run the macro:

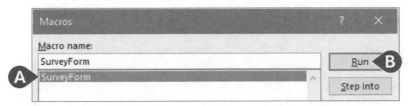

A Choose your **SurveyForm** macro.

B Click **Run**.

Your macro should create a copy of your survey form. The heading line is selected. You can click to deselect. If you made an error in the macro, you could delete the incorrect macro and record it again. Later in the chapter, you will learn to make minor edits in the VBA Editor.

16. Close the document without saving it and then create a new, blank document.

Editing Macros with the VBA Editor

Visual Basic for Applications (VBA) is a macro programming language that runs in Office 2016 applications. When you record a macro, you are creating a Visual Basic module containing program instructions that execute when you run the macro. This topic provides a brief introduction to Visual Basic, but a complete discussion is beyond the scope of this course.

You can edit a macro by displaying the Visual Basic module and modifying the code. The editor has its own menus, toolbars, and commands, which allow you to develop, edit, and test Visual Basic applications.

DEVELOP YOUR SKILLS: W11-D8

In this exercise, you will open the Visual Basic editor and revise your macro. Then you will run the modified macro.

1. Choose **View→Macros→Macros** 🔲.

2. Follow these steps to begin the editing process:

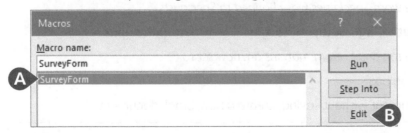

A Choose your **SurveyForm** macro.

B Click **Edit**.

3. Follow these steps to modify the code:

```
Al Normal  NewMacros (Code)

(General)

    Sub SurveyForm()
    '
    ' SurveyForm Macro
    '
    '
        Selection.Style = ActiveDocument.Styles("No Spacing")
        Selection.Font.Bold = wdToggle
        Selection.TypeText Text:= _
            "Raritan Clinic East Pediatric Diagnostic Specialties"   ◀ Ⓐ
        If Selection.PageSetup.Orientation = wdOrientPortrait Then
            Selection.PageSetup.Orientation = wdOrientLandscape
        Else
            Selection.PageSetup.Orientation = wdOrientPortrait
        End If
        Selection.WholeStory
        With ActiveDocument.Styles(wdStyleNormal).Font
            If .NameFarEast = .NameAscii Then
                .NameAscii = ""
            End If
            .NameFarEast = ""
        End With
        With ActiveDocument.PageSetup
            .LineNumbering.Active = False
            .Orientation = wdOrientLandscape
            .TopMargin = InchesToPoints(0.4)           Ⓑ
            .BottomMargin = InchesToPoints(0.4)
            .LeftMargin = InchesToPoints(0.5)
            .RightMargin = InchesToPoints(0.5)
            .Gutter = InchesToPoints(0)
```

Ⓐ Change the word *Specialties* to **Specialists**.

Ⓑ Change the TopMargin and BottomMargin settings from 0.4 to **0.5**.

4. Choose **File→Close and Return to Microsoft Word**.

The changes are saved automatically. Now you will test the edited macro.

5. Choose **View→Macros→Macros** 🖽, choose **SurveyForm** in the Macro Name list, and then click **Run**.

Notice that the word Specialties was changed to Specialists.

6. Choose **Layout→Page Setup→Margins** 🖽**→Custom Margins**.

Notice that the top and bottom margins are now set to 0.5.

7. Close the dialog box.

8. Close the document without saving; create a new, blank document.

Running Macros from the Quick Access Toolbar

When you create a macro to automate repetitive tasks, you are trying to increase efficiency. To make macros run more efficiently, you can assign them to a button on the Quick Access toolbar or to a shortcut keystroke. By taking advantage of these time-saving tools, you alleviate the tedious nature of displaying the Macros dialog box and selecting the macro each time you want to run it.

You can assign a toolbar button or keyboard shortcut to a macro as you record it. In addition, you can assign a toolbar button to an existing macro using the Quick Access toolbar commands in the Word Options dialog box. Word offers numerous button images that you can choose to help keep your macro buttons straight.

 View the video "Assign a Macro to the Quick Access Toolbar."

DEVELOP YOUR SKILLS: W11-D9

In this exercise, you will assign the SurveyForm macro to a Quick Access toolbar button.

1. Choose **File→Options** and then click the **Quick Access Toolbar** category.

2. Follow these steps to assign a macro button to the Quick Access toolbar:

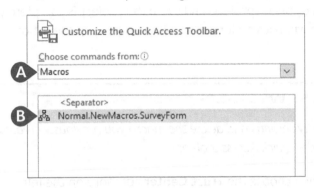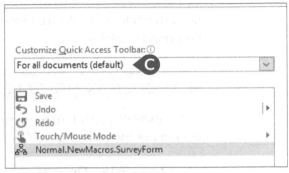

Ⓐ Choose **Macros** here.

Ⓑ Select the **SurveyForm** macro.

Ⓒ Ensure that **For All Documents (Default)** appears here.

3. Click the **Add** button in the middle of the dialog box to add the macro to the Quick Access Toolbar list and then click **OK**.

   Notice that a new button appears on the Quick Access toolbar.

4. Hover the mouse pointer over the button to see the button name in a ToolTip; click the button to run the macro.

   Leave the document open.

Macro Security

Macro attacks were more prevalent in earlier versions of Microsoft Office. Added security features in recent versions have caused virus creators to pursue other avenues; however, it's always better to be safe than sorry. The Trust Center in the Word Options dialog box contains security settings.

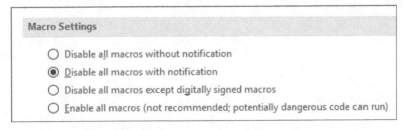

MACRO SETTINGS OPTIONS

Option	What It Does
Disable all macros without notification	Word disables all macros and does not notify users.
Disable all macros with notification	This is the default setting. It gives the user the option to enable or disable a macro.
Disable all macros except digitally signed macros	This option allows users to enable or disable only digitally signed macros.
Enable all macros (not recommended; potentially dangerous code can run)	This option significantly reduces security and could potentially cause serious damage.

Deleting Macros

You may create a macro for use in a special project, and when the project is complete you no longer need the macro. Deleting a macro when it's no longer required helps keep the list of macros from becoming unwieldy.

DEVELOP YOUR SKILLS: W11-D10

In this exercise, you will review security settings and delete the macro you previously created. Finally, you will remove the macro button from the Quick Access toolbar.

1. Choose **File→Options** and then choose the **Trust Center** category on the left.
2. Click the **Trust Center Settings** button and review the Macro Settings options at the top of the dialog box.

   You will not make any changes to security settings.

3. Click **Cancel** twice to close the dialog boxes.

   Now you will delete your macro.

4. Choose **View→Macros→Macros** .
5. Choose the **SurveyForm** macro in the Macro Name list, click **Delete**, click **Yes** to verify the deletion, and then close the dialog box.

   Now you will remove the macro button from the Quick Access toolbar.

6. Right-click the macro button and choose **Remove from Quick Access Toolbar**.
7. Exit Word without saving the document.

Self-Assessment

Check your knowledge of this chapter's key concepts and skills using the Self-Assessment in your ebook or eLab course.

REINFORCE YOUR SKILLS: W11-R1

Streamline Kids for Change Office Procedures

Kids for Change is streamlining its office procedures. Staff members will review various options to determine which changes will help them be more efficient. In this exercise, you will prepare screenshots of the features you would like staff members to consider for personalizing Word.

Before You Begin: *Be prepared to take notes of changes you make to settings so you can reset the options later if necessary.*

1. Start Word, open **W11-R1-WordOptions** from your **Word Chapter 11** folder, and save it as **W11-R1-WordOptionsRevised**.

   First, you will create an AutoCorrect shortcut for a Kids for Change Nature Hikes project.

2. Choose **File→Options→Proofing** and click the **AutoCorrect Options** button.

3. Type **kfcnh** in the Replace field, type **Kids for Change Nature Hikes** in the With field, and click **OK** twice.

4. Position the insertion point at the end of the document; then type **AutoCorrect Shortcut: kfcnh** and tap Enter.

   Now you will work with Save options.

5. Choose **File→Options,** choose the **Save** category, and change the AutoRecover interval to **15** minutes.

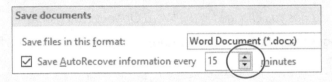

6. Check the **Save to Computer by Default** checkbox.

7. Click the **Browse** button to the right of the Default Local File Location field.

8. In the Modify Location dialog box, navigate to the **Desktop** and click **OK**.

   Now you will take a screenshot of the Word Options dialog box and paste it into your Word Options document.

9. Press Alt + PrtScn to take a screenshot of the dialog box and then click **OK** to close the dialog box.

10. Press Ctrl + V to paste the screenshot and then resize the screenshot to about a third of the original size.

11. Create a new, blank document so you can test the default local file location.

12. Choose **File→Save As** and click **Browse** at the bottom of the left-hand panel.

    Notice that the path at the top of the dialog box leads to the Desktop. The change worked.

13. Click **Cancel** to close the Save As dialog box.

14. Click **Close** in the far-left panel to close the blank document without saving it.

Customize the Recent Documents List

15. Choose **File→Options→Advanced** category.

16. Scroll down to the **Display** options and change the number of recent documents to **8**.

17. Press ⎡Alt⎤+⎡PrtScn⎤ to take a screenshot and click **OK**.

18. Ensure the insertion point is at the end of the document, tap ⎡Enter⎤, and paste the screenshot into your document, resizing the screenshot to about a third of the original size.

19. If necessary, resize the screenshots until they both fit on the first page of the document.

20. Choose **File→Open** and notice that a maximum of eight documents appear in the Recent Documents list.

Now you will pin a document to the Recent Documents list.

21. Hover the mouse pointer over a filename to display the pushpin icon at the right and then click the pushpin to pin the document to the list.

The document will remain in the list until it is unpinned.

22. Right-click the document you just pinned and choose **Unpin from List**.

You can clear all documents, except pinned documents, from the list.

23. Right-click any document in the Recent Documents list and notice (but don't click) the Clear Unpinned Documents command.

24. Tap ⎡Esc⎤ to close the menu.

Now you will restore the settings you changed in the Word Options dialog box.

25. Retrieve the list of changes that you noted earlier and, if necessary, restore the following options to their original settings:

- AutoRecover interval
- Save to Computer by Default checkbox
- Default Local File Location path
- Number of Recent Documents displayed

Create a Custom Property

26. Choose **File→Info**, click the **Properties** button at the top of the Properties panel, and click **Advanced Properties**.

27. Click the **Custom** tab and follow these guidelines to create a custom property:

- Choose **Checked By** from the Name list.
- Leave the data type at **Text**.
- Type **Reviewer Sean Oct 17** in the Value field.

You have requested that each reviewer sign in here so you can easily track who has already reviewed the document and when.

28. Take a screenshot of the dialog box, click **OK**, and then click **Back** ⎡←⎤.

29. Make sure the insertion point is at the end of the document.

30. Tap ⌈Enter⌉ and paste the screenshot in your Word Options document and resize to about a third of its original size.

This screenshot will appear on page 2.

31. Save and close the file.

REINFORCE YOUR SKILLS: W11-R2

Create Kids for Change Carbon Footprint Macro

Kids for Change operates on a tight budget, so it types its own document header information manually. The group is currently working on a carbon footprint project and wants that information to appear in the headers of documents related to the project. Because this is something it will do over and over, it knows it has a good candidate for a macro. In this exercise, you will create and test the macro.

1. Create a new, blank document.

2. Choose **View→Macros→Macros** 📖 **menu button ▾→Record Macro**.

3. Name the macro **Header** and verify that the **Normal** template is chosen in the Store Macro In field.

4. Click **OK** to start recording.

The mouse pointer now has a cassette tape attached to it indicating that your steps are being recorded.

5. Choose **Insert→Header & Footer→Header** 🗋 and then choose **Edit Header** at the bottom of the gallery.

6. Tap ⌈Tab⌉ to position the insertion point in the center of the header and type **Kids for Change**.

You can't double-click in the document body to close the header area. This is one of those mouse movements that the macro recorder can't record.

7. Choose **Header & Footer Tools→Design→Close→Close Header and Footer** ⊗.

8. Choose **View→Macros→Macros menu button ▾→Stop Recording**.

9. Close the document without saving; start a new, blank document.

Now you will run the macro.

10. Choose **View→Macros→Macros**, make sure the Header macro is chosen, and then click **Run** and observe the header.

11. Close the document without saving; start a new, blank document.

Use the VBA Editor to Modify the Macro

12. Choose **View→Macros→Macros**, verify that the **Header** macro is chosen, click **Edit**, and then locate the Kids for Change text.

```
End If
ActiveWindow.ActivePane.View.SeekView = wdSeekCurrentPageHeader
Selection.TypeText Text:=vbTab & "Kids for Change"
ActiveWindow.ActivePane.View.SeekView = wdSeekMainDocument
```

13. Position the insertion point to the right of the word *Change*, tap ⌈Spacebar⌉, and type **Carbon Footprint Project**.

14. Choose **File→Close** and Return to Microsoft Word.

Now you will assign the macro to a keyboard shortcut and run the macro to verify your editing changes.

Assign the Macro to a Keyboard Shortcut

15. Choose **File→Options** and choose the **Customize Ribbon** category.

Notice the Customize button next to Keyboard Shortcuts at the bottom of the left-hand panel.

16. Click **Customize**; scroll down and choose **Macros** from the Categories list on the left.

17. Choose the **Header** macro in the field on the right.

18. Position the insertion point in the **Press New Shortcut Key** field and press Ctrl + 9.

Below the Current Keys field at left, notice that the shortcut you entered is currently unassigned.

19. Click the **Assign** button to assign the shortcut to your macro, click **Close**, and then click **OK**.

Now you will test the macro.

20. Press Ctrl + 9 to run the macro and notice the editing change you made.

Review Macro Security and Delete the Macro

21. Choose **File→Options→Trust Center**, click the **Trust Center Settings** button, and review the Macro Settings at the top of the dialog box.

You will not change any security settings.

22. Click **Cancel** twice to close the dialog boxes.

23. Choose **View→Macros→Macros** 🔲, verify that the **Header** macro is chosen, and then click **Delete**.

24. Click **Yes** to confirm the deletion and then close the Macros dialog box.

25. Save the file as **W11-R2-Header** in your **Word Chapter 11 folder** and then close it.

REINFORCE YOUR SKILLS: W11-R3

Personalize Options and Create a Tutoring Schedule Macro

Kids for Change will participate in an after-school tutoring program. In this exercise, you will personalize Word to work more efficiently and create a macro that generates a table where you can set up the weekly tutoring schedule.

Before You Begin: *Be prepared to take notes of changes you make to settings, so you can reset the options later if necessary.*

1. Open **W11-R3-Tutoring** from your **Word Chapter 11** folder and save it as **W11-R3-TutoringRevised**.

2. Choose **File→Options→Save** and change the AutoRecover interval to **5** minutes.

3. Check the **Save to Computer by Default** checkbox.

4. Click the **Browse** button to the right of the Default Local File Location field, navigate to the **Desktop**, and then click **OK** twice.

Now you will observe the change to the default file location.

5. Start a new, blank document.

Remember, you saved the tutoring file outside of the default location; therefore, if you click Browse, you will access its original storage location. You will use the new, blank document to test the storage location you just set.

6. Choose **File→Save As** and note that *This PC* is highlighted.

7. Click the **Browse** button and notice that the path at the top of the Save As dialog box leads to the Desktop.

8. Click **Cancel** to close the Save As dialog box and then choose **Close** on the left to close the blank document without saving it.

Pin a Document to the Recent Documents List

9. Choose **File→Open**, hover the mouse pointer over a filename, and notice the pushpin icon to its right.

10. Click the pushpin to move the file into the Pinned category at the top of the list.

11. Click the pushpin again to unpin the document and return it to the main list.

Now you will restore the default settings that you noted earlier.

12. Click **Options** on the left and restore the following items to their original settings:
   - AutoRecover interval
   - Save to Computer by Default
   - Default Local File Location

Record and Run a Macro

Now you will create a table macro that Kids for Change can use each week to set up the tutoring schedule.

13. Position the insertion point at the end of the Tutoring document.

14. Choose **View→Macros→Macros** 🔲 **menu button ▼→Record Macro**.

15. Name the macro **TutorTable** and verify that the **Normal** template is chosen in the Store Macro In field.

Now you will assign the macro to a keyboard shortcut.

16. Click the **Keyboard** button.

17. Ensure that Macros appears in the left column and then choose the **TutorTable** macro on the right.

18. Position the insertion point in the **Press New Shortcut Key** field and press [Ctrl]+[8].

Notice that the shortcut is unassigned.

19. Click **Assign** and then click **Close**.

20. Choose **Insert→Tables→Table** 🔲 and drag in the grid to create a **5x7** table.

The insertion point should be in the first table cell. Macro recording limitations do not allow you to drag the mouse pointer to select cells, so you will need to use keystrokes instead.

21. Press [Shift] and tap [→] 5 times to select the first row.

22. Choose **Table Tools→Layout→Merge→Merge Cells** 🔲.

23. Choose **Table Tools→Layout→Alignment→Align Center** 🔲 and type **Weekly Tutoring Schedule**.

24. Enter the remaining text shown, using arrow keys to position the insertion point.

Remember, macro recording limitations don't allow you to position the insertion point with the mouse pointer.

Weekly Tutoring Schedule				
	Max	Allison	Manuel	Margarita
Monday				
Tuesday				
Wednesday				
Thursday				
Friday				

25. Choose **View→Macros→Macros** 🔲 **menu button ▾→Stop Recording**.

Now you will remove the table so you can recreate it with the macro. Nelly is replacing Allison while she is out of town, so you'll make that change to the macro first.

26. Select the table, right-click the table, and choose **Delete Table** from the pop-up menu.

27. Choose **View→Macros→Macros** 🔲, make sure the **TutorTable** macro is chosen, and then click **Edit**.

28. Locate Allison's name. (You may need to enlarge the Visual Basic window—Allison is near the bottom.)

```
End With
Selection.MoveRight Unit:=wdCharacter, Count:=5, Extend:=wdExtend
Selection.Cells.Merge
Selection.SelectCell
Selection.ParagraphFormat.Alignment = wdAlignParagraphCenter
Selection.Cells.VerticalAlignment = wdCellAlignVerticalCenter
Selection.TypeText Text:="Weekly Tutoring ScheduleMax"
Selection.MoveRight Unit:=wdCell
Selection.TypeText Text:="Allison"
```

29. Double-click *Allison* to select it and type **Nelly**.

30. Choose **File→Close** and Return to Microsoft Word.

Now you will run the macro to see your editing changes.

31. Click in the last blank line on the page and then press [Ctrl]+[8] to run the macro.

Notice Nelly's name in the table. Now you will delete the macro.

32. Choose **View→Macros→Macros** 🔲.

33. Make sure the **TutorTable** macro is selected, click **Delete**, and click **Yes** when the message appears confirming the deletion.

34. Close the Macros dialog box and save and close the file.

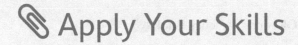 Apply Your Skills

APPLY YOUR SKILLS: W11-A1

Review Office Efficiency

The Universal Corporate Events office manager is reviewing various options to determine whether it is possible to make work more efficient for the company. In this exercise, you will create an AutoCorrect shortcut, change options for saving, and work with document properties.

Before You Begin: *Be prepared to take notes of changes you make to settings, so you can reset the options later if necessary.*

1. Open **W11-A1-Efficiency** from your **Word Chapter 11** folder and save it as **W11-A1-EfficiencyRevised**.

2. Open the **Word Options** dialog box, choose the **Proofing** category, and click the **AutoCorrect Options** button.

   Creating a shortcut for the company name will certainly be a time-saver.

3. Enter **uce** in the Replace field and **Universal Corporate Events** in the With field; click **OK** twice.

4. Position the insertion point at the bottom of the document and type **uce** ⏎Enter to test the shortcut.

5. Open the **Word Options** dialog box; in the **Save** category, change the **AutoRecover** interval to **30** minutes.

6. Check the **Save to Computer by Default** checkbox.

7. Use the **Browse** button to the right of the Default Local File Location and set the path to the **Desktop**.

8. Take a screenshot ([Alt]+[PrtScn]) of the **Word Options** dialog box, paste it at the end of your document, and resize it to about a third of its original size.

9. Create a new, blank document and choose **File→Save As**.

10. Click the **Browse** button to test your default file location (Desktop) and then cancel the dialog box and close the blank document.

    Now you will restore the default settings.

11. Retrieve your list of default settings you wrote down earlier and reset the defaults in the Word Options dialog box.

12. In the Properties panel in Backstage view, type **Efficiency** in the Tags field.

13. Use the **Properties** button to open the **Advanced Properties** dialog box.

14. Follow these guidelines to add a custom property:
    - Property Name: **Checked By**
    - Property Type: **Text**
    - Property Value: **Matt Robinson**

    As staff members review the potential procedural changes, they will enter their names in the Properties dialog box so you can tell when everyone has completed the review.

15. Take a screenshot of the **Custom** tab, click **OK**, and then click **Back** ⬅.

16. Position the insertion point at the end of the document, generate a blank line, and paste the screenshot, resizing it to about a third of its original size.

17. Save and close the file.

APPLY YOUR SKILLS: W11-A2

Create a Las Vegas Macro

Universal Corporate Events is preparing a Las Vegas tour for a corporate client. As agents are communicating via email with the travelers, they will paste the macro text into the email as needed. In this exercise, you will create and edit the macro and run it from the Quick Access toolbar.

1. Open **W11-A2-LasVegasMacro** from your **Word Chapter 11** folder and save it as **W11-A2-LasVegasMacroRevised**.

2. Start a new, blank document and then start the macro recorder.

3. Name the macro **LasVegas**, verify the **Normal** template is chosen, and then click **OK**.

4. Record this text in the blank document:

   Upon arrival at the airport, pick up your bags in the luggage area and then look for a limousine driver with a Silicon Tech Group sign. The driver will take you to the MGM Grand where you will stay during your visit.

5. Stop the macro recorder, tap Enter, and then test your macro to ensure it runs as expected.

   Now you will edit the macro and assign it to a toolbar button.

6. Open the macro editor and locate the word *airport* in the VBA code.

7. Position the insertion point in front of *airport*, type **Las Vegas**, and then tap Spacebar.

8. Close the macro editor and then open the **Word Options** dialog box.

9. Choose the **Quick Access Toolbar** category and choose **Macros** from the commands list.

10. Add your macro to the list on the right and then click the **Modify** button.

11. Choose the envelope button, change the **Display Name** to **Las Vegas**, and click **OK** twice.

12. Tap Enter and then run the macro from the Quick Access toolbar and verify your editing change.

13. Take a screenshot of the document you used to run your macro and then switch to **W11-A2-LasVegasMacroRevised**.

14. Position the insertion point at the bottom of the document and then paste the screenshot.

15. Delete the macro and remove the macro button from the Quick Access toolbar.

16. Save and close the file and close the other document without saving it.

APPLY YOUR SKILLS: W11-A3

Get Ready for the Corporate Trainer

Universal Corporate Events staff will have an opportunity to review some advanced Word features with the corporate trainer. The staff will practice with some of the features and note questions they have for the trainer. In this exercise, you will work with an AutoCorrect shortcut and the Word Options dialog box, and you will create and edit a macro.

Before You Begin: *Be prepared to take notes of changes you make to settings, so you can reset the options later if necessary.*

1. Open **W11-A3-BrownBag** from your **Word Chapter 11** folder and save it as **W11-A3-BrownBagRevised**.

   First you will create an AutoCorrect shortcut. You will soon be making travel arrangements for a new client, Morgan, Alexander, and Swift, and you will type the client name many times, so a shortcut will be a real time-saver.

2. Open the **Word Options** dialog box, choose the **Proofing** category, and click the **AutoCorrect Options** button.

3. Enter **mas** in the Replace field and **Morgan, Alexander, and Swift** in the With field; click **OK** twice.

4. Position the insertion point at the end of your document, type **mas**, and tap Enter to test the shortcut.

5. Open the **Word Options** dialog box, choose the **Save** category, and change the **AutoRecover** interval to **20** minutes.

6. Check the **Save to Computer by Default** checkbox.

7. Use the **Browse** button to change the default local file location to the **Desktop**.

8. Take a screenshot of the **Word Options** dialog box, click **OK**, paste it at the end of your document, and resize it to about a third of its original size.

9. Create a new, blank document so you can test your changes.

10. In the **Backstage, Save As** screen, click **Browse** and check that the path at the top of the Save As dialog box targets the **Desktop**.

11. Click **Cancel** to close the Save As dialog box and close the blank document without saving.

12. Restore the default settings in the Word Options dialog box.

Create, Run, and Edit a Macro

Now you will create a macro that you will use with another client whose employees will visit the Van Gogh Museum in Amsterdam. There is information that will be used in many letters, so it's a good candidate for a macro.

13. Position the insertion point at the end of your document and generate a blank line.

14. Turn on the macro recorder, name the macro **VanGogh**, and ensure the **Normal** template is chosen.

15. Click the **Keyboard** button and assign Ctrl+7 to the macro.

16. Record the following text:

The Van Gogh Museum is open daily from 9 am to 5 pm. It is located at Amstel 51, Amsterdam, and you can get there by boat shuttle or the Hop on, Hop off bus.

17. Turn off the macro recorder and tap ⎄Enter⎄ to generate a blank line.

18. Use ⎄Ctrl⎄+⎄7⎄ to test the macro.

Now you will enter additional information in the macro.

19. Open the macro editor and locate the word *bus* at the end of the macro text.

20. Position the insertion point after the period following the word *bus* and tap ⎄Spacebar⎄.

21. Add the following text and then close the macro editor:

Be sure to see The Potato Eaters and Starry Night.

22. Tap ⎄Enter⎄ and test the macro to verify your change and then delete the macro.

23. Save and close the file.

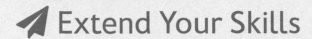 Extend Your Skills

These exercises challenge you to think critically and apply your new skills. You will be evaluated on your ability to follow directions, completeness, creativity, and the use of proper grammar and mechanics. Save files to your chapter folder. Submit assignments as directed.

W11-E1 That's the Way I See It

As the owner of a small business, you know it's important for your staff to operate as efficiently as possible. You're a whiz with Word, and you want to show your employees some features that can help them effectively organize the Word environment. Write a one- to two-page document explaining how the following might help them:

▸ When would it be beneficial to change the AutoRecover time interval?

▸ Under what circumstances would changing the default file location be helpful?

▸ What is the benefit of pinning documents to the Recent Document list?

▸ How can custom properties be useful?

Add two or three screenshots to help make your concepts come alive. Add your own Title and Comment to the Properties panel in Backstage view for the document you create. Save your file as **W11-E1-WordIdeas**.

W11-E2 Be Your Own Boss

As an administrator at Blue Jean Landscaping, you have found that macros can greatly increase efficiency. You want to create a macro that will rapidly create a letterhead, with the added benefit of avoiding printing costs. Create a new document named **W11-E2-BJLetterhead**. Record a new **Letterhead** macro and store it in the Normal template.

Type **Blue Jean Landscaping** as the company name and make up the rest of the letterhead content. Delete the text you used to create the macro and then test it. Delete the letterhead text and then edit the macro to add a comma, Spacebar , and **Inc.** at the end of the company name. Test the macro again; if it runs as intended, save the document.

W11-E3 Demonstrate Proficiency

The owner of Stormy BBQ just attended a Microsoft Word class at the local community college, and it opened his eyes to some of the beneficial features that he had not been aware of. Knowing that you are a very experienced Word user, he has asked you to record some ideas about how Word options and macros can benefit the business. Write a one- to two-page paper explaining what Word options (at least three) you would modify and why. Also, think of three different types of Word documents you use at Stormy BBQ and suggest at least one macro for each document type that would make creating the document more efficient. Don't forget to explain why. Use the Properties panel to add a Title and Tag. Save your file as **W11-E3-EfficientStormy**.

WORD

12 Integrating Word with Excel, PowerPoint, and the Web

One advantage to using a suite of applications is that they are designed to share data and information and to work together seamlessly. You can display data stored in an Excel worksheet in a Word document or use Excel data as the source document in Mail Merge. You can send a Word outline to PowerPoint to create a new presentation or insert a PowerPoint presentation in a Word document. You can open a PDF file in Word and edit it, and you can convert a Word document to a web page. In this chapter, you will explore the features that allow Word to interact with other Office programs.

LEARNING OBJECTIVES

- Embed and link Excel objects in Word
- Use an Excel worksheet as a Mail Merge data file
- Create PowerPoint presentations from Word outlines
- Insert PowerPoint presentations in Word documents
- Open a PDF file in Word for editing
- Convert Word documents to web pages

📁 Project: Multitasking with Word, Excel, and PowerPoint

You are an administrative assistant at Raritan Clinic East. An advisory committee meets quarterly to review the budget and clinic activities. In preparation for the upcoming meeting, you will help create the quarterly expense report. The data is in an Excel worksheet, so you will use the Excel data in the report that you will prepare in Word. You will add the chart contained in the Excel file to the report and prepare a PowerPoint presentation using an outline of headings from the clinic's Annual Report. You will generate a letter to all committee members using an Excel name and address file to address the letters. Then you will edit a press release in Word that was saved in PDF format. Finally, you will save your report as a web page for posting on the clinic website for others to review.

Embedding and Linking Excel Objects

You can share data and objects among the programs in the Office 2016 suite. Object is a term for an element that you share between files. For example, you can place data and chart objects from an Excel file in a Word document. You would choose to embed an object if you don't want it to change when the original source file is updated. On the other hand, if you want the Word document to stay current with any changes in the source file, you would link the object to its original file so your document will be updated when the source file is modified.

Link or Embed Data

Whether you are embedding or linking to files, there are two techniques for inserting data from other files:

▶ **Copy/Paste:** Using this procedure, you copy data from a source document, such as an Excel worksheet, and paste it directly into the Word document. Using the Paste Special command, you can choose to link the data or not at the time you paste it. This method is useful when you want to include only a portion of the file.

▶ **Insert Object:** You can insert a file, such as an Excel workbook, from within Word, and you can choose to link the data or not at the time you insert it. This procedure is useful when you want to include an entire file in a document.

DEVELOP YOUR SKILLS: W12-D1

In this exercise, you will embed an Excel worksheet in a Word document and test its static nature.

1. Start Word; create a new, blank document; and save it to your **Word Chapter 12** folder as **W12-D1-BudgetRpt**.

2. Type these heading lines:

   Advisory Committee Budget Report
   Third Quarter 2016

3. Tap [Enter] and then select both heading lines.

4. Choose **Home→Styles→More** ⬇ on the Quick Styles gallery and choose the **Title** style.

5. Position the insertion point in the blank line below the heading lines and type this introductory paragraph:

This report, produced by clinic staff, is in keeping with the Advisory Committee's decision to conduct quarterly reviews of the current year's budget. It provides a snapshot of expenses for the quarter and for the year-to-date.

6. Tap Enter and then choose **Insert→Text→Object**.

7. Follow these steps to identify the Excel file from which to embed the data:

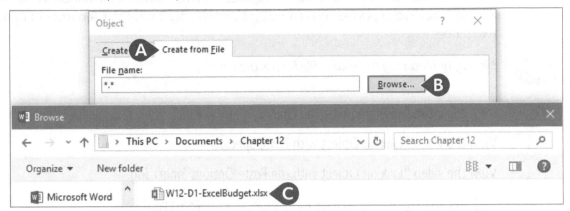

Ⓐ Click the **Create from File** tab.

Ⓑ Click the **Browse** button and navigate to your **Word Chapter 12** folder.

Ⓒ Double-click **W12-D1-ExcelBudget** and click **OK**.

Modify the Source File

8. Start Excel, open **W12-D1-ExcelBudget**, and save it in your **Word Chapter 12** folder as **W12-D1-ExcelBudgetRevised**.

9. Follow these steps to edit a value in the source file:

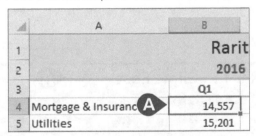 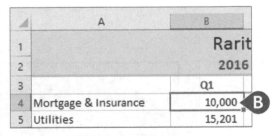

Ⓐ Click the cell for **14,557** (Q1, Mortgage & Insurance) and tap Delete .

Ⓑ Type **10,000** and tap Enter .

10. Switch to Word and verify that the value of Q1 Mortgagee & Insurance remains 14,557.

Because the table is embedded (not linked) in the document, the data in Word is not affected by changes made to the Excel file.

11. Switch back to Excel and click **Undo** ↺ twice to return the value to its original amount.

Because you actually want the report to reflect the most recent data in the worksheet, you will delete the embedded object and then link to the data in the next exercise.

12. Switch back to Word, click the embedded worksheet to select it, and tap Delete .

13. Save the Word file and leave all files open.

Link Objects

When you link data from another application, such as Excel or PowerPoint, to a Word document, the original information resides in Excel or PowerPoint. This is known as the source file because it is the source of the data. When you place the information (object) in a Word document, it becomes the destination file. By linking source files with Word documents, you create a dynamic tie between the two files.

For example, you might start working on a quarterly report before the end of the quarter, and, if there is a linked chart in the report, it updates with the current information as the numbers change in Excel. That way, updates are centralized, and you don't have to keep track of making changes in two places.

 Moving or renaming the source file breaks the link.

 View the video "Inserting a Linked Object."

 View the video "Link an Object with Paste Special."

 View the video "Link an Object with the Paste Options Smart Tag."

≡ Insert→Text→Object→Create from File→Link to File

DEVELOP YOUR SKILLS: W12-D2

In this exercise, you will link Excel data to a Word document using Paste Special. You will then modify the Excel worksheet and observe how the changes update the Word document. Then you will link an Excel chart to the document using the Paste Options smart tag.

1. Save your file as **W12-D2-BudgetRpt**.

2. Switch to Excel and follow these steps to select and copy the Excel data:

A1	▼	⋮	×	✓	*fx*	Raritan Clinic East

	A	B	C	D	E	F
1	Raritan Clinic East Ⓐ					
2	2016 Budget Summary					
3		Q1	Q2	Q3	Q4	Totals
4	Mortgage & Insurance	14,557	14,557	14,557		43,671
5	Utilities	15,201	18,200	21,000		54,401
6	Food	5,480	4,512	3,452		13,444
7	Staff Salaries	87,685	87,685	87,685		263,055
8	Maintenance & Repairs	16,982	17,458	15,225		49,665
9	Fundraising for Donations	820	2,006	67,325		70,151
10	Grand Totals	140,725	144,418	209,244	-	494,387 Ⓑ

Ⓒ

Ⓐ Click in the merged cell containing the heading *Raritan Clinic East*.

Ⓑ Press Shift and click the last cell in the worksheet, **494,387**.

Ⓒ Choose **Home→Clipboard→Copy**.

3. Switch to Word and position the insertion point at the end of the document.

4. Choose **Home→Clipboard→Paste** ![paste icon] **menu button** ▼**→Paste Special**.

5. When the Paste Special dialog box opens, follow these steps to paste the object:

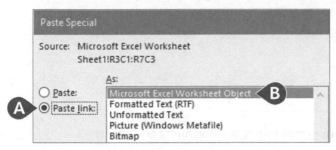

Ⓐ Choose **Paste Link**.

Ⓑ Choose **Microsoft Excel Worksheet Object** and click **OK**.

Now you will edit the worksheet and observe the change to the linked object in Word.

6. Switch to Excel and tap Esc to remove the marquee (animated dashed line) surrounding the table.

The marquee in Excel identifies the cells copied.

7. Click **cell E4**, which is the Q4 cell for Mortgage & Insurance.

8. Type the Q4 projections shown, tapping Enter after typing each number.

The formulas in the Totals cells automatically update as you enter the data.

Q4
11,337
1,750
4,975
17,685
2,543
1,529

9. Switch to Word.

The linked table updated with the additions you made in the Q4 column. If the Excel table failed to update on your computer, right-click the Excel object and choose Update Link.

10. Position the insertion point at the end of the document and tap Enter three times.

Link an Excel Chart in Word

Now you will use the Paste Options smart tag to link a chart to Word.

11. Switch to Excel, click the **Sheet 2** tab at the bottom of the Excel window, and click the pie chart border once to select it.

The mouse pointer becomes a four-headed arrow, and the selection handles appear in the border.

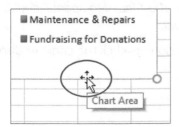

12. Choose **Home**→**Clipboard**→**Copy** and then switch back to Word.

13. Choose **Home**→**Clipboard**→**Paste** .

14. Follow these steps to paste a link for the chart object:

    Ⓐ Click the **Paste Options** smart tag at the bottom of the chart.

    Ⓑ Click **Keep Source Formatting & Link Data**.

15. Save the Word file.

16. Exit Excel, saving changes when prompted.

Open Excel and Chart Tools from Word

When data or objects from other sources are linked to Word documents, you can open source program tools directly from the Word document and use the tools to edit the object. Or, you can open the Excel application from within Word.

DEVELOP YOUR SKILLS: W12-D3

In this exercise, you will launch Excel from within Word and edit data in the worksheet. Then you will use Live Preview with Excel Chart Tools on the Word Ribbon to view potential formatting changes.

1. Save your file as **W12-D3-BudgetRpt**.

2. Double-click anywhere in the Excel worksheet table object to open the Excel file.

    At this stage, you can make editing changes that will be reflected in the Word document.

3. In Excel, click the Q1 cell for Staff Salaries (**cell B7**), type **1,000**, and tap ⌶Enter⌷.

4. Switch to Word and ensure that the data and chart both updated.

    If your table failed to update, right-click the Excel worksheet table and choose Update Link from the menu. It's possible the worksheet table will update but not the chart. If your chart failed to update, double-click the chart and from the Ribbon choose Chart Tools→Design→Data→Refresh Data.

5. Switch to Excel and click **Undo** .

6. Switch to Word.

    The chart and the worksheet data update to their original values. If your table failed to update, right-click the Excel worksheet table and choose Update Link from the menu. It's possible that the worksheet table will update but not the chart. If your chart failed to update, double-click the chart and choose Chart Tools→Design→Data→Refresh Data.

7. If you did not use Chart Tools in the previous step, double-click the chart to display the Chart Tools on the Ribbon.

8. Click the border of the chart to select the chart background.

   You should not see handles on objects within the border.

9. Choose **Chart Tools→Format→Shape Styles→Shape Fill** 🎨 **menu button** ▼.

10. Hover the mouse pointer over several different colors to see Live Preview display the effects as they impact the chart area background color.

11. Tap [Esc] to close the gallery and then tap [Esc] again to deselect the chart.

    The Chart Tools tabs disappear from the Ribbon.

12. Save and then close the Word file but leave the Excel file open.

Updating and Breaking Links

Linked objects in Word automatically update if the destination file is open at the time the source document changes. Naturally, the destination file is not always open when you modify the Excel source document; however, Word will prompt you to update links when you open a document containing links.

You can break the link between a linked object and its source document. Once the final figures for a period are in, you may want to break the link between Word and Excel so that the linked object is converted to an embedded object. Then, the Word report always reflects the closing numbers for that period.

DEVELOP YOUR SKILLS: W12-D4

In this exercise, you will modify the linked Excel file and observe the prompt to update links when you open the Word document. Then you will break the links to the worksheet data and test to see that the links are broken.

1. In Excel, click **cell C4** (Mortgage & Insurance for Q2), type **50,000**, and tap [Enter].

   You entered an overly large number so that the changes in the associated worksheet table and chart will be easy to see.

2. Open **W12-D3-BudgetRpt**, which contains the linked objects.

3. When the message appears prompting you to update links, click Yes.

   Observe the change in the worksheet data and in the chart. If your table failed to update, right-click the Excel worksheet table and choose Update Link from the menu. It's possible the worksheet table will update but not the chart. If your chart failed to update, click the chart border and choose Chart Tools→Design→Data→Refresh Data.

4. Save the Word file as **W12-D4-BudgetRpt**.

   Now you will break the link between the objects in Word and the Excel file.

5. In Word, right-click in the worksheet data to display a pop-up menu.

6. Slide the mouse pointer down to **Linked Worksheet Object** and choose **Links** from the submenu.

7. Follow these steps to break the link for the table:

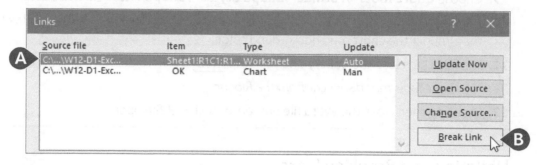

Ⓐ Make sure the worksheet object is selected.

Ⓑ Click **Break Link**.

8. When the message appears asking if you want to break the link, click **Yes**.

   The link disappears from the Links dialog box. The remaining link is already highlighted.

9. Click the **Break Link** button to break the link between Excel and the chart.

10. When the message box appears, click **Yes**.

    The Source File now displays the term NULL, indicating there is no source file attached.

11. Click **OK** to close the Links dialog box.

    Now you will test to see that the links are broken.

12. Right-click the worksheet object, review the menu options, and note that the Update Links option is gone.

13. Double-click the chart, choose **Chart Tools→Design→Data**, and notice that the Refresh Data button is grayed out, indicating that the link is broken.

14. Save and close the Word and Excel files but leave the program windows open.

Using Excel as a Mail Merge Data Source

You may recall the Word's Mail Merge feature is most often used for generating personalized form letters. Word can use a variety of file types as data sources, including Excel files. Whether you type a new data-source list from within Word or create your data source in Excel, the rules for effective data sources apply.

The more data is split into small segments, the more flexibility you have in the merge. A rule to remember is that you cannot merge part of a field. If the name field, for example, contains the title, first name, and last name, you will not be able to use those elements separately. For instance, in the greeting line, you will not be able to drop the first name and use Dear Title Last Name.

In Excel, the columns are treated as separate fields in a mail merge. Therefore, in a name and address list, it is a good idea to place the title, first name, and last name in separate columns, as shown in the following illustration.

	A	B	C	D	E	F	G
1	Title	First Name	Last Name	Address	City	State	Zip
2	Ms.	Sally	Redding	756 Locust Street	Los Angeles	CA	91025
3	Mr.	Jose	Lopez	7812 Olive Road	Los Angeles	CA	91357
4	Mr.	Charles	Douglas	91 Sycamore Ave.	Los Angeles	CA	91642

 Note! When an Excel file is used as a merge data source file, the first row of the worksheet must contain the field names. In addition, all columns and rows must be adjacent to each other for Mail Merge to identify all entries as part of the same data source. You cannot have blank rows and columns within the Excel worksheet data.

≡ Mailings→Start Mail Merge→Select Recipients→Use an Existing List

DEVELOP YOUR SKILLS: W12-D5

In this exercise, you will begin by examining the Excel worksheet that you will use as the data source. Next you will open a letter and designate it as the main document. Then you will connect the Excel data source to the letter and conduct the merge.

1. In Excel, open **W12-D5-CommAddress** from your **Word Chapter 12** folder.

   Each column represents a mail merge field; Title is a field, First Name is a field, and so forth.

2. Look at the bottom of the Excel worksheet and notice the tab labeled Sheet 1.

   This is the name of the page in the Excel workbook that contains the address list. You will see Sheet 1 again later in this exercise.

3. Exit Excel.

4. In Word, open **W12-D5-CommLtr** and save it as `W12-D5-CommLtrRevised`.

5. Choose **Mailings→Start Mail Merge→Start Mail Merge** 🖹 and then choose **Letters**.

   This designates the letter as the main document.

6. If necessary, display formatting marks.

   Being able to see the formatting marks will be helpful later in this exercise. Now you will connect to the Excel data source.

7. Choose **Mailings→Start Mail Merge→Select Recipients** 🗒 and then choose **Use an Existing List**.

8. Navigate to your **Word Chapter 12** folder and open **W12-D5-CommAddress**.

9. When the Select Table dialog box appears, notice that Sheet 1 is highlighted.

   Earlier you observed Sheet 1 as the name of the page in the Excel workbook that contains the address list.

10. Click **OK**.

11. In the letter, select the **Today's Date** text; delete it but don't delete the paragraph symbol at the end of the line.

    Deleting the paragraph symbol would throw off proper business letter spacing.

12. Type the current date in its place.

Insert Merge Codes

13. Select and delete the **Address Block** text but don't delete the paragraph symbol at the end of the line.

14. Choose **Mailings→Write & Insert Fields→Address Block** 🗎.

15. When the Insert Address Block dialog box appears, click **OK** to accept the default settings for the inside address.

16. Delete the **Greeting Line** text but not the paragraph symbol at the end of the line.

17. Choose **Mailings→Write & Insert Fields→Greeting Line** 🗎.

18. When the Insert Greeting Line dialog box appears, change the Greeting Line Format from a comma to a colon and click **OK**.

Conduct the Merge

19. Choose **Mailings→Finish→Finish & Merge** 🗎 and then choose **Edit Individual Documents**.

20. When the Merge to New Document dialog box opens, click **OK** to merge all of the records from the Excel file.

21. Turn off formatting marks and scroll through the letters to see the results of the merge.

22. Close the merge document without saving it.

23. Save and close **W12-D5-CommLtrRevised**.

Integrating Word with PowerPoint

PowerPoint is another program that Word can share files with. Word outlines can be used to create PowerPoint presentations. This hierarchical structure uses Heading 1 topics as the slide's title and headings such as Heading 2, Heading 3, and so forth as the bullet and sub-bullet entries in the slide.

Using Word Outline View

The following illustration is an example of an outline created specifically for generating a Power-Point presentation. Clicking or selecting entries in the outline displays the Word heading level in the Outlining tab on the Ribbon.

This field displays the Word heading style level of the highlighted heading.

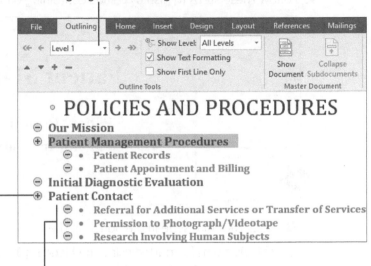

The plus (+) symbol indicates that there are lower-level headings below this heading.

Minus (-) symbols indicate that there are no lower-level headings below this heading.

Although you can use an existing document that contains Word headings to create a PowerPoint presentation, PowerPoint cannot extract just the headings from a document, so if you use an existing document with body text in addition to the headings, you will have to edit the PowerPoint presentation accordingly.

The procedures used to launch PowerPoint are the same as those used to launch Word. No special knowledge of PowerPoint is required to complete the following exercise.

 View→Views→Outline

DEVELOP YOUR SKILLS: W12-D6

In this exercise, you will use a Word outline to create a PowerPoint presentation. Then you will observe how the different heading levels are displayed in the presentation.

1. Open **W12-D6-ProcOutline** from your **Word Chapter 12** folder.
2. Choose **View→Views→Outline** 📄.
3. Click several different entries in the outline and notice the Word heading level indicated on the Ribbon.
4. Close the document and start PowerPoint.
5. Click the **Blank Presentation** template on the PowerPoint Start screen to open the PowerPoint window.
6. Choose **File→Open** and navigate to your **Word Chapter 12** folder.
7. In the bottom-right corner of the Open dialog box, click the file type drop-down list and choose **All Files (*.*)**.

WORD

8. Double-click **W12-D6-ProcOutline** to open it.

9. Follow these steps to display a slide containing a title and bullet points:

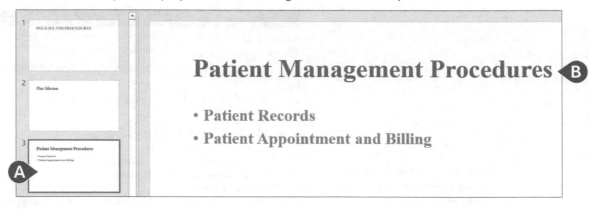

> **(A)** Click the third slide in the panel on the left.
>
> **(B)** This title was formatted using the Heading 1 style, and the bullet points are formatted using the Heading 2 style.

10. Exit PowerPoint without saving the file.

Adding a PowerPoint Presentation to a Word Document

When you create a document that will be distributed electronically, it could be useful to include a PowerPoint presentation within the document. For example, suppose you want to distribute a presentation and include a letter with it. You can create the letter and place the presentation in the body of the letter.

 When you insert a presentation into a Word document, only the first slide appears in the document. Double-clicking the slide image plays the show automatically.

≡ Insert→Text→Object→Create from File

DEVELOP YOUR SKILLS: W12-D7

In this exercise, you will insert a presentation into the letter being sent to board members.

1. Open **W12-D7-AdvisoryLtr** from your **Word Chapter 12** folder and save it as **W12-D7-AdvisoryLtrRevised**.

2. Turn on formatting marks and then position the insertion point in the middle paragraph symbol just before the complimentary close for the letter.

3. Choose **Insert→Text→Object** ▢ and click the **Create from File** tab.

4. Click **Browse** and navigate to your **Word Chapter 12** folder.

5. Double-click **W12-D7-IntroToRCE.ppt** (a PowerPoint file) and then click **OK**.

   Word adds a picture of the first slide in the letter. Notice that the image is large and makes the letter extend to two pages. Next you will size the image so that the letter fits on one page.

6. Click the slide image to display the sizing handles.

7. Drag the lower-right sizing handle diagonally up toward the center of the image until the letter fits on one page.

8. Double-click the slide image in the letter to start the slide show.

9. Click the mouse pointer anywhere on the screen to advance the slides.

10. When the black screen appears at the end of the show, click one more time to close it.

11. Save and close the file.

Opening, Editing, and Saving a PDF File

You can open, edit, and save a PDF file in Word 2016 without purchasing and learning separate, and often expensive, editing software. After editing the file, you can save it as a Word or PDF file. The file you open is considered a read-only file, so you must save it under a different name.

You can optimize a PDF file when you save it based on how your audience will likely read the file. And there are additional options, such as the range of pages you want to save and the ability to create bookmarks in the PDF file.

Choose additional publishing options here.

If your audience will be printing the PDF file, leave the option at Standard. If the file will be viewed only online, you can choose the Minimum Size option.

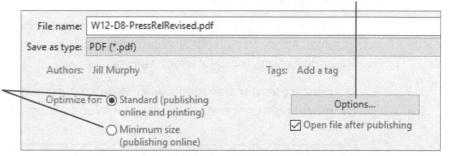

DEVELOP YOUR SKILLS: W12-D8

In this exercise, you will open a PDF file in Word and make editing changes. You will then resave the file as a PDF.

1. Choose **File→Open**, navigate to your **Word Chapter 12** folder, and open **W12-D8-PressRel**.

2. When the message appears, take a moment to read it and then click **OK**.

   The PDF file opens with all the Word editing and formatting tools available.

Note! *When you open a PDF file in Word, there may be formatting issues. Don't worry about that now. Concentrate on opening so, in the future, you know how to open and edit a PDF file for which you don't have the original Word file.*

3. Select the three lines at the top of the page.

4. Choose **Home→Font→Font Color** ▣ **menu button** ▾ and choose **Blue, Accent 1, Darker 25%**.

5. Choose **Home→Font→Font Size** and choose **16 pt**.

6. Choose **File→Save As**, navigate to your **Word Chapter 12** folder, save the file as **W12-D8-PressRelRevised**, choose **PDF (*.pdf)** from the Save as Type list, and then click **Save**.

7. If the PDF file opens in a PDF reader, close the PDF window.

   Remember, the original file is read-only, so saving it under a different name saved the changes in a new file.

8. The original file is still open in Word; close the file without saving.

Creating Web Pages from Word Documents

You can create web pages from Word documents. As you might imagine, this saves you the need to learn a more specialized web design or coding program. Another advantage is that Word can display a document in Web Layout view so you can make edits before posting the file on the web.

Format Web Pages

Web pages are often set up in tables to help align text in multiple columns, and the Table feature works well for this purpose. When you save a document as a web page, Word converts it to hypertext markup language (HTML), the authoring language for web pages. When you convert a document to HTML, some formatting features may be lost. However, most of your documents should translate cleanly into attractive web pages.

Add Alternative Text

Using alternative text helps people with limited vision understand the meaning of pictures and graphics. Although traditionally used with web pages, you can also add alternative text to regular Word documents for greater accessibility.

If a person uses a screen reader while viewing a web page, alternative text appears when hovering the mouse pointer over a picture or graphic. Some users won't see the text, but they'll hear it.

DEVELOP YOUR SKILLS: W12-D9

In this exercise, you will save a document as a web page and examine its format. You will also add alternative text to a picture in the document.

1. Open **W12-D9-RCEWalk** from your **Word Chapter 12** folder and save it as **W12-D9-RCEWalkRevised**.

2. If no gridlines appear, choose **Table Tools→Layout→Table→View Gridlines**.

   The document is set up in a table. The gridlines are visible so you can see the column with no content on the left side of the table. Web pages may appear too far to the left in a browser window, so the blank column is acting as a spacer to position the content farther to the right.

   Now you will add alternative text to the picture.

3. Right-click the picture and choose **Format Picture** to open the Format Picture task pane.

4. Follow these steps to add alternative text:

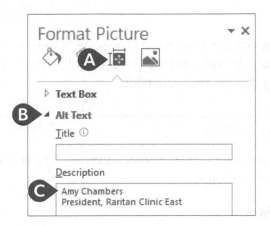

Ⓐ Click the **Layout & Properties** button.

Ⓑ Click **Alt Text**.

Ⓒ Type this text in the description field.

Note! *The title field should be filled in only if you are entering a detailed explanation in the Description field.*

5. Close the Format Picture task pane.

6. Choose **File→Save As** and navigate to your **Word Chapter 12** folder.

7. Follow these steps to set the format and title of the web page document:

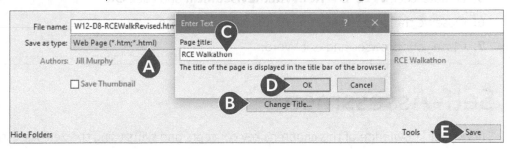

Ⓐ Choose **Web Page (*.htm;*html)** from the Save as Type drop-down list.

Ⓑ Click the **Change Title** button to open the Enter Text dialog box.

Ⓒ Type **RCE Walkathon** in the Page Title field.

Ⓓ Click **OK**.

Ⓔ Click **Save**.

8. Launch Internet Explorer or your default browser.

Steps for opening the file in your default browser may vary slightly. You may need to seek assistance to determine the correct method.

9. Press Ctrl+O and click the **Browse** button.

10. Navigate to your **Word Chapter 12** folder, double-click **W12-D9-RCEWalkRevised.htm**, and click **OK**.

If you do not see the .htm file extension, look closely, and you will see that the web page file has a slightly different icon than a Word file icon.

11. Review the document layout and notice that the gridlines do not appear.

12. Close the browser and the Word web page file.

Edit Web Pages in Word

When you create a web page in Word, you can use Word to edit the page as well. You open the *.htm* page from within Word, make the necessary changes, and then resave the file. When you open it in the browser again, you will see the editing changes that you made.

DEVELOP YOUR SKILLS: W12-D10

In this exercise, you will open the web page you created in the previous exercise and edit it. Then you will reopen the page in your browser and observe the change.

1. Open **W12-D9-RCEWalkRevised.htm**.

   If you do not see the .htm file extension, look closely, and you will see that the web page file has a slightly different icon than a Word file icon.

2. Change the walkathon date from March 1 to March **8**.

3. Save and close the file and then restart your browser.

   Steps for opening the file in your default browser may vary slightly. You may need to seek assistance to determine the correct method.

4. Press Ctrl+O and navigate to your **Word Chapter 12** folder.

5. Double-click **W12-D9-RCEWalkRevised.htm** and click **OK**.

6. Observe the date change you made in the web page.

7. Close your browser and exit Word.

Self-Assessment

Check your knowledge of this chapter's key concepts and skills using the Self-Assessment in your ebook or eLab course.

Reinforce Your Skills

REINFORCE YOUR SKILLS: W12-R1

Create a Consignment Shop Sales Report

Kids for Change operates a fund-raising consignment shop, Collectibles & Curiosities. In this exercise, you will prepare a static sales report and distribute it to the board members and then link the sales report data so you can start collecting data for your year-to-date report.

1. Start Word, open **W12-R1-Q1SalesRpt** from your **Word Chapter 12** folder, and save it as **W12-R1-Q1SalesRptRevised**.

2. Position the insertion point in the first blank line below the paragraph.

3. If necessary, choose **View→Views→Print Layout** 📄 to change from Web Layout view.

4. If necessary, turn on formatting marks, choose **Insert→Text→Object** 🔲, and click the **Create from File** tab.

5. Click **Browse**, navigate to your **Word Chapter 12** folder, and double-click **W12-R1-Collectibles**.

   Because you are embedding (not linking) the data in Word, you won't check the Link to File checkbox.

6. Click **OK** to close the dialog box and insert the table.

   Having distributed this report to the board members, you will now link this worksheet table in the Word document so you can begin collecting year-to-date data.

7. Click the embedded worksheet table and tap ⌨Delete.

Link Excel Data to a Word Document

8. Start Excel, click the **Open Other Workbooks** link at the bottom of the Recent list on the left of the Start screen, and navigate to your **Word Chapter 12** folder.

9. Open **W12-R1-Collectibles** and save it as **W12-R1-CollectiblesRevised**.

10. Make sure the **Collectibles and Curiosities** merged cell is selected and then press ⌨Shift and click the last cell in the table (value of **$1,464.00**).

11. Choose **Home→Clipboard→Copy**, switch to Word, and position the insertion point in the first blank line below the main paragraph.

12. Choose **Home→Clipboard→Paste menu button ▾→Paste Special**.

13. In the Paste Special dialog box, choose **Microsoft Excel Worksheet Object**, click the **Paste Link** option, and click **OK**.

    Now you will edit the worksheet in Excel and observe the change in the linked table.

14. Switch to Excel, tap ⌨Esc to remove the marquee surrounding the table, and click the cell at the top of the worksheet to select it.

15. Double-click the cell to position the insertion point in the cell and then click and drag to select **Quarter 1**.

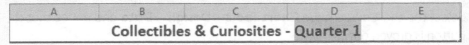

16. Type **Year-to-Date**, tap $\boxed{\text{Enter}}$, and then switch to **Word**.

    Notice that the linked table updated with the change you made. If the table failed to update, right-click it and choose Update Link.

17. Position the insertion point on the blank line below the table.

    Now you will link an Excel chart in Word using the Paste Options smart tag.

18. Switch to Excel, click the **Sheet 2** tab at the bottom of the workbook, and then click the chart to select it.

19. Choose **Home→Clipboard→Copy** and then switch back to Word.

20. Choose **Home→Clipboard→Paste** and click the **Paste Options** smart tag at the bottom of the chart.

21. Click the **Keep Source Formatting & Link Data** button. (If necessary, use ToolTips to identify the button.)

22. Switch to Excel, exit Excel, and save changes when prompted.

Open Excel and Display Chart Tools from Within Word

23. Double-click in the worksheet table in Word to open the Excel file.

    You realize that there is an error in the March sales figure for Glass & Crystal, so you will make that change in the worksheet.

24. Click **cell B7** (Glass & Crystal, March), tap $\boxed{\text{Delete}}$, type **1,500.00**, and tap $\boxed{\text{Enter}}$.

25. Switch to Word and ensure that the table and chart both updated.

    If your table failed to update, right-click the Excel worksheet table and choose Update Link from the menu. It's possible the worksheet table will update but not the chart. If your chart failed to update, click the chart and choose Chart Tools→Design→Data→Refresh Data.

26. Save the document and exit Word.

Update Links and Break a Link Between Word and Excel

27. In Excel, click to select **cell D5** (Vintage Jewelry, January), tap $\boxed{\text{Delete}}$, type **600**, and tap $\boxed{\text{Enter}}$.

28. In Word, open **W12-R1-Q1SalesRptRevised**; when the message appears prompting you to update links, click **Yes**.

29. If your table or chart failed to update, use the manual procedures you've used before to update.

30. In Word, right-click the worksheet table to display the pop-up menu.

31. Slide the mouse pointer down to **Linked Worksheet Object** and choose **Links** from the submenu.

32. With the worksheet selected, click **Break Link**.

33. When the message appears verifying the break, click **Yes**.

34. With the chart selected, click **Break Link**, click **Yes**, and then click **OK**.

    Now you will test to ensure that the links are broken.

35. Right-click the **worksheet table** in Word and notice that Update Links does not appear in the menu.

36. Select the chart and choose **Chart Tools→Design→Data** and notice that the Refresh Data button is grayed out.

37. Save and close the Word and Excel files.

Organize an Autumn Garden Cleanup for Seniors

Kids for Change volunteers assist senior citizens with autumn garden cleanup every year, and it's time to get that project rolling again. In this exercise, you will use Excel and Mail Merge to send letters announcing the volunteers' meeting. You will also convert a Word outline to a PowerPoint presentation for the meeting to review garden tasks needed at this time of the year. And finally, you will save a document as a web page so volunteers can go online to see which gardening supplies are needed for the project.

1. Open **W12-R2-GardenLtr** from your **Word Chapter 12** folder and save it as **W12-R2-GardenLtrRevised**.
2. Choose **Mailings→Start Mail Merge→Start Mail Merge**→**Letters**.
    Word will now recognize your letter as the main document.
3. If necessary, turn on formatting marks.
    Now you will connect an Excel file as the data source.
4. Choose **Mailings→Start Mail Merge→Select Recipients** and then choose **Use an Existing List**.
5. Navigate to your **Word Chapter 12** folder and open **W12-R2-AddressLst.xls** (an Excel file).
6. When the Select Table dialog box appears, make sure **Sheet 1**, which contains the address list, is selected and then click **OK**.
    Now you will insert the merge codes in your letter.
7. In the letter, delete the **Address Block** text but not the paragraph symbol at the end of the line.
8. Choose **Mailings→Write & Insert Fields→Address Block**.
9. When the Insert Address Block dialog box opens, click **OK** to accept the default formats for the inside address.
10. Delete the **Greeting Line** text but not the paragraph symbol at the end of the line.
11. Choose **Mailings→Write & Insert Fields→Greeting Line**.
12. When the Insert Greeting Line dialog box opens, choose **Joshua** from the drop-down list and click **OK** to insert the Greeting Line code.
    Now you will conduct the merge.
13. Choose **Mailings→Finish→Finish & Merge**→**Edit Individual Documents**.
14. When the Merge to New Document dialog box opens, click **OK** and then turn off formatting marks.
15. Scroll through the documents to see the results of the merge and then close the document without saving it.
16. Save and close **W12-R2-GardenLtrRevised**.

Create a PowerPoint Presentation from a Word Outline

Now you will create the PowerPoint presentation that Kids for Change will use during the meeting to remind team members of the various gardening tasks that must be completed during their cleanup project. You will generate the presentation from a Word outline.

17. Open **W12-R2-GardenTasks** and choose **View→Views→Outline**.

18. Click several different entries and notice the heading levels indicated on the Ribbon.

    Level 1 entries will provide slide titles, and Level 2 entries will provide bullet points.

19. Close the outline document.

20. Start PowerPoint and click the **Open Other Presentations** link at the bottom of the Recent list on the left of the Start screen.

21. Navigate to your **Word Chapter 12** folder; in the bottom-right corner, click the drop-down list and choose **All Files (*.*)**.

22. Double-click **W12-R2-GardenTasks**.

23. Click several slide icons in the left panel and notice that the titles are formed from the Level 1 outline entries and the bullet points come from the Level 2 outline entries.

24. Exit PowerPoint without saving.

Save a Document as a Web Page

In planning for the Kids for Change garden cleanup project, the project manager needs to determine which gardening supplies members can contribute to use during the project.

25. Open **W12-R2-GardenSupplies** from your **Word Chapter 12** folder and save it as **W12-R2-GardenSuppliesRevised**.

    The document is set up in a table, which is common for organizing data in web pages. If you cannot see table gridlines, choose Table Tools→Layout→Table→View Gridlines.

26. Choose **File→Save As**, navigate to your **Word Chapter 12** folder, and choose **Web Page (*.htm,*.html)** from the Save as Type list.

27. Click the **Change Title** button, type **Gardening Supplies** in the dialog box, and click **OK**.

    This text will appear in the title bar or as a tab in your default browser.

28. Click **Save**, and Word automatically switches to Web Layout view.

    Now you will open the document in your web browser. Steps for opening the file in your default browser may vary slightly. You may need to seek assistance to determine the correct method.

29. Start your browser, press [Ctrl]+[O], and click **Browse**.

30. Navigate to your **Word Chapter 12** folder and double-click **W12-R2-GardenSuppliesRevised**. (If necessary, use the file icon to identify the web page file.)

31. Observe the *Gardening Supplies* at the top of the browser and then close the browser.

32. Exit all programs.

Report on a Fund-Raiser and Work on Pending Projects

Kids for Change sells used books to raise funds for its projects. In this exercise, you will send a letter to the board members containing sales data from Excel. And you will use a PDF file, a PowerPoint presentation, and a web page to help pending projects move forward.

1. Start Word, open **W12-R3-BookSalesLtr** from your **Word Chapter 12** folder, and save it as **W12-R3-BookSalesLtrRevised**.

2. If necessary, choose **View→Views→Print Layout** to change from Web Layout view.

3. Start Excel and click the **Open Other Workbooks** link at the bottom of the Recent list on the left side of the Start screen.

4. Navigate to your **Word Chapter 12** folder, open **W12-R3-UsedBookSales**, and save it as **W12-R3-UsedBookSalesRevised**.

5. Press Ctrl+Home to select the first cell in the worksheet and press Shift and click the last cell in the table (**$1,424.00**).

6. Press Ctrl+C to copy the data.

7. Switch to Word, display formatting marks, and then position the insertion point on the second blank line below the letter closing.

8. Choose **Home→Clipboard→Paste menu button ▾ →Paste Special**.

9. Choose **Microsoft Excel Worksheet Object** from the list, click the **Paste Link** option button, and click **OK**.

10. Close Excel.

    Now you will open Excel from within Word.

11. Double-click the worksheet table in Word to open the Excel file.

    You need to correct the January sales figure for Historical Fiction.

12. Click **cell C3** (Historical Fiction, January), type **$385.00**, and tap Enter.

13. Switch to Word and verify that the worksheet table updated.

14. If your table failed to update, right-click the table and choose **Update Link**.

15. Save and close the Word document and exit Excel, saving the file when prompted.

Add a PowerPoint Presentation to a Word Document

Kids for Change will soon meet to discuss upcoming projects. You will paste a PowerPoint presentation that overviews the projects into a letter to the board members for their review.

16. Open **W12-R3-BoardMtgLtr** from your **Word Chapter 12** folder and save it as **W12-R3-BoardMtgLtrRevised**.

17. Position the insertion point at the end of the document.

18. Choose **Insert→Text→Object** and click the **Create from File** tab.

19. Click **Browse**, navigate to your **Word Chapter 12** folder, double-click **W12-R3-ProjectsPPT.ppt**, and then click **OK**.

20. Double-click the slide image to start the presentation and then click the mouse pointer on the screen to advance the slides. (Notice the Beach Cleanup and Golden Retriever Rescue projects as you view the presentation.)

21. When the black screen appears, click again to close the presentation and then save and close the file.

Edit a PDF File in Word

One of the upcoming projects is Beach Cleanup. Kids for Change wants to get local school kids involved. You will send an online letter to superintendents in the area requesting their support in this mission. You will use a PDF file as it's likely that the letter will be read on computers with varying operating systems and software. The date for the cleanup has slipped a week, so you need to update the file.

22. In Word, open **W12-R3-SuperLtr.pdf** from your **Word Chapter 12** folder.

23. When the message appears, click **OK** and change the date (second line of body paragraph) from September 3rd to September **10th.**

24. Save the file as a PDF file naming it **W12-R3-SuperLtrRevised**.

25. If the file opens in a PDF reader, close the reader.

26. Close the Word document without saving.

Create a Web Page from a Word Document

One of the pending projects is the Golden Retriever Rescue project. You've created a flyer announcing the Foster Home Fair for Golden Retriever Rescue, which will take place at the Community Center. You will save it as a web page so it can be posted on the Community Center website.

27. Open **W12-R3-FosterHomeFair** from your **Word Chapter 12** folder.

28. Choose **File→Save As** and navigate to your **Word Chapter 12** folder.

29. Name the file **W12-R3-FosterHomeFairRevised** and choose **Web Page (*.htm,*html)** from the Save as Type list.

30. Click the **Change Title** button, type **Foster Home Fair**, click **OK**, and then click **Save**.

    Now you will add alternative text to the picture to enhance accessibility.

31. Right-click the picture and choose **Format Picture**.

32. In the Format Picture task pane, click the **Layout & Properties** button and then click **Alt Text**.

33. Type **Olivia needs a good home!** in the Description field and then close the **task pane**.

    Seek assistance if you need help opening the file in your browser.

34. Start your default web **browser**, press Ctrl+O, navigate to your **Word Chapter 12** folder, and double-click **W12-R3-FosterHomeFairRevised**.

35. Review the web page and then close the browser.

    Now you will edit the web page. The Word web page should still be open.

36. Position the insertion point at the end of the last bullet point, tap Enter, and type **Fire Department BBQ Cook-off**.

37. Save and close the file.

    Seek assistance if you need help opening the file in your browser.

38. Start your browser, press Ctrl+O, navigate to your **Word Chapter 12** folder, double-click **W12-R3-FosterHomeFairRevised**, and click **OK**.

39. Observe the change you made to the web page and then close the browser.

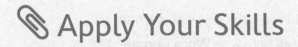
Apply Your Skills

APPLY YOUR SKILLS: W12-A1

Prepare a Report Comparing Tours

In this exercise, you will produce a report for the Universal Corporate Events management team comparing the sales of four tours over three months. You will embed an Excel worksheet table in a Word document and then link an Excel worksheet table and chart in the document. You will update links when changes are made in Excel, and finally you will break the link between Word and Excel.

1. Open **W12-A1-MgmtLtr** from your **Word Chapter 12** folder and save it as **W12-A1-MgmtLtrRevised**.

2. If necessary, choose **View→View→Print Layout** to change from Web Layout view.

3. If necessary, display formatting marks; then position the insertion point on the second blank line below the letter closing.

4. Start Excel, open **W12-A1-1stQSales** from your **Word Chapter 12** folder, and save it as **W12-A1-1stQSalesRevised.**

5. Press ⎡Ctrl⎤+⎡Home⎤ to select the cell at the top of the table, press ⎡Shift⎤, and click the last cell in the table, which displays the value of **$150,000**.

6. Copy the table and then switch to Word and make sure the insertion point is on the second blank line below the letter.

7. Click **Paste menu button** ▼→**Paste Special** and link the **Microsoft Excel Worksheet** object in Word.

   Now you will make a change to the Excel table and observe the change in the linked table in Word.

8. Switch to Excel and turn off the marquee.

9. Click **cell C3** (Hawaii Resort, January) and enter **40,000** to replace the current number.

10. Switch to Word and notice the change you made.

    If your worksheet table failed to update, use the Update Link command. Now you will link an Excel chart from the same file in the document.

11. In Excel, click the **Sheet 2** tab and then click the chart.

12. Copy the chart, switch to **Word** and paste it at the bottom of the document, and then use the **Paste Options smart tag** and the **Keep Source Formatting & Link Data** button to link the chart in Word.

13. Switch to Excel and save your changes; exit Excel.

    Now you will open Excel from within Word and edit the worksheet.

14. Double-click the worksheet table to open Excel and change the data in **cell B5** (Bahamas Cruise, March) to **45,000**.

15. Switch to Word, observe the change, and, if necessary, use **Update Link** to update the worksheet table and **Refresh Data** to update the chart.

16. Save and close the file; exit Word.

    Now you'll make a change in Excel and update links when you reopen the Word document.

17. In Excel, replace the data in **cell D4** (Florida Spa, February) with **40,000**.

18. Start Word, open **W12-A1-MgmtLtrRevised** from your **Word Chapter 12** folder, and update the links.

19. If necessary, use Update Link to update the worksheet table and Refresh Data to update the chart.

    Because you don't want the data to update any more, you will break the link between Word and Excel.

20. In the Links dialog box, break the link for both the worksheet and the chart.

21. Right-click the worksheet table and ensure that the Update Links command is not available.

22. Click the chart and choose **Chart Tools→Design→Data** and observe that the **Refresh Data** button is grayed out.

23. Save and close all files and exit Excel.

APPLY YOUR SKILLS: W12-A2

Prepare Documents for a Tour to Turkey

Universal Corporate Events reps are planning a tour of Turkey for a client. In this exercise, you will create a PowerPoint presentation from a Word outline. Then you will insert a PowerPoint presentation in a letter for tour members and create a web page from a Word document listing side tours in Turkey.

1. Open **W12-A2-TurkeyOutline** and switch to **Outline view**.

2. Observe the different heading levels indicated in the Outlining tab, which will become the title and bullet-point entries in the PowerPoint slides; close the outline document.

3. Start PowerPoint, click **Open Other Presentations** at the bottom of the left panel, and navigate to your **Word Chapter 12** folder.

4. In the bottom of the Open dialog box, choose **All Files (*.*)** from the drop-down list.

5. Double-click **W12-A2-TurkeyOutline** to open it; click through the slides in the left panel and observe the effect of the different heading levels in the outline.

6. Exit PowerPoint without saving.

    Now you will add a PowerPoint presentation to a letter you're sending as an email attachment to the tour members.

7. In Word, open **W12-A2-TurkeyLtr** from your **Word Chapter 12** folder and save it as **W12-A2-TurkeyLtrRevised**.

8. Position the insertion point at the end of the document, insert **W12-A2-TurkeyPPT.ppt**, and view the presentation.

    Now you will save the letter as a PDF file as tour members will likely have different types of computers.

9. Choose **File→Save As**, navigate to your **Word Chapter 12** folder, and save the file as a **PDF** file.

10. If your file opens in a PDF reader, close the reader.

11. Save and close **W12-A2-TurkeyLtrRevised.pdf**.

    The location for the meeting has changed, so you will edit the PDF file in Word and resave it as a PDF file.

12. Open the **PDF** file in Word and change *Lakeside* to **Harbor**.

13. Resave the file as a **PDF** file and name it `W12-A2-TurkeyLtrRevised2`.

14. If the file opens in a reader, close the reader.

15. Save the Word document as `W12-A2-TurkeyLtrRevised2`; make sure it's a *.docx* file and then close it.

Create and Edit a Web Page in Word

You have been asked to create a web page for the Universal Corporate Events website showing the side tours offered for the tour of Turkey.

16. Open **W12-A2-TurkeyWebPage**, save it as a **Web Page (*.htm,*.html)**, name it **W12-A2-TurkeyWebPageRevised**, and change the title to `Side Trips in Turkey`.

17. Open and observe the web page in your browser and then close the browser.

    Now you will add a side-tour destination to the web page. The web page document should still be open in Word.

18. Position the insertion point after *Turkish Bath*, tap [Enter], and type `Istanbul`.

19. Save and close the file.

20. Open the file in your browser again, observe the change, and then close the browser.

APPLY YOUR SKILLS: W12-A3

Plan an Australian Tour

A Universal Corporate Events representative is preparing an Australian tour for a client. You have been asked to prepare the documents associated with the tour. In this exercise, you will use an Excel name and address list for a mail merge and prepare a letter containing a PowerPoint presentation. Then you will prepare a web page about Australia for tour members to view online.

1. Open **W12-A3-AustraliaLtr** from your **Word Chapter 12** folder and save it as **W12-A3-AustraliaLtrRevised**.

2. Designate the letter as the main document in a mail merge.

3. Designate **Sheet 1** of the **W12-A3-AustraliaN&A.xls** Excel file as the recipient list.

4. Replace the **Address Block** placeholder text with the **Address Block code**, accepting the default formats for the inside address.

5. Replace the **Greeting Line** placeholder text with the **Greeting Line code**, accepting the default formats for the greeting line.

6. Finish the merge, choosing **Edit Individual Documents**, and merge all records.

7. Review the merged letters and then close the merged file without saving.

8. Save and close **W12-A3-AustraliaLtrRevised**.

Insert a PowerPoint Presentation in a Word Document

The tour members have now attended an orientation meeting, and the Universal Corporate Events representative has asked you to insert the PowerPoint presentation in a letter to members so they can review the topics covered in the meeting.

9. Open **W12-A3-OrientLtr** from your **Word Chapter 12** folder and save it as **W12-A3-OrientLtrRevised**.

10. Position the insertion point at the end of the letter, insert **W12-A3-AussiePPT.ppt**, and view the presentation.

11. Save and close the file.

Create and Edit a Web Page in Word

12. Open **W12-A3-AussieWebPage** from your **Word Chapter 12** folder, save it as a web page, name it **W12-A3-AussieWebPageRevised**, and change the title to **Australia Overview**.

13. View the web page in your browser and then close the browser.

    Now you will edit the web page in Word. The web page file should still be open.

14. Position the insertion point after the word *Territories*, tap Enter, type **History**, and then save and close the web page file.

15. View the web page in your browser, observe the change you made, and then close the browser.

16. Exit Word.

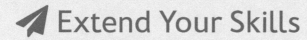 Extend Your Skills

These exercises challenge you to think critically and apply your new skills. You will be evaluated on your ability to follow directions, completeness, creativity, and the use of proper grammar and mechanics. Save files to your chapter folder. Submit assignments as directed.

W12-E1 That's the Way I See It

As a sales rep for a small business, you track your quarterly sales in Excel. It's the end of the third quarter, and you will submit the end-of-quarter figures and the associated chart to your boss in a Word file. Create a one-paragraph Word file indicating that you are submitting your third-quarter sales summary. Name the file **W12-E1-MyLetter**. Link the worksheet table and chart from **W12-E1-3rdQSales**. The product names are generic. Decide which products your company sells and change the product names in the Excel file accordingly; update the linked objects in your Word document, too.

Your boss has asked you to use Mail Merge to send a mailing to customers announcing a new product. Decide on the new product and then write a letter (one to two paragraphs) describing it. Save the file as **W12-E1-MyMergeLtr**. Designate the letter as the main document and **W12-E1-Address** (Word Chapter 12 folder) as the recipient list. Add the Address Block and Greeting Line merge codes; conduct the merge. Save the merged file as **W12-E1-Merged**.

W12-E2 Be Your Own Boss

As the owner of Blue Jean Landscaping, you plan to hold a seminar to discuss your products and services. You want a PowerPoint presentation to guide your seminar. Use the Word outline **W12-E2-BJLGardens** to create the slides and save the presentation as **W12-E2-BJL-PPT**. After the seminar, you will email a Word document to attendees with the presentation inserted. Create a letter (1–2 paragraphs) thanking customers for attending the seminar. Note that the presentation is included, and add instructions on how to play the slide show. Save the Word document as **W12-E2-BJLLetter**. Save the document as a web page and test it in your browser.

W12-E3 Demonstrate Proficiency

Stormy BBQ sponsors an annual rodeo. To encourage a big turnout, you've been asked to prepare a PowerPoint presentation to use as an email attachment for Stormy's customers. To begin, open **W12-E3-RodeoOutline** in PowerPoint. Save the presentation as **W12-E3-RodeoPres**. Then create a two- or three-paragraph Word document describing the rodeo and why people should attend. Save the file as **W12-E3-RodeoWordDoc**. Insert a PowerPoint presentation, **W12-E3-RodeoPPT.ppt**, in the document. Remember to include instructions on how to run the slide show.

There will be a Rodeo Raffle, and you've been asked to create a web page to put on Stormy's website listing the prizes. Convert **W12-E3-RodeoWebPage** to a web page named **W12-E3-RodeoWebPage**. Test it in your browser. Add a prize, a $50 Starbuck's gift card, to the bottom of the list of prizes in the web document and then test it again in your browser.

Glossary

Accessibility Checker Tells you about possible accessibility issues in your files so you can fix them so someone with a disability can read and access your content

alignment Horizontal placement of text relative to the left and right margins of a cell or a page, where text is left-, right-, or center-aligned; or vertical placement of text relative to the top and bottom margins of a cell or page, where text is top-, middle-, or bottom-aligned

AutoComplete A feature that offers to complete the typing for you when it recognizes certain words or phrases

AutoCorrect Predefined text used for automatically correcting common spelling and capitalization errors; can be customized with user-defined entries

block style Letter style that aligns all parts of a letter with the left margin

bookmark Selection of text or other objects identified by a name and location; enables quick navigation through long documents

captions Text added to a figure to describe or explain the figure; text formatted as captions can be used to create a table of figures

cell A box formed by the intersection of a row and column table, in which information is entered and displayed

character styles Styles used to format a single word or selected group of words with text formatting such as font, bold, font size, etc.; no paragraph formatting is included

citation(s) Reference to a source used in a document; contains information to locate the source

collaborating Working together with other people to edit and complete a document

column break Manual break of a newsletter column at a specified location; moves text at the break point to the top of the next column

columns Vertical arrangement of cells in a table

Comment Electronic note attached to a document

Compatibility Checker When a Word 2016 document is saved down to Word 2010 or an even earlier version, the Compatibility Checker notifies the user how features specific to Word 2016 will be handled

Compatibility Mode Opening a document that was created in Word 2010 or earlier opens it in Compatibility Mode; available features are limited to those found in the earlier versions

Compatibility Pack This free download from Microsoft allows a user to open a Word 2016 or 2013 document in an earlier version of Word

concordance A list of terms used to mark words or phrases in a document that are to be included in an index

contextual tab(s) Hidden Ribbon tabs that only appear when certain types of objects, such as pictures or tables, are selected

convert Feature that allows you to transform documents that were created in an earlier version of an application to the Office 2016 file format

cropping Cutting off parts of a picture to make certain other elements stand out or to remove unwanted elements

data source In Mail Merge, the variable data that merges with the main document; controlled by merge fields in the main document

demote To increase text indentation so it appears farther away from the left margin and, if numbered or bulleted, reduces the numbering or bulleting level to the next lower level

destination file A file on which an operation is performed or into which data copied from another document is pasted

digital signature Means of authenticating the identity of the originator of a document; a signed document cannot be modified

Document Inspector Reviews documents for hidden data or personal information

document properties Information about a document, such as the date and time it was last modified, the author's name, and the name of the last person who modified it

embed To incorporate within the body of a file or document

encryption Technique for encoding a document so it can only be read by the sender and the intended recipient

endnotes Notes that appear at the end of the document body in which the reference is made; numbered sequentially throughout a document

file format Type of method used for storing information in a file; each application normally has a special file format it uses by default

footer Text that usually, but not always, is located toward the bottom of a document and that repeats on all (desired) pages within a document

footnotes Notes that appear at the bottom of the page on which the reference is made; footnote numbers can start with 1 on each page or can be numbered sequentially throughout a document or individually

formatting marks Special characters such as spaces, tabs, and paragraph symbols made visible when the Show/Hide button is turned on

handles Small squares or circles on selected graphics that can be dragged to make the graphic larger or smaller

header Text that usually, but not always, is located toward the top of a document, slide, or handout and that repeats on all (desired) pages, slides, or handouts within a document or presentation

hyperlink A block of text or a graphic that jumps you to another location in a file, to another file, or to a web page when clicked

insert control Appears when the mouse pointer is outside the table, pointing between columns or rows; click the control to insert a new column or row at that location

line spacing Vertical space between lines of text

link A code or instruction that connects one part of a source file to a destination file; the destination file can be updated when the source file is modified

Live Preview Feature that allows you to you point at formatting commands on the Ribbon to show how the format would appear on selected text and objects without actually applying the format

Macro A series of frequently used commands grouped together and saved as a single command; used to speed up repetitive tasks

Mail Merge Feature used to personalize standard letters, envelopes, mailing labels, and other documents by combining a main document with a data source

main document In a Mail Merge, the document that contains the content that remains the same for each recipient; controls the merge with merge fields

manual page break Forced page break created by pressing Ctrl+Enter or choosing Insert→Pages→ Page Break

Mark as Final Command that makes a document read-only; places an icon on the status bar to let readers know they are viewing the final form of the document

merge fields Placeholders in a Mail Merge main document that instruct Word to insert information from a data source

merged document Document that results when you complete a merge of the main document and the data source

MLA style Modern Language Association Handbook for Writers of Research Papers; shows how to work with sources in expository writing

nonbreaking spaces or hyphens Spaces or hyphens inserted between two or more words to keep those words together on the same line

object Refers to graphical images such as shapes, WordArt, Excel spreadsheets, charts, and pictures; these elements can be shared between documents

One Drive A service offered by Microsoft that provides free online storage to those who have a Microsoft Account ID; allows you to get and share files from anywhere on any device

orientation Direction in which the page is turned for viewing and printing, either portrait (short edge on top) or landscape (long edge on top)

paragraph In Word, this is created anytime you tap [Enter]; it can consist of several lines, a single line, or a blank line

paragraph style Style used to format a paragraph or selected group of paragraphs; may include character formatting

promote To reduce text indentation so it appears closer to the left margin and, if numbered or bulleted, to elevate the item to the next higher level of bullet

round-tripping Converting a document created in Word 97-2003 to Word 2016 format and then saving it back to the Word 97-2003 document format

rows Horizontal groups of cells in a table

section break Position in a document where one section ends and another begins because page formatting is going to change, such as from single- to multiple-column layout

select To drag over the desired text with the mouse pointer or other techniques; used in preparation for tasks such as formatting and copying; also called highlighting

shapes Tool for drawing graphics in documents

Show/Hide button Feature that displays nonprinting characters such as tabs, spaces, and paragraph symbols onscreen for easy access.

smart tag Context-sensitive option button that appears on menus to provide easy access to commonly used tasks

SmartArt Predesigned graphic designs added to a document; categories include List, Hierarchy, Pyramid, and so forth

sort Process used to arrange data in a specific order, such as alphabetic, numeric, by date, or in ascending or descending order

source file The document in which data or copied text originally appeared

split To create two or more table cells from a single table cell

style Group of formats that allows you to quickly apply multiple formats at once; when a style is modified, all text with the style applied is updated with the modification; also known as Quick Styles

style sets Used to change font and paragraph properties, interact with themes; most effective when used in conjunction with Styles gallery

tab stops Preset stops along the horizontal ruler set at every half inch to control and align text; can be customized

table styles Styles applied to table cells, rows, or columns to ensure formatting consistency

template A preformatted document or workbook layout used as the basis for new documents to maintain consistency among documents and save the user time and that usually contains text, paragraph, table, graphical, and other types of formatting

theme Preset formatting selections you can apply to a document or presentation; include colors, graphic elements, and fonts all designed to work well together and quickly achieve the look of a professional design

title bar Appears across the top of the application window, contains the name of the application and the name of the current file

Track Changes Feature that, when activated, marks each change to a document; the changes can then be reviewed and either accepted or rejected

view Onscreen layout of a document optimized for performing specific tasks or for determining how the document will look in final form

Visual Basic for Applications (VBA) A programming language used by Office programs that creates modules containing macros

watermark Text or images placed in the header of a document so it appears faintly behind document text and graphics

Widow/Orphan control Prevents placing the last line of a paragraph at the top of the next page (widow) or the first line of a paragraph at the bottom of a page (orphan); ensures there are at least two lines of a paragraph at the top or bottom of a page

WordArt Feature for creating stylized formatting of text; often used for headings

Word Wrap Automatic moving of text to a new line when it extends beyond the right margin of a paragraph; eliminates the need to tap Enter at the end of lines within a paragraph

Index

Note: Page numbers ending with a "V" indicate that a term is discussed in the video referenced on that page.

A

academic papers. *See* research papers
accepting tracked changes, 222
Accessibility Checker, 244–245, 325. *See also* alternative text
address lists, working with, 128V–130
Advanced Properties dialog box, options in, 276
aligning
    data in tables, 37–39
    images in flyers, 79
    objects, 62–64
    text, 9–10, 21, 26, 30–31
alignment, explained, 325
alternative text, adding to web pages, 310–311. *See also* Accessibility Checker
artistic effects, applying to newsletters, 155
ATS (Application Tracking System), 3, 12, 18
AutoComplete feature, 7, 325
AutoCorrect feature
    customizing, 270V–271
    explained, 325
    using with lists, 13
AutoRecover interval, changing, 271–272

B

backward-compatible documents, preparing, 243, 258
BBQ-restaurant exercises. *See* Stormy BBQ exercises
Belize report, completing, 114–115
bibliographies, inserting, 100V–101, 112–113, 116–117
"bleisure" newsletter, creating, 163–164
block style
    explained, 325
    using with business letters, 2
Blue Jean Landscaping exercises
    business documents, 32
    collaboration tools, 238
    data source, 148
    long documents, 192, 216
    macros, 295
    newsletter, 166
    PowerPoint presentation, 322
    promotional brochure, 82
    research report, 121
    résumé in table, 56
    sharing and securing content, 267
Bold button, using, 22

bookmarks
    explained, 325
    navigating long documents with, 177–179, 184
borders, adding to tables, 41–43. *See also* page borders
bottom alignment, applying, 9–10
Break Link option, accessing, 304
brochures. *See also* flyers
    adding page background, 69–70
    adding shapes, 58–61
    inserting pictures, 62–64
    Page Setup options, 64–65
    using SmartArt, 65–69
    using text boxes, 64–65
    using WordArt, 62–64
bullet formats, customizing, 174–175, 183–184, 186
bulleted lists
    creating, 23
    demoting and promoting in tables, 40
    using, 12–13, 25
business letters. *See also* letters
    creating, 28–29
    elements of, 2–3
business reports, creating, 84–86. *See also* reports

C

captions
    explained, 325
    inserting, 101V–103, 109–111, 118–119
cells
    explained, 325
    merging and splitting in tables, 37–39
    merging in tables, 50–51
center alignment, applying, 9–10, 21
changes, allowing for parts of documents, 248–249
character styles, 89, 325
Chart Tools, opening from Word, 302–303
citation placeholders
    deleting and editing, 98–100
    inserting, 97
citations
    adding, 111–112
    editing and formatting, 98V
    entering, 116–117
    explained, 325
    inserting, 95V
    inserting in research report, 108–109

collaboration tools, 232–233, 236
    exercises, 238
    explained, 325
    highlighter pen, 218–219
    Track Changes feature, 219–221
collapsing heading topics, 89–90
colors, changing in flyers, 74. *See also* Page Colors gallery
Colors option, using with themes, 173
column breaks
    explained, 325
    inserting, 92
columns
    adding to recycling report, 106–107
    arranging text in, 92–94
    displaying in tables, 34
    explained, 325
    inserting in tables, 36
    resizing in tables, 51
    setting up in newsletters, 153–154, 159, 161
    sizing in tables, 39–40
comments
    adding to flyers, 106
    adding to Track Changes documents, 219V–221, 229–230
    inserting, 90–91, 120
Compatibility Checker, 244, 325
Compatibility Mode, 240, 325
Compatibility Pack, 240, 325
concordance
    explained, 325
    using to generate index entries, 203
confidential information, securing, 240
contextual tabs
    explained, 325
    using with tables, 34
Continuous section break, purpose of, 93
converting documents, 240–241, 325
cover letters, elements of, 3. *See also* letters
cover pages, inserting into newsletters, 156, 161, 163–164
cropping tool, using, 62
Cycle category, using with SmartArt, 65

NOTES

NOTES

NOTES

NOTES

NOTES

NOTES

NOTES

NOTES